A PERSON FROM ENGLAND

FITZROY MACLEAN

A PERSON
FROM ENGLAND

AND OTHER TRAVELLERS

Sweet to ride forth at evening from the wells,
When shadows pass gigantic on the sand,
And softly through the silence beat the bells
Along the Golden Road to Samarkand.

FLECKER

READERS UNION
JONATHAN CAPE
LONDON 1959

This Readers Union edition was produced in 1959 for sale to its members only by Readers Union Ltd at 38 William IV Street, Charing Cross, London, W.C.2 and at Letchworth Garden City, Hertfordshire. Full details of membership may be obtained from our London address. The book is set in 11 pt Bembo type and printed by The Alden Press, Oxford. It was first published by Jonathan Cape Ltd.

CONTENTS

ILLUSTRATIONS

Plates

between pages 192 and 193

In the text

To Orenbur

Astrakhan

Caspian

Kinderley Bay

AZERBAIJAN

Baku

Apsheron Pens.

Caucasus Mts

Sea

Krasnovodsk
Üzün Ada
Great Balkan Range

Kizil Arvat

R. Etrek
Etrek
Gömüshtepe
R. Görghen
Ashurada

Mazenderan

Elburz Mts.

Teheran

Kuchan

TUR

Kazal

Aral Sea

Irikibai

R. Y

Kungrad

R. Oxus

Shor Gol
Kaflankir Plateau

Kiva

Hazar Asp
Sheik Arık
Adam Kürülgan

Bu

Alty Kudak

Kara Kum

Little Balkan Range

Gök Tepe
Askabad
Lutfabad
Dushak
Kaka Kelat

DERGUEZ

Meshed

Rafita

Mer

Sarakh

R. Tejend

Penjdeh

Paro

Her

KHORASSAN

PERSIA

N

0   150   300
Scale of Miles

E. G. Morton

K E S T A N

rt No.1)

Fort Perovski (Fort No.2)

Kuldja•

aria   R. Syr Daria (Jaxartes)

izil Kak   •Turkestan

izil
au Mts.   Wells of
•Tamdy   Bukali
au   •Tashkent   Tien Shan
•
Aristan-Bel-
-Ata   -Kuduk   Khodjent KHODJENT •Kokand   CHINESE
K H   •Ferghana
R.Zerafshan   A   •Kashgar
khara Katta •Samarkand R   TURKESTAN
Kurgan   A
akol   Djam   Kafirnigan
rjui   •Karshi Husar •Yurchi
•Burdalik   •Dennau   Pamirs
Kerki   •Shirabad
Patta Hissar •Termez   Hindu Kush
ndkuy Balkh• •Mazar-i-Sherif

•Maimene

Mts.   Hindu Kush   •Kabul

I N D I A

•Kandahar
•Chaman   R. Indus

ACKNOWLEDGMENTS

MY warm thanks are due for the help and information given me by Mr Henry Drummond Wolff, Colonel F. M. Bailey, C.I.E., Mr Mandić, now of Sarajevo, Mr Patrick Macnaghten, Dr Arthur Ransome, C.B.E., and Mr Douglas Carruthers, to whom I am also indebted for permission to reproduce the magnificent photographs used as dust cover and end papers and also for the photograph of Bokhara reproduced at page 97. My thanks are also due to Mr Noel Blakiston and the Staff of the Public Record Office, the Librarian and Staff of the India Office Library, Mr D. E. Rhodes of the Printed Books Department of the British Museum, the Librarian and Staff of the House of Commons Library, General Sir James Marshall-Cornwall, K.C.B., C.B.E., D.S.O., M.C., and the Staff of the Royal Geographical Society, Miss M. Franklin and to Mr E. G. Morton for his care in preparing the map.

I also acknowledge with thanks the permission given me by Colonel Bailey to reproduce the photographs at page 336, by the National Portrait Gallery to use the portraits at page 49, by the Camera Press to use the photograph at page 289, by Hulton Picture Library to use the photographs at pages 112, 288 and 337, and the line drawings at pages 157 and 204, by Planet News to use the top photograph at page 352, and to Messrs Faber & Faber for permission to reproduce the photographs at pages 273 and 352 (below).

Finally, I also wish to record my gratitude to my secretary, Miss Jeanne Thomlinson, for her invaluable help in preparing the text.

FOR
CHARLES AND JAMES
WHO HAVE STILL
TO START
THEIR TRAVELS

A PERSON FROM ENGLAND

PROLOGUE

ROUND about the year 1890, the hero of an early novel by John Buchan finally redeemed the failures of an otherwise unsatisfactory life by repulsing single-handed a sizeable Russian army which he found, while on a shooting expedition, in the act of invading India. He did it with a sporting rifle and with a conveniently placed boulder which at the critical moment he toppled down on the intruders.

At about the same time, Kipling's *Man Who Was* crawled out of Central Asia and into the mess of his old regiment, the White Hussars, who happened to be stationed somewhere near the Khyber Pass. He had been so roughly handled over the past thirty years by some Russians, whose Colonel he had insulted, and more recently by the outposts of the White Hussars, who had unfortunately mistaken him for an Afghan, that he died three days later. But not before the circumstances of his brief reappearance had revealed in his true colours the apparently charming Cossack officer who happened to be visiting the White Hussars at the time and had also served to remind that dashing regiment that a couple of hundred miles to the north of the Khyber was an enemy worthier of their steel than the unruly tribesmen who periodically sniped at them from the neighbouring hilltops.

And then, of course, there was *Kim*, whose real name was Kimball O'Hara, and who at the age of seventeen managed, with his friend the *Guru*, completely to upset the plans of the Tsar's Intelligence Service.

But it was not only in the realms of romantic fiction that such characters had their being. They really existed. Even the invading Russian army was a reality, though the boulder that finally checked its progress was a diplomatic one.

For the greater part of the nineteenth century, and after it, up and down the length and breadth of Central Asia, from the Caspian to the Karakoram and from the Khyber Pass to the confines of Siberia, throughout the whole of the vast, but rapidly narrowing Tom Tiddler's Ground that separated their respective Empires, Englishmen and Russians, and men of other races and nationalities too, played what they and their contemporaries called The Great Game. Played it from various motives and with varying degrees of success. Played it, on the whole, with courage and resourcefulness, with dash and initiative, and with no great attention to any particular set of rules.

For a space, the attention of the world was focused on Central Asia. Men risked their lives to get there. Not many succeeded and not all of them returned to tell the tale. But, between them, both figuratively and literally, they put Central Asia on the map.

And then a strange thing happened. As the spheres of influence crystallized and the tension between Great Britain and Russia subsided, people forgot about Turkestan. Today, it is by no means everyone who knows where to look for Merv or Bokhara or is even sure to what country they now belong. And the men who for one reason or another once risked their lives to reach them have for the most part been forgotten too.

Because this seemed to me a pity, I conceived the idea of writing a book about some of them. The result is not a serious work of scholarship. Though it contains, it is true, the results of a certain amount of original research, much of what I have written has already been told. Much was known, seventy or eighty years ago, to every schoolboy. But I have enjoyed writing it and for my part I shall be content if I help to revive memories of some men who deserve to be remembered and at the same time manage to give my readers some idea of the regions to which they travelled, of the times in which they lived and of the restless, adventurous spirit that drove them on.

A PERSON FROM ENGLAND

'How extraordinary! I have two hundred thousand Persian slaves here; nobody cares for them; and on account of two Englishmen, a person comes from England, and single-handed demands their release.'

EMIR NASRULLAH OF BOKHARA

I F, as you are approaching Richmond Bridge from London, you turn aside from George Street and make your way through one of the narrow passages which lead off it to the right, you will find yourself on Richmond Green, a broad expanse of grass, fringed with trees and surrounded by handsome red-brick Georgian houses.

Anyone passing that way after breakfast on July 7th, 1843, might have seen the door of one of these houses open and a grubby, undersized, rather wild-looking man of about fifty emerge, garbed as a curate of the Church of England. The rain which had fallen earlier that morning had cleared away and, after glancing about him with an air of studied unconcern (for he did not wish his wife to think that anything unusual was afoot), the curate proceeded to stroll up and down the green, as though taking the air. But he did not remain alone for long. Before many minutes had passed, there arrived on the scene a gentleman of military bearing and appearance, looking about as though in search of somebody or something. The curate at once accosted him, and the two, having shaken hands, were soon engaged in animated conversation.

From their manner, an observer might have deduced that the curate and his companion were discussing some project or plan. This deduction would have been correct. But the project was no ordinary project. Nor could the curate by any stretch of the imagination have possibly been described as an ordinary curate.

By experience and outlook, no less than by origin and upbringing, the Reverend Joseph Wolff, D.D., lately Curate of High Hoyland in Yorkshire, was as different as he well could be from the mild young clerics who had already begun to provide a target for the wit of contributors to the daring new periodical which for the past two years had been appearing under the title of *Punch or The London Charivari*. His appearance and manner, too, were distinctly unusual. 'He is', wrote a female contemporary, 'a strange and most curious-looking man; in stature short and thin, and his weak frame appears very unfit to bear the trials and hardships to which he has been, and will be, exposed in his travels. His face is very flat, deeply marked with smallpox; his complexion that of dough, and his hair flaxen. His grey eyes roll and start, and fix themselves, at times most fearfully; they have a cast in them, which renders their expression still wilder ... His pronunciation of English is very remarkable; at times it is difficult to understand him: however, his foreign accent gives originality to his lectures, aided occasionally by vehement gesticulation. His voice is deep and impressive; at times, having given way to great and deep enthusiasm, and having arrested the attention of his hearers, he sinks at once down into some commonplace remark, his voice becomes a most curious treble, the effect of which is so startling, one can scarcely refrain from laughter.'

Born at Weilersbach in Bavaria in 1795, Joseph Wolff was the son of a rabbi. From an early age he had shown a keen interest in theological matters. Already at seven he had started to question the fundamental tenets of the Jewish faith (thereby causing his aunt by marriage, an impatient woman, to throw the poker at him). Subsequently, from a chance remark dropped by a barber named Spiess, he had conceived the desire to learn more about Christianity. Thenceforward he addressed himself to any Christian teachers who would be bothered with him, whether Lutheran or Catholic, and for the next ten years explored with them a wide field of doctrine and dogma, showing a pertinacity and a disputatiousness which left those whom he encountered exhausted and, as often as not, exasperated. It was not until 1812 that, having reached the age of seventeen, he finally decided to dismiss the claims of the Lutherans and was received into the Church of Rome by the Abbot of a Benedictine monastery in Prague.

No sooner had he embraced Christianity than Wolff, his imagination fired by the example of St Francis Xavier, conceived the desire to become a missionary and preach the gospel in distant lands. With this aim, he spent the next three or four years studying theology and oriental languages at the Universities of Vienna and Tübingen.

But his natural disputatiousness and his extreme independence of mind were soon to get him into trouble. He found it impossible, amongst other things, to accept the doctrine of papal infallibility. What is more, he said so. In Germany and Austria, where ecclesiastical discipline was comparatively lax, this irregularity seems to have passed practically unnoticed. If anything, it endeared him to certain influential Catholics who were themselves inclined to the same way of thinking. But in Rome, where Wolff was sent in 1816 to continue his studies at the Collegio Romano and the Propaganda, the reaction was less favourable.

Wolff liked Rome. He felt himself, he tells us, strongly drawn to Pope Pius VII; so strongly that at their first meeting he patted His Holiness affectionately on the shoulder. He also liked the Cardinals. But he could not help arguing. He argued with his fellow-students; he argued with his preceptors; he argued with the Cardinals. He would have argued with the Pope himself, had he been given the chance.

One day, after a particularly violent theoretical altercation regarding the Church's right to burn heretics, matters came to a head. Returning to his room, he found three men assembled there: a tailor, a hatter and a bootmaker. Silently they took his measurements and silently they left. Something, he decided, must be wrong.

It was. The suit of clothes for which he had thus involuntarily been measured was destined to take the place of his cassock. Called before the Cardinal-Prefect, Cardinal Litta, he was told, amiably enough, that he must go. He must leave the Propaganda and leave Rome. Then after he had been given a glass of Tokay to refresh him and had been fitted out in his new clothes, he was in his own words, 'rolled out of the Holy City' in a coach under an escort of twenty-five Swiss Guards, one dwarf and one member of the Holy Office.

He came to rest a few months later in a Redemptorist monastery in Switzerland. But it was not long before the Rector of the monastery arrived in his turn at the conclusion that this new recruit was not really fitted for the monastic life, and having given him a testimonial of good conduct, sent him on his way.

It was at this stage of his life — he was now twenty-four — that Joseph Wolff recalled the invitation of an Englishman he had met in Rome,

Henry Drummond, the banker, to visit him in England. He decided, characteristically, to go there immediately. On the way over he became involved in yet another religious discussion, this time with a Protestant, a Mr Haldane, a member of the Church of England. He was impressed by what he heard and, on reaching England, attended divine service in an Anglican church. His first favourable impression was confirmed. He had at last found a religion that suited him.

In England, Wolff found something else as well: the means of becoming what he had long wanted to be — a missionary. After two years at Cambridge, where he continued his theological and oriental studies and also learned English, he set out in the spring of the year 1821 for the East on a mission to the Jews.

For the next five years he travelled continuously, visiting Palestine, Egypt, Mesopotamia, Persia, the Crimea, Georgia and Turkey. In the course of his travels, he met (and argued with) innumerable people and encountered innumerable adventures. In the summer of 1826 he returned to England, already, in his way, something of a celebrity. There was a fashion at the time for travellers, and he, for his part, had a weakness for the great. As he himself put it, he had 'ever sought the friendship of those who adorn their aristocratic birth with high talents and virtues; for Wolff believes the aristocracy on earth to be a type of that in heaven'. Now that he was back in civilization, he went out into society whenever the opportunity offered. At a dinner party in London he met and was strongly attracted to Lady Georgiana Walpole, the sister of Lord Orford. The attraction was mutual. A few months later they were married.

But Wolff did not allow matrimony to interfere with his missionary activities. Early in 1827 he was off again to the Levant, accompanied this time by his bride. 'Lady Georgiana', we are told, 'tried dromedary riding, which she much preferred to the camel.' A first child, a daughter, was born to them towards the end of 1827 in Malta, but died. In 1829 a son was born at Alexandria and christened Henry Drummond out of affection for his father's friend and banker.

Leaving his wife and child at Alexandria, Wolff now set out once more on his travels. 'Bokhara and Balkh,' he said to Lady Georgiana, 'are very much in my mind, for I think I shall there find the Ten

Tribes.' 'Well,' she replied, 'I have no objection to your going there.

On this, his second voyage, his encounters and adventures were even more varied and remarkable than they had been on his first. In addition to Bokhara, he visited Kurdistan, Persia, Afghanistan and India. In the course of these travels, he was shipwrecked; and poisoned; and robbed by Skupliot pirates; and stung half to death by wasps. He was laden with chains by one Kurdish tribe and bastinadoed by another, receiving, or so he said, two hundred lashes on the soles of his feet. He was flogged, enslaved and tied to the tail of a horse by a robber chieftain in Khorassan. In Afghanistan he narrowly escaped being burnt alive. On at least three occasions he was stripped completely naked 'like Adam and Eve, without even an apron of leaves' and left to fend for himself in the most unpromising surroundings.

But, wherever Wolff went, he made friends. He made friends with Goanese monks and Coptic patriarchs; with mullahs and dervishes and rabbis; with an Abyssinian chieftain named Hyloo; and a beautiful but intolerant Greek widow called Mrs Katziflis; with a black lady married to a French physician, who 'spoke very affectingly about Christ' and was 'beyond all doubt the handsomest black woman Wolff ever saw'; with the Ganz Awra, a high Christian dignitary at Basra who, in the course of his ecclesiastical duties, 'wrote some mysterious characters upon a part of the Governor's wife's body usually concealed from sight', in order to provide a charm to ensure pregnancy ('for which the Governor gave orders to cut off his right hand, and he writes therefore with his left'); with General Borowsky, a Jewish soldier of fortune in the service of the Shah, who wore a British general's uniform and claimed to be the son of Prince Radziwill; with another Jewish general who had married Borowsky's wife for her money, only to be later disappointed by discovering that she had none; with the Governor-General of India, Lord William Bentinck, and with hosts of lesser British officers and officials, such, for example, as 'Mr Smith, the judge, whose wife, Mrs Smith, was related to the Marquis of Hastings and united beauty, amiability, modesty, dignity and chastity with elegance, piety and zeal for the glory of God', and at whose house, he tells us, he 'drank chocolate and ate the best curry he ever tasted in his life'. And wherever he went, Wolff argued. He argued with Christians and Jews, with Hindus and Mohammedans, with Catholics and Protestants, with Sunnis and Shiahs. He argued about almost everything: about the Pope, and the Millennium, and Mohammed, and the Lost Tribes, and the Second Coming, and the End of the World, and about what would happen to all the fishes when the sea dried up. He argued good-humouredly, tirelessly and without any regard whatever for the consequences.

After a brief visit to England in 1835, Wolff set out yet again. This time his travels took him to Abyssinia, to India, to North America and to Arabia. On his way through Arabia he engaged in a series of theological discussions which, even by his standards, were unusually lively. One of these was with a dervish, who, on being asked politely whence he came, replied: 'Dust is my native land and to dust I shall return. Ho! Ho! HO!', the last 'HO!' being 'uttered in such a powerful voice that it produced an echo'. Another was with 'a swarm of Rechabites' who rushed at him exclaiming 'Hoo! Hoo! Hoo! A Jew! A Jew!' And yet another with some Wahabites to whom he had given some copies of the New Testament. 'The books you gave us', said the Wahabites severely, 'do not contain the name of Mohammed, the Prophet of God.' 'This circumstance', Wolff rejoined, 'should bring you to some decision.' 'We *have* come to a decision!' replied the Wahabites, 'with fury stamped upon their faces', and, 'having horsewhipped Wolff tremendously, went about their business'.

Wolff did not return to England again until the beginning of 1838, when, having been ordained by the Bishop of Dromore, he was appointed to the living of Linthwaite in Yorkshire. But the stipend at Linthwaite amounted only to twenty-four pounds a year and 'from the exposed position of the locality' he and Lady Georgiana were 'constantly attacked with quinsy'. And so in 1840 he moved to the curacy of High Hoyland in the same county, where, he tells us, his predecessor showed his disapproval of the appointment by rather pointedly taking as the text of his farewell sermon: 'After me ravening *wolves* will come to devour the flock.'

According to Wolff, the three years which he spent at High Hoyland were amongst the happiest of his life. To his parishioners they brought a number of novel experiences, as when their curate's old friend

Athanasius, Bishop of the Jacobites in Mesopotamia, visited him there and preached in Arabic to a crowd of three thousand, 'the sermon being interpreted, sentence by sentence, by Wolff'. But, for all his strange ways, the people of High Hoyland seem to have been as fond of him as he was of them, and it was, Dr Wolff tells us, purely on account of renewed financial difficulties that he applied to his diocesan, the Bishop of Ripon, for a transfer to a foreign chaplaincy.

Certainly he and his parishioners parted on the best of terms and, before he left High Hoyland, there was a little ceremony at which a suitably inscribed piece of plate was presented to him and a number of speeches made. But were the motives which dictated his departure in reality purely financial? Was it perhaps not rather a return of the old urge to wander that possessed him? Had not a friend, after all, once said of him that he was no more suited to be a parish priest than a dancing-master?

The fact remains that, having reached the temporary lodgings which he had taken at Richmond, he at once sat down and wrote the following letter to the *Morning Herald*, or rather, for such was its superscription, 'to all the Officers of the British Army':

July 2, 1843   *Richmond Green, Richmond*

Gentlemen,

Though a missionary and a clergyman myself, and not an officer, I do not take up my pen in order to excite your sympathy in behalf of a clergyman or missionary, but in behalf of two of your fellow-officers, Captain Conolly and Colonel Stoddart, who are at present captives in the great city of Bokhara; but having been myself two months at Bokhara; and knowing, as I do, the character of the inhabitants of Bokhara, I am fully convinced that the report of their having been put to death is exceedingly doubtful, — much more so by the source from which the report originated.

If, therefore, one of you, gentlemen, would be inclined to accompany me to Bokhara, or merely pay the expenses of my journey, I am ready to go there; and I am fully confident that I shall be able, with God's help, to liberate them from captivity, with the assistance of my Turkomaun friends in the desert of Khiva, and one of the derveeshes; but I would undertake the journey without making myself responsible to the British Government, and entirely on my own responsibility.

I merely want the expense of my journey and not *one single farthing as a compensation*; even in case of complete success.

I shall be ten days more at Richmond, Surrey; if therefore, one of you brave officers is now ready to accompany me, or to assist me in making the journey, let him come to me, and we may talk over the matter more fully.

I am, Gentlemen,
Your humble servant,
JOSEPH WOLFF,

Late Curate of High Hoyland, Yorkshire, formerly
Missionary in Persia, Bokhara, and Affghanistaun.

It was this letter which led a few days later to the appearance at Richmond of Captain Grover, for such was the name of the Doctor's military-looking companion. And the project which, unknown to Lady Georgiana, the two were discussing as they walked up and down Richmond Green on that pleasant July morning, was none other than the early departure of Dr Wolff for the great city of Bokhara in search of Colonel Stoddart and Captain Conolly.

Who, it may be asked, were Colonel Stoddart and Captain Conolly and how had they come to be captives in the great city of Bokhara?

For hundreds of years, Bokhara, like the rest of Turkestan, had been almost completely cut off from the West. Once the centre of a mighty empire stretching from Delhi to Moscow and from Byzantium to Peking, the splendid capital of Genghiz Khan and Tamerlane had with the passage of the centuries come to be the chief city of a remote and relatively unimportant Central Asian Khanate situated to the north of Afghanistan, midway between Khiva and Kokand.

Surrounded by waterless deserts infested with marauding tribes, a prey to constant civil and dynastic strife, at enmity with its neighbours, enthralled by religious fanaticism, ruled over by bloodthirsty tyrants, this ancient centre of learning and civilization had grown ever harder of access to the outside world. More often than not the caravans of merchants or pilgrims which set out for Bokhara from Persia or China, from India or Afghanistan, would fall into the rapacious hands of Turkoman robbers or perish miserably of hunger and thirst in the desert. The walled city with its domes and minarets, its mosques and palaces, its harems and religious colleges, its pleasure-gardens and its bazaars, had, with time, become to the West a legend scarcely more substantial than the glittering mirage of houses and trees and water that so cruelly beguiled the thirsty traveller in the parched wastes which surrounded it.

Through the centuries no more than a handful of Europeans attempted the journey. At the end of the thirteenth century Marco Polo and his brother spent three years in Bokhara on their way to China and in the fourteenth Don Ruy Gonzalez de Clavigo made his way there as Spanish Ambassador at the Court of Tamerlane. After that there is a gap of two hundred years before we come upon any trace of another traveller from the West, though a number of poor wretches were doubtless dragged there against their will to be sold as slaves. Then, in April 1558, we find an English Merchant Adventurer, Mr Anthony Jenkinson, setting out for Bokhara from Moscow with a cargo of English cloth and other merchandise and with letters of recommendation from Tsar Ivan the Terrible.

Jenkinson's account of his expedition leaves no doubt as to the hazards and hardships which the journey involved. From Moscow he and two other Englishmen, Richard and Robert Johnson, travelled by river to Astrakhan, where, having reached the limit of the Tsar's dominions, they bought a ship to carry them across the Caspian Sea. But half way across, their ship was boarded by thirty 'rovers', 'gentlemen, banished from theyr countrey, and out of living', who 'came to see if there were any Russes or other Christians in our barke', and in the event the travellers were only saved from slavery or death by the benevolence and ready wit of a 'holy Tartar' who swore black and blue that they were all good Moslems. The inhabitants of the eastern shore of the Caspian they found on arrival to be 'very badde and brutish people, for they ceased not dayly to molest us, either by fighting, stealing or begging, raysing the prise of horse and camels, and victuals double, and forced us to buy the water that wee did drinke'. But the party's troubles had scarcely begun. Five days' journey farther on, they encountered 'certain Tartars on horseback', who 'stayed our caravan in the name of their prince, and opened our wares, and took such things as they thought best for their said prince without money'. There then followed '20 dayes in the wilderness from the sea side without seeing towne or habitation, carying provision of victuals with us for the same time, and were driven by necessitie to eate one of my camels and a horse, and during the said 20 dayes we found no water, but such as we drewe out of olde deepe wells, being very brackish and salt, and yet sometimes passed two or three dayes without the same'. After this there was yet another encounter with brigands. 'They willed us', writes Jenkinson, 'to yeeld ourselves, but wee defied them, wherewith they shotte at us all at once, and wee at them very hotly and so continued our fight from morning untill two hourse within night, divers men, horses and camels being wounded and slaine on both partes: and had it not been for 4 hand gunnes which I and my company had and used, we had been overcome and destroyed.' At last, on December 23rd, 1558, Jenkinson reached the 'great Citie' of Bokhara with its 'high walls of earth, with divers gates into the same' and its 'many houses, temples and monuments of stone sumptuously builded and gilt'. The King, to whom, as the Tsar's Ambassador, he formally presented his letters, 'interteined us', he writes, 'most gently, and caused us to eat in his presence, and divers times he sent for me and devised with me familiarly in his secret chamber, as well of the power of the Emperour, and the great Turke, as also of our countreis, lawes, and religion'. 'But', adds the Merchant Adventurer, 'after all this great intertainment he shewed himselfe a very Tartar: for he went to the warres owing me money, and sawe mee not paid before his departure.'

Jenkinson's return journey was no less adventurous. After narrowly escaping 'the danger of 400 rovers, which lay in waite for us back againe', he found, on reaching the Caspian, that his barque now had 'neither anker, cable cocke nor saile'. Having 'made us a sail of cloth of cotton wooll and rigged our barke as well as we could', he and his companions finally set sail, and after passing 'in this voyage various fortunes' arrived at last 'in safetie at Astracan'. 'Note', writes Jenkinson, 'that during the time of our navigation, wee sette uppe the redde crosse of S. George, in our flagges ... which I suppose was never seene in the Caspian sea before.' On his return to Moscow, one year, five months and nine days after he had set out, Jenkinson dined in state at the Kremlin with Ivan the Terrible who 'sent him meate by a Duke' and questioned him graciously about the countries he had visited, while he, for his part, gave the Emperor 'a white cowes taile of Cathay and a drumme of Tartaria, which he well accepted'.

Jenkinson's example did not encourage others to emulate him. Two or three times during the next hundred and fifty years a Russian envoy or merchant braved the perils of the desert and reached the capital of the Emirs. But there is no record of any traveller arriving there from Western Europe until the year 1732, when the journey was apparently made by a Colonel Harber or Garber, though what took him to Turkestan or how he fared when he got there does not appear. He was followed in 1741 by Mr George Thompson, an English merchant, who spent several months in Bokhara, reaching the conclusion that 'no foreign commodity bears a price proportionable to the risque of bringing it to market'. After which, almost another century went by before the next bold travellers from the West, taking their lives in their hands, set out once more for the legendary cities of Turkestan.

The reason for the sudden awakening of interest which now ensued is not far to seek. With the simultaneous advance of the Russians from the north and of the British from the south, Central Asia had in the second quarter of the nineteenth century become all at once an area of great strategical and political importance. Pushing forward across the desert from their base at Orenburg, the Russians were already actively threatening the independent Khanates of Khiva and Kokand, while the British, seeing in this advance and in Russia's intrigues in Persia and Afghanistan a threat to their own possessions in India, sought by means of direct intervention in Afghanistan to establish 'a permanent barrier against schemes of aggression upon our North-West Frontier'. 'If we go on at this rate, Sir John,' said a Russian diplomatist to a member of Lord Melbourne's Government, 'the Cossack and the Sepoy will soon meet on the banks of the Oxus.' 'Very probably, Baron,' was the cool and confident reply. 'But, however much I should regret the collision, I should have no fear of the result.'

Caught between the two advancing colossi, Bokhara, after centuries of tranquil isolation, now found itself placed in a most exposed and precarious position, while for Russians and British alike it became of paramount importance to gain a foothold there as speedily as possible.

The Russians were first in the field. A military expedition dispatched by Alexander I in 1803 had, it is true, been obliged to turn back far short of its objective. But a first diplomatic mission in 1820 was followed in 1835 and 1843 by others, of which the ostensible purpose was to set free a number of Russian subjects who had at one time or another been carried off by robbers and taken to Bokhara to be sold as slaves.

On the British side, a semi-official journey to Bokhara was undertaken in 1824 by a Mr Moorcroft who succeeded in reaching his destination but died, with both his companions, Mr Trebeck and Mr Guthrie, on the return journey. He was followed in 1832 by Lieutenant Alexander Burnes of the Bombay Infantry who, after various adventures, not only successfully reached Bokhara, but, unlike his less fortunate predecessors, lived to tell the tale. In the same year Bokhara was, as we have seen, also visited by Dr Wolff, who was likewise given a not unfriendly reception and allowed to depart unmolested. Another traveller, Lieutenant Wyburd, of the Royal Indian Navy, fared less fortunately. Having set out into the desert entirely alone, riding a grey horse and disguised as a Mohammedan, he was either taken prisoner by Turkoman robbers or, according to another account, by the Emir's soldiers, and, after various adventures, brought to Bokhara, where he was thrown into jail. 'If you become a Mussulman and enter my service,' said the Emir, 'I will treat you well.' 'Understand,' replied Wyburd, 'that I am an Englishman and therefore I shall neither change my religion nor enter the service of a tyrant.' 'See,' he added, as they led him out to execution, 'how an Englishman and Christian can die.'

It was not, however, until 1838 that the British, now seriously disturbed by the Russian advance in Central Asia and by Russian intrigues in Persia and Afghanistan, and fearing for the security of

India, finally decided to dispatch an official emissary to the Court of the Emir. Their choice fell on Lieutenant-Colonel Charles Stoddart, a young officer of the Royal Staff Corps, who had served of late in Persia and Afghanistan. There, as it happened, it had fallen to his lot to deliver to the Shah of Persia the ultimatum which had brought about the prompt withdrawal of the invading Persian army from Herat — an episode which seems to have given him decided ideas as to the best methods of dealing with oriental potentates.

Colonel Stoddart received his final instructions from Sir John McNeill, British Ambassador in Persia, on whose staff he was serving at the time. These directed him to do what he could to secure the release of any Russian slaves or prisoners there might be in the Emir's dominions and thus deny to the Russians a pretext for invading them; to offer the Emir British assistance in case his country was attacked by a foreign power; and, finally, to assure him that he had nothing to fear from British influence in Afghanistan, which Great Britain was at that moment preparing to invade.

Bokhara in the year 1838 was ruled over by the Emir Nasrullah, who had ascended the throne twelve years earlier, having first murdered his father, his elder brother and, as an added measure of precaution, his three younger brothers. After this somewhat lurid start, Nasrullah is said, during the early years of his reign, to have displayed a certain moderation, both in his dealings with foreigners and in his private life. 'Before he came to the throne,' wrote a young Indian who visited Bokhara in 1832, 'he loved boys, but now religion.' It was not long, however, before his behaviour again reverted to normal. Ever more tyrannical towards his subjects and ever less restrained in his personal habits, he became increasingly truculent both in his relations with his lesser neighbours and with the great powers, with whom he now imagined himself able to deal on equal terms. By the year 1838 he could justly be described as an ugly customer, in an ugly frame of mind.

Having successfully crossed the intervening wilderness, Charles Stoddart reached Bokhara on December 17th, 1838. Despite, or indeed because of, his previous diplomatic experience in Persia and Afghanistan, he was perhaps not ideally suited for the difficult mission which he had been chosen to undertake. 'Stoddart', in the words of a friend, 'was a mere soldier, a man of the greatest bravery and determination, with a delicate sense of a soldier's honour; but he was a man of impulse, with no more power of self-control than an infant. To attack or defend a fortress, no better man than Stoddart could have been found; but for a diplomatic mission, requiring coolness and self-command, a man less adapted to the purpose could not readily have been met with.'

The Russian envoys had readily complied with the elaborate usages of the Emir's Court; but from the reports which in due course reached London it appeared that Stoddart had brushed these impatiently aside. Wearing uniform and a cocked hat, he had insisted on riding his horse right into the Registan or main square before the Palace, a privilege reserved by tradition for the Emir and his Grandees. Moreover, on the Emir's appearance, he had refused to dismount but had simply given an ordinary military salute and later, when about to be presented to the monarch, had hit out irritably at a Court official who came too near to him.

The Emir, it seemed, had merely smiled at this display of independence, but his subsequent audience with Stoddart was only fairly friendly and became less so when he discovered that his visitor had brought him no presents and that the letter of which he was the bearer had not been signed by Queen Victoria in person. Yet another factor weighed heavily against the success of Stoddart's mission. Unknown to his master, one of the servants he had brought with him from Afghanistan was the bearer of a letter to Nasrullah from Yar Mohammed Khan of Herat describing him as a dangerous spy and advising Nasrullah to do away with him without delay.

Nor indeed was it long before Colonel Stoddart's fortunes took a sharp turn for the worse. From information which eventually filtered through to Kabul, it appeared that two or three days after his audience with the Emir he had on some pretext or other been invited to move his quarters to the house of a certain high functionary. There, a night or two later, he had suddenly been set upon and bound hand and foot, 'but not', said the reports, 'until after a violent struggle with many men'. After this, he had been hurried through rain and darkness to the City Jail and there consigned to the notorious *Siah Cha* or Black Well. This was a noisome pit, twenty-one feet deep, full of men's bones, decomposed animal matter and other indescribable filth, and swarming with a mass of specially bred vermin and reptiles, kept by the Emir in order the better to torment his victims, and including enormous sheep ticks that burrowed deep into the flesh, producing terrible sores.

Again and again during the long months of torment that followed, Stoddart was told that, unless he abjured Christianity and entered the service of the Emir, he would be put to death. But this, in spite of everything, he resolutely refused to do.

At length, after terrible sufferings, he was taken from the jail, his grave was dug before his eyes, and he was told that, unless he did what was desired of him, he would now be buried alive. Hitherto, through all his sufferings, Stoddart's resolution had not failed him. But now all at once his powers of resistance gave way. Weakened in body and mind by what he had endured, he had reached the point where human nature could stand no more. In his own phrase, the grating of the spades against the sides of the grave jarred beyond endurance on his shattered nerves. In a moment of weakness, for which he was never to forgive himself, he had, or so it seemed, capitulated. 'I argued', he wrote, 'hard and long with them till they brought the Executioner with spade and pick to dig the grave near the prison. I told them that the Ameer must know it was a false pretence, my service to him; but it ended in my release.' His position was evidently still precarious. 'I write', he added, 'at risk of my life.' His letter, which bore the date July 31st, 1839, had somehow been smuggled out and had eventually reached his family in Norwich.

Subsequent letters showed that, though he was no longer in prison, his position remained highly insecure. Nasrullah played with his unfortunate victim like a cat with a mouse, varying his treatment of him in accordance with the varying reports he received of the progress of British arms in Afghanistan. 'Here I am', he wrote at the end of August, 'nominally free, but in fact a prisoner at large ... The news of the probable fall of Cabool has been widely spread here and has caused great alarm ... My release will probably not take place till our forces have approached very near to Bokhara. This Ameer is mad ... My hope of release is in the Almighty and in the approach of our Army, for Government must support its own honor and therefore release me or my bones.' 'The Ameer', he wrote again ten days later, 'is mad', and underlined it twice.

But whether mad or sane, Nasrullah showed no signs of letting his victim go. Messages of protest from the British authorities in India remained unanswered, nor did he take any more account of the representations addressed to him by the Sultan of Turkey and the Tsar of Russia, let alone by his neighbours, the Khans of Khiva and Kokand. To him ambassadors were no more than pawns in a game or animals in a zoo. 'You have one English Envoy', he replied to the Khan of Khiva. 'What do you want with another? Do you grudge my having one?' At the end of 1839 it became known that Stoddart had once more been imprisoned and rumours reached England that he was dead.

But these rumours proved in due course to be unfounded. In October 1840 the prisoner was again released and the letters which he managed to send out now took on an astonishingly cheerful tone. 'Thank God', he wrote in January 1841, 'I have fought my way from my imprisonment and insult to the highest favour with the Emir.'

The latter's earlier treatment of him had, he now believed, been due to 'the dreadful ignorance of these people' and to a misunderstanding of the nature of his mission. His Majesty, it seemed, was now most friendly and anxious to conclude an alliance with Great Britain. 'I am confident', he wrote, 'that, if Government will only do, what it can easily do, make its demands, and send me a few presents (not at first but after the first negotiations, and the Ameer has apologized) such as a Barouche, to give this Chief, all will be right.' Meanwhile he had shown the Bokharans how to plate glass ('It has long been an object of anxiety and desire with the Ameer to know how this was done') and had himself made a looking-glass for the Emir, which had delighted him. 'It may seem trifling and ridiculous', he went on, 'to dwell on a looking Glass, but my object being his favour, I am glad by all means to have secured it.' 'I consider', he concluded courageously, 'that the interests of Government, (especially in keeping the Russians out of this, who hitherto have no hold whatever here) will best be answered by my stopping here, and doing my best to keep the Ameer to us, till all is satisfactorily straight, and till Government are perfectly firm in their relations with this man.'

In February of the same year he reported that the Emir's kindness was 'daily on the increase' and that his comforts were being attended to. 'My dearest Jane,' he wrote to his sister in Norwich, 'I now have to inform you how agreeably and satisfactorily my time passes, and that the Ameer has given to me employments which enable me to render him service, and to show that I am his well-wisher and also promise to obtain for me a good name.' And, anxious no doubt still further to enhance this good name and keep the Emir in a happy frame of mind, he went on to ask her to send him from England a wide variety of unlikely objects: books, seeds, plants, medicines, prescriptions, detonating powder, 'models of Steam Engines and rail roads', 'models with detailed descriptions of Gas, Gasworks and portable gas, how a City and a room are lighted by it ... and of the system and pipes by which the houses of a City are supplied with water'. 'I know', he added, perhaps a little anxiously, 'that my friends and acquaintances will be glad to do for me what they can to enable me to prove the sincerity of my service and well-wishing towards the Ameer.'

Stoddart was now living in a garden, a mile outside the city, as the guest of the Nayeb Abdul Samut Khan, the *Topshi-Bashi*, as he was called, or Commander of the Royal Artillery. It was to this personage, whom he had formerly regarded as an enemy, that he attributed the recent change in his fortunes. The Nayeb, a Persian of dubious antecedents, now in command of the only trained troops in Bokhara, had, or so he told Stoddart, succeeded in persuading the Emir that he ought to keep in with the British and that his ill-treatment of their envoy had been a serious mistake. 'The Naib', wrote Stoddart, 'has been of great service, and hereafter will, I feel confident, do whatever he can at my desire to add to my comfort and assist my duties at Bokhara.'

The Emir, for his part, now seemed genuinely anxious for a Treaty and kept pressing for a reply to the proposals for one which he had first formulated in October. 'The Ameer', wrote Stoddart in an official dispatch to Lord Palmerston dated March 15th, 'daily exhibits the

THE GARDEN OF THE NAYEB WITH BOKHARA IN THE DISTANCE

greatest anxiety to have a treaty of peace concluded', and in a second dispatch, dated March 16th, enclosed an elaborate missive addressed by the Emir to Queen Victoria, 'whose place is on the Throne of Greatness and Sovereignty supported by the Four Pillars of State and Royalty, the Sun of the Sky of Exaltedness and Fortune, the Jewel of the Sea of Glory and Greatness, increasing the Splendour of the High-Starred Crown, great as Jamshid, graceful as Feridon, Chief among the Sovereigns of the Messiah's Faith, Selectest among the Famed of the Religion of Jesus, the Example-giver of the Doctrine of Government and Customs, the Strengthener of the Principles of Britain and Europe'. In this letter, Nasrullah, having first briefly explained that, once he had grasped the nature of Colonel Stoddart's mission, he had at once 'restored him to his own condition', went on to declare once again his readiness to conclude a treaty with Great Britain and to ask in return for an assurance that 'the exalted State of Britain' reciprocated this desire.

But, despite the improvement in his prospects, Stoddart's sufferings had left their mark on him. A letter written in July 1841 and received several months later by a friend in London left no doubt as to this. 'A painful three years', it began, 'have passed away without my being able to hear or give any news ... To me all that is left in this world of change is to the good; for I was gone myself for a time and had fairly counted not what I left behind, but those I was hoping to rejoin in the mercy we rejoice in, assured that the loiterers would soon follow and top Death's grizzly fence. My time, however, is not yet come; and I have again advanced "once more into the breach" before me; and whenever that call may come, pray that my heart may be well strung with joy in Him that has led us, and whom we know we never should leave as our only hope and strength.'

Meanwhile, the news of a British victory at Herat had still further improved his position. 'These people', he wrote, 'who, on my arrival, professed never to have heard who the English were, tremble at their new neighbours and now deprecate their wrath.' 'I am now', he added hopefully, 'only waiting a letter from the Government to leave the field we have won.'

Subsequent messages echoed this same optimistic note and contained further references to his own early departure from Bokhara, possibly in company with a Bokharan Ambassador. He was, he wrote during the summer of 1841, now trusted and acknowledged in his official character by the Emir and he gave it as his view that a sound foundation had been laid for friendly relations between the two Governments. He believed this favourable change on the part of the Emir to be the result of better information and of a more just and rational perception of the views of the British Government and of his own interests; and he therefore had no doubt that it would be permanent. For his own liberty or safety he now had no apprehensions. Indeed, he considered his liberty perfect and his influence all that could be desired. He was, he added, cheered by the conviction that the public objects of his journey to Bokhara had been attained and that he was now about to leave with honour the city where he had suffered so many indignities. 'The Ameer', he wrote on July 11th, 'is impressed with a full confidence that the friendly relations now established are sincere and will be kept up, and believes that whatever answer comes to his letter to Her Majesty will confirm and strengthen those relations.'

But still there was no answer to the Emir's letter and still Stoddart's departure was postponed from day to day. And now, as he was waiting to leave, came the news that a Russian Envoy, a Colonel Butenyov, was approaching Bokhara bound on a mission which was precisely the converse to his own, namely to forestall British expansion in Central Asia and to substitute Russian for British influence at the Court of the Emir. Needless to say, the possibilities implicit in such a situation did not escape Nasrullah, who at once perceived that Stoddart's continued presence in Bokhara might well be of advantage to him in his negotiations with the Russians and vice versa.

Colonel Butenyov reached Bokhara on August 17th, 1841, and from now onwards the Emir amused himself by trying to play the two envoys off against each other. The Russians having, on instructions from their Government, asked that Colonel Stoddart should be allowed to leave, Nasrullah, with an appearance of frankness, at once inquired of the latter whether he wished to go or not, adding that, as he had received no answer to the letters he had addressed to the British Government, and, as the Russians had shown themselves more forthcoming, he, for his part, saw no further reason for retaining a British Envoy at his Court. To this Stoddart, whose sense of duty forbade him to leave Bokhara without express instructions from his own Government, returned a non-committal reply, with the result that the question was left in abeyance. It was still in abeyance when on September 18th the Emir set out at the head of his troops on one of his periodic military expeditions against his neighbour the Khan of Kokand.

At the instance of the Emir, Stoddart now moved into the house occupied by the Russian Mission with whom his relations were excellent. 'A very clever, well educated and agreeable man', wrote Colonel Butenyov, 'who, to my great pleasure, has by order of the Emir been removed this day to the house we occupy.' 'I came here on Sunday', wrote Stoddart, 'and experience much kindness from M. Boutinief.'

It is at this stage in our story that a new figure appears upon the scene, the second of the two officers for whose safety Dr Wolff was concerned: Captain Arthur Conolly of the Bengal Light Cavalry. A young man of a strongly adventurous, but at the same time romantic and religious disposition, Arthur Conolly was a true product of the transitional period in which he lived, half Regency adventurer and half Victorian empire-builder, but first and foremost an enthusiast — an enthusiast and a visionary.

In 1823, when barely sixteen, Arthur Conolly had gone out to India to be a cornet in the Sixth Bengal Cavalry. He travelled in the same ship as Bishop Heber, the author of *From Greenland's icy mountains*, and on the long voyage out the older man's influence seems still further to have strengthened the already strong religious enthusiasm of the younger. Returning to England on leave four years later, Conolly formed the resolve to make his way back to India by way of Russia, the Caucasus, Persia and Afghanistan. He himself has left us a characteristic description of his departure from Moscow in October 1829. 'From the last of a succession of hills', he writes, 'we looked back upon the painted and gilded roofs and cupolas of the city, which lay *en masse* on either side of the river Moskva, backed by a deep blue sky that told of snow: while we looked, the flakes began to fall thick about us; so, wrapping ourselves in our fur cloaks, we set our faces resolutely towards Asia, and bade the *isvoschtshiks* give the rein and whip to their horses.' It was a fitting start of an adventure which was to be a signpost for his whole career.

Once arrived in Persia, Conolly made in the spring of 1830 a determined attempt to reach the Khanate of Khiva. Disguised as an Indian merchant, he managed to penetrate a considerable distance into the Turkoman Desert before being captured by robbers and forced, after many adventures, to turn back. On reaching Delhi in January 1831 he made a full report to the Governor-General. He also recorded his travels and adventures in a most readable and entertaining book, and in 1834, on the strength of his reputation as a Central Asia expert, was posted to the Political Department of the Government of India. But for him this was only a means to an end. Like all who have once been to Central Asia, he longed to return there. 'I trust yet', he wrote to Alexander Burnes, 'to pitch a tent among some of our long-bearded friends of the mountains.'

But for a time other emotions were to drive even these engrossing thoughts from Arthur Conolly's mind. While in India, he chanced to meet and lose his heart to 'the daughter of a man in high position there, a member of a noble family'. In due course she returned to England with her parents and in January 1838 he followed, believing, 'as he had good reason to believe', that their reunion would soon be followed by marriage. They met again in her father's house and for a while he was supremely happy. He was doomed, however, to bitter disappointment. Something — we know not what — came between them. 'It is not', in the words of a contemporary, 'a history to be publicly related.'

Now that the betrothal was at an end, the young officer, we are told, 'said to her whom he had lost that, although there was cause for sorrow on both sides, there was none for reproach on either; that with God's comfort he should not fail to find happiness in single life, especially if he could feel assured of God's restoring hers'. After which, 'chastened and subdued; full of the deepest love for the one and of boundless charity for the many; not at all exasperated, not at all embittered', Authur Conolly, hoping to find an outlet for his emotions in the excitement of vigorous action, went back to the 'solitude of public life' and to the promising career which he had been on the point of abandoning in favour of matrimony.

Circumstances favoured his resolve. As part of their forward policy in Central Asia, the British Government were at this moment planning to invade Afghanistan with the object of deposing the reigning monarch, Dost Mohammed Khan, and putting in his place a former king, Shah Soojah. A man who knew that wild country as well as he did was welcomed in Whitehall with open arms, while he for his part was delighted at the idea of a British advance into Afghanistan. It should, he declared in a long memorandum which he drew up for the India Board, be accompanied by a simultaneous diplomatic offensive in Khiva, Bokhara and Kokand, designed at once to suppress slavery, increase trade, spread Christianity, promote steam navigation on the Oxus and counter Russian influence by forming from the countries of Turkestan, at present hostile to each other, a stable confederation capable, with the help of Great Britain, of resisting Russian penetration and preserving their own independence.

And who, after all, could be better suited than he himself to carry this grand design into execution? His enthusiasm, his abundant, irrepressible enthusiasm, was infectious. At first the India Board even considered dispatching him direct to Turkestan. In the end, however, after first furnishing him with five hundred pounds as journey money, they sent him back to India to lay his proposals before Lord Auckland, who had recently succeeded Lord William Bentinck as Governor-General. 'Captain Conolly', they wrote in a dispatch dated January 24th, 1839, 'will himself be the bearer of this despatch and, having been in free communication with us and having our entire confidence, he will be able to put you more fully in possession of our views upon all the points discussed in this letter.'

Having called on Prince Metternich in Vienna and spent some time in Constantinople where, somewhat to the irritation of his superiors, he engaged, on his own initiative, in prolonged private discussions with an envoy of the Khan of Kokand, Conolly finally reached Bombay in November 1839. Thence he made his way to Calcutta and was received by the Governor-General, who at once sent him on to Kabul now occupied by a victorious British expeditionary force, which had by this time successfully ousted Dost Mohammed and installed Shah Soojah in his place. It looked as though the stage were set for the immediate implementation of his plans.

Many months, however, were to elapse before a final decision was reached, and in a letter to a friend the young cavalryman wrote impatiently of 'the easy-going secretaries, who, quietly entrenched within the Ditch, rave about economy and sententiously recommend prudence'. 'If we treat the Toorkistan question liberally,' he continued, managing to combine high-mindedness with hard-headedness in the manner of his age, 'we shall, I think, secure the great position which we have now gained and make our jealousy of Russian advance in this direction the means of purifying and enriching to our future advantage the whole of Oosbeg Tartary.' 'I feel very confident', he wrote on another occasion, 'about all our policy in Central Asia; for I think that the designs of our Government there are honest and that they will work with a blessing from God, who seems now to be breaking up all the barriers of the long-closed East for the introduction of Christian knowledge and peace.'

But there were others who did not share his views. In Afghanistán, his fellow-explorer, 'Bokhara' Burnes, now Sir Alexander and a considerable power in the land, was strongly opposed to the project. In Burnes's opinion, the right policy was for the British to concentrate on strengthening their position in Northern India and Afghanistan rather than seek belatedly to forestall Russia in Central Asia. Having been there himself, he thought nothing of Conolly's schemes for 'purifying Tartary'. 'You will guess', he wrote, 'what I think of any of our officers going in any capacity to Turkistan, to Khiva, Bokhara or Kokund ... Is England to become security for barbarous hordes some thousands of miles from her frontier? ... It must be at London or St Petersburg, and not at Kokund, Bokhara or Khiva that we are to counteract Russia ... we should have done with dealing with the Oosbegs, for it is time ... At Bokhara poor Stoddart's captivity reflects seriously on our character and damages it here.'

In St Petersburg, meanwhile, the Imperial Russian Government, irritated by continued Khivan forays and attacks and by the constant kidnapping of their compatriots by the Khivans, and also, it must be added, seriously alarmed by the British advance into Afghanistan, had lost patience and had finally resolved to launch a full-scale military expedition against the Khanate of Khiva. 'Every means of persuasion', they declared in a state paper, 'has now been exhausted. The rights of Russia, the security of her trade, the tranquillity of her subjects, and the dignity of the state call for decisive measures. The Emperor has accordingly judged it to be time to send a body of troops to Khiva, to put an end to robbery and exaction, to deliver those Russians who are detained in slavery, to make the inhabitants of Khiva esteem and respect the Russian name and finally to strengthen in that part of Asia the lawful influence to which Russia has a right and which alone can ensure the maintenance of peace.'

At the beginning of December 1839 a Russian expeditionary force of 5000 men with twenty-two guns and a transport train of 10,000 camels set out for Khiva from Orenburg under the command of General Count Perovski. The menace which had for so long threatened Central Asia from the north seemed about to materialize.

General Perovski had calculated that it would be easier to cross the desert in winter than in summer; but by the middle of December the temperature had dropped to 32 degrees below zero and snow began to fall heavily. As the Russians advanced, they encountered worse blizzards and more intense cold. Soon their camels were dying at the rate of a hundred a day. By the beginning of February 1840 they had lost half of them and half their men were casualties to frostbite or disease. While still five hundred miles from Khiva, Perovski decided to turn back. The ensuing withdrawal was even more disastrous than the original advance. Without so much as coming in sight of the enemy, the Russians had suffered a serious reverse.

Amongst the British in Afghanistan the Russian expedition against Khiva was the great topic of discussion during the winter and spring of 1839-40, the news of its final failure only reaching them in the course of the following summer. 'Everything', wrote Sir Alexander Burnes in December 1839, 'has been cast into the shade by the expedition which the Russians have now pushed into Central Asia.' In the hope of patching things up between the contestants and so removing the pretext for any further Russian penetration in Central Asia, an officer of the Royal Artillery, Captain James Abbott, was hurriedly dispatched to Khiva, to be followed later by Lieutenant Richmond Shakespear, both, we are told, 'men of ability, of enthusiasm and of high courage'.

Setting out from Herat shortly before General Perovski left Orenburg, Abbott, another romantic, highly imaginative character of the stamp of Arthur Conolly, reached Khiva in January 1840. There he was received by the Khan, a stout, clumsy, easy-going, amiable man of about forty-five with a round face, slit eyes and a black beard, who, after a great deal of prevarication, finally overcame his natural suspicion of any *Ferenghi* to the extent of agreeing that his British visitor should propose to the Russians on his behalf an exchange of prisoners in the hope that they would then call off their expedition. But, before Abbott could establish contact with the Russians, who had by now in any case abandoned their campaign, he was ambushed by nomad raiders on the shores of the Caspian and, after enduring appalling hardships, narrowly escaped with his life.

Shakespear, who reached Khiva in June of the same year, fared better. He possessed, according to a contemporary, 'qualities of a more serviceable kind, more practical and more judicious'. Starting where Abbott had left off, he eventually succeeded in bringing about an agreement between the Russians and the Khan of Khiva under which the Khan agreed to give up all his Russian prisoners, while the Russians in return withdrew all their troops from Khivan territory. This, it was hoped in Delhi, would render less likely a fresh Russian attack on Khiva, at any rate for the present.

While Stoddart languished in Bokhara and while Abbott and Shakespear were engaged on their respective missions to Turkestan, Arthur Conolly was still in Afghanistan, still waiting for permission to set out and still encountering determined opposition from Sir Alexander Burnes. 'Arthur Conolly', wrote Burnes in March 1840, 'has gone to Jellalabad. He is flighty, though a very nice fellow. He is to regenerate Toorkistan, dismiss all the slaves, and looks upon our advent as a design of providence to spread Christianity. "Khiva is subdued by Russia", said I, "Bokhara is her ally, and Kokan is not inimical if not friendly. How, then, is the league to be formed and how are you to get two hundred thousand Kuzzilbach slaves given up for nothing?" "It must be done!" "Yes, with the wand of a Prospero!" '

At one moment it began to seem to Conolly as though his opponents in Kabul and Delhi had won the day, and for a time unhappy memories from the recent past once more gained the upper hand. 'I was greatly disappointed', he wrote to a friend, 'when Lord Auckland's prohibitory letter arrived; for I had set my heart upon this nobly stirring employment; and when the chance of it seemed removed, I felt the blank that a man must feel who has a heavy grief as the first thing to fall back upon.' But with characteristic persistence he returned to the attack and throughout the spring and summer of 1840 various fresh projects were at his instigation considered and reconsidered — much to Sir Alexander's disgust. 'There is something new', wrote Burnes in May; 'Kokan pronounced impracticable, and Conolly going on a mission to the Russian camp.' 'Of the Khivan expedition under Conolly,' he wrote a fortnight later, 'I have nothing new to communicate ... I think they cool upon it, but perhaps I am wrong.'

Meanwhile the news of Abbott and Shakespear which reached Kabul from Khiva filled Conolly with envy and made him more anxious than ever to be off. 'Spite all the encouragements to persevere that Todd's letters from Abbott and Shakespear afford', he wrote to a friend in July 1840, 'Burnes persists in believing that all interference in Toorkistan on our part has been and will be "insanity". "Our rear", he says, "is not secure enough." Then make it more so. But don't, for this imperfect reason, give up as lost the important ground in front, upon the independence of which from Russian control depends your retaining the necessary footing that you have gained in Afghanistan.' 'I think', he continued pertinaciously, 'that it *must* end in my going to Khokund, probably *via* Khiva with the Envoy thence, Yakoob Bai, with whom I have established great croneyism.' And then, reverting to an earlier idea, 'Perhaps', he added, 'I may come round by Bokhara.'

For, apart from high politics and strategy, apart from what he and his contemporaries called 'The Great Game', Conolly had another, more personal reason for wishing to go to Bokhara. At the beginning of

June 1840 one of Stoddart's servants, a certain Rujub Bey, had arrived at Kabul, having made his escape from Bokhara concealed in a camel panier. From him Conolly had learned something that had hitherto not been entirely clear, namely that, in addition to his undertaking to serve the Emir, Stoddart, worn down by the sufferings he had endured, with his grave ready dug and the executioner standing over him, had actually repeated the *Kulna* or Mohammedan profession of faith. 'There is', he had solemnly declared, 'no God but God. And Mohammed is His Prophet.' And thereafter, though refusing to take a Mohammedan wife, he had been publicly subjected to the rite of circumcision and had subsequently worshipped in public with the Emir and his Court. 'Bravo!' the Emir had exclaimed, on first hearing of his conversion. And, later, when Stoddart had sought to complain to him, he had merely replied: 'Cease such talk, *now that you are one of us.*'

To a man of Conolly's temperament and religious feelings this was a challenge. At once he seems to have formed the resolve personally to release Stoddart from captivity and restore him to the Christian faith. And it was thus that to the general project of a mission was now added the specific purpose of securing Stoddart's redemption and release, and that a dispatch was sent to Delhi, transmitting 'the spirited offer of Captain Conolly to proceed in person to the Court of Bokhara'.

Burnes, for his part, continued vigorously to oppose the whole idea. 'Conolly', he wrote in June, 'having been beaten out of Kokan … has chalked out for himself a mission to Bokhara to release Stoddart, but it does not seem to be entertained. He will stand a fair chance of keeping Stoddart company if he goes.' Nor did he keep his views to himself, but blazoned them forth to all and sundry on every possible occasion. 'Poor Stoddart's health', wrote Conolly a week or two later, 'was drunk last night … after a briefly eloquent speech by Sir Alexander, who concluded by expressing a hope that if the last of Sir William Macnaghten's amicable endeavours to bring the Ameer to reason should fail, our gallant and unfortunate countryman should be released from captivity by *Baron Bokhara*. You may imagine the accent and energy with which Burnes thundered out the last two words … I thought as we rode home, in the loveliest of calm nights, how very much English gentlemen let themselves down by these vulgar outbreaks.' Burnes's heavy sarcasm was evidently beginning to rankle. 'I remain', Conolly added, 'in uncertainty about the Toorkistan journey.'

But Arthur Conolly had a useful ally in his cousin, Sir William Macnaghten, British Minister and Envoy at the Court of Shah Soojah, to whose Staff he was temporarily attached. Sir William had at one time half entertained the idea of sending a British brigade across the Hindu Kush to Bokhara to rescue Stoddart. He also happened to be Burnes's official superior. Soon Conolly's prospects had undergone a marked improvement. 'Hip, hip, hurrah!', he wrote on August 4th, 1840, 'I do believe that I am fairly going now', and, like all sensible emissaries, at once sat down to draft his own instructions.

These were drawn up in the broadest terms. He was to establish wherever he went a correct impression of British policy and strength; to reach amicable arrangements with the rulers of Khiva and Kokand; to discourage them from giving the Russians any further reason for attacking them; and, if circumstances permitted, to return to Afghanistan by way of Bokhara.

Conolly's instructions were later amplified by an official dispatch to Sir William Macnaghten from the Chief Secretary which ran as follows: 'As in the present aspect of affairs it does not seem necessary to continue the restriction which had at first been imposed, his Lordship in Council authorises you to permit Captain Conolly to proceed from Khiva to Kokund, if he should think it expedient, and if he finds that he can do so without exciting serious distrust and jealousy at the former place. In his personal intercourse with the Khan of Kokund, he will be guided by the instructions which have been issued, prescribing the purport of his written communications. Captain Conolly may, in such a journey, find increased means of using a useful influence at Bokhara for the release of Colonel Stoddart; and, his Lordship in Council need not add, that he would wish every such means to be employed with the utmost earnestness and diligence for that purpose.'

Whether, in fact, either Sir William Macnaghten or the Governor-General were themselves ever very enthusiastic about the proposed mission seems doubtful. It is more probable that the former allowed himself to be over-persuaded by his enthusiastic relative, while Lord Auckland, for his part, ultimately yielded to Sir William's representations. But, for all this, their consent, though given reluctantly and against their better judgment, was nevertheless in the end forthcoming.

The first of September 1840 found Conolly, following a last-minute hitch, still at Kabul, 'bothered', as he put it, 'and detained'. But two days later he was ready to start. His party consisted of his 'croney' the Khivan Envoy, an Ambassador from Shah Soojah, one Allahdad Khan, an Afghan of the Populzye tribe — 'a scrubby-looking little man, with a scant beard and a restless eye, which seems to indicate all the disposition of intrigue' — and a train of no less than eighty servants, with an immense quantity of baggage.

The mission on which he was now setting out was a perilous one. The experiences of his forerunners left no doubt as to that. And so it was only natural that, before starting, he should wish to send some kind of message to the young lady in England on whom his thoughts still centred. 'Those feelings', he wrote to a mutual friend, 'have more force with me than ever now, because I am about to undertake a journey, which is not without risk to life, and if mine should end in Tartary, I would not have her fancy it shortened or carelessly ventured in consequences of my disappointed love for her ... The cause I go upon is one which every man must be proud and eager to peril his life for — the noblest in which he could fall ... I have regained a cheerful mind and only hope that the same unfailing spirit of goodness who has surrounded me ... will give her the best gifts of earth, and make her eternally happy in heaven, where all separations and disquietudes will be healed.'

Leaving behind him the jagged mountains of Afghanistan, and striking across the dreary expanse of the Turkoman Desert, Arthur Conolly made first for the oasis of Merv, the capital of the turbulent Tekke-Turkomans and an important centre of the slave-trade. Thence in due course he reported that he had seen 'enough to sicken and shame the coarsest heart'. In particular, he had observed female captives being taken into 'small pens' and there stripped naked and handled like cattle by purchasers who fancied them. No one, he was glad to notice, was louder in his expressions of horror at these proceedings than his old croney, the Khivan Envoy. But his opinion of that dignitary soon suffered a severe setback when he discovered that, for all his elevated sentiments, he had himself bought up all the children offered for sale in the market 'on a speculation'.

From Merv, Conolly travelled northwards across the desert to Khiva, which he reached at the beginning of 1841. There he was courteously received by the Khan, 'a dignified and gentlemanlike person, gentle in his manner, kindly and affable in his address, with a low pleasant voice, and a habitual smile upon his face'. But for all the Khan's habitual smile and gentle manners, Conolly found him obdurate, unimpressionable and bellicose, and responsive neither to his visitor's idea of an Uzbeg Confederation nor to his urging that he should do nothing to antagonize the Russians. He was, he declared, determined to 'punish' his neighbours the Khokundees; and, 'as to the Persians and the Russians, let them come'. Had not the Russians after all attempted only a few months ago to invade his country and had they not been obliged to retire in confusion? Why should he be afraid of them? As for his visitor's impassioned representations on the subject of the slave-trade — his country's national industry — they clearly made not the slightest impression on him. From Khiva Conolly went on to Kokand. But here again the Khan, who at that moment was actually at war with Bokhara, showed no more interest than his neighbour had done in his visitor's project of a Central Asian Confederation.

After this somewhat unpromising start, it struck Conolly as a good omen when, while still at Kokand, he received a number of letters from Stoddart, of which one conveyed to him a personal invitation from the Emir to visit Bokhara on his way home. 'The favor of the Ameer', Stoddart had written on June 8th, 'is increased in these days towards me. I believe you will be well treated here.'

Ignoring the repeated warnings of the Khans of Khiva and Kokand who had both besought him on no account to go to Bokhara, Arthur Conolly at once seized on this opportunity of extending his mission. Setting out from Kokand by a roundabout way, made necessary by the hostilities in progress between the two countries, he finally crossed the Bokharan frontier just in time to meet the Emir as he was returning to his capital from his victorious campaign against the Khan of Kokand. On November 10th, 1841, together with the Royal Party, he entered

Bokhara and on orders from the Emir was installed in the house of that highly equivocal character, Abdul Samut Khan, the *Topshi-Bashi*. There he was joined by Stoddart, who had left the relative security of the Russian Mission in order to be under the same roof as his fellow-countryman. Shortly afterwards both officers moved to another house in the city which had been placed at their disposal by the Emir. Nasrullah now had not one but two British envoys at his mercy.

During the month of November the Emir received Stoddart and Conolly on four or five occasions. Though not openly hostile, his attitude at these interviews suggested that he entertained grave suspicions as to the true nature of their mission. In old times, he announced, there had been friendship between Mussulmans and infidels and there was no particular reason why friendly relations should not be established between Bokhara and England. He would, however, like to know the purpose of the journeys made by Englishmen to different parts of Turkestan. Was it in order to spy out the land with a view to its eventual conquest, as had been the case in Afghanistan, or for some other purpose? Were their intentions friendly or hostile? That was what he wanted to be told. And at subsequent interviews he asked why he had had no answer to the letter which he had sent to the Queen, why Conolly had travelled by way of Khiva and Kokand, and why he had no proper credentials. His intention, he confided at about this time to one of his suite, was 'to give the English a few more rubs and then be friends with them again'.

But there was worse to come. Some months earlier, Stoddart had reported that the news of the British victory at Herat had caused Nasrullah to adopt a more favourable attitude towards him. Now fresh reports from beyond the Oxus led him drastically to revise his attitude. The British, he learned towards the end of November, had suffered a disastrous reverse in Afghanistan. Kabul and the surrounding country had risen against them. Their protégé, Shah Soojah, had been overthrown. Sir Alexander Burnes and many others had, it seemed, been massacred and the British army defeated in battle. Characteristically, the Emir lost no time in drawing from this intelligence the conclusion that he now had nothing to fear from the British and could treat their emissaries as he chose. On December 2nd he again sent for Stoddart and Conolly and this time violently upbraided them, alleging that through Conolly the British had incited the Khans of Khiva and Kokand against him and once again brusquely demanding to know why he had received no reply to the letter which he had addressed to Queen Victoria. In vain they sought to reason with him. He brushed their explanations angrily aside. He wanted, he said, one of two things: positive friendship or positive enmity. If the British Government wanted the former, why had no answer come to his letter?

A week later, on December 10th, a packet was handed to Stoddart by an official of the Court. It had, he said, been brought from Persia by a Jew, and the Emir wanted an accurate translation made of the document which it contained. Accurate, he emphasized – they had means of checking its exactitude.

The document proved on inspection to be a dispatch from Lord Palmerston dated August 3rd, which, while it acknowledged receipt of Stoddart's dispatch of March 16th transmitting the letter which the Emir had addressed to Queen Victoria, contained no direct reply to that flowery communication. On the contrary, it administered what to a power-drunk maniac could seem dangerously like a snub. 'As it is found by the British Government convenient', it ran, 'that the political intercourse which may take place between Great Britain and the States of Central Asia should be carried on through the Governor-General of India, copies of your despatches and letters and their inclosures have been transmitted to the Governor-General of India in order that His Excellency may reply on behalf of Great Britain as may appear to His Excellency most conducive to the general interests of the British Government in India, to the overtures which the Ameer of Bokhara has made through you. You will accordingly acquaint the Ameer of Bokhara that Her Majesty has empowered His Excellency the Governor-General of India to communicate with the Ameer on the several points in his letter to Her Majesty.'

The dispatch, unhelpful as it was, was duly translated and forwarded with an encouraging commentary from Stoddart to the Palace. After this, another week went by before the two officers' next audience with the Emir. This took place on December 19th, when His Majesty 'talked long and graciously with us about the continued bad rumours from Cabul'. As Stoddart and Conolly were leaving, Nasrullah sent after them to ask if he might see Conolly's gold watch. Taking the hint, Conolly asked him if he would accept it as a present. This he graciously consented to do, remarking that he had always had a high opinion of British workmanship.

Next morning early, both officers were arrested and imprisoned in the private jail of the *Topshi-Bashi*, the Nayeb Abdul Samut Khan. The reason for this, they were told, was that 'no proper answer' had been sent to the Emir's letter by Queen Victoria. At the same time all their servants were also arrested, some being subsequently released, while others, including Long Joseph, a Greek in Conolly's service, were executed.

It was several months before any reliable news of Stoddart and Conolly reached Persia. Meanwhile, for the rest of the winter of 1841-42 they led a miserable existence in a damp, unheated cell with a leaky roof, short of food, in filthy rags without a change of clothing, infested with nauseous vermin, racked with fever and ague.

Occasionally a Chamberlain or other court official would be sent to visit them on some pretext or other. The Emir, they would be told, wanted a plan of the castle and city of Kabul, or of Herat, or a detailed description of the Peacock Throne of India. One messenger brought Stoddart his own thermometer and invited him to say how cold it was; another the gold chronometer which Conolly — or Khan Ali, as the Bokharans called him — had given to the Emir, and asked him to mend it. Each time their hopes would momentarily be raised, only to be dashed again almost immediately by the realization that these visits were not inspired by any interest in their well-being but rather by idle curiosity or a sadistic delight in their sufferings.

Every seven or eight days the *Topshi-Bashi* himself would visit them. But when they begged him to intercede with the Emir on their behalf, he would reply that it was well known that His Majesty's mind dwelt both on great matters and on small, that he must therefore be well aware of their condition, and that in these circumstances there could be no question of raising the matter with him until he mentioned it first. On another occasion, after first ostentatiously setting before him his axe of office and prefacing his remarks by a portentous pause, Abdul Samut asked Conolly if he would become a Mohammedan 'and remain in the enjoyment of favour at Bokhara'. But to this Conolly's only reply was that his religion was a matter between him and his God and that he would rather suffer death than change.

Hitherto Stoddart and Conolly had contrived to send out occasional reports and messages. It now became almost impossible for them to communicate with the outside world. But somehow, Conolly managed to obtain some sheets of paper and a reed pen with which, in tiny characters, he secretly kept a journal of their imprisonment, and somehow, during the long months that followed, he contrived to smuggle instalments of this and an occasional letter out of their prison and thence by a trusted messenger to Afghanistan or Persia. Some of the sheets, written closely on both sides, were cut into three pieces and sent by as many messengers. Other messages were written in a primitive kind of invisible ink. 'White paper reaching you with a Greek letter on it', wrote Stoddart, 'is written with sugar water and must be rubbed with powder of charcoal.'

In general these messages reflected extraordinary patience and fortitude. Only one letter, addressed by Stoddart to the Secretary of Government in India, betrayed the resentment that he felt at the Government's failure to back him up or come to his assistance:

Sir,

The Governor-General in Council will be informed by the accompanying abstract how far my position here (and that of Captain Conolly) has been sacrificed.

I have the honour to be, Sir,

Your obedient, humble servant,

CHARLES STODDART

The words within brackets had been erased, probably by Conolly. Two other notes had been written by the prisoners on the back of the letter: one to Miss Stoddart at Norwich and the other to Conolly's brother John at Kabul. 'Don't believe all you hear or may hear', wrote

Stoddart to his sister. 'Keep all friends informed of my health, and don't let them be disturbed by rumours', wrote Conolly to his brother.

In the second week of March 1842 both prisoners were struck down with fever. In their weakened state, and in the appalling conditions under which they lived, their prospects of survival did not seem good. A letter from Conolly to his brother struck a gloomy note.

11th March, 1842　　　　　*From our Prison in Bokhara Citadel*

My dear John,

This will probably be my last note hence, so I dedicate it to you, who now, alas! stand next to me. We both dedicate everything we feel warmest to William, whom may God bless in all belonging to him, for his long and untiring brotherly affection to us all! Send my best love to Henry and to all our dear sisters.

This is the eighty-third day that we have been denied the means of getting a change of linen from the rags and vermin that cover us; and yesterday, when we begged for an amendment in this respect, the Topshee-Bashee, who had before come occasionally as our host to speak encouragingly, set his face like a flint to our request, showing that he was merely a vane to the withering wind of his heartless master, and could not help us thus, so that we need not ask him to do so. This, at first, astonished and defeated us; we had viewed the Ameer's conduct as perhaps dictated by mad caprice; but now, looking back upon the whole, we saw instead that it had been just the deliberate malice of a demon, questioning and raising our hopes, and ascertaining our condition, only to see how our hearts were going on in the process of breaking. I did not think to shed one warm tear among such cold-blooded men; but yesterday evening, as I looked upon Stoddart's half-naked and nail-lacerated body, conceiving that I was the special object of the king's hatred because of my having come to him after visiting Khiva and Kokund, and told him that the British Government was too great to stir up secret enmity against any of its enemies, I wept on entreating one of our keepers, the Gunner's brother, to have conveyed to the chief my humble request that he would direct his anger upon me, and not further destroy by it my poor

brother Stoddart, who had suffered so much and so meekly here
for three years. My earnest words were answered by a 'Don't cry
and distress yourself'; he also could do nothing. So we turned and
kissed each other, and prayed together, and then said, in the words
of the Kokunders, *My-bish!*[1] Let him do as he likes! he is a demon,
but God is stronger than the devil himself, and can certainly
release us from the hands of this fiend, whose heart he has perhaps
hardened to work out great ends by it; and we have risen again
from bed with hearts comforted, as if an angel had spoken to them,
resolved, please God, to wear our English honesty and dignity to
the last, within all the filth and misery that this monster may try
to degrade us with.

We hope that, though the Ameer should now dismiss us with
gold clothing, the British and Afghan Governments will treat him
as an enemy; and this out of no feeling of revenge. He treacherously caused Stoddart to invite me here on his own Imayut-
Nameh; and after Stoddart had given him a translation of a letter
from Lord Palmerston, containing nothing but friendly assurances,
which he could have verified, with our entire consent, at the Russian embassy, he pent us both up here, because we could not pay
him as a kidnapper for our release, to die by slow rot, if it should
appear that he might venture at last to put us altogether out of the
way. We hope and pray that God may forgive him his sins in the
next world; but we also trust that some human power will soon
put him down from his oppressive throne at this capital.

I feel sure [he added on March 12th] that Government will
forgive me for not being able to make an account of my steward-
ship during my Toorkish mission and that it will use every exertion
to get free and to reward all who have suffered with me, but
remained alive ... Stoddart and I will comfort each other in
every way till we die.

But by the end of the month the prisoners had shaken off their fever.
'I am now', wrote Conolly on March 28th, 'almost well in health
again ... Stoddart, also ... is, I rejoice to say, convalescent. We are

[1] Obscure in MS.

both in a very uncomfortable state, having been ninety-nine days and nights without a change of clothes; but we are together. Stoddart is such a friend as a man would wish to have in adversity, and, our searchers having missed the little Prayer Book which George Macgregor gave us (tell him), we are able to read and pray as well as to converse together.'

There were, they reported, moments when it seemed possible that the Emir might release them. The longing to rid themselves of their verminous rags was becoming an obsession with them and they constantly begged their gaolers to give them clean clothes. '*Sewonchee!*' said the *Topshi-Bashi* cheerfully, entering their cell one morning. 'Reward me for good tidings. I represented your great want of clothes and proposed to buy shirts and trousers for you from the bazaar, but His Majesty said, "They won't wear bazaar clothes; in three or four days, I'll give them dresses of honour and dismiss them."'

But the days had gone by and there was still no change in their condition. 'This', wrote Conolly, 'is the hundred and seventh day of our confinement without change of clothes, but the weather having become warmer, we can do without the garments that most harboured the vermin that we found so distressing, and we are both now, thank God, quite well.'

All this time the two captives had been receiving such help and comfort as was possible from an unexpected quarter, namely from the Russians. Despite the tension existing between their two countries, personal relations between the rival Missions had from the start been friendly and, ever since his British antagonists had been imprisoned, Colonel Butenyov had done his utmost to maintain contact with them and to obtain their release. But in April 1842 came depressing news. The Russian Mission was preparing to leave.

Having treated the Russians well enough at first and kept them not unskilfully in play for eight months, while exploiting their presence there for his own purposes, Nasrullah had, in answer to repeated requests, finally granted Colonel Butenyov a brief audience at which he had informed the Tsar's plenipotentiary that for the settlement of his business he might in future address himself to the head *Destur Khandji* or 'Table-coverer', in other words to his butler. From this

Colonel Butenyov had concluded that his continued presence in Bokhara would serve no useful purpose and had begun to make arrangements for his departure. 'The Russian Mission', wrote Stoddart in May, 'left this toward the end of April. I feel convinced that Colonel Buteneff's kind desire to obtain our release failed solely in consequence of the unreasonableness of the Ameer.' The outlook was now less promising than ever; and there was still no sign of help or word of comfort from their countrymen in Afghanistan or India.

Towards the middle of April the Emir, as was his habit, declared war on the Khan of Kokand. 'Early next morning' (April 14th), wrote Conolly, 'the Ameer marched out to the sound of his palace kettle-drums and trumpets, leaving us in the filthy clothes which we had worn for one hundred and fifteen days and nights.'

Soon came news of the progress of the campaign: 'From the 4th to the 7th of May the palace drums were continually sounding for intelligence that Khokund had been taken.' The Emir, it seemed, having killed in cold blood the Khan of Kokand, his son, his brother and his maternal uncle, was proposing to return to Bokhara 'after the despatch of another week's business'. 'No change', wrote Stoddart on May 28th, 'has taken place in our treatment, though hopes, so long found to be deceitful, are held out to us, on the return of the Chief, said to be about to take place very soon.'

This was the last direct communication that had been received from either Stoddart or Conolly. Even the first news of their arrest had taken four months to reach London and had not been officially confirmed until two months after that. The Russian Mission had in due course arrived in St Petersburg. There they had reported that, before leaving Bokhara in April, they had sought to induce the Emir to allow the two British officers to return with them. But the Emir's answer had been that the Englishmen had presented a letter to him to the effect that the Queen desired to be on friendly terms with Bokhara; in consequence of this he had himself written to the Queen; on receiving an answer, he would dispatch both officers direct to England. And that was all they had been able to get out of him. Apart from that, they could only confirm that, although in considerable peril, both prisoners had been alive when they left.

Since then, there had been more fighting in Afghanistan and communications with Bokhara had broken down completely. A letter dispatched to the Emir by Lord Ellenborough, the new Governor-General of India, on October 1st, 1842, urging him to release Stoddart and Conolly, whom it somewhat ineptly described as 'innocent travellers' had remained unanswered. Meanwhile, in Whitehall, consideration was at long last being given to the proposal that a letter might actually be sent to Nasrullah by the Queen.

Such were the situation and the sum total of concrete information available in London concerning Stoddart and Conolly, when in November 1842 a young Persian, known variously as Saaleh Mahommed or the *Akhoonzadeh*, who had at one time been employed by Conolly, arrived in Meshed from Bokhara with the story that, after further ill-treatment, both officers had been publicly executed in June of that year. He had not himself witnessed the execution, but claimed to have obtained a first-hand account of it from one of the executioners.

In due course Saaleh Mahommed's story had been forwarded to the Foreign Office by Colonel Justin Sheil, Her Majesty's Ambassador in Teheran, who in a covering dispatch had given it as his view that 'the appearances and manners of the *Akhoonzadeh*, who is a most intelligent and prepossessing young man, contribute highly in strengthening the impression in favour of his veracity'. No confirmation of the story was forthcoming and subsequent reports from a number of other sources seemed to cast doubt on the veracity of the prepossessing young Persian, who, it was pointed out, had been handsomely paid for his story by Colonel Sheil. But the competent authorities had, on the strength of it, nevertheless felt justified in assuming Stoddart's death. A personal letter which, after much deliberation had finally been drafted for dispatch by Queen Victoria to the Emir, urging him to release the prisoners, remained in the end unsent, and the following entry was duly inserted in the Army List for March 1843:

Deaths. — Lieut.-Col. Stoddart, H. P.
Royal Staff Corps. Bokhara. Persia.

Conolly's death was also taken for granted. What is more, the authorities in Delhi now somewhat surprisingly declared that he had never in fact been authorized to go to Kokand or Bokhara. Indeed, they said, he had been expressly instructed not to go there, and 'in all probability owes all his misfortunes to his direct transgression of that instruction'. In spite of this, the Governor-General was in his wisdom prepared to pay the wages of the native servants who had accompanied him as far as Kokand and 'are not responsible for the indiscretion of their master'. But, said the Chief Secretary in a letter to the Commander-in-Chief, the sums disbursed 'will be made a charge against Lieutenant A. Conolly, who will be required to refund the amount, as well as all sums which may have been drawn on account of such an unauthorized extension of his mission'.

And there, so far as the competent authorities were concerned, the matter might have rested, had it not been for a number of friends of the two officers who felt that further investigation was called for.

Foremost amongst these was Captain John Grover, a retired officer of over thirty years' service, who, as he put it, had received his first commission from King George the Third, during whose reign 'British envoys were safe from insults; or had an insult been offered, an attempt would most certainly have been made to obtain reparation for the injury inflicted on our national honour'. In June 1843, Captain Grover, who was a personal friend of Colonel Stoddart, had informed the Foreign Office — where, with the return to power of Sir Robert Peel, the bellicose Lord Palmerston had been replaced by the more pacific Lord Aberdeen — that he was himself prepared to leave immediately for Bokhara at his own expense, at his own wish and on his own responsibility, for the purpose of discovering what had happened to Colonel Stoddart and Captain Conolly. He only asked that the Government should 'authenticate' his mission. To this the Foreign Office had with characteristic caution replied that there would be 'no objection whatever' to his proceeding to Bokhara 'as a private traveller', but that 'Lord Aberdeen ... would not feel himself justified in investing Captain Grover with an official character.'

Captain Grover was now in a dilemma. 'Excessively disgusted at the official indifference of the authorities at the Foreign Office', convinced in his own mind that if he himself were to undertake the journey as a private traveller it could only 'lead to his destruction', and assured by 'all those best qualified to give an opinion' that 'the thing was impossible', the gallant Captain had next examined the possibility of 'attempting disguise', only to reach the strange conclusion that 'even had I possessed a sufficient knowledge of the language and customs of the country and could I even have been sure of success, I would not have practised a deception to save the life of a friend'. It was while he was 'in the midst of these doubts and anxieties' that a copy of the *Morning Herald* had been brought to him, containing Dr Wolff's letter of July 2nd. Here was the answer to his dilemma. Seizing his pen, he at once wrote off to Dr Wolff to say that he was prepared to furnish the necessary funds for his journey and that he would himself visit him at Richmond on the following day.

As they walked together up and down Richmond Green, Captain Grover soon found all his doubts and anxieties resolved. 'The worthy Doctor' at once dismissed as 'madness' the idea that the Captain should proceed to Bokhara as a private traveller. As to his own journey, Dr Wolff's mind was already completely made up. He knew Bokhara and he knew the Emir. He also knew Arthur Conolly. He had stayed with him at Cawnpore in 1833 and had conceived for him the most friendly feelings. Conolly, he recalled, used in his light-hearted way, to tease him for being so dirty. 'Have we put on clean stockings?' he would inquire every morning when he came down to breakfast. 'And have we used the sponge and basin?' And the Doctor had thought it a capital joke. Conolly was also a devout churchman. What could be more natural than that he should set out in search of him? At once the Doctor turned his attention to practical details. 'He intended wearing his canonicals and, as a *moolah* (minister of religion), his sacred character would protect him.' 'From his knowledge of the country, of the King, and of the language, he had', we are told, 'no doubt whatever but, with the blessing of God, he should succeed in clearing up the dreadful mystery that enveloped the fates of the captives.'

Having once set his mind to a project, Dr Wolff was not a man to be worried by doubts or anxieties. Before the two took leave of each other it had been decided that Dr Wolff should proceed to Bruges where he was to fill in time by assisting in the duties of the English

Church, while Captain Grover set about collecting the five hundred pounds which they estimated would be necessary to cover the cost of the journey. Dr Wolff had meanwhile taken the somewhat overdue step of 'communicating with Lady Georgiana', who, he tells us, 'felt reluctant to my encountering the matter'. Her objections, however, do not seem to have weighed with him more heavily than any of the numerous other obstacles which confronted him, and from Bruges he continued to keep up a regular and lively correspondence with Captain Grover.

After first issuing 'a hasty pamphlet' describing the events leading up to Dr Wolff's mission in terms far from flattering to Lord Aberdeen or to the Foreign Office, Captain Grover's next step was to call a public meeting to take place on September 7th at the Crown and Anchor Tavern in the Strand. Although the Foreign Office, apparently in the hope of taking the wind out of Captain Grover's sails, had caused the *Akhoonzadeh's* story to be published in full in *The Times* and other papers, and although Sir Robert Peel, while talking of 'an outrage on humanity', had, in reply to a question in the House of Commons, skilfully sought to dispose of the whole affair once and for all, public opinion was now thoroughly roused. The meeting at the Crown and Anchor was an unqualified success, being attended by such distinguished personages as Admiral Sir Edward Codrington, the hero of Navarino, Major-General Sir Jeremiah Bryant, Mr J. Silk Buckingham, the celebrated traveller, and many others. In the course of the proceedings the choice of Dr Wolff was, it is true, criticized at one moment on the grounds that he was 'a wild enthusiast'. But the critic was at once effectively silenced by the unanswerable retort that a 'wild enthusiast' was precisely what was wanted for this particular mission and that 'none but an enthusiast would leave his country, his home, his wife and only child, to expose himself to all the dangers of a journey to Bokhara, there to meet with probable imprisonment and death, without even the protection of a letter from the British Government, which would alone ensure his safety'. After this a subscription was opened, to which no less a person than Lord Melbourne contributed the sum of twenty pounds, and a Committee formed, with Captain Grover as President and including amongst its members,

Admiral Codrington, General Bryant and Mr J. S. Buckingham, for the purpose of sending Dr Wolff to Bokhara and, in general, 'of taking such measures as may be necessary'.

When, some weeks earlier, Captain Grover had asked for an interview with the Secretary of State for Foreign Affairs, his request had been refused and he had been 'unceremoniously handed over to irresponsible subalterns'. Now, as President of the Stoddart and Conolly Committee, he and the members of his Committee were admitted without difficulty to the presence of Lord Aberdeen, who, while careful to undertake no new commitments beyond promising to provide Dr Wolff with a passport free of charge, made himself so agreeable to his visitors that Captain Grover 'for the first time felt sorry' that he had 'handled his Lordship so roughly' in his Appeal and, on leaving the Foreign Office, went straight to his publishers and 'committed to the flames all that was left of the impression of that pamphlet'.

The Committee's interview with Lord Aberdeen took place on September 26th. Five days later, on October 1st, Dr Wolff returned to England from Bruges and on October 3rd was formally handed a cheque for £500 by Captain Grover. On October 11th another public meeting was held, this time at the Hanover Square Rooms, in order that he might publicly take leave of his friends, the chair being taken by Major-General Sir Jeremiah Bryant. Speeches were made on this occasion by the Chairman, who spoke at some length about Stoddart and Conolly, and by Dr Wolff who spoke at much greater length about his own travels and experiences, about the Diaspora and the Lost Tribes, and about his disbelief in the *Akhoonzadeh's* account of the execution of the two officers.

The next two days were taken up with packing and other last-minute preparations. 'I shall take with me', Dr Wolff had written to Captain Grover, 'my clergyman's gown and cassock, my hood and a shovel hat.' And he had gone on to enumerate the other articles of equipment which he considered necessary for his mission: 'one dozen or two of Hebrew Bibles and Testaments and of the Common Prayer Book in Hebrew for the Jews of Bokhara, Shahr Sabz, Khiva, Samarcand, Balkh and Khokand ... Two or three dozens of silver watches, for the Grand-mullah and mullahs of Bokhara, the Khans of Khiva, Shahr Sabz and Kokand. The Ameer of Bokhara shall not get one single thing, in case he was the cause of their death ... Three dozens of Robinson Crusoe, translated into Arabic.' Finally, having 'expedited matters with all possible despatch' and having duly received his free passport from Lord Aberdeen and a free passage from the newly established Peninsular Steam Company, Dr Wolff set out for Southampton where he was due to embark on October 14th on the steam packet *Iberia*, bound for Gibraltar, Malta and Constantinople.

The scenes which attended the Doctor's departure were, by all accounts, worthy of the occasion. There was Captain Grover, plagued as usual by 'feelings of great anxiety and uneasiness'. There was Lady Georgiana. There was little Henry, who had been granted special leave of absence from Rugby. There was 'the celebrated authoress of *The Undying One*, the Honourable Mrs Norton', who had come to shake hands with the Doctor and wish him well. There was 'a young gentleman of high birth and noble family — the Honourable Frederic Walpole — as fine a fellow as ever breathed', who expressed the wish to accompany him. ('Thank God', remarked Dr Wolff, 'he did not, for I never should wish any young man to enter Bokhara. If it were possible, in the present state of the world, to conceive scenes that would justify to the full the awful injunctions in Leviticus against the Canaanitish nations, they are certainly enacted in that atrocious city.') There were 'crowds of ladies and gentlemen' who 'came from the shore to have a peep at Joseph Wolff and to shake hands with him'. There were, finally, his fellow-passengers: 'one lady of rank' and her daughter; 'a fat Methodist woman, wife of one of the engineers, who sat on deck upon her husband's knee'; Captain Evans, 'an intelligent gentleman'; and some 'no doubt respectable people who were going to Constantinople to be employed there, in the fabrics and mills established by the Sultan'.

'Any stranger on witnessing Dr Wolff's departure would', Captain Grover tells us, 'have thought that he was merely taking a trip to the Isle of Wight ... There was no weeping or wailing. Neither Lady Georgiana nor the Doctor's son shed a single tear.' But at the last moment Dr Wolff gave Captain Grover his blessing 'in such a solemn manner that the sailors left off their work and all heads were un-covered'. After which he fell on his neck and kissed him. The visitors then left the ship, the anchor was weighed, and soon the *Iberia*, with the worthy Doctor on board, was making her way out past the Needles and into the open sea beyond.

For Dr Wolff the three weeks which it took the *Iberia* to reach Constantinople passed pleasantly enough. He spent the first day conversing with the 'lady of rank', Lady Augusta Paget. On the second, 'the ominous evils of a sea voyage began to indicate themselves and her Ladyship took to her berth'. But sea-sickness had no terrors for the Doctor, who 'walked about the deck without a hat', 'slept on the sofa in the dining-room' and 'had sea-water poured over him every morning'. As often as the opportunity offered, he lectured or preached. On Sunday, October 16th, he tells us, 'my poor fellow passengers were too ill to admit of my performing divine service'. And 'matters had not mended' when they slipped into the Bay of Biscay. But on Monday the 17th, while they were rounding Cape Finisterre he gave a lecture. On Tuesday the 18th, with Cape St Vincent in sight, he lectured again. And on Wednesday the 19th, 'when off Cadiz', he continued his lecture. He also preached on Conversion, on the Apostolic Succession, on the Authority of the Church and on the Divine Right of Episcopacy. And when there was nothing better to do, he would wrangle merrily with his Methodist and Baptist fellow-passengers, whom he dismissed as 'a canting and whining set', and in particular with the fat wife of the engineer, who when it came to a theological argument could give as good as she got. 'Your friend Dr Hook', she announced, 'places the sacraments above Christ and so does Dr Pussy!'[1] And on being told by Dr Wolff that this was a lie and that 'even the most ill-informed Roman Catholic' did not hold such views, 'You ought not', she replied, 'to say to a lady that she lies.' To this Dr Wolff in his excitement retorted, 'You are as much of a lady as I am a gentleman!' After which, amid general merriment, he 'apologized to the good woman for his rude-ness and they parted friends'.

And indeed, wherever they landed, Dr Wolff made new friends or

---

[1] Dr Pusey, the well-known divine.

found old ones: the Bishop of Gibraltar; the Governors of Malta and Gibraltar; Captain Tidy; a Mr Levy; Madame Blosco; the King and Queen of Greece; a number of unspecified Maltese, who, remembering him from a previous visit, swarmed round him in the street exclaiming: 'How are you, Sir? And how is the Lady?'; his old friends Temple and Calhoun, agents of the American Bible Society; and Bishop Neophitos, the President of the Greek Synod. It was while he was visiting and, one suspects, arguing with the latter, that he suddenly found that the *Iberia* had sailed without him. However, with the timely help of Commodore Sir James Stirling and the Royal Navy, he succeeded in catching her up forty-eight hours later at Syra where, as one can well imagine, his reappearance was 'hailed with cheers by the whole ship's crew and passengers'.

On November 2nd they reached the Dardanelles and on the 3rd Dr Wolff landed at Constantinople, where he was at once invited to dinner by Her Majesty's Ambassador, Sir Stratford Canning, and Lady Canning, who, he tells us, 'acted towards Wolff like a mother, advising him how he should manage with his luggage and buying him flannels in order that he should not catch cold'.

Besides these creature comforts, Dr Wolff received while he was at Constantinople a letter from the well-known traveller and Orientalist Henry Layard, who was at that time living at Buyuk-dere on the Bosphorus. This brought him more encouraging news of Stoddart and Conolly than had been received for a long time. 'Reverend Sir,' wrote Mr Layard, 'I have much pleasure in informing you that I have received additional accounts of Messrs Stoddart and Conolly; and that all these accounts tend to prove that those gentlemen are still alive. As far as Colonel Stoddart is concerned, I do not now feel a doubt but that he was alive four or five months ago. I have learned today that a native of Bokhara, who quitted the city about five months ago, states that he was well acquainted with an Englishman there, who had turned Mussulman. That he enjoyed perfect liberty, and was not only permitted to live in the city, but was furnished with money, and all necessaries, by the principal people of Bokhara.' Of the various other rumours circulating at this time in Constantinople, some seemed to bear this out. Others did not. The general opinion, the Doctor records, was that the fate of Colonel Stoddart and Captain Conolly was 'very uncertain'.

Before leaving Constantinople on the next stage of his journey, Dr Wolff, in the absence of any recommendation from the British Government, took the precaution of providing himself with letters from the Sultan of Turkey to the Kings of Khiva and Bokhara and from the Sheikh ul Islam to the Mullahs of Khiva, Bokhara and Kokand, recommending him to them and inviting them to help him in his mission. 'It is', wrote the Sultan to the Emir of Bokhara with, for an oriental sovereign, surprising directness of approach, 'a thing incompatible with the principles observed by Governments and with the dignity of sovereignty to arrest and imprison such *Moussafirs*; and it is fit that your Greatness should cause them to return whence they came.'

On November 24th, after Lady Canning had sewn these letters into his coat and presented him with tea and sugar and a saddle and bridle, and Sir Stratford had given him a telescope and compass, Dr Wolff embarked on the *Metternich*, an Austrian-owned steamship, provided, as an added aid to navigation, with staysails, which plied regularly between Constantinople and Trebizond on the Black Sea. On board Dr Wolff found the poop reserved for first-class passengers. Dogs and second-class passengers berthed forward. The tickets, which also bore a pictorial representation of the *Metternich* under full steam, expressly invited passengers to keep their dogs tied up and on no account to go to bed, or even lie on the sofas, with their boots on. Chancing to look through the Captain's visitors' book, he discovered, under the date August 24th, 1839, the following entry:

I beg to add my thanks to Captain Clician for his kindness during a passage from Constantinople to Trebizond.

ARTHUR CONOLLY

From Trebizond, with its red-roofed, whitewashed houses nestling round the harbour, Dr Wolff set out on December 1st across the mountains for Erzerum. He was accompanied by a Serbian attendant named Michael, whom he had engaged at Constantinople, by a

Tartar, placed at his disposal by the Pasha of Trebizond, and, last but not least, by Omar, 'an excellent Turk', who walked by his side when they came to any precipices, seizing his horse's bridle if it stumbled and crying out reassuringly, 'Sarar yok, Beyk Zadeh! — No danger, Son of the Bey!' The Doctor, however, 'generally preferred walking'. The road he tells us was 'horrid' and he himself 'a more wretched horseman than I ever was before'. But, for all this, he somehow or other managed to 'climb over various precipices, where I was compelled for safety to creep upon my stomach', and on December 9th, after a week's hard travelling, came in sight of the minarets and fortifications of Erzerum with its surrounding circle of snowy mountains rising steeply all round it.

As the state of the weather made it inadvisable for him to continue his journey immediately, Dr Wolff, having been hospitably welcomed by the British Consul and promised 'a good Christmas dinner, roast-beef, plum-pudding, mince pies, etc.', settled down to spend Christmas in Erzerum, passing the time by lecturing, preaching, dining out, holding services, baptizing babies, discussing Arabic and Persian literature with the local Pasha, telling humorous anecdotes and writing long letters to Lady Georgiana, Captain Grover, Henry Drummond and the Bishop of London.

While he was at Erzerum, in addition to 'a slight earthquake', there was a further 'tremendous snow storm'. The passes were blocked up, there were avalanches and from all sides came stories of travellers who had perished in the snow. On December 27th, however, the storm having somewhat abated, Dr Wolff, now 'feverishly anxious' to proceed on his way, set out through the snow for Tabriz. As he had failed to bring any winter clothing with him, his friends in Erzerum took it upon themselves to make him 'snow-proof' and he left 'clothed in the following manner: in an *aba* — trousers made immensely large, a waistcoat and coat of the same. The coat is precisely the form of a shooting jacket: over this a large loose coat, sleeves and body entirely lined with fur of wolf's skin. On my feet, first of all some thick worsted stockings, light boots lined with fur, over all large leather boots like the Horseguards, that came up to my hips. Attached to my fur coat was a fur hood, to draw over my fur cap when travelling, and a large pair of fur gloves sewed to my coat'. 'I was', he adds with irrepressible facetiousness, 'a Wolff in wolf's clothing'.

Thus equipped, Dr Wolff, skirting round the massive cone of Mount Ararat, 'waded through the snowy mountains from Armenia unto the frontier of Persia'. It was not an agreeable journey. All at once there would be shrieks of '*Koolagh! Koolagh! Koolagh!*' and the little party would find themselves enveloped in a sudden tornado of freezing, blinding snow, in imminent danger of blundering over a precipice. Nor did they meet with at all a friendly reception from the Kurdish inhabitants of some of the villages through which they passed, their escort being obliged on at least one occasion to 'convince the Kurd, with a whip, of the necessity of affording the Grand Dervish shelter'. At Khoi, however, the Doctor was hospitably received by the Persian Governor, his old friend Soleiman Khan, a freemason, who, 'as a proof of his progress in civilisation, though a Muhammadan, treated Wolff at supper with excellent wine'. That night a fire broke out in the Governor's beautiful house and destroyed the greater part of it; but Wolff slept so soundly from being tired out by the journey and cold that he knew nothing about it till next morning.

At Tabriz, which he reached on January 12th, he met another old acquaintance, Mohammed Khan Kerahe, otherwise known as 'the Head-Tearer', the very same robber chieftain, whose tribe had made him a slave in 1832, and who, having fallen on evil times, was now a prisoner in the State Jail. The encounter was a most friendly one. Mohammed Khan, a gigantic man with a pipe in his mouth and chains on his hands and feet, shook hands cordially with his former captive. 'That time', he remarked philosophically, 'you saw me a great man, now you see me a little man. One must have patience in this world.' Dr Wolff, as befitted so experienced a traveller, was the soul of discretion and confined himself to asking the Head-Tearer for his autograph. 'As Orientals', he writes, 'have long recollections, and one may meet them in out-place regions and rather unexpectedly, I omitted to revive any unpleasant reminiscences.'

Dr Wolff's departure from Tabriz for Teheran took place on January 20th. It was marked by an unseemly episode in which the central part was played by his Serbian servant Michael. The latter had already been incapably drunk the day before, which was celebrated as a feast day by the local Christian community and, on being reproved, had replied impenitently, 'What should one do else on such a grand day?' Now, as the little party was setting out, Michael was once again so drunk that he could hardly stay in the saddle. On being told by Wolff to dismount, he descended unsteadily from his horse and proceeded to knock his master down, after which he collapsed in the snow and went to sleep. Having waited for him to come round, the long-suffering Doctor sought to extract from him a promise that he would not get drunk again. But Michael indignantly rejected this suggestion. 'I am determined', he replied, making the sign of the cross, 'to be drunk whenever the feast of the Holy Virgin Mary is celebrated.' This was too much for the Doctor. 'Wolff', he tells us, 'then dismissed him and entered into conversation on religion with a dervish.'

Dr Wolff reached Teheran at midday on February 3rd and, at the invitation of the Ambassador, Colonel Sheil, put up at the British Embassy. Here and there in the course of his journey from Constantinople he had come on rumours of Stoddart and Conolly. At Trebizond there had been eight Bokhariots, newly arrived from their native land, who said that both officers were alive and that Colonel Stoddart was now in command of the Emir's artillery with Captain Conolly to help him. At the village of Ashkaleh he had found three dervishes who had left Bokhara four months earlier and who said that it was true that both the tall Englishman and the short had been imprisoned, but they were now once more at liberty and were employed as military advisers. At Erzerum there had been a traveller from Bokhara who said that he had heard that Colonel Stoddart was dead, but there had also been others who maintained that he and Conolly were still alive. At Teheran the news was a good deal less encouraging. Colonel Sheil, while admitting that there were conflicting accounts of what had happened to Stoddart and Conolly, made it clear that 'in his own mind, he had not the slightest doubt that both had been killed'. The Bokharan Ambassador in Teheran had, it is true, told him that he 'did not believe that they were killed, but kept in prison'. But he had equally told the Russian Ambassador that both Englishmen were dead.

As for Wolff, despite his resolute refusal to accept the accounts of their death, it seems that by now in his mind, too, the fear was beginning to grow that his mission would prove to have been in vain. 'But', he tells us, 'he withheld this conviction, because he was afraid that if he was to return, acting upon this conviction, from Teheran to England, everyone would say that the whole of his attempt to go to Bokhara had been a piece of humbug, and was the work of a braggart.' There could be no turning back now. 'To Bokhara! To Bokhara!' he writes, 'was my firm resolve; and even if the Ameer should tell me that they were dead, I was determined to demand their bodies, and put them in camphor and carry them with me to Constantinople, and thence to London.' Such was the mood in which he now embarked on the desperate venture which lay before him.

The first thing was to see the Shah, who, he was gratified to find, remembered their previous meeting and recalled that Lady Georgiana was 'sister to the Earl of Orford'. Although at one stage Dr Wolff so far 'forgot himself' as to shout His Majesty down and had to be called to order by a push from Colonel Sheil, the audience was a success. At any rate he left it the bearer of an extremely flowery letter recommending him, Wolff, 'the High in rank, the Possessor of Genius and understanding, the Endowed with sagacity and judgment, the Prop of the learned among the followers of Messiah, the Chief among the wise people of Christendom' to 'the Enlightener of the Dawn of Sovereignty and Dominion, the Exalted Star in the heaven of splendour and greatness, the illustrious Sun in the firmament of magnificence and felicity', in other words, the Emir of Bokhara. Equipped with this and with his innumerable other letters of introduction, he left Teheran for Meshed on February 14th. 'Colonel Sheil', he tells us, 'could scarce conceal his grief at losing me', and gave him three lengths of rather cheap cloth and a silver watch as presents for the Emir.

The journey from Teheran to Meshed, the capital of the Persian province of Khorassan, took nearly a month. Before starting Dr Wolff had been asked how he felt about travelling through Khorassan. 'Very uncomfortable', he had replied; adding reminiscently, 'It was in Khorassan that they stripped me and tied me to the horse's tail; and it was in Khorassan that they put me into a dungeon; and it was in Khorassan that they offered me for sale for £2 10s. And now I am afraid that I shall again meet with dreadful hindrances in that horrible country; however' — and here he snapped his fingers — 'I am determined to continue my journey.'

But in the event his fears proved to be groundless and he was welcomed by the inhabitants of Khorassan 'in the most cordial manner' — a change for the better which, rightly or wrongly, he attributed to Lord Napier's recent victories in Afghanistan. At Meshed, which he reached on March 11th, the *Assaff-ood-Dowla* or Governor-General, lost no time in assuring him of his own good intentions towards him and of his solicitude for his safety. 'You go', he said to him, 'to the dangerous town of Bokhara. There are about 50,000 Marwee, the worst of people, but very rich and of great influence with the King of Bokhara. And if one goes among *rascals*, one must take a *greater rascal* to protect one. I shall therefore send with you nine rascals of the Marwee tribe; and if they don't behave well I will burn their wives and children who remain in my hands.'

Gratefully accepting this kind offer, Dr Wolff set out from Meshed at the end of March, taking with him the nine Turkomans from Merv, one of whom, Dil Assa Khan, was a Chieftain in Merv and a personage of some importance, and two servants: Hussein, an 'amiable rogue' who never allowed anyone to cheat him but himself and 'was not devoid of that kind of affectionate spirit I have noted in some very depraved men', and Abdullah, 'a fellow of the worst character and the worst appearance'.

From the start he had, not unnaturally, considerable trouble with his retinue. Dil Assa Khan, in particular, caused him constant annoyance. First of all he did everything in his power to delay their departure, and, once they had started, he began to pester the Doctor with incessant demands for money. However, an appeal to the *Assaff-ood-Dowla* produced the desired result. By return of courier came a letter for Dil Assa Khan with a copy for Dr Wolff running as follows: 'I will ruin you and your family if you ask one single farthing from my friend Joseph Wolff and do not discharge well your business.' 'Dil Assa Khan', noted the Doctor in his diary that evening, 'is now very humble and submissive.' But his troubles with that wily Turkoman had scarcely begun.

Dr Wolff was now entering on the final stage of his journey. Since leaving London he had travelled more than five thousand miles. Less than five hundred, he calculated, separated him from his destination. On April 2nd the little caravan reached the frontier fortress of Masteroon built high up in the border hills, from which the Persian garrison could watch the movements of the Turkomans in the plain below and seek to prevent them from plundering passing caravans. Thence, on April 3rd, they set forth, wending their way down from the hills into the plain and on towards the neighbouring oasis of Sarakhs, some twenty-five miles distant. From Sarakhs their route lay across rather more than a hundred miles of desert to the river Murgab and the oasis of Merv. Approximately the same distance separated Merv from the next oasis of Charjui, or Four Wells, where they would be on Bokharan soil. Yet another hundred miles separated Charjui from the city of Bokhara itself.

They were now traversing Turkoman territory, infested with fierce tribes of marauding nomads, notorious throughout Central Asia for their cruelty, rapacity and treachery, and owing, despite the repeated attempts of their neighbours to subdue them, lasting allegiance to none. The region through which they were travelling was as inhospitable and as forbidding as its inhabitants: a vast expanse of stony, waterless desert stretching away as far as the eye could see in every direction and varied only by occasional stunted bushes or patches of dried up grass and gnarled and wizened scrub, by low stony ridges or by dunes of soft, shifting sand, shaped by the wind into forms resembling the waves of the sea. The wells upon which travellers depended for water were many miles apart and often proved on investigation to have dried up or to be in the hands of hostile tribesmen. The climate was scorchingly hot in summer and bitterly cold in winter. Even now, in the first half of April, there were heavy falls of snow, which delayed the travellers and kept them huddled in their tents for days at a time.

On April 12th, after suffering considerable privations, and being 'bothered every day to death' by repeated requests for presents from the importunate Dil Assa Khan, Wolff reached Merv, the crumbling capital of the Tekke Turkomans. Here, amid the ruins of the oldest of cities, once famous as The Queen of the World, he spent two agreeable days as the guest of the Khalifa Abd Awahman, whom he had met on his previous visit to Merv twelve years earlier, 'a venerable old Turkoman, worthy of his office — a man without many words, without covetousness, given to prayer, and a friend of hospitality'. The Khalifa, or Successor of the Prophet, whose high religious standing caused even the unruly nomads to treat him with a respect which they accorded to no one else, did his best to persuade Wolff to abandon his project. He himself took a gloomy view of the fate of Stoddart and Conolly and was clearly convinced that, if he continued on his way, Wolff would come to an equally unpleasant end. 'Youssuff Wolff', said the old man entreatingly, 'you are a dervish like myself; permit me to save you ... Do not go to Bokhara.'

But to this, as to all other attempts to dissuade him, the Doctor turned a deaf ear. 'To Bokhara', he replied, 'I must go.' After which, having induced the Khalifa to provide him with some letters of introduction, having written to Lady Georgiana and to Captain Grover, having indulged in some abstruse three-cornered theological arguments concerning the twelfth chapter of Revelation with a dervish and an elderly local Jew, having disposed of the rumour current in Merv that Lady Hester Stanhope was likely to marry the Messiah at the Second Coming, and, finally, having witnessed a spirited display of whirling by a company of dancing dervishes from Yarkand in Chinese Turkestan, he set out once again on his way.

Soon after leaving Merv, Wolff and his little party fell in with a large caravan of merchants and other travellers from Bokhara, Kokand, Tashkent and Herat, with their long strings of well-laden camels, mules and horses. With these they now joined company. Henceforward there were plentiful opportunities for conversation. His new companions entertained the Doctor with stories of Alexander the Great and Tamerlane, speaking of them as though they were still alive and showing him whole bags full of ancient Greek coins. And he for his part, we may be sure, was not silent.

More than once they were held up by heavy falls of snow and once they went for three days without water. There was, too, a fearful rumour that the people of Khiva were in the neighbourhood and marching with six thousand men towards Merv, and, though they did not themselves encounter this formidable force, they heard afterwards that a caravan which followed them two days later had been less fortunate. Finally, as he progressed farther and farther from the restraining influence of the *Assaff-ood-Dowla* and nearer and nearer to his own stamping-grounds, Dil Assa Khan 'grew worse and worse', annoying Dr Wolff 'with every inconvenience that [his] knavery could throw in my way'. He stole his tea and sugar and sold them to the other travellers. He made him give him money to buy sheep and then pocketed it himself. He hired camels for him and then used them himself, charging him, needless to say, more than double the usual price. He was, in short, 'incessantly committing some act of villainy'. Meanwhile, the worthy Doctor could only comfort himself with the thought that 'if the Assaff-ood-Dowla catches him at any time, I would not give a *para* for his life'.

In a short note dispatched to Grover on April 15th ('I cannot write much for the Turkomauns sit near me on the ground'), Dr Wolff had described himself as 'advancing confidently towards Bokhara'. But by now his early optimism had largely vanished and, though as determined as ever to proceed, come what might, with the perilous undertaking to which he had set his hand, he found the serenity of his thoughts more and more troubled by gloomy forebodings. So far, it was true, he had found no one who had actually witnessed the execution of Stoddart and Conolly, and it was usual in Bokhara to execute Europeans in public. Had not, he reflected, Conolly's Greek servant Joseph, or Youssuff, been so executed? But this line of argument only made him think of 'another poor Youssuf', who might shortly share the same fate. At least, he reflected more cheerfully, strangling had been abandoned by the present monarch and 'slaughtering with a knife substituted in its room'. 'That was one comfort, for I have a strong antipathy to hanging.' Even so, it was with mixed feelings that he reached Charjui and so entered the dominions of the Emir.

Scarcely had he done so than his tent was besieged by a number of local Jews whom he had met on his previous journey. Having first expressed their joy at finding him in good health, and waited for all the Bokharans present to leave the tent, these now addressed him as follows: 'Joseph Wolff, Joseph Wolff, Joseph Wolff! you are a son of death as soon as you enter Bokhara. For God's sake do not enter; there still is time to retrace your steps: this night we will fly with you to Organtsh,[1] or send a man with you to Organtsh, with one of our friends. The King of Organtsh is a friend of England and to Conolly, but for God's sake do not go on to Bokhara. Stoddart has been put to death, — Conolly also; and some years before both of them, Lieutenant Wyburd, who was on his way to Khiva, but was brought to Bokhara, and put in prison there, and some years after his throat was cut; and five other Englishmen have been put to death at the gate of Jehaar-Joo, only ten months ago. Poor Conolly, poor Conolly, poor Conolly! was dragged to the place of execution. His words were, "*Wail, wail, wail! Kee Aftadam bedaste Szaalem.*" "Woe to me, woe to me, woe to me! that I have fallen into the hands of a tyrant!"'

But to this outburst Dr Wolff replied only, 'I shall go on; I must be more certain as to this subject.' At this instant, he tells us, there entered his tent a dervish who was considered to stand in immediate communication with God and had the title of *Baba*. 'Go on', said the dervish to Dr Wolff, 'and prosper.'

Not long after leaving Charjui, Dr Wolff and his companions reached the Oxus, at this point a muddy, strongly flowing river nearly half a mile wide, fringed with jungle and reeds, and, having been ferried across, came to the town of Karakol. There they found that rooms had been prepared for them and Wolff, tired from his long and arduous journey, was glad of a good night's rest. They were now only thirty miles from their destination.

When he awoke next morning, Dr Wolff called his servants. For a long time nothing happened. Then Abdullah appeared. 'I can no longer be your servant', he said, 'I have eaten dung, because I came with you.' Whereupon he seized his bag and made off. Some time after his other servant, Hussein, the 'amiable rogue', made his appearance. 'Have you

[1] Khiva.

also left me?' asked the Doctor. 'I will speak to you words of wisdom', replied Hussein. 'One's own life is very sweet. I see you now in danger, and therefore I stand aloof from you. Should I observe that the King of Bokhara cuts off your head, I will run away as fast as I can. Should I observe that fortune again smiles on you, I shall be again your humble servant.' His other companions, too, deliberately avoided him.

It was not long before Dr Wolff found out what had happened. While he had been asleep, the abominable Dil Assa Khan had secretly visited the Governor of Karakol and had, it seemed, been told by him that both Stoddart and Conolly were dead and that Dr Wolff was likely to share their fate. In these circumstances, he had decided to disassociate himself from the Doctor without delay and had advised the others to do the same. When next morning they left Karakol, the rest of the party shunned Wolff as though he had the plague, keeping at a safe distance from him, while he, for his part, rode on alone to meet whatever fate awaited him.

Dr Wolff had been told at Karakol that before reaching Bokhara he would meet some horsemen carrying baskets. These baskets, it appeared, would contain bandages with which he would be blind-folded, chains with which he would be chained and knives with which he would be slaughtered. And now, as he approached the village of Shahr Islam, some eight or ten miles from Bokhara, he suddenly caught sight of three horsemen galloping towards him. Of these one proved to be the King's Grand Chamberlain. The other two, he noticed, carried baskets.

After greeting him by touching his hands and stroking his beard, the Grand Chamberlain said to Wolff, 'The King of Kings, the Prince of the Believers, Nasrullah-Bahadur, feels great kindness towards you. He has declared you his guest.' He then opened the baskets and produced, not bandages, chains and knives, but delicious pomegranates, apples, pears, melons, cherries, roasted horseflesh, veal, tea with milk, grease and salt and (especially for Wolff) tea with milk and sugar. As they continued on their way, Wolff, chancing to look round, observed that his companions had once again moved up closer to him.

They had now left the desert behind them and were travelling through green, well-watered country. Tall poplars lined the roads and the water-courses. In the fields the corn was green and the cotton plants were in bud, while the orchards and gardens were gay with apple and apricot blossom. Smoke rose from the farmsteads and, as they made their way along the road, they encountered strings of camels and donkeys, herds of sheep and goats, and wayfarers of every rank and kind riding horses or camels, mules or donkeys or travelling in high-wheeled native carts or *arbas*.

Ever since leaving Merv, Dr Wolff had worn full canonicals, and now, with his shovel hat and Doctor's hood and his Bible open in his hand, he presented a striking and unusual appearance. The weather was brilliantly fine and as he approached Bokhara more and more people turned out to stare at him. By the time he reached the massive outer walls and watch-towers of the city and entered one of its great gates, he was the centre of a seething, yelling crowd. '*Salaam aleikum!*' they shouted to him, as he rode on his way, 'Peace be with you!'

'It was', in his own words, 'a most astonishing sight: people from the roofs of houses, the Nogay Tatars of Russia, the Cassacks and Girghese from the deserts, the Tatar from Yarkand or Chinese Tartary, the merchant of Cashmere, the Serkerdeha or grandees of the king on horseback, the Affghauns, the numerous water-carriers, stopped still and looked at me; Jews with their little caps, – the distinguishing badge of the Jews of Bokhara – the inhabitants of Khokand, politely smiling at me; and the mullahs from Chekarpoor and Scinde looking at me and saying, "Inglese Saheb"; veiled women screaming to each other, "Englees Eljee" [English ambassador]; others coming by them and saying, "He is not an Eljee, but the Grand Derveesh, Derveesh Kelaun of Englistaun".' But, as he anxiously scanned the sea of faces, brown and brownish-yellow under their turbans and skullcaps, he could see no sign of the two faces he was looking for: those of Charles Stoddart and Arthur Conolly.

No sooner had he entered the city, with its narrow, crowded streets, its walled gardens, its pools and rivulets of water, its covered bazaars and its multitude of ancient mosques and minarets, than Dr Wolff was at once conducted *Bala*, 'Up', to the royal palace or Ark.

The Ark stood near the gate by which Dr Wolff had entered the city, on an eminence dominating the Registan or main square of the city. It was a thousand years old. Its entrance gate was flanked on either side by twin turrets and surmounted by a loggia in which hung a clock made for the Emir a few years earlier by a captive Italian watchmaker, Giovanni Orlandi from Parma. On the other two sides of the Registan stood massively built *medressehs* or religious colleges, while on the fourth there was a fountain and a pool of water shaded by lofty trees. From early morning, when the tea drinking began and the boys with their donkeys brought in the milk from the country, until evening, when the King's Drum beat at dusk, there was assembled here a vast, disorderly, diversely garbed concourse, Persians, Indians, Afghans, Armenians, Turkomans, Jews and even a few captive Russians mingling with the native Bokharans in their turbans and gaily coloured robes. 'From morn to night', wrote a traveller, 'the crowd which assembles raises a humming noise, and one is stunned at the moving mass of human beings.' Here and there the multitude would part to make way for a light two-wheeled cart or for a horseman pushing his way roughly through the throng. The women rode astride like the men, enveloped from head to foot in an impenetrable black horsehair veil, entirely unapproachable. Under awnings in the centre of the Registan all kinds of fruit were exposed for sale: grapes, melons, peaches, apples, apricots, pears and plums. Near by, tea was being made in samovars. Next to the sellers of tea, *rahat i jan* could be bought, the Delight of Life, grape syrup mixed with crushed ice. Neighbouring stalls displayed books, sweetmeats, spices, cutlery and trinkets of the most varied kinds and countries of origin. And all around, in the brilliant sunlight of Central Asia, the crowd surged and scuffled and chattered tirelessly in the high-pitched querulous tones of their race.

As Wolff and his companions approached the gate of the palace, there was a stir and a stately band of *Serkerdeha* or Grandees of the Kingdom rode out of it, splendidly mounted and dressed in magnificent striped robes of shot silk and cloth of gold. In their hands they carried wands, bearing the names of the tribes to which they belonged, and on their passage the crowd bowed down before them. But no sooner had they passed, than the populace turned their attention to Wolff, crowding round him and asking him what book it was that he carried in his hand, and trying to touch it. At the entrance to the Ark, Wolff was required to dismount, only the *Serkerdeha* and the ambassadors of the Sultan and the Shah being allowed to enter the palace on horseback. He was next informed by a Chamberlain that the Emir wished to know whether he would 'submit to the mode of *selaam*', as Stoddart, it seemed, had refused to do so. On asking what this involved, he was told that he would be placed before the Emir; the *Shekhane* or Minister of Foreign Affairs would then take him by the shoulders, after which he would be required to stroke his beard three times and bow three times, saying each time '*Allah Akbar, Selaamat Padishah*' — 'God is great. Peace to the King'. To this inquiry Wolff wisely replied that he would do it thirty times if necessary. He was then taken up through the gate and, after being left for a few minutes sitting on a stone seat, was asked to send up his letters. He produced them. After this there was a further delay and he was then brought before the King. The date was Friday, April 27th, 1844.

Nasrullah was seated on a balcony of his palace, looking down on them — a short, stout man of about forty, with a short black beard, a dark complexion and small, beady black eyes, dressed in the plain white turban and robes of an ordinary mullah. The muscles of his face twitched convulsively and he wore a forced smile. He spoke rapidly in rather a low voice. To the Doctor's discerning glance he seemed to have 'all the appearance of a *bon-vivant*'.

THE
EMIR

As Wolff drew near, still arrayed in full canonicals and with his Bible still in his hand, the assembled onlookers watched spellbound to see how he would behave. The Doctor did not disappoint them. Having bowed the prescribed three times with the help of the Foreign Minister, he went on bowing repeatedly of his own accord, at the same time shouting out, again and again, '*Selaamat Padishah!*' 'Peace to the King!' until in the end the Emir burst out laughing and cried 'Enough! Enough', at the same time observing to those who stood near him, 'What an extraordinary man this Englishman is, in his eyes, and in his dress and the Book in his hand!'

Once the presentation was over, Wolff was taken, together with Dil

Assa Khan, to a small room in the palace which served as an office. Here he found awaiting him the Foreign Minister and a Persian slave who acted as his secretary. The Foreign Minister first addressed himself to Dil Assa Khan who, much to Dr Wolff's indignation, declared that he was the leader of the mission, having come as an emissary from the *Assaff-ood-Dowla*, and that the Doctor was merely a member of his

 retinue. There followed a sharp exchange between his two visitors, after which the Foreign Minister turned to Wolff and asked him to state his request. Wolff then spoke of the 'commotion' that had been caused in England by the reports that Stoddart and Conolly had been killed and of the thousands who had cried 'War with Bokhara!' on hearing them; of his own mission and of his personal conviction that the Bokharan authorities could never have violated the laws of hospitality. 'My object', he concluded, 'is, first, to ask, where are my friends Colonel Stoddart and Captain Conolly? Are they alive or dead? If alive, I beg His Majesty to send them with me back to England; if dead, His Majesty will state his reasons for putting them to death and also send with me an ambassador to England.'

At the mention of war, the Foreign Minister interrupted Wolff to inquire the distance from England to Bokhara and later asked for more information about the 'commotion' caused by the reports of the death of Stoddart and Conolly. He also inquired what credentials his visitor carried from the British Government. After which, having duly noted the Doctor's replies, he dismissed him, leaving all his questions unanswered.

On leaving the Foreign Minister, Wolff was taken to the house which had been assigned to him as a dwelling-place and which had formerly belonged to one of the King's murdered brothers. Thenceforward his freedom of movement was severely restricted and he was watched day and night by the King's Chamberlains.

That same evening he was visited by one of these who told him that the King had been graciously pleased to order him to answer two

78

questions. The first was: 'Are you able to awake the dead?' And
the second: 'When will the day of resurrection take place?' To the first
of these Wolff replied without hesitation that, with God's power, one
could do anything, but that so far God had not granted him power
to raise the dead. The second he found not quite so easy to answer,
having on his previous visit to Bokhara somewhat rashly announced
that the Second Coming was due to take place in exactly fifteen years'
time. He now explained that since then he had 'had some doubts of
the correctness of my calculation', but that he was still convinced
'by the signs of the times' that the coming of Jesus was at hand. All
of which was taken down in writing by a secretary.

On the following day, after he had again made obeisance before the
Emir, another Chamberlain was sent to ask him on behalf of His
Majesty why he was dressed in black and red and what meaning this
had. To this he replied that his dress was that of the Grand Mullahs of
England and that he wore black in token of mourning for his dead
friends and red to show that he was ready to shed his blood for his
faith.

On the day after, a Chamberlain called at his house and told him
to follow him. 'Where', asked Wolff, 'shall we go?' 'This', replied the
Chamberlain, 'you will see.' At which the attendants trembled and
the guard commander whispered to him in tears, 'Why did you come
here? Stoddart Sahib and Conolly Sahib have thus been taken out of
the house where they will now bring you.' In the meanwhile, much to
Wolff's rage, the unspeakable Dil Assa Khan had mounted his horse
and ridden arrogantly off in front of him, his servants driving the unfortunate Doctor back if he came
too near to him. In this manner they arrived at the
country residence of the Nayeb Abdul Samut Khan
the *Topshi-Bashi*, or Master Gunner, who for so
long had been the jailer of Stoddart and Conolly.

ABDUL
SAMUT
KHAN

Abdul Samut Khan, Commander of the Emir's
Artillery, was a Persian of about sixty years of age,
a handsome enough man, though portly, with a
flowing black beard and a roving eye, and wearing

his ceremonial bonnet perched at a jaunty angle on the side of his head. Having at one time or another served with European officers in Persia and elsewhere, he affected a number of European mannerisms and on occasion even sought to pass as a European by birth. After an adventurous military career in his native land, he had, in order to avoid having his ears cut off by an enraged patron, fled to India. Thence he had fled for similar reasons to Afghanistan where he had placed his talents at the disposal of Dost Mohammed. From Afghanistan he had fled to Bokhara, where, having entered the service of the Emir, he had in the space of nine years risen to exalted rank and amassed a vast fortune. A year or two earlier he had fallen into disgrace for embezzling the troops' pay and had narrowly escaped execution; but at the last minute the Emir had found that he needed his advice for the conduct of his latest campaign against the Khans of Khiva and Kokand, with the result that he was now once more in favour, enjoying considerable political as well as military power and living in great magnificence and pomp on his estate outside the city.

It was here, in an upper room of the luxurious house in which he had so often conversed with Stoddart and Conolly, that this highly equivocal character now received Dil Assa Khan and Dr Wolff. Having only 'slightly embraced' Dil Assa Khan, he gave the Doctor a much warmer welcome, pressing him to his heart, kissing him 'for about ten minutes' and pinching his hands and fingers, 'as', his guest supposed, 'the freemasons do'. After this he invited them to sit down with him

to an excellent breakfast of *kebab* and rice with coffee and tea, while a secretary, sitting cross-legged on the floor, prepared pen, ink and paper in readiness to take down all that was said. A Royal Chamberlain, Makhram Kasem, was also present.

The Nayeb opened the conversation. 'Now Mullah Youssuf Wolff', he said, eating as he spoke, 'I have known you twelve years; ay, I saw you at Peshawar, and I know all about you.

At present England and Bokhara are at war, and are enemies; but after you have heard how the two officers, Colonel Stoddart and Captain Conolly, treated His Majesty and how they have treated me, England and Bokhara shall be friends, which I heartily wish. By the Usbeks I am suspected of being an Englishman, and by the English I am suspected of being an Usbek; but I am neither the one nor the other. All I wish is, that the truth should be known, and now I will tell you all about it.' And, so saying, Abdul Samut Khan set out to tell to his visitor the story, or at any rate his version of the story, of Charles Stoddart and Arthur Conolly.

When Colonel Stoddart arrived at Bokhara, said the Nayeb, the Emir had sent a guard of honour of soldiers to receive him. The moment of his arrival had happened to coincide with the Emir's return from a pilgrimage and, as he approached the Ark, the Minister of Foreign Affairs and some of the other Grandees had gone up to him and said: 'This is His Majesty; you must dismount.' But this Stoddart had refused to do, saying that he was without instructions on this point. He had likewise refused to submit to the ceremonial of *selaam*, drawing his sword as soon as the Foreign Minister took him by the shoulders. These early breaches of etiquette had, according to the Nayeb, been overlooked, the Emir only smiling and saying: 'He is a guest.' But more ill feeling had been caused when the Colonel, on being asked by a high Moslem religious dignitary whether he was a merchant or an ambassador, had replied with military succinctness: 'Eat dung.' After which things had gone from bad to worse. Though the Nayeb did not dwell on this, Stoddard had, it seemed, indeed been consigned to the well twenty-one feet deep in which the Emir kept his selection of specially bred vermin and reptiles and had, after a time, as the Nayeb put it, agreed 'from fear' to turn Mohammedan. 'And', he added, 'according to the Mohammedan religion if a man says he will turn Mohammedan, he must either do so or die.'

Thereafter the Emir's treatment of his prisoner had varied. At times Stoddart had been confined in a noisome dungeon. At others he had been set free and favours heaped upon him. He had been told that all would be well if the British Government would send letters accrediting him as their representative at the Court of the Emir and recognizing the latter as the supreme ruler of all Turkestan. To this he had replied that he would obtain such letters in four months, and the Emir had ordered a series of *japar-khanas* or post-houses to be established all the way to the Persian frontier in readiness for their arrival. But fourteen months had gone by and still there had been no answer, and when at length a letter had arrived for the Emir it had been signed not by the Queen of England but by Lord Ellenborough, the Governor-General of India. Worse still, it had described Colonel Stoddart as a 'private traveller'. Once more the rage of the Emir had descended on the unfortunate Colonel and once more he had been consigned to the deepest of the Palace dungeons.

Stoddart had now been joined by Conolly. But Conolly had not, any more than Stoddart, been officially accredited to the Court of Bokhara. On the contrary, said the Nayeb, his mission, in so far as he had one, had been to the Emir's bitterest enemies, the neighbouring Khans of Khiva and Kokand. Surmising that his purpose was to stir these up to attack Bokhara and generally to intrigue against him, the Emir had readily granted him permission to visit Bokhara and had then promptly cast him into the same dungeon as Stoddart.

So long as the Russian mission under Colonel Butenyov had remained in Bokhara, their presence had, it seemed, acted to some extent as a restraining influence on Nasrullah. With the departure of the Russians in April 1842 the last restraint had been removed. Stoddart and Conolly had been sent back to endure the torments of the Black Well for another two months, until 'masses of their flesh had been gnawed off their bones'. Already they were doomed. It only remained to choose a pretext for executing them.

To a man like Nasrullah this presented no difficulty. During their imprisonment both officers had sought to communicate by stealth with the outside world. This had been reported to the Emir, recently returned with great sounding of trumpets and beating of drums from his victorious campaign against the Khan of Kokand. 'On this account', said the Nayeb, concluding his narrative, 'His Majesty became displeased, and both Captain Conolly and Colonel Stoddart were brought, with their hands tied, behind the Ark in the presence of Makhram Saadat. They then embraced each other and Colonel Stoddart said to

Saadat: "Tell the Ameer that I die a disbeliever in Muhammed, but a believer in Jesus; that I am a Christian and a Christian I die." And Conolly said: "Stoddart, we shall see each other in Paradise near Jesus." Then Saadat gave the order to cut off first the head of Stoddart, which was done; and in the same manner, the head of Conolly was cut off.'

There was a pause. 'I thought', said Dr Wolff, 'that strangling was the mode of killing in Bokhara.'

'Strangling', replied Abdul Samut Khan, 'was formerly used; but the King of Bokhara said: "Strangling gives more pain, and the rascally Khan of Khiva strangles his people; and therefore, out of mercy, I command the heads of evil-doers to be cut off with a common knife."'

The Nayeb next asked Dr Wolff if he had anything to say. To this the Doctor replied that it was strange that the Emir should ever have expected the British Government to enter into correspondence with him so long as he was holding their envoy a prisoner. In any case, had not Lord Ellenborough written to the Emir? At this the Nayeb showed signs of embarrassment. 'What', he finally asked, 'is to be done?'

By this time it had become clear to Dr Wolff that, so far as he himself was concerned, 'there was now nothing else to be done but to contrive to get away from Bokhara as soon as possible and in the best and safest manner I could'. Accordingly, taking advantage of the note of anxiety he now discerned in the Nayeb's manner, he boldly replied: 'Let the King send with me an ambassador to apologize in England for his conduct.'

Meanwhile there were signs that the King shared the Nayeb's anxiety. During breakfast no less than three Royal Chamberlains had arrived at the Nayeb's house to inquire what progress the two of them were making. Makhram Kasem and the secretary were accordingly now sent back to the Palace to report, while the Nayeb asked Dil Assa Khan and the others present to take a walk in the garden.

So long as Dil Assa Khan and the Makhram had been present, Abdul Samut had defended the conduct of the Emir. Now that he was alone with Dr Wolff, he completely changed his line. 'Both Colonel Stoddart and Captain Conolly', he cried, bursting into floods of tears, 'have been put to death without a sin or crime on their part.' Stoddart,

when he had last seen him, had, he said, been in a pitiful condition, without a shirt on his back and as white as a wall. It had all been the work of the Emir. He himself had even offered Nasrullah one hundred thousand ducats for their release, but he had only replied: 'They are spies, and as spies they must die.' He, Abdul Samut, was now himself in danger, and had only narrowly escaped having his head cut off. 'Let the British Government', he continued, 'send one officer to Khokand, another to Khoolom, and another to Khiva, and thus let those Khans be induced to march against Bokhara; and let the British Government only give me twenty or thirty thousand ducats, I am ready to support them.' 'I make, he shouted, breaking into English, "Halt! Front!"' 'There is a custom', he went on, 'on the circumcision of a son to invite some great man, who takes the child upon his knees. I intend, if the British Government gives me twenty thousand ducats, to invite the King, place him upon a seat undermined, and, the moment he sits down, I will blow him up.'

Having somewhat sanctimoniously replied that the British Government would certainly not approve of such a scheme, Dr Wolff now took the opportunity to bring the conversation back to himself. What, he asked, had the Emir said on learning of his arrival?

The Nayeb's reply was far from reassuring. 'If he brings no letters from the British Government', the Emir had said on hearing of his approach, 'he shall fare like his predecessors. I shall kill him.' Then, being restless in his mind, he had assembled about twenty Grandees and asked them for their opinion. And they, too, had been in favour of killing him, one adding that, while he was about it, he might as well kill the Nayeb, too. 'But fear not,' said the Nayeb reassuringly, 'I will stand by you.' And, as proof of his reliability, he produced a number of signed testimonials including one from Colonel Stoddart bearing witness to his kindness and to the service he had rendered him in his attempts to obtain permission for Stoddart to leave Bokhara.

These highly misleading documents seem, for the time being at any rate, to have somewhat allayed the justifiable apprehensions which the Doctor was now beginning to feel in regard to his own safety. He was also, as evening approached, agreeably surprised to hear the familiar strains of 'God Save the Queen' rising from the Nayeb's garden, where that stirring melody was being accurately rendered, presumably in his honour, by a 'musical band of Hindus from Lahore', formerly in the service of Ranjit Singh. By the time he sat down to supper in the garden with the Nayeb and Dil Assa Khan, he was feeling rather happier, and his mood still further improved when at midnight Makhram Kasem, the King's Chamberlain, came panting in from Bokhara with tidings from the monarch, who had caused the gate of the city to be especially opened in order that he might deliver his message without delay. On his return to the Palace, said Makhram, he had found His Majesty sitting with his head in his hands. Suddenly he had started up and exclaimed, 'What did Youssuff Wolff say?' Then, after reading the account of their conversation, he had at once given orders that an ambassador should be ready in a few days to leave with the Doctor for England carrying presents for the Queen. 'You have', said the Nayeb, 'permission to leave.'

On the strength of this, Dr Wolff now sat down and wrote what he described as an 'official' letter to Captain Grover. 'I write this letter', he began, 'in the house of Nayeb Abdul Samut Khan, the Chief of Artillery and of the Arsenal of His Majesty the King of Bokhara, a sincere and excellent friend of the British nation.' He was, he said, writing 'by order of the King' to whom he was giving a copy of what he wrote. He then went on to report briefly and in extremely guarded terms the execution of Stoddart and Conolly, adding that he himself had now received permission from the King to leave Bokhara on May 9th. 'From Meshed', he concluded, 'I shall write everything more fully.' After which the Hindu band once again played 'God Save the Queen'.

But looking back on the events of the evening Dr Wolff realized that he had made at least one tactical error. In the course of his conversation with the Nayeb, he had, in an unguarded moment, let fall the remark that, had he found Stoddart and Conolly alive, he would have been ready to pay a large sum to obtain their release. The implications of this were not wasted on Abdul Samut Khan. 'How much', he at once asked, 'would *you* pay if *you* were imprisoned?' No sooner were the words out of his mouth than the Doctor realized what a mistake he had made. 'Here', he tells us, 'I perceived the height of my unguarded observation, and I began to tremble and was already somewhat afraid that the Nayeb was not quite sincere.' His forebodings were soon to prove abundantly justified.

Meanwhile, to judge by appearances, Wolff's position had somewhat improved. The Nayeb and the Royal Chamberlains went out of their way to be agreeable to him, and Dil Assa Khan, who always reflected

the prevailing trend, no longer kept at a distance from him when they rode abroad. Every day emissaries arrived from the King on the most diverse errands. How, His Majesty wanted to know, did the Christian Mullahs prove the truth of their religion? Would Dr Wolff write a short life of Mohammed from the English point of view? Why was England ruled over by a Queen? Had she the power to kill anyone she liked? How did a railway work? How fast did a steamship go? Were there witches in England? How were ambassadors treated there? Was an ambassador from Bokhara likely to be killed? Who were the richest Jews in England? Why did the English like old coins? Who were Darius and Genghiz Khan? Who were the members of Her Majesty's Government?

Dr Wolff was never at a loss. The information for which he was asked, whether theological, historical, political or general, was always forthcoming. He told the Emir about constitutional monarchy, and the Salic Law, and the Witchcraft Act, and King James VI of Scotland, and coin-collecting, and the Rothschilds and the Cohens and Sir Moses Montefiore. He wrote for him a non-controversial, but highly readable, life of Mohammed in Persian which caused an 'immense sensation' and was widely distributed all over Central Asia. He told him, for no very good reason, that Genghiz Khan was really a Jew.

Some things Nasrullah found a little hard to understand. He was worried about the Prince Consort. 'What kind of husband', he asked, 'is he that is under the government of his wife!' while one of the Chamberlains exclaimed indignantly, 'What kind of Sovereign is this that cannot take away any life that she pleases!' And the Doctor also had 'to write an immense time before he comprehended our railway travelling' and even then 'His Majesty could not understand why we had no camels in England'. But it was only when he sent him a list of the members of Sir Robert Peel's Government that he ran into real trouble. Immediately the Royal Chamberlain returned 'in a fury'. His Majesty, he said, had found Wolff out a liar. He happened to know that the four Grand Viziers were not, as he pretended, Sir Robert Peel and his colleagues but 'Laard Maleburne, Laard Jaan Rawsall, Laard Malegraave and Seere Jaan Habehaase'. Colonel Stoddart had told him so. And Wolff was obliged to hurry round to the Palace in person and give the Emir 'a complete idea of the Constitution of England' before Nasrullah could be finally satisfied as to his good faith. 'Though His Majesty could not understand it fully, I yet convinced him', he tells us, 'that my list might be true also, especially as I was able to tell him the names of the Whig administration.' But it had been a near thing.

While thus playing the part of a latter-day Scheherazade, the Doctor was gradually building himself up a special position in Bokhara. He was now comfortably installed in the Nayeb's house. He was allowed to ride freely about the town without the constant surveillance to which other foreigners were subjected. And more and more people now came to see him or spoke to him in the street. In this manner he obtained access to the innumerable rumours and whispers which flew about the bazaars and so received more information about the end of Stoddart and Conolly and about a variety of other subjects.

He met and talked to two Jews who had actually seen Stoddart and Conolly executed. Makhram Saadat, they said, had displayed their two heads to them, 'with the delight of a demon', exclaiming glee-fully, 'Here are the heads of the infidels!' He met some other Jews who wanted to know about Sir Moses Montefiore and who, referring to the English Rothschilds, remarked that in a country where one can so openly make such a display of one's property, the religion of that nation must be better. He met an old Russian woman, a slave, aged one hundred and eleven, who remembered Catherine the Great and who had no wish to return to Russia. He met Giovanni Orlandi, the captive watchmaker from Parma who, some years before, had saved himself from execution by making the clock over the gate of the Ark but was nevertheless to be executed in due course for refusing to become a Mohammedan or, according to another account, for allowing the Emir's watch to stop. He had, in his own words, been *un povero miserabile* in his own country and was now, he said, *un povero miserabile* in Bokhara.

He met, too, a number of people who told him much that was to the credit neither of the Emir nor of Abdul Samut Khan; who told him, for example, about the *Dastar Khanjee*, who, at the age of twenty was in charge not only of the Royal Kitchens, but also of the Customs and Excise Department and occupied in fact the position of King's Vizier. This promising young statesman had, it appeared, been raised to the high office which he now held 'for demerits unmentionable in any journal or narrative'. But, Wolff tells us, 'when he is older, it is generally hoped by the inhabitants and confidently expected by them, that the King will decapitate him and seize on his enormous wealth'.

Wolff also learned something of the elaborate network of espionage which existed in Bokhara and of the fear and suspicion which it engendered. The King, it seemed, employed innumerable boys as *akbar newees*, or 'news-writers'. These reported to him everything that the other boys said in the streets and even what their own families said at home. The servants, too, in the houses wrote down everything their masters said, taking note of every conversation between husband and wife, 'even in bed', and passing it all on to the Emir.

Nor was the Emir the only one to have his private intelligence service. Just as he spied on his Ministers, so they spied on him, Abdul Samut openly boasting that he knew of 'every sentence and every half sentence' uttered by His Majesty. And there were plenty of people, too, who kept a close watch on Abdul Samut Khan. Every time that, as Chief of the Royal Artillery, he caused the Royal cannon to be fired, the Emir would send a Royal Chamberlain to ask the reason. Of late, his long private conversations with Dr Wolff had aroused comment, and the report was going about Bokhara that they sat together all day in a room and practised witchcraft.

Even the Emir had by now realized that in Dr Wolff he had got hold of someone quite out of the ordinary. Each time he saw him, he found him more remarkable and, when the Doctor called on him dressed as a Bokharan, he burst into fits of uncontrollable laughter. Wolff, he told the Nayeb, was the most singular being he had ever seen — 'a Star with a Tail' — quite unlike an Englishman, or a Jew or a Russian, either in his conduct or in his outward appearance. He was also a little surprised and perhaps a little alarmed, at the fact of his being there at all. 'How extraordinary!' he had exclaimed on first learning of his arrival, 'I have two hundred thousand Persian slaves here, — nobody cares for them; and on account of two Englishmen a person comes from England and single-handed demands their release.' And on another occasion: 'I have done myself terrible harm by killing Stoddart and Conolly.' There were other times, however, when His Majesty seemed less contrite, as for example when Wolff asked for permission to take back with him the bones of Stoddart and Conolly and received in reply the jocular answer, 'I shall send *your* bones!'

Meanwhile May 9th had arrived, the day on which Wolff was to leave. But Wolff did not leave. His departure, he was told, had been postponed until the fourteenth, when he would be accompanied by a great Turkoman Chief, bearing presents and a letter for Queen Victoria. His hosts, in the meantime, remained, to all appearances, as friendly as ever. He still lived in luxury at the house of the Nayeb. The Royal Chamberlains still arrived daily from the Palace with

their variegated questionnaires. And when from time to time he called on the King in Bokharan dress, His Majesty still laughed heartily at his appearance, leading Wolff, for some reason, to the conclusion that he was 'wholly uneducated, but not without talent'.

Another five days went by. It was now May 14th. Wolff went to see Abdul Samut Khan. 'Will permission be given today?' he asked. 'Yes', replied the Nayeb, 'and for this reason I beg you to give me a receipt for five thousand ducats.' 'Great God!' said Wolff and asked him to give him the account. 'Not now,' replied Abdul Samut, 'but give me your receipt.' 'You are dealing', he added coyly, 'with the Nayeb, who will not deceive you.' And in the end Wolff gave him the receipt he asked for. All day Wolff waited for word to start, but none came. Instead, in the evening, Makhram Kasem arrived with a message from the King, a message that caused Dr Wolff the deepest concern.

'His Majesty', it ran, 'has already ordered the letters to be written to the Queen of England, and the presents which were intended for Her Majesty the Queen of England were already prepared; but His Majesty has just been informed that the British Ambassador at Teheran has offered one thousand tillahs as a daily compensation, as long as the Bokharan Ambassador is detained within the confines of Persia. His Majesty the Ameer is therefore determined to keep Joseph Wolff at Bokhara as long as his Ambassador is detained in Persia.'

No sooner had Dr Wolff received the Emir's message than he sat down to write to Colonel Sheil at Teheran, asking him to do everything in his power to secure the early release of the Bokharan Ambassador. 'You must', he wrote, 'pardon my confused style, for I am in a great stew.' And he went on to ask Colonel Sheil to honour his bills, adding, a little prematurely as it turned out, that there was no longer any probability of his being put to death. 'Pray get the Ambassador soon sent off', he concluded, 'and be kind enough to send a copy of this letter to Lady Georgiana also.' Then he went off to see Abdul Samut Khan to try to get back his receipt for the five thousand ducats. In this, needless to say, he was unsuccessful and had in the end to be content with a solemn oath, sworn by the head of Abdul Samut's four-year-old son Abdullah, that the Nayeb would on the following Sunday approach the Emir on Dr Wolff's behalf for permission to depart.

On the following Sunday, Abdul Samut Khan went to see the King, as he had said he would, and returned two hours later with the news that Wolff would be able to leave in four or five days' time. But four and then five days went by, and the end of the month came, and nothing happened. On the contrary a much stricter watch was now kept on Wolff. Visitors were discouraged and three guards accompanied him wherever he went.

It was at about this time that the Doctor seems first to have entertained serious doubts as to the reliability of Abdul Samut Khan. Certainly, if he still preserved any illusions on this subject, it was not from any lack of telling. Again and again people he had met, including the Nayeb's own officers, had warned him against him. 'The Nayeb', said one officer, 'will do with you as he did with Stoddart and Conolly. He killed them, and he will kill you.' And as the two of them stood talking in the Nayeb's pleasant garden, a shrieking and howling and wailing fell on their ears. 'What is that?' asked Wolff. 'That', replied the officer, 'is the prison kept by the Nayeb for those whom he suspects, and whom he suffers to starve from hunger.' Whereupon, happening to look round, they found that they had been joined by the Nayeb in person, and their conversation ceased abruptly. Later, another of the Nayeb's officers had taken Wolff aside and had also tried to put him on his guard. 'You will find at last', he said, 'that the Nayeb is a *haram-zadeh*, a bastard, who behaved towards Stoddart and Conolly as he does [to] you, detaining them as long as he could and always pretending to be their friend.' Certainly there was an ominous similarity between what he had been able to find out about the Nayeb's behaviour towards Stoddart and Conolly and the way in which that dignitary was now treating him.

For Wolff, by now, almost the only source of encouragement was the presence in Bokhara of an Ambassador from the Shah of Persia, a certain Abbas Kouli Khan, who had recently arrived with instructions to secure his release. But scarcely had Abbas Kouli reached Bokhara on his errand of mercy than there also arrived there no less than three Ambassadors from Yar Mohammed Khan of Herat for the express purpose of advising the Emir to cut off the Doctor's head. In apprising him of the arrival of these ominous Afghans, the Nayeb, as usual, took the opportunity to assure him of his own friendship and anxiety to help. 'Now remain with me here in the garden', he said, 'and if the King does not send for you in a few days, I will let you escape, either to Shahr-Sabz or to Khiva. I swear to you by the head of Abdullah Khan — by the Koran, that I will do so; and if the King will take you by force, I will beat the drum—drum! drum! drum! and say, "Halt, Front!" for I know that the King will send you home.' At the same time he did his best to poison the Doctor's mind against Abbas Kouli by telling him that the latter, far from having come to intercede for his release, was in fact the bearer of a request from the Shah to put him to death. 'But fear not,' he added, as reassuring as ever, '*I* shall see the King next Sunday.'

But when next day a Chamberlain arrived with orders from the Emir that Wolff was to be taken back to Bokhara, the Nayeb, for all his assurances of support, only urged his guest to obey the Royal command. This was too much for Wolff. 'I now see', he suddenly shouted at Abdul Samut, 'that the people are right who say that you are the cause that Colonel Stoddart and Captain Conolly have been killed.' 'You', he continued, getting angrier than ever, 'are the murderer of Stoddart and Conolly. You are a bloodhound. You are a liar, a traitor and a rascal. You intend to kill me too.' To which the Nayeb, his features distorted with rage and fury replied, 'Yes, I killed them; I know how to manage you Englishmen; and I will pay you out for having insulted me.' At this Wolff gave him a push, shouting, 'You murderer!' to which the Nayeb, with refreshing frankness, replied, 'Yes, I am.' 'It is', Wolff tells us, 'utterly impossible that Wolff could give a description of the countenance of the blood-hound when he said these words. His whole face became convulsed, distorted and crooked, and pale with anger and rage; grinning, laughing, raging, just like an apparition from hell!!'

The Royal Chamberlain, who had been a witness of this remarkable scene, now sought once more to induce Dr Wolff to accompany him to Bokhara in compliance with the command of the Emir. But the Doctor, beside himself, shouted 'No!' and, jumping over the Nayeb's garden wall, took to his heels.

He did not get far. On the other side of the wall was the garden of a pavilion which the Nayeb was building for his little son Abdullah, or, according to other accounts, as a fortress for use in case of trouble with the Emir. Here Wolff was overtaken by one of the Nayeb's officers, who, assuring him that he was helping him to escape, hurried him through a water-hole into the house of a major who lived near by. There he remained until evening, when his new-found protectors returned with the story that the Emir, believing him to have escaped, had sent out troops in all directions to scour the roads for him. Once the pursuit had died down, they said, they would help him to escape to India. In fact, they would come with him themselves.

But it was not long before the Doctor discovered that he was being played with. No sooner had his new friends left the room than 'a female, in the most coquettish manner and unveiled, entered it'. But, says Wolff, 'I at once observed the trap, and exclaimed in a loud voice and with great apparent rage, "Go to hell!"' And when the two officers came running in to see what was the matter, he told them that he had recognized this as an old trick of the Nayeb's and that he was not going to be taken in by it.

Next day, on orders from the Emir, he was conducted back to the city, where, he was told, he would occupy the same room in which Stoddart and Conolly had been kept immediately before their execution. On his way there he was taken to the Palace to make obeisance to the Emir. This time he was not taken inside, but was made to wait outside the gate. He noticed that the Emir, when he appeared, looked sternly at him and was visibly displeased. He was then taken to the house in which Stoddart and Conolly had awaited their end and told to stay there.

That evening he received a message from the Emir. There were in

Bokhara, said the message, a number of foreigners. None of these foreigners had been molested by the Emir. All of them enjoyed his protection. His Majesty, therefore, felt 'greatly incensed' that Dr Wolff should have seen fit to declare that it was his intention to put him to death. His Majesty had been red in the face from anger. He would now like to know whether Dr Wolff wished to leave Bokhara 'without honour and in disgrace or with honour and filled with favour'.

Dr Wolff had by now learnt to receive announcements of his impending release and departure from Bokhara without undue enthusiasm. He accordingly replied that he would leave His Majesty to decide the mode of his going from Bokhara and then settled down to await developments.

He had been right not to let himself be over-excited by the Emir's message. On the next day that unpredictable potentate set forth at the head of his army to attack the new Khan of Kokand. Before leaving, he doubled Wolff's guards and at the same time let him know that his prospects of release, indeed of continued survival, would depend on the success of the expedition. 'I am still', wrote Wolff to Lady Georgiana, 'detained at Bokhara and the King has now marched against Khokand. Whatever may happen to me, dearest wife and son, remember that you yourselves have nothing to reproach yourselves ... God had given me strength to await his will with patience and resignation. Pray amuse yourself and go to Wiesbaden in summer.' To Captain Grover he wrote: 'I am in the greatest danger ... The Persian Ambassador, Abbas Kouli Khan, is kind to me, but I think he will not have it in his power to rescue me ... Pray console my dear wife and child as much as you can.' To Colonel Sheil also he dispatched a brief report of his predicament:

Bok hara June 8, 1844

My dear Colonel Sheil

I am now a prisoner at Bokhara in spite of all

*the promises of the King and the
Nayeb and do not know
what shall happen to me.
I have not the least hope
of being soon released*

*Yours affectionately
Joseph Wolff*

It was now June, the brazen, blazing June of Central Asia. For Wolff the weeks that followed were a nightmare. Soon he found that he had completely lost count of the days. He came to wish that they would kill him and have done with it. Closely guarded and continually spied on, he lived in constant uncertainty of what each day would bring forth. Cut off from outside contacts, he was forced to live at close quarters with companions who had long been uncongenial to him. As usual when things were going badly for him, the detestable Dil Assa Khan and the others became more infuriating than ever, pestering him for money and depressing him with their gloomy prognostications. 'The whole town of Bokhara', said his servant Abdullah, 'speak with certainty that the Ameer will put you to death, for it is the wish of Abdul Samut Khan and all the Grandees; and the King of Persia, being a Shiah, has no influence at Bokhara; but if you satisfy our demands, we will save your life.' Next came the Nayeb's tailor on a similar errand and then two of Dil Assa Khan's Turkomans, who, their minds clearly working on the same lines, addressed him as follows: 'Mullah Youssuff Wolff, ducats are sweet; we dream of ducats day and night, and we dreamed last night that you, on your return to England, sat near your monarch, and all the grandees of your country kissed the hem of your garment. The most beautiful women crowded around you, and desired to be your wives, and you took the daughter of the

Queen as your lawful wife ... You will live in the finest palace except the Queen's and be fanned by dancing girls; and if you say to her: "Oh, my Queen, cut off the head of this or that person", she will immediately follow your advice. Both of us, Kaher Kouli and I, Amir Sarog, dreamed this at one and the same time, and therefore it will become true.' Even the guards pestered him continually for bribes.

During these difficult weeks Wolff derived much comfort from the kindness and devotion of Abbas Kouli Khan, the Persian Ambassador, who, fortunately for him, happened to be living in the same house as he was. In order to show the falseness of Abdul Samut Khan's slanderous

THE PERSIAN
AMBASSADOR

assertions, Abbas Kouli now produced the written instructions given him in Teheran, ordering him to do everything in his power to secure Dr Wolff's release. 'I swear to you,' he said, 'by God and the Koran, that I will not leave Bokhara without you.' In the meantime he did what he could to protect Wolff and to make life more agreeable for him, reading to him, sending him food from his own table to prevent him from being poisoned, and setting one of his own servants to watch over him at night so that he should not be murdered in his sleep. Wolff was also visited at this time by certain of the Jews of Bokhara who managed to convey to him much useful information by chanting it in Hebrew under the very noses of his Bokharan guards who thought that they were singing psalms.

Now and then news would trickle through from the Kokand front, where the Emir had now been joined by the Nayeb with four pieces of cannon and two hundred disciplined troops. It was for the most part not very reassuring news. There was a report that Kokand had surrendered. There was another not very convincing report that the Emir had reached Kokand and had then withdrawn his troops out of pity for the inhabitants. And there was a third report, which turned out to be true, that the Emir had been heavily defeated and had lost twelve of his generals. Finally, there was a story that the Emir, either of his own accord or at the instance of Abdul Samut Khan, had decided to put Wolff to death as soon as he returned to Bokhara.

No sooner had this last story reached Bokhara than Wolff's servant Abdullah burst angrily into his room shouting: 'Now they are going to kill you, and what shall I do here? I have no money for going back. Give me a letter to the Ambassador of your nation at Teheran to make me a present of two thousand ducats; if not I will kill you now.' This was too much for Wolff. Without a moment's hesitation he 'took a stick and gave him such a beating as he never gave anyone in his life'. During these anxious weeks he also took to singing to keep up his spirits, one of his favourite songs being the robber chorus from *Rinaldo Rinaldini*. This he sang so loudly that 'the whole Palace resounded with it and Abbas Kouli Khan, the Persian Ambassador, his great friend, was rejoiced to perceive him bear up against his dreadful state'.

At length, towards the end of July, some six or seven weeks after setting out, the King and Abdul Samut Khan returned to Bokhara. As they approached the Ark, Wolff was waiting for them by the gate. But the King, as he passed him, deliberately looked away, and the onlookers, seeing this, said to each other, 'It will not go well with that Englishman.'

And indeed the very next day Wolff was visited by a *mullah* sent by the King to ask whether he would turn Mussulman. 'Tell the King,' replied Wolff, 'NEVER! NEVER! NEVER!' At this the *mullah* asked whether he had not a more polite answer for His Majesty. 'Decidedly not,' said Wolff and the interview was at an end. A few hours later the executioner arrived. 'Joseph Wolff,' he said, 'to thee it shall happen as it did to Stoddart and Conolly.' After which he made a sign at Wolff's throat with his hand and withdrew.

The end had come. Dr Wolff now prepared for death. He had with him some opium and this he first decided to take in order to alleviate the pain in case his throat should be cut. Then, on further consideration, he threw it away and said his prayers and wrote the following words inside his Bible:

> My dearest Georgiana and Henry,
> I have loved both of you unto death.
> Your affectionate husband and father,

Bokhara 1844   J. WOLFF

In the meanwhile, however, an important development had taken place. The Persian Ambassador had received by secret courier from Meshed a personal letter from the Shah for the Emir and on this very same day sent word to Nasrullah asking for an audience in order that he might deliver it to him. On receiving the answer that he could give it to the Minister for Foreign Affairs, he replied that his orders were to deliver the letter to the Emir in person. Again there came the message from the Palace to say that he should send it, and again he replied that it must be delivered in person. Only then did the Emir finally consent to receive him. But the letter, once delivered, was not without its effect. 'Well,' said the Emir, having read it through, 'I will make you a present of Joseph Wolff. He may go with you.' And this time, it seemed, he really meant it.

Before Dr Wolff set out, the Emir, as unpredictable as ever, presented him with ninety ducats, a Persian manuscript bearing his personal seal, a shawl and a horse with a silver saddle. He also sent with him, as his Ambassador to Queen Victoria, Amir Abul Kasem, one of the Court Chamberlains. When the Doctor went up to the Palace for the last time to pay his respects, he was allowed to ride through the gate without dismounting, a privilege scarcely ever accorded to a foreigner. 'Stoddart and Conolly', the Emir said to him on taking leave, 'excited Khokand and Khiva to war, and therefore were put to death. You, Joseph Wolff, proved yourself to be a man of understanding and knowledge, and therefore I treated you with honour.'

There was also a last encounter with Abdul Samut Khan. The *Topshi-Bashi* went straight to the point. 'I give you', he said, 'one thousand ducats more, which you will deliver with the other two thousand; and three thousand ducats you have to give me for my trouble, including a present of eight hundred ducats to my son

Abdullah Khan; and two thousand two hundred ducats I have spent for you among His Majesty's officers. You must, therefore, give me now a note of hand for six thousand ducats.'

'Give me back my other notes of hand,' said Wolff and, on being given them, at once tore them into small pieces.

'Why', asked the *Topshi-Bashi*, 'do you tear them before you have written the other?'

'I will now write you another,' said Wolff, and, taking a pen, wrote as follows:

> In the garden of the infamous Nayeb, Abdul Samut Khan, surrounded by his banditti, and compelled by him, I write that he forced from me a note of hand for six thousand ducats.
>
> JOSEPH WOLFF, Prisoner.

Dr Wolff finally left Bokhara on August 3rd. A crowd of many thousands flocked to witness his departure, crying out in amazement at this unexpected act of clemency on the part of the Emir. In addition to Abbas Kouli Khan, who continued to display the utmost solicitude for his well-being, Wolff was accompanied by the unspeakable and apparently inescapable Dil Assa Khan; by Amir Abul Kasem, the Emir's newly appointed Ambassador to the Court of St James; by his Ambassador to Persia; by Mirza Abdul Wahab, a painter, who in return for thirty tomans had, at the Doctor's request, drawn from life a number of masterly portraits of the Emir and his principal advisers;[1] by a large number of ransomed slaves; by some Afghan merchants and some fakirs and dervishes from India; and finally by some professional murderers, who, Wolff was reliably informed, had been hired by Abdul Samut Khan to kill him at a convenient moment during the journey. On being invited by these to join up with them, the Doctor prudently replied that he preferred to stay with Abbas Kouli.

Their caravan, which numbered no less than two thousand camels, made its first halt at Jesman-Doo, a village not far from Bokhara, where they rested in a garden beside a lake. Here they were overtaken by one Mohammed Taki, an astrologer from Herat, who had come from Persia with Abbas Kouli for the purpose of rescuing his wife, who

---

[1] Reproduced at pp. 34, 84 and passim.

had been kidnapped and made a slave by the Turkomans. Not only had Mohammed Taki found his wife, but he had also received from the Emir a present of a hundred ducats. But now that he had caught up with them, his companions noticed that his wife was not with him.

'Where', asked Abbas Kouli, 'is your wife?' At this the astrologer looked a little shifty. 'For two or three nights successively,' he replied, 'I looked in the stars and saw one star with a black tail. From this I perceived that misery was *entailed* upon her. And so I have resold her for forty ducats and for a beautiful high-bosomed slave girl, only seventeen.' This was too much for Abbas Kouli. Jumping to his feet, he threw down his pipe with such violence that it broke to pieces. 'God burn you and your stars!' he shouted. 'You rascal! You did not look on the stars but on the money and the beauty of the young girl. I spit in your beard!' At which, we are told, 'the astrologer went out quite mortified'.

While they were waiting to go on, Dr Wolff was addressed by a Turkoman from Sarakhs who sniffed the air and said, 'I smell a caravan of Uzbeks.' And, sure enough, a few hours later a caravan of Uzbeks arrived from Khiva. At Jesman-Doo, Dr Wolff was visited by a dervish from Yarkand, by an Afghan Seyd and by some yellow-coloured Calmucks. 'Ay, you Infidel,' said the Afghan vindictively, 'have you succeeded in cheating the Emir so that he let you go? If he had only given you into my hands, I would soon have made away with you by my javelin.' 'A dervish!' he went on; 'I know these English dervishes. They go into a country, spy out mountains and valleys, seas and rivers; find out a convenient adit and then go home, inform a gentleman there — a chief, who has the name of Company, who sends soldiers and then takes a country. Tell him what I say.' Whereupon he withdrew.

From Jesman-Doo they made their way to Shahr-Islam. Here Dr Wolff had more trouble with the murderers, who once again sought to edge him away from his friend Abbas Kouli. He was, they kept telling him, a much greater man than Abbas Kouli or anyone else in the caravan and it was therefore only proper that he should keep aloof and pitch his tent in an isolated position. But Dr Wolff was not so easily taken in. 'I know your villainy,' he replied. 'You do not have to tell me where I am to pitch my tent. I shall ride with Abbas Kouli Khan.'

As the great caravan made its way across the desert, the tinkling of the camel bells was cheerful and encouraging. At sunrise and sunset they would halt. The cry of '*Allah Akbar!*', 'God is Great!' would resound. And, turning towards Mecca, the travellers, solemnly stroking their beards, would repeat the prayers and perform the genuflexions prescribed by their creed.

At Karakol Dr Wolff received a further warning from the Governor of that place who told him that he was in greater danger than ever, in greater danger even than at Bokhara. Abdul Samut Khan, he said, had given specific instructions that he should be murdered in the desert. And, indeed, from now onwards the murderers who accompanied him did not give the unfortunate Doctor a moment's peace. Finding that the trunks in which he kept his money had been broken open, he decided to buy himself an extra mule, so that he might keep it constantly under his own eyes. But a day or two later he saw the murderers clustering round his mule and next day, when the time came for the caravan to start, the mule was lame. The good Abbas Kouli Khan, as resourceful as ever, had the mule, lame or sound, dragged along with his own mules, while he and his brother took Dr Wolff's own horse on a leading rein so as not to lose him. But even this did not deter the murderers who, choosing a moment when the caravan had lost its way in the dark, sought to separate the Doctor from his escort, first by jostling him, and then by means of a fictitious message, asking him to wait behind. They next tried poison, but here again were frustrated by Abbas Kouli who provided Dr Wolff with specially cooked food, at the same time taking charge of his money for him so as to keep it out of harm's way.

On reaching Charjui, the murderers decided to take the bold step of telling Dr Wolff to his face that, if he did not hand his money over to them, they would kill him. But Abbas Kouli, hearing of this, summoned them and denounced them to the principal people of the caravan, who replied in chorus: 'We will burn the father of the first rascal that touches him.' Whereupon the murderers loudly protested that they had never had any intention of harming Dr Wolff.

From the great tower of Charjui, meanwhile, came the watchman's ominous cry: 'Watch! watch! For the people of Khiva may come to kill your cattle and destroy the child in the mother's womb.' Nor was this all. So as to deny water to their traditional enemies the Khivans and thus hamper their movements, the Turkomans, they found, had filled up the wells at the oasis of Rafitak, which lay directly on the caravan's route across the waterless desert. To help the travellers on their way, the Governor of Charjui now sent an advance party of fifty horsemen to Rafitak to clear the wells in preparation for their arrival. As soon as this had been done, they set out and reached Rafitak after riding for two days and two nights without stopping, for fear of the Khivans.

Before long Dr Wolff, who had suffered a serious internal injury through a fall from his horse some weeks earlier and was in considerable pain, found himself wondering if he would ever get home alive and whether even capture by the Khivans might not be preferable to the hazards and hardships which he was enduring. At Rafitak there were more rumours of an impending Khivan attack and not long afterwards the appearance of some horsemen on the horizon was greeted with anguished cries of 'Organtshee! Organtshee!' 'The Khivans! The Khivans!' But on closer inspection they turned out to be a party of tax-collectors sent after them from Bokhara to levy a charge in respect of every liberated slave who crossed the Oxus.

Even now their troubles were not over. On reaching Merv, Wolff and his companions were once again hospitably received by his old friend the Khalifa. But this did not prevent the latter's sons from declaring them prisoners and endeavouring to extort money from them by threats of violence. At Merv, Wolff also got wind that a new plot against his life was being hatched by two of the Turkomans who accompanied them and that the Turkoman tribes through whose territory they were passing were planning an attack on the caravan. In fact, neither of these threats materialized, but on his arrival at Sarakhs Dr Wolff was hooted by a mob of Turkoman boys, egged on by Dil Assa Khan and Abdullah. The Doctor dealt with this situation in a highly original manner. Fearing that the crowd, which was becoming more and more hostile, might rush him, he 'suddenly conceived the brilliant idea of playing the madman' and, dressed as usual in the gown of a Doctor of Divinity, started to dance and leap, singing, as he danced, the following Persian song which he had learnt a few days before from a dervish:

> *Had Khoda Khahe, Ham Donyae Dun,*
> *Een Khyal ast, een Mohal ast, een Jenoon.*
>
> His fancy's wild, his mind distraught,
> Who casts on God and Earth his thought.

And, sure enough, his strange behaviour produced the desired effect. 'This', said the Turkoman boys, 'is a *Dehli*, a possessed dervish,' and dispersed in terror. 'I cannot', was Wolff's comment, 'bear the Turkomauns. They are a covetous, treacherous and at the same time stupid, race of people.'

At length they came once more to Masteroon, where the Persian frontier fortress on its rocky eminence towered high above the plain. 'Thank God!', they said to each other, 'we are on Persian ground.' The worst part of their journey was over.

As Dr Wolff approached Meshed a day or two later, the inhabitants flocked out to meet him. 'Praise be to God!', they said, 'that you come back with your head from that accursed city, Bokhara! We have heard how shamefully you have been treated by those scoundrels, Nayeb Abdul Khan and Dil Assa Khan. The *Assaff-ood-Dowla* has sworn by God, the Prophet and Ali, to burn the father and wife of Dil Assa Khan.' And, indeed, no sooner had they entered the city than both the abominable Dil Assa Khan and his henchman Abdullah were seized and clapped into irons. As Dil Assa Khan had a wife and children, the Doctor interceded on his behalf, but Abdullah he caused to be bastinadoed and sent to jail for forty days. After which, those two unpleasing characters passed finally out of his life.

At Meshed, where he remained for just over three weeks, Dr Wolff received a letter from Colonel Sheil, brought by a special courier with instructions to escort him back to Teheran, and containing a cordial invitation to stay at the Embassy. He reached Teheran on November 3rd. For some weeks past he had been far from well, suffering from vomiting and various other disorders. But though 'ill, miserable, bilious and excited', he 'still bore up against all', and on November 4th, at the invitation of Colonel Sheil, preached at the Embassy, though the Colonel, being a Roman Catholic, did not himself attend. A day or two later he preached at the Russian Embassy in the presence of the Russian Ambassador and all his staff, and later attended a public dinner given for him by the Ambassador. Once again he called on the Shah who graciously gave him his autograph, and said that he supposed that by now he had had enough of Bokhara and would not be in a hurry to go back there. He also asked him why he had shaved his beard off. 'My beard', replied Wolff, never at a loss for an answer, 'was so full of lice, that I was afraid that they would drag me back to Bokhara!'

Wolff's next visit was to his old friend Khosrow Khan, the Chief Eunuch, a Georgian by birth, secretly a Christian with a tendency to be Swedenborgian. Khosrow, it appeared, had recently seen and conversed with both Moses and the Prophet Samuel, whom he described to Wolff in considerable detail. Moses, he told him, never smiled, being still greatly incensed at the ingratitude of the Jews.

Although Wolff stayed at the Embassy, his relations with his host, Colonel Sheil, seem to have been somewhat strained. Apart from religious differences, there seem to have been a number of subjects on which they did not see eye to eye, notably the Colonel's attitude towards his mission. 'The more I reflect on Colonel Sheil's conduct,' writes the Doctor, 'the more do I perceive his culpable neglect and indifference.' He also complained of his manners, adding, however, that 'his bilious maladies and gout must plead an apology for all this'. And it is indeed not hard to understand that to a functionary of Colonel Sheil's disposition, with a tendency to biliousness and gout, an enthusiast of the calibre of Dr Wolff might at times have been a severe strain on the nerves.

Dr Wolff left Teheran on November 7th. He was accompanied for some of the way by the faithful Abbas Kouli Khan, who, before turning back, gave him two Cashmere shawls for Lady Georgiana and a letter in which he compared her to the Queen of Sheba.

Dr Wolff's journey from Teheran to Tabriz was, as usual, marked by encounters with a variety of improbable characters. The first of these was with a Georgian Colonel serving in the Persian Army who was secretly a Christian and undertook to profess Christianity openly *and in uniform* if Dr Wolff would only obtain for him from Queen Victoria a commission as a Colonel in the British Army. 'I could not', wrote the Doctor, 'give him any encouragement.' At the same place he met another Georgian who told him that, if he did not take him with him to England and 'put him in the way to make money', he would turn Mohammedan out of sheer spite. 'I told him', wrote the Doctor, unmoved by this religious blackmail, 'that he was welcome to do so.' A little farther along the road he met two travellers who turned out to be American missionaries, Mr Perkins and Mr Stocking. 'You are Dr Wolff, I guess,' said Mr Perkins. 'It's Dr Wolff, if I guess right,' said Mr Stocking. But a violent snowstorm made any further conversation impossible. And, after handing him a slice of delicious plum-cake, they took leave of him.

On November 24th, just before reaching Tabriz, Dr Wolff was again taken ill, 'vomiting immensely' and being seized with 'a terrible shivering' so that he was obliged to exchange his horse for a litter. His temporary indisposition did not, however, prevent him from enjoying to the full the social amenities of Tabriz, where he was once more received 'not only with hospitality, but with great cordiality' by Mr Bonham, the British Consul-General, and his 'amiable lady'. These included a public dinner given for him by the principal Armenians of Tabriz, the christening of the Bonham baby, at which he himself officiated, and a ball given in his honour by Mr Bonham.

The dancers at the ball, at which the band of Prince Bahman Mirza, the Governor of Azerbaijan, played European music, were, we are told, 'not ladies and gentlemen, but all gentlemen', and included 'the Russian Consul-General, Mr Osrov, with all his attachés' and 'the respectable Greek merchants of the house of Ralli — a firm established at Tabreez, Constantinople, Marseilles, London and Manchester'. In order to make things still livelier, some of the guests dressed up in Dr Wolff's Turkoman *khalats* and in the robe given him by the Emir of Bokhara. 'It was', he tells us, 'a most funny sight.' Mrs Bonham, for her part, 'kept herself in another room, as some Persians were present'.

Poor Mrs Bonham! She had only a few more weeks to live being 'removed from us' on December 30th by the typhus fever. 'She was', writes Dr Wolff in an enthusiastic little character sketch, 'one of the most pious, sensible, virtuous and kind-hearted ladies I ever met with — exquisitely beautiful with a childlike simplicity. She was daughter to Sir William Floyd, Bart., residing at Brussels.'

After attending 'a third dinner' given in his honour by the Russian Consul-General and being cured from 'a second dangerous attack oɪ bilious fever' by a Maltese physician named Casolani, Dr Wolff set out from Tabriz in his litter on December 9th. All his friends came to see him off: the British and Russian Consuls-General, Dr Casolani, a Georgian Colonel, the Greek merchants and all the Russian attachés. On his departure he was loudly cheered by all the Europeans, 'with', he tells us, 'many a hearty hurrah'.

A week later he was twenty-four miles beyond Khoi. Before him rose once again the snowy mountains of Armenia. The cold was intense and he felt more bilious than ever. In view of the precarious state of his health, he now stayed only in Christian houses in order that, if he died, he might be given a Christian burial. This, in practice, meant staying with Armenians and, though 'rather partial to Armenians in general', he very soon came to the conclusion that their filthiness was 'inconceivable' and that their priests were 'most depraved', being principally concerned to cater for the temporal needs of any Europeans who happened to be 'of a gay disposition' rather than to minister to their spiritual requirements.

To add to his discomfort, the snow now began to fall in earnest. In order to get across the mountains he was obliged to abandon his litter and once more take to a horse. In the mountains the snow was 'prodigious' and it was 'horridly cold'. *Koolagh* after *koolagh* overtook him. The Armenians he encountered were dirtier than ever, 'so dirty that it would be actually indecent to describe it'. His horse fell on him, knocking him senseless. When he came to, he found that he had been laid in a stable among cows and horses. By the time he reached the outskirts of Erzerum on January 5th, he was in a sorry condition indeed, being 'in such a state of debility and nervousness and so eaten up by vermin all over the body' that he could scarcely stand, and it was with feelings of thankfulness and joy that, looking out from his litter, he saw his friend Colonel Williams, and some other members of the British Colony who had ridden out to meet him. On seeing the state he was in, Colonel Williams rode on ahead into Erzerum to get ready some clean linen and 'a good Turkish bath'. But even the best of Turkish baths was not enough. For the next five days Colonel Williams, later to become famous as the heroic defender of Kars, was fully occupied in personally picking the vermin off his guest and even then final victory was only achieved by means of a 'special ointment' provided by the English doctor.

After three weeks spent recuperating in Erzerum under Colonel Williams's hospitable roof, Dr Wolff was ready to continue his journey to Trebizond. This appears to have been relatively uneventful. Taking the route across the mountains followed by Xenophon and the Ten Thousand, he reached his destination and the Black Sea on February 7th.

At Trebizond, he had a last moment of uneasiness, for there he received a visit from a man who introduced himself as a Chamberlain of the Emir of Bokhara and, despite his visitor's pleasant manners, he could not help wondering whether he was perhaps not a member of the Ismaeli, a sect entrusted by the Emir with the task of tracking down his enemies, wherever they might be, in order to murder them. It was not until he set sail for Constantinople that he felt completely safe.

Dr Wolff reached Constantinople on February 23rd. Again he was hospitably entertained by Sir Stratford and Lady Canning, by M. Titov, the Russian Ambassador, and by a number of other members of the diplomatic corps. Again he preached repeatedly and at length in Embassies and private houses and again he called on the Grand Vizier, the *Reis Effendi* and the *Sheikh ul Islam*. He also visited, in the congenial company of Lord Clarence Paget, Lord Maidstone, Lord Anson and Mr Rashleigh, M.P., the great Mosque of St Sofia and was duly impressed by its enormous size. Finally, on March 20th, after Lady Canning had once more personally supervised the packing of his trunks, he set sail for England in the Oriental Peninsular Company's steamer, *The Duke of Cornwall*, arriving on April 11th at Southampton.

At Southampton Dr Wolff was greeted by Captain Grover and his friends, all cheering him, and, a few minutes later, by his wife and child. Captain Grover, he was glad to find, had arranged with the Treasury that the presents he had received from the Emir of Bokhara and other potentates he had encountered should be let through the Customs free of duty.

On reaching London, Dr Wolff lost no time in repairing to the Church of Holy Trinity in Grays Inn Lane Road, where he gave thanks for his preservation and later preached to a numerous congregation. He also spoke for several hours at a public meeting organized by the Stoddart and Conolly Committee in the Exeter Hall.

Dr Wolff's travels were over. 'I now hope', he wrote, 'to end my days quietly in England, and to give up migrating altogether, for my natural inclinations are all in favour of comfort and ease ... I ever detested travelling for travelling's sake, for I dislike uncivilised life and uncivilised habits; and it is altogether an absurdity to talk of the sacredness of "the word of an Arab", or "the noble character" of a rapacious robber Kurd, or "the generosity" of a treacherous Turkomaun, who invariably require for their hospitality tenfold the price of what they tender to the weary wanderer. But I was carried onwards by the object; and should I ever be again called on to be the instrument of ransoming English or other captives from the hands of the vile Khyburees or the merciless Affghauns, or from the power of the blood-hound Abdul Samut Khan, I trust never to be wanting at my post.'

His wishes were to be fulfilled. The call to further action in strange climes and distant lands never came. Nor did the opportunity present itself for a second round with 'the bloodhound Abdul Samut Khan'. The latter, as was only to be expected, came to a bad end, his intrigues carried to such lengths that in 1847 'the King did at last take an axe and actually cut him in two with his own hands'. Nasrullah, on the other hand, continued to prosper. He reigned until 1860, committing up to the last the most appalling atrocities. As, finally, he lay on his death bed, scarcely able to speak, he ordered his wife to be brought in and had her stabbed to death before his eyes.

Dr Wolff, meanwhile, had been given the living of Ile Brewers in Somerset, where he spent the remainder of his life and where in 1862 he died. Lady Georgiana had predeceased him in 1859. As for little Henry, he grew up in due course to be Sir Henry Drummond Wolff, the prominent diplomatist and politician.

One day in the late summer of 1862, just twenty years after Stoddart and Conolly had been beheaded in Bokhara and a few months after the death of Dr Wolff, a parcel was delivered at 25 Chester Square, the house of Arthur Conolly's sister, Mrs Francis Macnaghten. It contained — now much battered and soiled — the small prayer book belonging to her brother which he and Charles Stoddart had read together in prison. It also contained a letter. The letter, which was dated August 18th, 1862, from St Petersburg, ran as follows:

Mistress!

You know by the means of Messrs Boutinoff that in the year 1848 during my sojourn in Bokhara, a lucky hit gave in my possession the prayer-book that belonged to a man of great merit, to your unhappy brother Mr Arthur Conolli, cast into the prison by Ameer. Mr Conolli sought a religious consolation in this small book, upon which pages he underlined the passages having reference to his woeful position, and noted the events of his sojourn and barbarous treatment at Bokhara, hop thoses last words will reach his fatherland. After the barbarous murdering by Ameer of M. M. Stoddart and your brother the book passed from hands to hands and is now at last fallen into the possession of the sardars (soldiers of the Ameer) who born in Poland and after the year 1831 sended in the steppes of Orenburg has fallen into the hands of the Kirghisian robbers, and was sold off into a slavage to Bokhara. Ameer allowed him among the others to return in the Russia. The compassion from my part towards my unhappy compatriote called forth his attachment to me. He brought me the prayer-book and talked very much about your unhappy brother's fate. This small book was for me the dearest remembrance of my journey to the Central Asia. Yet as Mr Boutinoff informed me your desire to possess this last memory of yr unhappy brother I decided without hesitation to put this book into your hands. Mr Gaugart, the friend of mine going into the London in the purpose of visiting the great Exhibition was so good and purposed me to put the book into your hands, and I think it is my duty to render to the sister the property of her brother. I remain with all possible regard yr most obedient servant—

VICTOR SALATZSKY

Mrs Macnaghten opened the prayer book. 'Thank God', her brother had written in it all those years ago, 'that this book was left to me. Stoddart and I have found it a great comfort. We did not fully know before this affliction what was in the Psalms or how beautiful are the prayers of our Church.' And in another place: 'Desiring that the circumstances of our last treatment at Bokhara should become known, and conceiving that a record made in this book has a better chance of preservation than one made upon loose paper, I herein note the chief occurrences since my arrival.' There followed his will and a kind of diary of several thousand words written during his last imprisonment in the margins and on the fly-leaves and end-papers of the little book. The writing, Mrs Macnaghten noticed, ended abruptly in the middle of a sentence, as though the writer had been suddenly disturbed at his work. The book itself was later lost, but not before a copy had been made of what was written in it.

A DERVISH FROM TURKEY

'*Smotrite kakoi bieloi etot Hadji!*' — 'Look how white that pilgrim is!' These words, casually addressed to a companion by a Russian naval officer as he looked over the side of his ship, caused the most acute embarrassment, nay trepidation, to the person to whom they referred — one of a boatload of dervishes returning from a pilgrimage to Mecca and now undergoing a routine examination at the hands of the Russian naval authorities off the Island of Ashurada, at that time (the year was 1863) Russia's only outpost in the Southern Caspian.

The pilgrim in question was a bearded man of about thirty with a marked limp, wearing an immense turban and the traditional garb of an itinerant dervish, and known to his companions as Hadji Reshid. His skin, though deeply burned by the sun, was, as the keen-eyed Russian had noticed, a shade or two lighter than those of his dusky companions, and it might have been observed that during the whole of the inspection which now ensued he remained huddled in his place, leaving any discussion or negotiation that was necessary to his fellow pilgrims and taking care to present to the Russians no more of his face or features than was absolutely necessary.

Not that Hadji Reshid was afraid of the Russians. From them he had nothing to fear. What disturbed him was the thought of the doubts to which such a chance remark might give rise in the minds of his fellow pilgrims, the twenty-four devout Mohammedans in whose company he was travelling. For Hadji Reshid was not a real pilgrim; nor was he, as he let it be supposed, a Turk. He was not even a Mohammedan. And the discovery of these facts by his present companions or by anyone else he might encounter during the journey on which he was now setting out would not only ensure the failure of his enterprise but would almost certainly condemn him to a singularly unpleasant death.

Arminius Vambery, to give 'Hadji Reshid' his true name, had been born in a small town in Hungary in 1832. Though lame from birth, he was otherwise robust and his unusual intelligence quickly attracted the attention of his teachers. Apprenticed at the age of twelve to a ladies' dressmaker, he nevertheless managed by his own exertions to continue his education and eventually made his way to Pressburg where he earned his living by teaching, while at the same time pursuing his own studies. 'Impelled', he tells us, 'by a particular inclination to linguistic science', he 'occupied himself with several languages of Europe and Asia'. But it was to the East in particular to which he felt himself drawn. 'All my musings, endeavours, thoughts and feelings', he writes, 'tended towards the Land of the East, which was beckoning to me in its halo of splendour.' In 1854, at the age of twenty-two, he was enabled by the generosity of a compatriot to fulfil his long-cherished desire. Setting out with little luggage save some old clothes and a knapsack of books, he travelled by way of the Danube and Black Sea to Constantinople, arriving there practically penniless.

In Constantinople he at first earned a precarious living as a teacher of languages. But, soon after his arrival there, he had the good fortune to be appointed tutor to the family of a rich and influential Turk. For the next six or seven years the Hungarian lived as a Turk amongst Turks, speaking Turkish, inhabiting the Turkish quarter, frequenting Moslem libraries and places of learning and finally even entering the service of the Turkish Government. For convenience he now changed his beribboned Hungarian hat for a fez, took to using the name of Reshid Efendi and, while remaining at heart a Hungarian, became outwardly in almost every respect a Turk. He was thus able to penetrate to circles which would normally have been closed to anyone but a Moslem. Even the most fanatical *mullahs* welcomed him to their cells and there discoursed to him on obscure questions of Mohammedan doctrine and told him fascinating tales of their pilgrimages to the Holy Cities of Arabia and Turkestan.

In this manner he was all the while increasing his mastery of Oriental philology and acquiring a minute and far-reaching knowledge of the languages, customs and religious beliefs of the countries of the Middle East. In particular he became interested in the affinity that seemed to exist between the Turco-Tartar dialects of Central Asia and his own native Hungarian. Soon he felt ready to carry his investigations a stage farther and, in the year 1860, conceived the daring project of visiting Turkestan, the cradle, if not the birthplace of the Turanian race.

For nearly twenty years now, no one had been found bold enough to follow in the footsteps of Dr Wolff. Travellers from Europe had shunned Central Asia. The murder of Stoddart and Conolly and the disasters which had overtaken the British expedition to Afghanistan had given an evil reputation to the whole area which lay between Russia and India, a reputation which had been further darkened by reports of the thousands of unfortunate Persians who each year were kidnapped and carried off into slavery by the man-stealing Turkomans of Transcaspia. Turkestan was more than ever a region which no European, indeed no foreigner, could visit without risking death or slavery.

Politically and strategically, on the other hand, Central Asia was growing daily more important. The Russian forward movement towards India, temporarily checked by the Crimean War, had been resumed. Each year since 1860 had brought news of fresh clashes between the ever-advancing troops of the Tsar and those of the Central Asian Khanates, of the establishment of fresh Russian outposts and the preparation of fresh expeditions. Soon it became clear that the continued independence of the Khanates was gravely threatened. In London serious alarm was felt at the course of events. To many it seemed that, if Khiva, Bokhara and Kokand, let alone Afghanistan, were to fall under Russian domination, the British position in India would be directly menaced. Soon many were asking whether the time had not come to take active measures to check the Russian advance before it went any farther.

Such was the background against which Arminius Vambery, impelled partly by scientific, but partly also by political curiosity, had formed the resolve to visit Turkestan. One thing was clear enough. If he was to reach his destination and return from it alive, it would be necessary for him to make the journey in some kind of disguise. To travel openly as a European in search of knowledge was an impossibility.

It remained for him to make up his mind which character he could assume with the least danger of discovery and, having taken this decision, to find a suitable jumping-off place from which to start.

Here his unrivalled knowledge of the language, customs and religions of the East and the numerous connections which he had formed during his years in Constantinople stood him in good stead. In the summer of 1862 he made his way from Turkey to Persia, reaching Teheran towards the middle of July. On arrival in Teheran, he at once repaired to the Turkish Embassy, where he was hospitably received by the Ambassador, Haidar Efendi, a former acquaintance from Constantinople.

Vambery spent the next eight months in Persia. During this period he made the Turkish Embassy his base. It was an old custom that the Sultan's Ambassador should extend his help and protection to the many Mohammedan pilgrims of various nationalities who passed through Persia on their way to and from Mecca, and amongst its visitors the Embassy counted a wide assortment of holy men, *hadjis* and dervishes, from different parts of Central Asia. To Vambery these 'ragged wild Tartars' were a source of unending delight. He made it his business to see and talk with as many of them as possible and so gleaned much valuable information concerning the regions which he intended to visit, while at the same time adding to his store of philological knowledge. The dervishes, for their part, were glad of his help and grateful for the interest which he took in their affairs, and soon the word went round the *caravanserais* of Teheran that Reshid Efendi (as he now called himself) was a good friend to dervishes, that indeed he was perhaps himself a dervish in disguise. Thus it was that on the morning of March 20th, 1863, a party of four *hadjis* presented themselves at the Embassy, asking to see Reshid Efendi in order to seek his help and in particular to complain to him of their treatment at the hands of the Persians, who, as Shiahs, had little sympathy for the Sunni pilgrims who traversed their country on their way to Mecca.

The dervishes' spokesman was a *hadji* from Chinese Tartary, wearing a green robe over his rags and on his head a great white turban. His fiery glance and proud bearing proclaimed him a personage of considerable importance. He was, he announced, no less a person than Hadji Bilal, Court Imam to the Vang of Aksu and, as one who had twice made the pilgrimage to Mecca, a *hadji* twice over. He and his twenty-three companions were now returning to their homes in Eastern Turkestan. 'Our company', said he, 'consists of young and old, rich and poor, men of piety, learned men and laity. And yet we live together on good terms with each other, since we are all from Kokand and Kashgar and have amongst us no Bokhariot, no viper of that race. From Teheran to our homes', he continued, 'there are four roads that we can take: the first, by Astrakhan, Orenburg and Bokhara; the second by Meshed, Herat and Bokhara; the third by Meshed, Merv and Bokhara; and the fourth through the wilderness to Khiva and Bokhara. The first two are too costly and the fighting now taking place round Herat is also an obstacle. The last two are, it is true, very dangerous, but we are bound to take one of them and we wish, therefore, to ask your friendly counsel.' And so they fell to discussing the arduous journey which lay before the pilgrims and the difficulties and dangers which it presented.

It was as they sat there talking that an idea began to take shape in the mind of Arminius Vambery. At first sight his visitors were far from prepossessing. Their wild demeanour and strange features, the extreme filthiness of the rags in which they were clothed, the indelible marks which their long and arduous travels had left on their persons, gave them an outlandish, an almost forbidding appearance. And yet, it was impossible not to like their frankness, impossible not to be pleased at the ready confidence which they showed in their new-found friend. Might they not, Vambery reflected, perhaps provide the answer to his problem? Might they not exactly serve his purpose? What, he asked himself, if he were to journey with them into Central Asia?

Having once formed such a project, it was necessary to proceed with extreme caution in order not to arouse their suspicions or wound their susceptibilities. Vambery chose his line of approach with care. After they had been talking for more than an hour, he observed that he had himself always cherished the desire to visit Turkestan. Not only did he long to see the only source of Islamic virtue and inspiration which still remained undefiled; it was also his wish to behold with his own eyes the saints of Khiva, Bokhara and Samarkand. It was with this object in view, he said, that he had left Turkey. He had now been waiting for a year in Persia. He thanked God for having at long last granted him fellow-travellers such as they with whom he might proceed on his way and accomplish his wish.

Having once recovered from their surprise at this announcement, the four Tartars showed every sign of delight. They were, they announced, now quite sure of what before they had only suspected, namely that he was a dervish in disguise. It gave them infinite pleasure that he should regard them as worthy of the friendship implied by his readiness to undertake so distant and perilous a journey in their company. 'We are all ready', said Hadji Bilal, 'to become not only your friends, but your servants. But we must draw your attention to the fact that the routes in Turkestan are neither as commodious nor as safe as those in Persia and in Turkey. On that which we shall take, travellers meet often for weeks with no house, no bread, not even a drop of water to drink; they also run the risk of being killed, or taken prisoners and sold, or of being buried alive under storms of sand. Ponder well, Efendi, the step which you propose to take. You may later have occasion to rue it, and we would not wish to be regarded as the cause of your misfortune. Above all, you must not forget that our countrymen at home are far behind us in experience and worldly knowledge, and that, in spite of all their hospitality, they invariably regard strangers from afar with suspicion. And besides, how will you be able without us and alone to make the long journey back?'

But Vambery was not to be deterred. He declared that, in order to achieve his desire, he was ready to bear any fatigue, to give up any of the comforts which he now enjoyed. Such things meant nothing to him. 'I know', he went on, 'that this world below resembles a hostelry, in which we take up our quarters for a few days and whence we soon move on to make room for others. Yes, my dear friend, take me with you. I must hasten away from this horrid Kingdom of Error, for I am too weary of it.' These well-chosen words were more than the pious Tartars could resist. Without further ado they formally accepted 'Hadji Reshid' as their travelling companion and all four of them then fell upon his neck, kissing him and embracing him with every show of affection — a proceeding the delights of which were tempered as far as Vambery was concerned by the overpowering stench which exuded from their bodies and clothing.

Having temporarily taken leave of his new friends, Vambery at once acquainted his host, Hajdar Efendi, with his plan. The Ambassador received his announcement with dismay. It was, he said, the act of a lunatic to want to go to a place from which so few travellers had ever returned, and, not content with that, to choose as guides men who 'for the smallest coin' would gladly take his life. But, seeing that nothing that he could say would shake Vambery in his resolve, he decided to do what he could to help his headstrong guest in his perilous venture. At Vambery's request he received the Hadjis and warmly recommended him to their hospitality, adding that they would be duly requited for any service they might render to the Efendi, the servant of the Sultan, who was now entrusted to their charge. After which he asked to be told the names of all the pilgrims and made them a present of some fifteen ducats, while to Vambery himself he gave an official passport bearing the *Tugra* or seal of the Sultan.

It was decided that they should set out in a week's time. Vambery spent the days that followed preparing for the journey and making the acquaintance of the remainder of the party whom he found huddled together in two tiny cells of a caravanserai, 'dens filled with filth and misery'. But, for all the squalor of their surroundings, the pilgrims seemed cheerful enough and readily interrupted their never-ending search for lice to give him a hearty welcome and brew him some rather unappetizing green tea.

They were, as their leader had told him, a strangely assorted company. There was Hadji Yusuf, a rich peasant from Chinese Tartary; and his nephew Hadji Ali, a boy of ten with little narrow eyes like a Kirghiz; and Hadji Yakub, a hereditary mendicant; and Hadji Kurban, a knife-grinder, who had in his time traversed the whole of Asia, travelling to Mecca and Constantinople, to Tibet and Calcutta, to Orenburg and Taganrog. There was an infirm lad of fourteen named Hadji Abdur Rahman whose feet had been badly frostbitten in the mountains near Hamadan and who had been in agony ever since; and 'an enthusiastic young Tartar' called Hadji Sheikh Sultan Mahmoud, the son of a poet and descendant of a famous saint; and a Chinese musketeer; and a man who knew the whole Koran by heart; and another who, having shouted 'Allah!' precisely two thousand times, would foam at the mouth and fall into a state of ecstatic blessedness; and a dozen others, some rich and some poor, some possessing a mule or donkey and some with no possessions save their beggar's staff, but all, it seemed, on good terms with each other and all well disposed towards their future travelling companion.

After they had drunk their tea and after he had broken bread with each of them individually, they sat down in a circle to discuss which way they should go. The choice, it will be recalled, had already been narrowed down to two possible routes, both dangerous and both leading across the Turkoman desert. The way by Meshed and Merv to Bokhara was the shorter but would lead them through the territory of the Tekke Turkomans, the fiercest of all the Turkoman tribes, of whom it was said that they would not hesitate to sell the Prophet himself into slavery if he fell into their hands. The alternative route lay through the territory of the Yomud Turkomans, a relatively hospitable people, but it involved a journey of forty stations through the desert without a single spring of sweet drinking water. In the end they decided to take the second. 'It is better, my friends,' said Hadji Bilal, 'to battle against the wickedness of the elements than against that of men. God is gracious and on this His journey He will certainly not abandon us.' After which he invoked a blessing, the whole company raising their hands in the air, and, when he had finished, grasping their beards and crying 'Amen!'

During the two last days which remained before his departure there were moments when Arminius Vambery was assailed by doubts. Hadji Bilal had shown himself so very agreeable, so very anxious to please. Could it be that the Ambassador was right after all? Might not the pilgrims be deliberately luring him on, in order to rob him or hold him to ransom, once they had him in their power? And his health? Would he, with his lame foot, have the physical strength to endure the hardships that lay before him? And worse than hardships. 'When you see that preparations are being made to torture you to death,' said his friend Dr Bimsenstein of the Austrian Legation, handing him some strychnine pills, 'and when you cannot see a ray of hope anywhere, then take these pills; they will shorten your agony.'

But the time for doubts was past. When he thought of the fruits that his journey might produce, his mind was made up. Fighting back any lingering qualms, he speedily completed his remaining preparations. Having, on the advice of Hadji Bilal, shaved his head, he exchanged the semi-European costume of a Turkish Efendi for the ragged robes and tremendous turban of a Tartar dervish, and, after bidding farewell to his friends at the Embassy, betook himself on the early morning of March 28th to the caravanserai. Here he found the remainder of the company already assembled and impatient to start. Once again Hadji Bilal invoked a blessing, and no sooner were the words out of his mouth than there was a wild rush of pilgrims through the gate, as those on foot struggled and strove to get ahead of their more fortunate companions on horseback.

Two or three hours later the travellers had reached the mountain pass from which they could take their last look at Teheran. As he looked back on the domes and minarets of the city, bathed in the bright Persian sunlight, Vambery reflected with a momentary sinking of the heart that he was leaving behind him the last outpost of civilization. Before him lay in his own words 'the extremes of savageness and barbarism'.

But he was not left to himself for long. Noticing his depressed mood, the other pilgrims at once flocked round him, assuring him of their brotherly love and doing their best to comfort him. From then onwards, whether he rode in company with the richer pilgrims or tramped on ahead with the poorer members of the party, he was never alone, but remained an object of delighted interest to his companions, who, gazing at him in admiration, kept exclaiming, 'Hadji Reshid is a true dervish; one can make anything out of him!' He, meanwhile, did his best to live up to their high opinion of him, screaming out *'Allah, ya Allah!'* at the top of his voice whenever it seemed appropriate.

After climbing for five days through rocky gorges, the pilgrims at last reached the lonely caravanserai which stands at the head of the pass leading through the Elburz Range into Mazenderan and, leaving behind them the arid mountains and tablelands of the Iranian plateau, plunged suddenly downwards into the startlingly luxuriant vegetation of the Caspian littoral. At first their way took them through green subtropical forests and once, while in search of water to make tea, they came on two 'splendid tigers' which bounded away into the bushes while Vambery, in his alarm, hurriedly seized a rusty sabre with which to defend himself. Thereafter they traversed a belt of orange groves and tea plantations and then making their way through a region of marshes and morasses, came at length to the seashore and to the little town of Karatepe, whence they hoped to take ship across the Caspian.

Though still on Persian soil, the pilgrims had now reached the fringes of Central Asia. The neighbouring shores and waters of the Caspian were infested with man-stealing Turkoman pirates and slave-traders, and in Karatepe Vambery found himself surrounded by bigoted Sunnis whose unwelcome curiosity about his origins and provenance gave him a disagreeable foretaste of the searching scrutiny which from now onwards he must expect to encounter.

Scarcely had he found somewhere to live, than his room filled with visitors who squatted down in a row all round the walls, staring at him, discussing him amongst themselves and then loudly proclaiming the conclusions they had reached. 'A dervish', they announced emphatically, 'he is not. His appearance is anything but that of a dervish. The wretchedness of his dress contrasts too plainly with his features and his complexion. He must, as the Hadjis told us, be a relative of the Ambassador who represents our Sultan in Teheran.' And at this they all rose to their feet. 'Allah', they added, 'alone knows what a man of such distinguished antecedents has to do amongst the Turkomans in Khiva and Bokhara.'

But Vambery refused to be drawn. To contradict them would, he felt, only serve to confirm his visitors in their suspicions. It was far better that his identity should remain impressively and conveniently shrouded in mystery. And so, assuming what he hoped was an air of Oriental inscrutability, he sat as though plunged in thought, oblivious to all that was being said — greatly to the disappointment of his visitors.

At last Hadji Bilal came to the rescue. Hadji Reshid, he told the assembled company, was in fact an *Efendi*, a servant of the Sultan. But, in response to divine inspiration, he had withdrawn himself from the deceptions of the world and was now engaged on a pilgrimage to the tombs of the Saints. At this the serried rows of Turkomans squatting round the walls shook their heads and left it at that, for, when told of divine inspiration, the true Mohammedan must never express disbelief, but, whatever his inward doubts, must exclaim '*Mashallah! Mashallah!*' in a tone of delighted admiration. For Vambery, Hadji Bilal's happy intervention had come not a moment too soon. When, after two hours of questioning and chattering, his visitors finally withdrew, it was with feelings of considerable relief that he settled down to brew himself some tea.

For the pilgrims the next step was to find a ship to take them across the Caspian to the Turkoman settlement of Gömüshtepe, the Hill of Silver. There was, it seemed, an Afghan whom the Russians at Ashurada employed to supply them with provisions and who was said to be ready to ferry the pilgrims across in return for a small sum. But here again Vambery found himself an object of unwelcome attention. When approached by the pilgrims, the Afghan captain declared that, while glad to take the rest of the party, he could not give a passage to Hadji Reshid, for he had heard that he was a secret emissary of the Sultan and was afraid that if he were to carry such a passenger the Russians might take away his livelihood.

It began to look very much as though 'Hadji Reshid' might find himself left behind. But, to his great relief, his companions loyally declared that nothing would induce them to go without him and at once started to look for another ship. And that very evening, as it turned out, came news of a pious Turkoman named Yakub who was prepared to carry the whole party to Gömüshtepe free and for nothing.

The pilgrims' leaders at once interviewed Yakub and found him quite ready to fall in with their plans. He was a voluble young man with a flashing eye and an 'uncommonly bold look'. But, for all his bold bearing, he proved on closer acquaintance to possess a romantic disposition. After he had been duly blessed by Hadji Bilal, he took Vambery aside and confided in him that he had long entertained an unhappy passion for a maiden of his own race by whom it was not returned. It appeared that an accomplished Jewish magician at present in the neighbourhood had told him that if he could procure thirty drops of attar of roses fresh from Mecca he could prepare him an irresistible love potion. 'We know', he said, 'that the Hadjis bring back with them from the Holy City essences of roses and other sweet perfumes. As you are the youngest of their chiefs, I address myself to you and hope that you will heed my entreaty.' Fortunately the necessary attar of roses was forthcoming and Yakub's wish could thus be gratified, though, whether the love potion produced the desired effect, is not related.

Two days later the pilgrims assembled on the seashore early in the morning, each with a sack of flour. A precarious-looking boat, hollowed from the trunk of a tree, was there to carry them to Yakub's ship which lay about a mile out. Once on board, they were packed in two rows like salted herrings, so tightly that they could scarcely move. At midday on April 10th they set sail. It was a fine spring day, and a favourable wind drove the little vessel before it like an arrow. Vambery, for his part, was in high spirits. There could be no drawing back now from his dangerous venture. Regrets were useless. And indeed he felt no regrets, but rejoiced in his own enterprise and in the goodwill and good faith of his fellow pilgrims.

Towards nightfall the wind dropped and they cast anchor and made tea. Vambery, who had stowed away some sugar in his girdle, invited Yakub to join him in a bowl of tea. As they sat talking under the brilliant stars, the young Turkoman, anxious to shine before the holy men, launched into a long account of his piratical exploits, of the marauding expeditions in which he had taken part, and of the numbers of heretics he had killed or taken prisoner. As he talked, he became more and more excited and his eyes flashed more than ever. One by one the pilgrims dropped off to sleep until at last only Vambery was left listening late into the night to these tales of murder and rapine.

On the evening of the following day they reached the Russian outpost of Ashurada, with its harbour, its European buildings and its steamships setting out to patrol for pirates. Here Yakub cast anchor and here it was, in the course of the routine examination by the Russian authorities which all ships had to undergo, that Vambery, crouching anxiously amongst his fellow pilgrims, overheard the remark of the Russian officer which momentarily caused him such alarm. So long as the examination was in progress, he kept as much of himself as possible out of sight. Then, once they had left the side of the Russian warship, he sat up and breathed a heartfelt sigh of relief. The breeze now freshened and after another hour's sailing they were in sight of the Turkoman coast: a long line of low-lying land, with hills rising here and there in the background. Immediately ahead of them, spread out on either bank of the River Görghen, lay the settlement of Gömüsh-tepe, a cluster of circular tents like beehives. The sails were taken in, the anchor lowered, and soon three insecure-looking craft were ferrying the pilgrims boatload by boatload to the shore.

Waiting to greet the pilgrims as they landed was Khandjan, a local Yomut chieftain whom Yakub had warned of their arrival. A tall, handsome man of about forty, he was modestly attired and wore a long black beard reaching down to his chest. As the boat approached the shore, Khandjan was seen to be prostrated in prayer, but, having completed his devotions, he now rose to his feet and, having solemnly embraced Vambery and the other leaders of the party, led them off in the direction of his encampment.

Here the news of the pilgrims' arrival had spread like wildfire and at their approach a noisy crowd of men, women and children, with dogs yapping at their heels, came pouring out of the tents, jostling each other in their anxiety to see and, if possible, embrace the holy men and so acquire a share in their merit. Though a little bewildered by this sudden onrush, Vambery, before being led away to the tent that had been allotted to him, had time to notice with pleasure that many of the young women, who were falling over each other in their desire to embrace him and who in accordance with Turkoman custom were unveiled, were possessed of very considerable personal attractions.

Scarcely had the pilgrims taken possession of their tent, after first ceremoniously walking twice round it and peeping in at all four corners, than they were overrun by the usual crowd of visitors who lingered on for hours, plying them with endless questions until even the long-suffering

Hadji Bilal lost patience. That night supper was served to them by Baba Djan, Khandjan's twelve-year-old son. It consisted of boiled fish and sour milk in a large wooden dish, which was brought in by a Persian slave, heavily laden with chains. After Baba Djan had set this before them he went and sat down by his father and both father and son looked on with obvious satisfaction while the hungry pilgrims ate their fill. Arminius Vambery slept soundly that night, his first amongst the Turkomans.

The pilgrims were to spend several weeks at Gömüshtepe as the guests of the hospitable Khandjan. Now that he was on Turkoman territory, Vambery made it his business to lay aside completely the character of an Efendi and become 'body and soul a dervish'. At the suggestion of Hadji Bilal, he now began to bestow blessings, to breathe on the sick and to beg for alms in true dervish fashion, with such success that his tent was for ever besieged by a numerous clientele all clamouring for blessings, talismans and 'holy breath' from 'the Turkish hadji', and he soon amassed a small fortune in alms, not to mention the dried fish, felt mats and other useful gifts with which his grateful patients rewarded him. What is more, he rapidly won the confidence and admiration of his hosts, who took him with them on visits to neighbouring tribes and even consulted him, as 'the best informed and most experienced dervish', regarding the construction of their new mosque.

Soon he had made any number of friends and acquaintances and was much in demand as a guest at the incessant banquets of horse-flesh, camel-flesh and other less appetizing delicacies which were given in honour of the pilgrims. In vain he would seek to limit his attendance at these functions to two or three a day. Despite all his efforts, he found himself literally elbowed out of his tent by his would-be hosts who in accordance with local practice would dig him unmercifully in the ribs until he yielded to their entreaties. 'The harder the push,' runs an old Turkoman saying, 'the heartier the invitation.'

Meanwhile time was passing, the weather was growing unpleasantly hot for desert travel, and, while most of his new friends saw in Vambery only a pious dervish, there were others who were inclined to lend credence to the persistent rumour that he was an envoy of the Sultan engaged in some kind of intrigue against the Russians. It was clearly time to be off and it was therefore with satisfaction that he learned that the *Caravan-Bashi* or chief caravan-leader to the Khan of Khiva would shortly be setting out for Khiva from Gömüshtepe. The Khan, it seemed, had been advised by his physicians to drink buffalo milk as a sovereign remedy against impotence, and, as there were no buffaloes in his own dominions, had dispatched his *Caravan-Bashi* to Gömüshtepe to buy him two couple of these animals. His mission successfully accomplished, the *Caravan-Bashi* was now returning post-haste to Khiva taking the buffaloes with him. What better travelling companion could the pilgrims hope to find on their road to Khiva than a professional *Caravan-Bashi*, with his unrivalled experience of the desert and with fear of his royal master's wrath to spur him on?

For all this, the plans for the pilgrims' departure, like most projects in Central Asia, took some time to materialize. There were preparations to be made. There were camels to be hired and bargained over. There was the sudden dilatoriness of Hadji Bilal to be overcome. 'Thy haste', he announced to Vambery with maddening detachment, 'is all to no purpose. Thou must perforce remain on the banks of the Görghen until Fate decrees that thou shouldst drink water in another place. And who can tell whether this will be in the near or in the distant future?'

In the end, however, the necessary preparations were made. The appropriate number of camels were hired, one to every two pilgrims; the provisions collected and packed. All was ready for their departure. Only one final precaution remained to be taken. The caravan was to assemble at Etrek, some twelve miles away in the territory of the Karaktchi, a particularly ferocious Turkoman tribe. Khandjan had therefore undertaken to recommend the pilgrims to the hospitality of Kulkhan, the Chief of the Karaktchi, with the request that he should grant them a safe-conduct through his territory. Once again Vambery was to experience a moment of acute uneasiness. When 'the Turkish dervish' was presented to him, Kulkhan, a man of sombre, repulsive physiognomy, showed no enthusiasm whatever for his would-be *protégé* and, having subjected him to a long and careful scrutiny, which he from time to time interrupted in order to whisper in

Khandjan's ear, finally announced that this was not at all his idea of a Turk.

But at this very moment there was a most fortunate diversion, the attention of all present being suddenly distracted by the return of Kulkhan's son Kolman or Kulumali from a horse-stealing raid across the Persian frontier. As the crowds gathered by the river to welcome him, Kolman and seven other mounted Turkomans with ten led horses came into sight on the far bank and, dashing into the river, swam their horses across. They were handsome, bold-looking youths with long, curling hair reaching down to their shoulders, heavily armed and wearing large sheepskin hats. At the sight of them and of the splendid animals which they had succeeded in carrying off, even the gloomy Kulkhan grew more cheerful, while the greedy-eyed crowd looked on in silent admiration and Hadji Bilal gave them his solemn blessing. As for Vambery, the distraction which their arrival afforded could not have come at a more opportune moment. Next day at noon the pilgrims, with Kulkhan, his son and the stolen horses, set out for Etrek on the first stage of their journey to Khiva.

At first the route they followed took them north-eastwards through a flat expanse of well-watered meadows knee-high with fragrant grass and broken only by occasional ancient Turkoman burial mounds. Next came reed-covered marshland swarming with wild pig. As Vambery, riding one of the stolen horses, was making his way through the reeds, his mount suddenly shied and threw him. With the laughter of his companions were mingled a series of piercing squeals. His horse had shied at a wild sow and in his fall he had landed on two of her brood. The outraged mother now rushed to her offspring's rescue and he was only saved from her tusks by one of his companions who held her at bay with a lance while he scrambled to safety. As he helped him to remount, Kulkhan's son pointed out to him that, as a holy man, he had had a most fortunate escape, for death from the tusks of a wild pig was enough to send even the most pious Moslem unclean into the next world, where a hundred years in the fires of purgatory would not suffice to cleanse him.

They spent that night in the tent of an aged Turkoman who killed a goat in their honour. The sombre Kulkhan, for his part, took advantage of their halt to torture a newly captured Persian slave with the object of ascertaining what relatives he had and what ransom they would be ready to pay for him. Though Kulkhan showed himself an exceptionally proficient torturer, the Persian, cunning even in misfortune, proved a difficult subject, with the result that they were held up for a whole day and it was not until the morning after that they set out again.

After an hour or two of slithering across a succession of salt flats and marshes the travellers eventually reached Etrek. No sooner had they arrived there than Kulkhan immediately led Vambery to his tent and told him not to leave it. He then went out and from inside the tent Vambery could hear him cursing at his womenfolk for 'always mislaying the chains'. This was scarcely reassuring and it was with feelings of considerable relief that shortly afterwards Vambery saw the unfortunate new slave enter the tent, his wounded feet now laden with heavy fetters, and realized that it was for the latter and not for himself that the chains had been needed. Shortly after, Kulkhan arrived to tell him that a tent had been prepared for him and that tea was ready. It was, he said, in order that this might be a surprise for him that he had temporarily shut him in.

Once out of danger himself, Vambery could not but feel pity for the poor Persian slave, who was brutally maltreated by everyone, and by no one more than Kulkhan's second wife, herself a Persian and a former slave. With tears streaming down his bearded face, the wretched man, forced to work all day in the melon fields and fed on a diet of salt fish, would beg piteously for a drop of water, and Vambery, with one eye on the door, for fear of being caught in such an impious act, would briefly pass him his water-skin. Already at Gömüshtepe he had become used to seeing slaves, but at Etrek he could not pass a tent without catching sight of two or three heavily chained Persians. And not only Persians. One day, while he was visiting a local Turkoman Khan, his host announced that he had a special treat in store for him. 'We know', he said, 'the relation in which the Osmanlis stand to the Russians. Thou shalt behold one of thy arch-enemies in chains.' At this a captured Russian sailor was led in, heavily laden with chains and sickly and sorrowful of countenance. Though deeply moved at the sight of a fellow European in such a plight, Vambery was careful not to betray his feelings, but behaved on the contrary as though he was highly delighted. 'Go and kiss the Efendi's feet,' said the Khan to the Russian and the Russian at once made as if to obey. But Vambery waved him back. He had, he explained, only that day begun his ceremonial purification and so did not want to soil himself by contact with an unbeliever. It would, he said, give him still greater pleasure if the Russian were at once removed from his sight, for there was no race he more heartily disliked. At this the Russian was hustled out, shooting at Vambery a glance of undisguised hatred as he went.

Now that the rest of the caravan had assembled at Etrek the news was received that the *Caravan-Bashi* was on his way to join them and would meet them in two days' time on the far bank of the River Etrek, which was to be the starting point for their journey across the desert. That evening was spent in preparations, in baking bread and salting down camel flesh, and next day they set out for the rendezvous, spending a night on the way. Vambery and Hadji Bilal shared the same camel, balancing in panniers one on each side. On the following day, having duly forded the Etrek, they were rewarded by the welcome sight of the *Caravan-Bashi*'s party advancing in their direction, preceded by three buffaloes.

The *Caravan-Bashi* proved on arrival to be a portly, amiable-looking Turkoman called Amandurdi. But, although he greeted the rest of the pilgrims with the greatest cordiality, his manner towards Vambery was markedly cold. Clearly somebody had told him something.

The trouble maker, it turned out, was Emir Mohammed, a crazy, opium-eating Afghan, who had joined their party at Karatepe and had been a source of constant annoyance ever since. A native of Kandahar, he had seen a number of Europeans during the British occupation of that city and had consequently been able to recognize Vambery as a *Ferenghi* by his features. After seeking unsuccessfully to blackmail him, he was now determined to make as much trouble for him as possible and had accordingly told the *Caravan-Bashi* that he was a European. 'I bet you', Vambery heard him saying, 'that he is a *Ferenghi* or Russian spy, and with his pencil he makes a note of all the mountains and valleys, all the streams and springs, so that the Russians can later on come into the land without a guide to rob you of your flocks and children. In Khiva, thanks to the precautions of the Khan, the rack will do its part, and the red-hot iron will soon show what sort of metal he is made of.'

It was not easy, Vambery found, to show no trace of uneasiness while such things were being said about him. But he did his best to affect indifference. And fortunately Hadji Bilal and the other pilgrims, without any prompting on his part, at once came to his rescue, indignantly rejecting the story that he was a European and threatening its author with an unpleasant fate when they reached Khiva. 'We'll teach him', they exclaimed indignantly, 'to represent a pious Moslem as an unbeliever!' Once again his luck had held — for the time being.

Having formally assumed command of the caravan, the *Caravan-Bashi* now caused its members to be counted. There were forty travellers and eighty camels. Before starting the pilgrims bade a formal farewell to Kulkhan. A prayer was said and both parties stroked their beards. After this Kulkhan and his followers turned back in the direction from which they had come, while the pilgrims, with the rest of the caravan, set out on their journey to the north.

One evening, some days later, while they were gathered round their camp fire, an idea occurred to Vambery. Sitting next to him, as it happened, was his tormentor, the Afghan, quietly drinking tea and smoking opium. By the glimmer of the coals on his water-pipe he could see his eyes, dull and glazed by the fumes of the drug. He was not more than half conscious. In his hand was his bowl of tea. What could be easier than to slip into this one of the strychnine pills he had been given by his friend Dr Bimsenstein and thus rid himself for good of a most dangerous enemy? Taking a pill from the wadding of his cloak, Vambery held it between his fingers above the bowl. Then, just as he was about to drop it in, he happened to look up, and saw, spread out above him, the moon and stars in all their beauty. For some reason, he felt a twinge of compunction and hid the pill away again in the lining of his cloak.

The pilgrims were now entering the true desert, the Kara Kum or Black Sands. Between them and Khiva lay some four hundred miles of howling wilderness, of salt flats and dunes of shifting sand and great, windswept expanses of hardened clay, from which the regular tread of the eighty camels echoed back monotonously as though in the surrounding stillness someone were endlessly beating time. During the day they set their course by the sun and at night by the Pole Star — *Temir Kazik*, as the Turkomans call it — the Iron Peg.

For Vambery, with his lame foot, crossing the successive stretches of dunes and shifting sand was a severe ordeal. In order to spare the weary camels, roped nose to tail, struggling along one behind the other under their heavy loads and refreshed only by scanty meals of thistles or dried-up scrub, the pilgrims were obliged to dismount and plod beside them for hour after hour, up hill and down, under the glare of a merciless sun, through the deep, soft sand. Nor was this his only trouble. The fear of discovery still weighed constantly upon him. At their very first camp he observed the *Caravan-Bashi* in earnest conversation with the pilgrims' leaders, and, from the glances which they cast in his direction, it was clear enough that he himself was the subject of their conversation. At first he pretended to pay no attention, but sat seemingly immersed in the pages of his Koran. Then, anxious to ascertain what was going forward, he walked over as though to join their little group. He was met half way by two of his friends, who, drawing him aside, confided to him that the *Caravan-Bashi* had had second thoughts and was now objecting to his remaining with the caravan. He considered his appearance suspicious and was afraid of incurring the wrath of the Khan of Khiva if he allowed him to accompany them. It seemed that once before he had accompanied a foreign envoy to Khiva and on that occasion the foreigner, with diabolical cunning and the help of a lead pencil, had somehow contrived to make a pictorial record of the whole route. This had so incensed the Khan that he had had two other members of the caravan put to death on the spot and he himself only escaped execution through the intervention of powerful friends. He did not wish to run the same risk again. In the end the pilgrims had persuaded the *Caravan-Bashi* to change his mind and not to leave their poor friend to his fate in the middle of the desert, but only on condition that he should be searched for hidden lead pencils and should promise to make no secret notes or drawings.

Having listened in silence to what they had to say, Vambery, on the principle that attack is the best form of defence, now suddenly began to shout and yell as though in a terrible rage. 'Tell the *Caravan-Bashi*,' he bellowed, so loud that the whole caravan could hear him, 'tell the *Caravan-Bashi* that it ill becomes him to listen to a drunken sinner like that Afghan. Religion, he will find, is no laughing matter. He will not have the chance to treat anyone like this again. He shall learn in Khiva with whom he has to deal.'

These words and the tone in which they were uttered quickly produced the desired effect. Roused to fury, the pilgrims were with difficulty restrained from assaulting the malicious Afghan. The *Caravan-Bashi*, a good-humoured, easy-going man, was, for his part, somewhat bewildered by the turn which events had taken. '*Khudaïm bilir*', he said resignedly, 'God knows.' And from then onwards he went out of his way to make himself agreeable to Vambery and even turned to him for religious advice. But, for all that, it was clear that deep down in their mystery-loving minds, he, and many others too, still clung to the notion that 'Hadji Reshid' was some kind of stranger in disguise, with the result that from now onwards he had to be more careful than ever not to be caught making drawings or taking notes or even showing undue curiosity about his surroundings. His spirited conduct had tipped the balance in his favour, but he could not for a moment afford to relax.

The caravan's progress was slow. One of the Khan's buffaloes was in calf and this considerably retarded the pace. There were stops, too, to bake bread, and a stop to look for the grave of the brother of one of the pilgrims who had been killed by brigands, and, on finding it, to exhume the corpse. There was also a stop to buy some more camels, of which Vambery took advantage to inspect a number of towers and domes and walls and columns which appeared to him to be ancient Greek ruins but which his companions urged him to shun as 'the abode of Djinns'. Once, at night, when clouds obscured the stars, they wandered from their course and were obliged to wake Vambery, asleep in his pannier, in order to consult his compass. Sometimes, too, at night, the camel-chain would break and someone would have to go back in the darkness to look for the missing beasts. As the caravan continued on its way, the searcher, so as not to lose his bearings, would shout at intervals to his companions and they would shout back to him, their cries echoing mournfully in the night.

After they had been going for four or five days the cow buffalo gave birth to a calf, which was packed into the pannier on the other side of Vambery's camel. Here it kept him awake at night by its constant bleating, and upset him during the day by the smell which it gave off under the blazing sun; but not for long, for the unfortunate little creature succumbed on the second day of its journey across the desert.

It was now May 18th. From where they were, they reckoned that it would take them two days to reach the twin mountain ranges of the Little and Great Balkan, which run parallel to each other a little way inland from the Caspian Sea, and another twelve days after that to reach Khiva. During the whole of this time they would come to only four brackish wells; and already the supplies of foul muddy water which they carried in skins on their camels were growing painfully short.

They had now established a regular routine. Each day they made three halts: the first before sunrise to bake bread; the second at noon to seek some respite from the scorching heat; and the third before sunset, to devour their scanty supper. On May 19th they caught their first sight of the Little Balkan range suspended between earth and sky like a dark blue cloud on the northern horizon. But that night disaster almost overtook them. The *Caravan-Bashi* having fallen asleep, the guide at the head of the line of camels led them in the darkness into a salt morass. All at once the camels stopped and refused to go on and their riders, leaping down, felt the ground moving under their feet as though they were in a ship at sea. Amid general consternation, the *Caravan-Bashi* now awoke and shouted to them all to stay where they were, and they spent the rest of the night standing there miserably, afraid to move in any direction. Only next morning, when it grew light, did they finally succeed in extricating themselves from their predicament. Had they gone any farther in the darkness, they would all have been sucked down into the morass.

All next day and all the day after they skirted along the foothills of the Little Balkan range, its glistening peaks and shady valleys furnishing a welcome contrast to the dreary flatness of the surrounding plain. Then on May 21st they came to the southernmost spur of the Great Balkan and, leaving both ranges behind them, turned late that evening north-eastwards into the true desert.

Before they started, the *Caravan-Bashi* addressed them. In order not to betray their position to any marauders, they should not, he told them, make any loud noise or light a fire at night, but should pray to God to watch over them and to grant them courage in the hour of danger. After this, some swords, a lance and two guns were distributed amongst them, Vambery receiving one of the guns and a good supply of powder and shot, and they set out. 'The more', he wrote afterwards, 'the Balkan disappeared in the blue clouds in our rear, the greater and more awful became the majesty of the boundless desert ... I often tried to brighten the dark hues of the wilderness by picturing, in its immediate vicinity, cities and stirring life, but in vain; the interminable hills of sand, the dreadful stillness of death, the yellowish-red hue of the sun rising and setting, yes, everything tells us that we are here in a great, perhaps the greatest, desert on the surface of our globe!'

During the days that followed, Vambery and his companions suffered all the torments of thirst. The sun blazed down mercilessly upon them. The heat during the day-time was scarcely endurable. Soon the supplies of water they carried with them were exhausted. The wells they came to were few and far between and yielded a bitter saline liquid which afflicted those who drank it with the most violent diarrhoea. With no water to wash it down, they could scarcely swallow their dry bread. Rancid mutton-fat was more than their stomachs could bear. Parched with thirst, without proper nourishment, they grew so weak that they could hardly stand. Underfoot the sand was burning hot.

At length, after three deadly days, the recent tracks of gazelles and wild asses brought them hope: somewhere not far away there must be water. Some hours went by and then all of a sudden there was a shout from the *Caravan-Bashi*. His practised eyes had spied in the distance a little lake of rain-water. '*Su! Su!*' they all cried, 'Water! water!' and, reinvigorated by the mere sight of water, pushed on joyfully towards the lake. Not long after they had reached its edge and were slaking their thirst in its waters. That night they pitched their camp in a green meadow amid countless little lakes. To complete their happiness, they were told that henceforward they need have no further fear of attack. Having filled their water-skins, they set out again in excellent spirits.

For the time being their sufferings were at an end. From now until they reached Khiva their water-skins were never empty. The route they followed led first across the Kaflankir, or Tiger Field, a high grassy plateau abounding in herds of antelopes and wild asses; then on to Shor Gol, a rectangular salt lake where they halted to wash and perform their ceremonial purification and where all save Vambery put on clean shirts; and then on across what remained of the desert to Khiva.

At length they came to the nomad encampments and outlying villages which lay on the fringe of the oasis and were hospitably received by the inhabitants, who, in return for their blessings, loaded them with bread, meat and fermented mare's milk or *kumiss*. As they approached the city itself the vegetation grew more and more luxuriant. For some time before reaching their destination their way took them through green fields and fruitful gardens and orchards and past poplar-shaded farmsteads until at last through the trees they caught sight of the minarets and watchtowers of the city.

So large a troop of Hadjis had not arrived in Khiva for many years and as they entered the city gates an excited crowd of citizens pressed round them, kissing their hands and feet, passing up gifts of fruit and food to them as they sat on their camels, and greeting them with noisy shouts of welcome. 'Ha Shah bazim!' they cried, 'Ha Arszlanim!' — 'Ah, my falcon! Ah, my lion!' At which Hadji Bilal intoned a chant, while Vambery joined in so vigorously that his voice could be heard above them all. Once again he was feeling somewhat uneasy, having heard that the Khan, whose cruelty was notorious throughout Central Asia, was in the habit of immediately making a slave of any visitor to the city who struck him as being at all suspicious.

At the Customs House they were met by the Royal Chamberlain who was responsible for examining new arrivals. But scarcely had he addressed himself to the *Caravan-Bashi* than an uncouth figure pushed himself forward. It was the drunken Afghan opium-addict. 'We have brought with us to Khiva', he shouted, indicating the buffaloes, 'three interesting quadrupeds.' '*And*', he added venomously, '*a no less interesting biped.*' At once all eyes turned to Vambery and amid the murmuring of the crowd it was possible to discern the words, '*Djansiz!*' 'Spy!' '*Ferenghi!*' 'European!' and '*Urus!*' 'Russian!' As Vambery, in consternation, made as if to withdraw, the Chamberlain, turning on him savagely, ordered him to stay where he was. At this very moment, however, one of the leading pilgrims, Hadji Salih, happening to come in and, not knowing what had passed, at once presented him to the Chamberlain in the most flattering terms. Amazed, the latter at once changed his attitude and, with an agreeable smile, invited Vambery to sit down beside him. But Vambery, assuming an air of injured dignity, gave him in return an angry look and left the building.

He now made his way to the house of one Shükrullah Bey, an aged and distinguished Khivan, who had once spent ten years as Khivan Ambassador in Constantinople and was therefore regarded by his compatriots as an expert on everything Turkish. To him he announced himself as an *Efendi* from Stamboul, adding, a little less than truthfully, that they had met there and that he had accordingly come to pay him his respects. Amazed that a Turkish *Efendi* should have come to Khiva, Shükrullah Bey at once came out to meet him, only to be even more astonished at the sight of a wild-looking mendicant in filthy rags. But to the old man's delight his visitor at once launched into a flood of reminiscence about mutual friends and recent events in Constantinople and had soon gained his complete confidence. Vambery now had at least one highly placed friend in Khiva and, on repairing to the monastery where his companions had established themselves, he was further gratified to learn that after his departure from the Customs House all present had turned on his Afghan detractor and driven him away with curses and blows. After a shaky start, he could congratulate himself on having completely restored his position.

And indeed next day he was visited by a Court official who brought him a gift from the Khan and an invitation to present himself the same evening at the Palace, 'as His Majesty attached great importance to being blessed by a dervish born in the holy country of Turkey'.

That evening Vambery made his way through the narrow winding streets of the city and the vaulted passage-ways of the bazaar up to the Royal Palace or Ark, a massive, strongly fortified citadel surrounded by a high double wall. Passing through a narrow gate flanked by two handsomely decorated cannon, he entered, first an outer courtyard crowded with soldiers of the Royal Bodyguard, then a second, more spacious enclosure occupied by a variegated collection of officials, servants, soldiers, executioners and others, awaiting orders from their royal master. Thence a small gateway led directly to the residence of the Khan.

At Vambery's approach the crowd in the outer apartments made way for him respectfully and he was at once ushered into the presence of the *Mehter* or Minister of the Interior, a dark, bearded man in voluminous robes and a great fur hat. On catching sight of him the *Mehter* turned with a laugh to the officials standing near him, but Vambery, going straight up to him, saluted him with due solemnity and then, without a moment's hesitation, assumed the place of honour due to him as a dervish and intoned a prayer, at which all present stroked their beards and exclaimed 'Amen'. He then produced his passport, bearing the Sultan's seal. This was received with reverence by the *Mehter* who kissed it and rubbed it against his forehead and then invited him to enter the hall of audience. Once in the hall, two court officials took hold of his arms, a curtain was rolled up, and he found himself face to face with the Khan of Khiva.

As the curtain went up, the Khan was discovered seated on a raised platform or dais. His left arm was supported on a round silk-velvet pillow. With his right he held a short golden sceptre. The impression which he made on Vambery was unpleasant in the extreme. Indeed it was a long time before the latter was able to rid himself of the memory of those deep-set eyes, of that degenerate, dissolute face, of those cruel white lips, of that imbecile chin thinly covered with hair and of that trembling, effeminate voice.

On the appearance of the sovereign, Vambery at once raised his hands, being imitated in this by the Khan and the others present. He then recited a short *sura* from the Koran, then two *Allahumu Sella* and then a prayer beginning with the words '*Allahumu Rabbena*' and concluding with a loud 'Amen' amid general stroking of beards. While the Khan was still stroking his beard, the rest of the company cried out, 'Kabul Bolgay' – 'May thy prayer be heard'. Vambery next moved forward a few paces and spread out his hands, the Khan doing the same. After this Vambery moved back a few paces and the ceremony was at an end.

The Khan now engaged his visitor in conversation, questioning him closely about the reasons for his journey and the impressions made on him by what he had seen. To this Vambery replied that he had suffered much, but had been richly rewarded for all he had undergone by being allowed to look upon *Hazrets Djemal* – the Beauty of Majesty. 'I thank Allah', he continued politely, 'that I have been allowed to partake of this high happiness and I discern in this special favour of Fate a good omen for the rest of my journey.'

The Khan next asked him how long he proposed to stay in Khiva and whether he was provided with money for his journey. To this he replied that he wished first to visit the tombs of the Saints who were buried in the soil of the Khanate and that after that he would go on his way. As to the present state of his finances, 'We dervishes', he said, 'do not trouble ourselves with such trifles. The Holy Breath imparted to me for my journey by the Chief of my Order will support me without nourishment for four to five days.' His only wish, he added, was that God would allow His Majesty to live a hundred and twenty years.

At this the Khan seemed well satisfied and gave orders that he should be given twenty ducats and a stout ass. The ducats he declined on the grounds that it was a sin for a dervish to keep money. As to the ass, he said that he would be glad to accept the Khan's gracious offer. He would only draw his attention to the holy commandment which prescribed the use of a white ass on pilgrimages. After the Khan had insisted that he must be his guest at any rate during his stay in the capital, Vambery once again thanked him profusely, bestowed his blessing on him and took his leave.

Outside, in the forecourt and bazaar, the crowds greeted him respectfully as he hurried home. Once back between the four walls of his cell, he drew a long breath. 'How fortunate', reflected the convinced freethinker, with the sinister image of the Khan still floating before his eyes, 'that gloomy superstition often imposes limits to the might and bloodthirstiness of such tyrants!'

From now onwards 'the dervish from Turkey', as they called him, was much in demand. Everybody wanted to have him as their guest. Every day he was forced to accept six, seven or eight invitations and to eat something in every house. Again and again, before sunrise, at three or four in the morning, he would find himself seated in front of a colossal dish of rice, swimming in fat from the tails of fat-tailed sheep, until he came to long for the dry, unleavened bread of the desert. 'To be able to eat no more' is to this day an expression which is regarded in Central Asia as indicative of low breeding and it was generally felt to be most astonishing that one so well educated should fall so short of polite practice in this important respect. But if Vambery himself was a disappointment, his friends the pilgrims, their appetites sharpened by their journey across the desert, gave, as he put it, 'the most brilliant proofs of their *bon ton*', each consuming at a sitting a pound or more of fat sheep's tail, two pounds of rice, a large quantity of bread, carrots, turnips and radishes and fifteen or twenty large bowls of green tea.

No less exacting was the constant cross-examination to which he was subjected on religious questions and points of procedure. For the Khivans, Stamboul set the standard in all such matters and the Sultan of Turkey, as the successor of Mohammed, was the ultimate authority on their practical application. How, they wanted to know, should a truly devout man wash his hands, his feet, his face and his head? How should he sit, walk, lie and sleep? Was it true that the Sultan wore a turban at least fifty ells in length, that his robe reached down to his toes and his beard half way to his waist? Was it also true that a specially consecrated dinner arrived for him miraculously from Mecca every day, performing the journey from the Kaaba to Stamboul in a single minute? Vambery, for his part, answered these questions as best he could, being careful to say nothing that would upset his audience, and in particular not to reveal that in fact the Sultan had his clothes made for him in Paris by Dusetoye, that his hair and beard were trimmed *à la Fiesko*, and that the table of Mohammed's successor was lavishly provided with the finest vintages of Margaux and Lafite.

The seekers after knowledge were followed by the seekers after healing. The courtyard of the mosque with its elm-shaded pool was a favourite public resort and from morning to night his monastic cell was besieged by men and women clamouring for blessings and for Holy Breath or Holy Dust, the men in their sheepskin hats or turbans, the women heavily veiled and wearing their characteristic high head-dresses.

Amongst those whom Vambery encountered by the side of the water under the elm-trees was a certain Hadji Ismael, who it appeared, had spent many years in Stamboul, where at one time or another he had plied the trades of tutor, leather cutter, calligrapher, bath-keeper, conjuror and chemist, on the strength of which he had since his return acquired a considerable reputation in Khiva and had been appointed Court Physician to the Khan. On meeting Vambery, Hadji Ismael, to his surprise, at once claimed to know him well and his father too, who, he said, was a *mullah* in Topkhane. At this, Vambery, realizing that his new acquaintance was as impudent a liar as he was himself, rose nobly to the occasion and, instead of refuting his statements, embraced him tenderly and assured him that he was remembered with affection in Stamboul and that his return there was anxiously awaited.

But the danger of discovery and of all that it entailed was ever-present. The *Mehter* or Minister of the Interior was, as it happened, a bitter enemy of Vambery's friend Shükrullah Bey and, out of hatred for him, was determined to do his *protégé* such mischief as he could. With this object, he now sought to plant in the mind of his master the Khan the idea that 'Hadji Reshid' was only a sham dervish, in reality probably a secret agent of the Sultan's. Forewarned of these intrigues, Vambery was not surprised to be summoned once again to the Palace and questioned by the Khan on various political subjects, while the *Mehter* stood by, waiting hopefully for him to put a foot wrong. For anyone who knew how many of the Khan's audiences ended with the fatal words, '*Alib barin*', 'Take him away', followed by his visitor's immediate execution, such an interview was bound to be something of an ordeal. But once again Vambery behaved with prudence and assurance and, before withdrawing, was ordered by the Khan to apply to the Keeper of the Treasure for a regular daily allowance for his food and lodging.

It was while he was on his way to the Treasury that he saw a sight which filled him with horror and heightened his own feeling of insecurity. In one of the courts of the Palace were assembled about three hundred prisoners of war who had been captured during some recent fighting and already looked half dead from hunger and fear. They had been divided into those over and those under forty years of age. Those under forty were being chained together by the neck in batches of ten or fifteen and led away to be sold as slaves. Those over, the *Aksakals* or Grey-Beards, patiently awaited punishment as leaders. As Vambery watched, some of them were hanged and some beheaded. Then, at a sign from the executioner, eight aged men lay down on the ground on their backs. They were bound hand and foot. The executioner then gouged out the eyes of each in turn 'kneeling on his victim's chest as he did so and then wiping his bloodstained knife on the poor wretch's beard'. After they had been blinded, the old men were set free. Groping round with their hands, they tried to get to their feet. But, in their agony, they fell one against another, their heads bumping together as they did so, while some lay moaning on the ground, powerless even to raise themselves up.

At the Treasury, Vambery found the Treasurer sorting out a number of *khalats*, or robes of honour, which, it seemed, were to be awarded to those who had particularly distinguished themselves in the campaign. Some of these robes, made of the finest silk and heavily embroidered with gold, were, Vambery noticed, much more magnificent than others. He heard them described as four-head, twelve-head, twenty-head and even forty-head robes. On asking why, he was told that the reason was quite simple. A man who had cut off the heads of four enemies received a four-head robe, and so on. The more the heads, the finer the robe. The robes would, said his informant, be distributed next day. It might interest him, as a foreigner, to witness the ceremony.

Next morning he reached the main square in time to see the arrival of about a hundred horsemen. Each of these had a prisoner or two with him, tied to his horse's tail, men, women and little children, or to the pommel of the saddle, and each carried a sack. First they handed over their prisoners as presents to the Khan. Then, opening their sacks, shook out the contents on to the ground. They contained human heads, some bearded, others beardless. These an accountant now kicked on to a pile, at the same time issuing a receipt for the number of heads delivered, to be exchanged in due course for a robe of appropriate quality.

In spite of 'these startling scenes', and of the ever present danger of discovery, Vambery enjoyed his stay in Khiva. However bloodthirsty they might show themselves in other contexts, the Khivans had treated him and his companions with the greatest kindness and generosity; his healing activities had brought in no less than fifteen ducats; and he had only to show his face in public to be literally pelted with presents by the passers-by. But it was now the beginning of July; the heat was becoming ever greater and his companions ever more anxious to start for Bokhara.

From this project his friend Shükrullah Bey did everything he could to dissuade him, recounting to him the horrible fate which had overtaken other travellers to the capital of the Emirs and actually shedding a tear when the time came for them to part. Indeed he showed such solicitude for his welfare that Vambery could not help wondering if he had not perhaps penetrated his disguise and realized the true nature of the dangers that beset him.

Before setting out, Vambery bestowed a final blessing on the Khan, who urged him to come back to Khiva on his return journey. To this he replied with the single, well-chosen word '*Kismet*', 'Fate', thereby implying that it was sinful to seek to look too far into the future.

The pilgrims were far better provided for when they left Khiva than when they arrived there. Even the poorest now had a donkey to ride, as well as a change of clothing, a supply of food and some money. Thus equipped, they set out late one Monday afternoon through the Urgendj gate. For the first mile or two they were accompanied by a crowd of the faithful who ran beside them in tears, seeking to embrace them and crying: 'Who knows when Khiva will again have the great good fortune to harbour so many pious men?' In the end this proved too much for Vambery's special white donkey. With an ear-splitting bray, it set off at full gallop, leaving its pursuers far behind.

The route they had chosen led first almost due east through fertile, well-cultivated country to the Oxus, and Vambery was able to pick ripe mulberries from the trees as he rode along. Far away to the north beyond the Oxus some blue mountains rose above the haze. On the second evening they reached the banks of the great river, its muddy yellow stream being here so wide that the far bank was scarcely distinguishable to the naked eye. Next morning they found the ferry and, after some argument, succeeded in convincing a reluctant ferry-man that it was his duty to take them across for nothing.

The crossing took all day under a blazing sun. First, their boat was carried too far down stream and they were obliged to turn round and come back again. Then, in the labyrinth of side-channels on the far side, they ran aground on one sandbank after another. Each time this happened, pilgrims and donkeys had to be unloaded and the boat floated off again. And each time, despite much shouting and beating and prodding, some of the donkeys refused to budge and had to be carried bodily through the water on the backs of the pilgrims and bodily back again. By dusk they were all exhausted.

After waiting another whole day for the trans-shipment of the camels, the pilgrims now set out in a south-easterly direction along the right bank of the Oxus with the desert on their left hand. It was their intention to follow the river southwards as far as they could and then strike due east across the desert to Bokhara at the narrowest point. In this way they would only need to spend the last two days of the journey in waterless desert and for the rest of the time would be plentifully supplied with water. Along the river bank grew a jungle of willows, rushes and high grass. Setting out before sunset, they marched all night, the long string of camels winding away into the distance under the moon. By day they camped by the river bank and so escaped the worst of the heat.

For the first two days all went well. Then, just before dawn on their third night's march, the caravan was hailed from a distance by two men. On coming closer, these proved to be half-naked and in the last stages of exhaustion. 'Bread! Bread!' was all they could say, as they sank exhausted to the ground at the pilgrims' feet. As soon as they had been given something to eat, they told their story. They were boatmen from farther down the river who had been set upon by a band of Tekke Turkoman marauders, stripped of boat, clothes, food and everything else they possessed and left to starve. The robber band, a hundred and fifty strong, was, it seemed, still in the immediate vicinity. 'For God's sake,' they cried, 'fly or conceal yourselves, or in a few hours you will encounter them.'

Scarcely had these words left their lips than the *Caravan-Bashi*, who had had previous experience of the Tekke Turkomans, gave the order to turn about. With their heavily laden camels, they could not hope to outdistance the Turkoman raiders on their swift horses, but, if they could get back to their last halting-place and there replenish their supplies of water, it was possible that they might have time to throw themselves into the desert before the pursuit caught up with them. And once in the desert, their prospects of escape would be better.

There followed an agonized rush back over the ground they had just covered, the panic-stricken pilgrims goading their tired, overloaded beasts to the point of breakdown. Once at their destination, three anxious hours were needed before the necessary water-skins were filled and men and animals were ready to set out on their perilous venture. Then, at the last moment, some of the party lost heart and sought to hide themselves in the rushes by the river's edge rather than face the rigours of the wilderness, while others, catching sight of a boat, urged that they should abandon their journey and return to Khiva. For Vambery, determined to press on at all costs, these were anxious moments. But in the end, after much wavering, most of the pilgrims followed the lead of the *Caravan-Bashi* and by sunset they had already advanced some distance into the desert.

All that night they marched in silence lest any sound should betray them to the Turkomans. As they plodded along, the sand became ever softer until at last the camels were sinking in up to their knees. Still they struggled on. First light revealed a sea of sand, stretching away as far as the eye could reach. On the one side, the sand was piled up into high dunes, like waves in a storm. On the other it lay as flat and smooth as the surface of a lake, scarcely rippled by the wind. Nowhere was there the slightest sign of life, only, here and there, a pile of bleaching bones. On inquiring where they were, Vambery was told by his companions that they had come to *Adam Kürülgan* — The-Place-Where-Men-Perish.

From where they were, they calculated, it should take them about five days to reach Bokhara, marching both at night and during part of the day as well. Their supplies of water, already dwindling under the blazing sun, could last them for only a fraction of the journey. The camels, hard-driven for a day and two nights on end, were becoming ever more distressed. By the time the caravan had reached its next halting-place, two were dead. Here they had hoped to find a salt well, but when they got there it was choked with sand.

Their supplies of water were now beginning to run very short, and at night each traveller slept with his own water vessel tightly clasped to him. Already two of the poorer pilgrims, obliged to trudge the whole time on foot, had finished all their water and were now so weak from thirst and exhaustion that they could no longer stand. Their companions accordingly bound them with ropes on to the backs of two camels, and there they remained, crying feebly for water as long as they could articulate. After a day or two, one died. 'I was present', writes Vambery, 'when the unfortunate man drew his last breath. His tongue was quite black, the roof of his mouth a greyish white; in other respects his features were not much disfigured, except that his lips were shrivelled, the teeth exposed and the mouth open. I doubt much whether, in these extreme sufferings, water would have been of service; but who was there to give it to him? It is a horrible sight to see the father hide his store of water from the son, and brother from brother; each drop is life and when men feel the torture of thirst, there is not, as in other dangers of life, any spirit of self-sacrifice or any feeling of generosity.'

'I', his narrative continues, 'had still left about six glasses of water in my leathern bottle. These I drank drop by drop, suffering, of course, terribly from thirst. Greatly alarmed to find that my tongue began to turn a little black in the centre, I immediately drank off at a draught half of my remaining store, thinking so to save my life; but oh! the burning sensation, followed by headache, became more violent towards the morning of the fifth day and about midday I felt my strength gradually abandon me.'

After four days spent in crossing the sand sea, they were now once more on firmer ground and could just distinguish far away in the mist on the horizon the Khalata Mountains, which they knew, were situated at a distance of some forty miles north-west of Bokhara. But by now both they and their beasts were at their last gasp and their progress had slowed down to a painful crawl. It was at this juncture that the *Caravan-Bashi* pointed to a swiftly moving cloud of dust in the middle distance and they scarcely had time to dismount and lie down behind their crouching camels before a burning, blinding, stifling sandstorm was upon them. Had it struck them two or three hours earlier, while they were still amongst the shifting dunes of the sand sea, they must all have perished.

Towards midnight on the fifth day they set out once more. After all their mishaps and misfortunes, they were almost within reach of Bokhara. But Vambery, broken in body and spirit, now felt that life was fast ebbing away from him. He could no longer mount or dismount without help. Lying prostrate on the ground, he decided that his last moment had come. Somehow they got him on to a camel and then he lost consciousness.

When he next came to, he was in a mud hut surrounded by men with long beards. '*Shuma ki hadji nistid*', they said to him in Persian, 'You are certainly no *hadji*', and then, seeing that he was too weak to answer, at once poured down his throat a strengthening draught of *airan*, a mixture of sour milk, water and salt. By great good fortune the caravan, when at their last gasp, had fallen in with a party of Persian slaves whom their masters had sent out into the desert from Bokhara to tend sheep, and these, in the kindness of their hearts, had given them shelter and shared with them their own meagre supplies of food and drink.

When they had rested, the pilgrims set out once more and, after spending another night on the way, came in the morning to the splendid profusion of green orchards and fields and gardens which lie on the outskirts of Bokhara.

By the time they encountered the Customs officers of the Emir, sent out from the city to meet them, Vambery, eternally resilient, had regained his good spirits. On being told to open his trunk, as 'his sort of people' — meaning, he suspected, Europeans — always had 'fine things' with them, Vambery replied that he indeed had fine things with him and, running out, came back with his donkey, which, amid the loud laughter of his companions, he led upstairs into the room in which they were sitting and formally presented to the assembled company. After which his friend Hadji Salih, who possessed considerable influence in Bokhara, intervened once more to explain who he was and how he came to be there, all of which highly misleading information was duly noted down by the conscientious excisemen for transmission to their superiors.

Proceeding on their way, the pilgrims soon caught sight, through the trees, of the mosques and minarets of Bokhara and, skirting round the walls, entered the city by the Dervaze Mezar. Hadji Salih now led Vambery to the Tekkie of Khalfa Husein, a spacious monastery built round a great courtyard and well planted with trees. Here he was allotted a cell and made welcome by the religious head of the Tekkie, an agreeable personage in a large white turban and robes of fine silk, who, he learned, was Court Imam to the Emir and also the grandson of the saint after whom the Tekkie was called. In the cells all round him were Moslem ecclesiastical dignitaries of great learning and high distinction. He had fallen into a veritable hot-bed of religious fanaticism.

For an impostor like Vambery this was a solemn thought. But his position also had its advantages. In this ecclesiastical stronghold the power of the civil authorities and even of the Emir was less effective than elsewhere. The Vizir, who in the temporary absence of the Emir, was conducting the government of Bokhara, had directed that the origins of the dervish from Turkey were to be carefully investigated and his companions closely questioned concerning him. But in the event little heed was paid to these instructions. 'Hadji Reshid', came the uncompromising reply, 'is not only a good Mussulman, but also a learned *mullah*. To have any suspicion of him is a mortal sin.'

During the three weeks which he spent in Bokhara Vambery assumed the garb of an *ishan* or *sheikh*, wearing on his head an immense turban and suspended from his neck a large copy of the Koran. This still further increased his reputation for sanctity, and, wherever he went, people pressed round him to ask his blessing, to praise him for his holiness, to listen to his preaching and to beg him to take them with him to Mecca. 'What extreme piety to come all the way from Stamboul to Bokhara!' onlookers would say as he passed by. 'These people's whole life is prayer, piety and pilgrimage.'

The Vizir, it is true, continued his investigations, setting spies to watch him and *agents provocateurs* to try to catch him out. Of these, some sought to trap him by engaging him in conversation on the subject of Europe and Europeans, while others questioned him on points of religious doctrine. But to the former he replied that he had deliberately left Constantinople in order to get away from the accursed *Ferenghis* and that he did not wish to poison his stay in Bokhara with the recollection of them, while on the latter he turned the tables by himself assuming the initiative and subjecting them to a vigorous cross-examination on their own religious tenets and principles.

When not performing his duties as a dervish, he would spend his time inspecting, sometimes alone and sometimes with Hadji Salih or some of the other pilgrims, the sights of the city which he had travelled so far to see. They did not inspire him with any great degree of enthusiasm. He was horrified by the unedifying spectacles he witnessed in the slave-market, disgusted by the unhygienic water-system and appalled at the thought of all the terrible things that had happened in the Citadel. Nor did he like the all-pervading espionage, the atmosphere of religious bigotry, the ubiquitous beggars, the meanness of the inhabitants, the heat, the dust and the dirt and the ever present threat of tapeworms and other even more disagreeable parasites. He was, it is true, interested to observe the diversity of the crowd which thronged the streets and bazaars and, after the hazards and hardships of the desert, he found it agreeable to sit drinking green tea and eating confectionery beside the tranquil elm-shaded waters of a cistern. But the bazaars seemed to him wretched places compared with those of Isfahan and Tabriz and almost the only thing that seems to have pleased him was the discovery that some of the goods displayed for sale had been made in England. 'How my heart beat', he writes, 'when I read the words "Manchester" and "Birmingham" and how apprehensive I was of betraying myself by an imprudent exclamation!'

Meanwhile the time had come to move on. For all his complaining, Vambery was beginning to find life in Bokhara not entirely unpleasant. He had had two shirts made and enjoyed his daily fare of good bread, tea, fruit and boiled meats. But his friends were anxious to reach their distant homes in Eastern Turkestan before winter set in and it was his intention to accompany them at any rate as far as Samarkand where he expected to encounter the Emir, an interview at which he felt that their support would be desirable. At Samarkand he would decide whether to continue with them to Kokand and Kashgar or to part company with them and make his way back to Persia alone by way of Herat.

Owing to the relative meanness of the Bokharans, the pilgrims' finances were by now sadly depleted. Such money as they had been able to earn in Khiva was exhausted and many of them, including Vambery himself, had been forced to sell their donkeys. Their numbers, too, were by now considerably reduced, some of their company having already dispersed to their homes. But Hadji Bilal and Hadji Salih and their companions from Chinese Turkestan still remained and for the next stage of their journey they decided to hire two two-wheeled carts or *arbas*. In these they now set out for Samarkand, shaded from the sun by an awning, but continually shaken and thrown against each other by the violent jolting of their primitive vehicles.

The road from Bokhara to Samarkand, following as it does the valley of the Zerafshan, runs for the most part through well-watered country. On either side were fields and gardens and at frequent intervals the pilgrims came to villages and *chai-khanas* or tea-shops at which they were able to refresh themselves. On the sixth morning, reaching the top of a hill, they gained their first sight of the city of Tamerlane spread out below them with its minarets and its glittering turquoise domes set against a background of green gardens and trees.

From where they stood, they could distinguish the three great *Medressehs* or religious colleges, which form three sides of the *Registan* or principal square. The *Medresseh* of *Shir dar*, the Lion Bearer, with a great yellow lion, worked in mosaic, sprawling across its façade, the *Medresseh* of *Tilla Kari*, which, as its name betokens, is richly decorated with gold; and the *Medresseh* of Ulug Beg, built by Tamerlane's grandson Ulug. Near by rose the ruins of the great *Medresseh* of Bibi Khanum, built in honour of a Chinese princess who became Tamerlane's wife, the remains of its vast shattered blue-tiled dome towering above the surrounding buildings. To the south they could see the smaller blue-domed tomb of Tamerlane himself, and facing them to the south-west, the Ark or Citadel standing on a hill with other buildings clustered round it. Outside the city, to the north, was the *Hazreti Shakh Zinda* or Shrine of the Living King, a succession of tombs and shrines built on a hillside on either side of a flight of forty marble steps near the site of Tamerlane's summer palace.

Though not an admirer of ancient monuments, even Vambery felt some pleasure at this sight. 'I must confess', he wrote later, 'that the first impression produced by the domes and minarets with their various colours, all bathed in the beams of the morning sun — the peculiarity, in short, of the whole scene — was very pleasing.' His enthusiasm, however, was soon to wear off. 'But alas!' he continues, 'why need I add that the impression produced by its exterior was weakened as we approached and entirely dissipated by our entry into the place itself?' And he goes on to tell us that his disappointment at the 'miserable appearance' of this famous city was so bitter and his sense of anti-climax so acute after all the efforts it had cost him to get there that he could not refrain from bursting into a fit of loud and sardonic laughter. His equanimity was, however, soon restored by the news that he and his friends were not to live, as they had originally thought, in the common caravanserai, but were to be the guests of a high court official.

The Emir, it appeared, was expected to arrive shortly from Kokand, where he had just won a great victory, and Vambery and his friends decided to await his return. A week later the monarch entered Samarkand in triumph at the head of his troops. Large crowds assembled in the Registan to welcome him and the day was made a public holiday, great mountains of *pilaf* being distributed to all and sundry. On the following day it was announced that the Emir would hold a public audience. But when Vambery and his friends presented themselves at the Palace they were informed by a Chamberlain that His Majesty wished to see Hadji Reshid apart from his companions. With a sinking heart, he followed the Chamberlain.

Half an hour went by and then an hour. And still he was kept waiting. Nervously he wondered what fate held in store for him and experienced a further moment of panic when one of the court officials, touching the nape of his neck, remarked to his companion, 'Unfortunately I have left my knife at home today.' Perhaps, he reflected, it was just a casual remark, but it had an ominous ring about it. Then suddenly the summons came and he was finally ushered into the presence of the Emir.

The Emir Mozaffer-ed-din of Bokhara, son of the infamous Nasrullah, was at this time a man of forty-two, pleasant enough looking, of middle height and with a tendency to corpulence. He had fine black eyes and a thin beard. A pious Moslem, he had the reputation of enforcing both civil and religious laws with severity, but also with justice. In marked contrast to that of his royal father, his private life was reputed to be blameless to the point of austerity. The ladies of his harem were both chaste and well trained and were kept fully occupied making their own clothes and those of the Emir. The meals served in the Royal Palace consisted almost exclusively of rice boiled with mutton-fat. A close watch was kept on the accounts. Undue luxury or display on the part of others was also sharply discouraged and, while showing relative clemency towards the poor and weak, the Emir would inflict the most severe punishments on the rich and powerful. In this way he had won for himself amongst the people the title *Filkush va Mushpewer* — 'Killer of Elephants and Protector of Mice'.

On entering the royal presence, Vambery found the Emir seated on an ottoman of red cloth, surrounded by books and papers. With his usual presence of mind, he immediately recited a short *sura* or prayer for the welfare of the Sovereign and, as befitted a holy man, went, uninvited, and sat down next to him — a proceeding which did not seem to displease the Emir. There ensued between them the following dialogue, during which the Emir stared fixedly at Vambery, possibly with the object of disconcerting him.

'You have come, I hear, from Stamboul in order to visit the tombs of the Saints.'

'Yes, but also to rejoice in the contemplation of Your Majesty's sacred beauty.'

'Strange! And you had no other motive in coming here from so far away?'

'No, Sire. It has always been my most fervent wish to behold noble
Bokhara and enchanting Samarkand. Besides I have long been a world-
pilgrim. I have no other business in life.'

'What, thou, with thy lame foot, a world-pilgrim! That is really
most surprising.'

'Forgive me, Sire, your glorious ancestor, Tamerlane, suffered from
the same infirmity, and he became a world-conqueror.'

Pleased at this last answer, the Emir next asked his visitor some
questions about his journey and about his impressions of Bokhara and
Samarkand and then sent him away with a handsome present. Once
again our hero had skilfully allayed suspicion. Nevertheless his friends,
on learning of his good fortune, advised him to leave Samarkand with
all possible speed, before the Emir changed his mind.

For a time he played with the idea of accompanying Hadji Salih to
Kokand or Hadji Bilal to Aksu and of then returning home as best he
could by way of Tibet or Peking. But in the end more prudent counsels prevailed and he decided, less ambitiously, to travel back to Persia
by way of Karshi and Herat.

It was with genuine grief that Vambery took leave of Hadji Bilal
and Hadji Salih. The hazards and hardships which they had shared
during the last six months had forged between them the strongest bonds
of friendship and many tears were shed on both sides when they said
farewell outside the city gate in the certain knowledge that they would
never meet again. After he had gone a little way, Vambery looked back
and saw them still standing where he had left them, with their hands
raised to heaven, asking for Allah's blessing on his journey.[1]

Vambery's journey from Samarkand to Herat was in the main uneventful. Water was plentiful for most of the way and there was
relatively little danger from robbers. Three days after leaving Samarkand he came to Karshi, a rambling town noted for the beauty of its
gardens and for the cheerfulness of its inhabitants, and, after another
night's journey, to the frontier fortress of Kerki, where he crossed the

[1] Many years later Vambery had news of Hadji Bilal. He had, it appeared, always
steadfastly refused to believe that he was anything but a Moslem and insisted that if he had
gone under a disguise at all it was in Europe rather than in Asia.

Oxus. Here he narrowly escaped arrest as a runaway Persian slave, but his indignant protests eventually succeeded in persuading the bewildered Governor that he was nothing of the sort. Here, too, he laid in a stock of haberdashery, cutlery, pins, needles and coloured beads to sell along the route and thus supplement his steadily diminishing earnings as a *hadji*.

A few miles from Kerki he crossed the Bokharan frontier and entered Afghanistan. 'Whilst my heavily laden ass was trotting on in the still night,' he writes, 'the joyful thought for the first time occurred to me that I had turned my back upon the Khanate of Bokhara, and that I was actually on my way to that West that I loved so well. My travelling experience, thought I, may not be great, but I carry back with me what is worth more than anything — my life.'

From Kerki, Vambery and the caravan which he had joined made their way to Andkuy and thence to Maymene where they halted for ten days. They had now reached the foothills of the Paropamisus and henceforward their route lay through increasingly mountainous country. For part of the way they followed the valley of the Murgab River, making their way through high mountain pastures beside its clear, swift-running waters. Then, crossing a last snow-topped mountain range, they descended precipitously into Djölghei Herat, the fertile plain which surrounds Herat, with its sparkling network of water-courses, its gardens, meadows and vineyards and its scattered groups of villages.

Only a few weeks before, Herat had, after a siege and much fierce fighting, been finally brought under Afghan domination. The city lay in ruins. The citadel and bazaar had been half demolished by the Afghan artillery and whole quarters of the town completely devastated. The Afghans, easily distinguishable from the more humble Heratis, swaggered about the streets in their native dress or in uniforms modelled on those of the British Army — scarlet tunics and smart black shakos. In the *Charbag* or Palace the sixteen-year-old son of the King of Afghanistan now ruled over the newly conquered province.

In the hope that the young prince might help him on his way, Vambery at once sought an audience of him. He found him, dressed in uniform and surrounded by a numerous retinue, sitting at an open window watching his troops at drill in the courtyard below. Outside a band was playing and through the window came the words of command, delivered by the Afghan officers in impeccable English, as their troops marched and counter-marched and wheeled to the left and right.[1]

On the Prince's right hand sat the Vizir, a corpulent, coarse-featured Afghan who, on being consulted about anything, invariably returned the same answer: '*Her tehi pish bud*' — 'Everything as before'. Having made the usual salutation, as became a dervish, Vambery, with characteristic assurance, walked straight up to the Prince and, pushing the Vizir out of the way with his foot, sat down next to him. He then raised his hands and recited a prayer.

Only now did he notice that the Prince was looking at him with evident surprise. Clearly something was puzzling him. Finally, as he came to the concluding Amen and all present started to stroke their beards, the Prince half rose from his chair and, pointing at him with his finger suddenly called out, '*Vallahi, billahi Shuma Ingiliz hestid!*' — 'By God, I swear you are an Englishman!' After which, jumping down, he came over and stood immediately in front of him and, clapping his hands with delight, like a child that has made a clever discovery, asked him in the most engaging manner, 'Tell me, you are an Englishman in disguise, are you not?'

Vambery did his best in distinctly difficult circumstances. 'Have done, Sire,' he replied solemnly, as though the joke had gone too far, 'You know the saying: "He who takes, even in sport, a believer for an unbeliever is himself an unbeliever." Give me rather something in return for my blessing, so that I may continue on my way.' At this the young man, who in his innocence had come so near to divining the truth, sat down again in confusion, observing shamefacedly that he had never before seen a *hadji* from Bokhara with features like that. After this, Vambery explained that he was from Stamboul and displayed his Turkish passport, which was examined admiringly by all present; the Prince gave him some money and invited him to come back and visit

[1] It was some time before Vambery, for all his expertise, could divine the provenance of the strange words used by the Afghans to denote their senior military officers: *Djornel*, *Kornel* and *Mejir*. Then it dawned on him. Like the uniforms and the words of command, they were of British origin.

him again frequently; and the audience was at an end. Not for the first time he had extricated himself from an awkward predicament.[1]

On November 15th, 1863, Vambery left Herat for Meshed with a great caravan numbering two thousand pilgrims and merchants. From some travellers encountered en route he learned of the presence in Meshed of an acquaintance of his, a certain Colonel Dolmage, an Englishman in the service of the Shah, and, on reaching Meshed after a twelve-day journey, at once called at his house. Colonel Dolmage, to whom he had been announced as 'a singular dervish from Bokhara', did not at first know what to make of him, but, as soon as he opened his mouth, he recognized him and made him most hospitably welcome.

While he was at Meshed he called on the Prince-Governor, Sultan Menad Mirza, the uncle of the Shah, who listened with interest to the account of his adventures and whose delight knew no bounds when he learned that his bigoted and suspicious neighbour, the Emir of Bokhara, who, to the disgust of the Persians, claimed the title of Prince of the Faithful, had actually let himself be blessed by an unbeliever. After spending Christmas with Colonel Dolmage, Vambery set off once more and on January 20th, 1864, arrived at the Turkish Embassy at Teheran, whence he had started out just ten months before.

On June 9th, after a leisurely journey back by way of Stamboul and Budapest, Arminius Vambery arrived in London, where he found himself greatly in demand, being invited to dine with the Royal Geographical Society at Willis's Rooms in St James's Square and to lecture to them at Burlington House, and being in general much sought after by hostesses, publishers and other lion-hunters. 'Invitations to dinner-parties and to visit in the country', he tells us, 'literally poured in upon me.' And it was not long before his new friends had managed to 'shape out of the rough material of the *ci-devant* dervish the lion of the London season'. He met the Prince of Wales; and Charles Dickens; and Sir Richard Burton; and a 'slender youth' called Swinburne, who recited his yet unpublished poem *Atalanta in Calydon*. He became a

[1] Many years later the Prince explained to an English officer that he had guessed Vambery was a European, because he beat time to the music with his foot, a thing no Asiatic would ever do.

member of the Athenaeum. He swopped bons-mots and racy stories with Lord Palmerston. He took part in a heated religious argument between Lord Stanley of Alderley, who was a fervent Mohammedan, and the Bishop of Oxford, Dr Wilberforce, usually known, it seems, as Soapy Sam.

But it was a long time before he could accustom himself to civilization. To sleep once more under a roof, to wear European clothes, 'particularly the necktie and stiff linen', to eat European food, and eat it with a knife and fork instead of with his fingers, all now seemed irksome to him. The traffic, too, bewildered him. 'Standing', he writes, 'at the corner of Lombard Street or Cheapside, or mixing with the crowds madly hurrying along Ludgate Hill, I felt like a man suddenly transported to pandemonium.' 'My wanderings', he tells us, 'have left powerful impressions upon my mind. Is it surprising if I stand sometimes bewildered, like a child, in Regent Street or in the saloons of British nobles, thinking of the deserts of Central Asia, and of the tents of the Kirghiz and the Turkomans?'

SPECIAL CORRESPONDENT

A BRIGHT, sunny afternoon — the afternoon of April 19th, 1873. All round about, a wide expanse of plain, intersected by irrigation ditches and dotted with tufts of greyish-green scrub. Farther away, to the south, a sedgy marsh with flocks of wildfowl flying over it. To the west, a caravan with its string of camels creeping slowly along the horizon. To the east, the walls of a mud-built town, and beyond them, rising from the river, the tall, slender masts of ships, like spears against the sky. In the immediate foreground, a swiftly running stream, and, half way across it, a *tarantass* — a long, low, black wagon drawn by half a dozen horses, now plunging wildly about in the fast-flowing water, while four or five Kirghiz postilions, some mounted and some standing in the water, sought unavailingly with discordant cries and savage blows from their whips to make the harassed animals pull together.

In the *tarantass*, meanwhile, wrapped in rugs and sheepskins, sat two disconsolate-looking American gentlemen, waiting resignedly for the water to pour in over their feet and over the arms and provisions with which the *tarantass* was piled; waiting, while the postilions quarrelled and fought and argued amongst themselves; waiting until in the end more horses were fetched, their carriage extricated from midstream, and they themselves enabled at last to continue their journey towards the near-by town of Kazala, whose mud-built walls they could see on the horizon.

Of these two American gentlemen, one was Mr Eugene Schuyler, the American *chargé d'affaires* at St Petersburg, at present on an official tour of Central Asia and at this actual moment bound for the seat of the Turkestan Government at Tashkent. His companion, with whom we are more immediately concerned, was Mr Januarius Aloysius Mac-Gahan, special correspondent of the *New York Herald*, bound, for his part, for the oasis of Khiva.

Year by year, during the decade which followed Vambery's journey

JANUARIUS ALOYSIUS MacGAHAN

to Khiva and Bokhara, the Russians had relentlessly continued their progress southwards into Turkestan, pushing their way steadily forward and encroaching ever farther on the territories of the Central Asian Emirates. A circular addressed to the Powers by Prince Gorchakov in 1864, explaining that Russia's aim in Central Asia was not to extend her dominions but to protect her existing frontiers, had certainly not been borne out by events. Already, the year 1864 had been marked by the capture of the sacred city of Turkestan. In 1865 General Chernayev had, with barely a thousand men, defeated the Khan of Kokand and stormed Tashkent. In 1866 General Romanovski had routed forty thousand Bokharans at Irdjar and reduced the fortress of Khodjent. In 1867 General Kaufmann had been appointed Governor-General of the newly formed Russian province of Turkestan. In 1868 he had, with a mere handful of men, captured and annexed Samarkand, thus dealing a decisive blow to the power of the Emir of Bokhara who, under the terms of the treaty which he was now forced to conclude, became no more than a Russian satellite. In 1869 a new Russian base had been established at Krasnovodsk on the Caspian, thus completing the conquest of the East Caspian littoral. In 1870 General Abramov had intervened to help crush the rebellious subjects of the Emir of Bokhara at the Heights of Kulikhan, thereby still further strengthening Russia's hold on that monarch's domains. In 1871 Kuldja in Eastern Turkestan had been seized from the Chinese, while, far to the West, the Turkoman territories lying between the mouth of the Atrek and Kizil Arvat had also been annexed by Russia.

To the north, meanwhile, remote behind his barrier of sands, the Khan of Khiva still retained his precarious independence; still made slaves of captured Russians; still defied his mighty neighbour.

For centuries the Russians had sought to bring his dominions under their sway. In the seventeenth century a famous chieftain of the Ural Cossacks had swooped down on the Khanate, and, taking the Khan by surprise, had driven him out and for a time ruled in his place. Then, finding that he could maintain himself no longer, he had started back for the Urals, laden with booty. Whereupon the Khan, who in the meanwhile had assembled a sizeable force, fell on the retreating Cossacks and slaughtered them to a man. In the years that followed, two more Cossack raids had ended in disaster; a military expedition sent to Khiva by Peter the Great in 1717 had been completely wiped out; and in 1840 General Perovski's ill-fated force had, as we have seen, been obliged to turn back when still five hundred miles short of its objective. Small wonder that the Khivans had come to regard themselves as well-nigh invincible.

But now, in the spring of 1873, after much preparation, a force of ten thousand Russians under the supreme command of General Kaufmann was marching on Khiva in five converging columns: one from the Caucasus under Colonel Markosov; one from Orenburg under General Veryovkin; one from Kinderly Bay on the Caspian under Colonel Lomakin; one from Kazala under the Grand Duke Nicholas; and one from Tashkent under General Kaufmann himself. No one knew which route offered the best chance of success, and, in order to ensure against failure, the Emperor had decided to launch not one, but five separate expeditions. To England, meanwhile, where rumours of the projected expedition were causing serious alarm, His Imperial Majesty had sent a special mission under Count Shuvalov to explain that his purpose was simply to punish acts of brigandage and rescue Russian prisoners and not — he was particularly insistent on this point — not to annex Khiva.

It was in order that he might report on the Khivan campaign and, if possible, enter Khiva with General Kaufmann's victorious troops that the proprietors of the *New York Herald* had dispatched to Central Asia one of the most celebrated special correspondents of his day, Mr J. A. MacGahan.

Born twenty-nine years before on a farm in Perry County, Ohio, Januarius Aloysius MacGahan had gone as a young man to Europe to learn languages, improve his education and study the law. While he was there, the Franco-Prussian War had broken out, and, being by nature adventurous and enterprising, he had managed, with the help of his famous and influential cousin, General Sheridan, to get himself appointed special correspondent of the *New York Herald*, now, under the stimulating if eccentric management of James Gordon Bennett, Junior, at the height of its fame.

Almost immediately, MacGahan's eye for news and gifts as a descriptive writer caught the attention of the American public. At first he followed the campaign in the field with the Army of General Bourbaki. Next he made his way to Lyons and Bordeaux, where, in the confusion then prevailing, he managed to secure sensational interviews with a number of leading public figures. Finally, reaching Paris, he remained there for the whole period of the Commune, was imprisoned by the Versailles troops, narrowly escaped death, and was only released thanks to the intervention of the United States Minister. His dispatches were eagerly read by a wide public. By the end of the war he was famous.

Always ready to pay lavishly for unusual news and good reporting, Gordon Bennett, enthusiastic and unaccountable, now sent the

Herald's new discovery on one assignment after another. From Paris he went to Geneva, from Geneva to the Crimea, and from the Crimea to the Caucasus, earning fresh laurels at every step.

While at Yalta in the Crimea, MacGahan had become a favourite with the Imperial Court and had in turn taken a great liking to Russia and the Russians. He had also met and subsequently married a Russian girl of noble parentage, Barbara Nikolayevna Elyagin. What then could be more natural than that James Gordon Bennett, Junior, on hearing of the forthcoming Russian expedition to Khiva and of the Russian refusal to allow any foreign journalists to accompany it, should at once have thought of MacGahan? If anyone could get round the Russians, beat the High Command's ban on journalists, find Kaufmann, get to Khiva, and get the news back in a form the public would enjoy, it was Januarius Aloysius MacGahan, with his youth, his mixture of American drive and Irish charm, his ingenuity, his determination and his flair for the unusual. Within a matter of days, MacGahan had left his bride and his comfortable hotel in Paris and was on his way to St Petersburg en route for the far-off town of Kazala, poised midway between Europe and Asia.

Fort No. 1, round which the town of Kazala had gradually grown up, had been built by the Russians some twenty years earlier as an entering wedge into Central Asia. Apart from its strategic importance, it lay at the junction of all the main trade routes in Northern Turkestan, of the roads from Orenburg, Khiva, Bokhara and Tashkent.

Round the little fort, with its ditch and its earthworks, from which projected a few light cannon, a flourishing Tartar town had come into being: thronged streets of flat-roofed, mud-built houses; strings of laden camels arriving from the desert; piles of outlandish merchandise; a bazaar where grave, long-bearded men in brightly coloured robes sat drinking tea among their wares. Beyond the town was the river, the Syr Daria or Jaxartes, a fast-flowing, muddy stream a quarter of a mile wide with a jungle of reeds and scrub on either bank. In the distance, beyond the river, the sands of the Kizil Kum stretched away to the south until they melted into the hazy sky.

When MacGahan had started from St Petersburg nearly a month

earlier, he had hoped to reach Kazala in time to join the Kazala column before it set out for Khiva under the command of the Grand Duke Nicholas. But he had long since abandoned that hope.

From St Petersburg he and his companion had travelled by train to Saratov, a distance of 940 miles, arriving there three days later. Their journey thus far had been uneventful and expeditious. Almost the only other passenger in their comfortable railway carriage had been a cultivated-looking oriental gentleman who was returning to his estates after a visit to the capital and who spent most of his time deep in a French novel. His name, they found on inquiry, was Genghiz Khan. This they took to be a good omen for their journey.

But after Saratov the two Americans had run into trouble. Three weeks of exasperating travel by *tarantass* across the frozen, wind-swept steppe, in bad weather, with poor horses and dilatory postilions, had shown them all too clearly that in these regions things did not always go according to plan. When finally they reached Kazala, they found that the Grand Duke's column had long since started. The only question was how far it had gone and what chance, if any, there was of overtaking it.

After a bath, a sleep and a dinner of juicy roast duck at the Hôtel d'Europe, the travellers made their way up to the fortress to call on the Commandant, a genial old gentleman called Colonel Kosarev. From him they learned over an excellent supper that the campaign against Khiva was already far advanced. The Grand Duke's detachment had left Kazala nearly a month ago, on March 21st. On April 6th, they had, it seemed, arrrived at Irkibai on the Yani Daria, where they had built a fort. When last heard of, on about April 9th, they had reached the Wells of Bukali, in the Bukan Tau Mountains, and were not more than a hundred miles from the Oxus. There it had been arranged that they should await the arrival of General Kaufmann who was in personal command of the Tashkent column, and of whom nothing had been heard since his departure from Tashkent.

The news was scarcely encouraging. Three hundred miles of desert now lay between MacGahan and the column which he had hoped to find at Kazala, three hundred miles of what must be regarded as enemy territory, for the Kirghiz of the Kizil Kum were hostile to the Russians, besides being traditionally robbers and marauders who would regard any small party of travellers as fair game. But MacGahan, having thought things over, decided that he would still try to cross the Kizil Kum, if need be alone, in the hope of catching up with the Kazala column before it reached Khiva. With swift horses and a good guide, he should, he reckoned, be able to reach the Oxus in a week. If, on reaching it, he found that General Kaufmann had already crossed the river, why then he would make his own way across as best he could and hope somehow to avoid the hordes of Khivan cavalry which would almost certainly be hovering round the rear and flanks of the advancing army.

It was a dangerous course, but it seemed the only one open to him if he was not to give up altogether. 'Remaining here', he wrote afterwards, 'or going on to Tashkent was equivalent to staying in St Petersburg. I had already spent so much of the *New York Herald*'s money, that I felt morally obliged to push forward; and I was very certain that anything less than my entry into Khiva would not be a satisfactory conclusion to my undertaking. The position of a correspondent is often a very embarrassing one. He embarks, perhaps, on an enterprise without fully counting the cost, or foreseeing or appreciating half the difficulties to be encountered in its accomplishment, and then feels obliged to put on a brave face and carry it out at whatever risk, when in his inmost self he knows that, if he were a free agent, he would be among the very last to undertake it.'

This bold decision MacGahan soon found was easier to take than to carry out. While still looking for horses and a guide, he received a visit from a Captain Vereschagin who, it seemed, was in charge of the rear party of the Expeditionary Force and who informed him in the most charming manner possible that he unfortunately could not take the responsibility of letting him start on so dangerous a journey without first obtaining General Kaufmann's express permission. As no one knew where General Kaufmann was or how to get into touch with him, and as time was of the essence if he was to achieve his purpose, this amounted in practice to saying that MacGahan must abandon his project. Certainly in so small a place there could be no question of slipping away across the river unnoticed.

But MacGahan had another plan. His friend Schuyler was going to

Tashkent. Having ascertained that there was no official objection to his accompanying him as far as that city, he handed to Captain Vereschagin, for transmission to General Kaufmann, a formal application for permission to visit Khiva, with the request that the answer should be forwarded to him at Tashkent. Then, piling his belongings back into the *tarantass*, he set out once again with Schuyler along the post-road that followed the course of the Syr Daria.

Ostensibly, he, too, was bound for Tashkent. In reality, however, his purpose was different. A hundred miles or so up-stream from Fort No. 1 lay Fort No. 2 — Fort Perovski. Except that more valuable time would be needed to get there, he calculated that Fort No. 2 would make as good a jumping-off place for his journey as Fort No. 1.

The four days which it took to reach Fort Perovski were for MacGahan 'days of intolerable anxiety and suspense', but in the end he arrived there and early next morning sent off his rascally old Tartar servant, Ak Mamatov, to find horses and a guide.

In the evening Ak Mamatov returned. He had, he said, not been able to find a guide and there were no horses to be had in Perovski. This was an unexpected blow. At a pinch he might have dispensed with a guide, but he could not do without horses. Might there, he asked Ak Mamatov, be camels? Ak Mamatov replied that there might, but that it was now too late to start looking for them. He would make further inquiries in the morning.

MacGahan spent the next day inspecting Fort No. 2. It was very like Fort No. 1: the same little fortress; the same mud houses; the same bazaar; the same acrid Eastern smells; the same bright costumes and swarthy faces; the same broad river flowing by. In the evening Mamatov returned with the same story: no guide; no horses; and no camels. A second precious day had been wasted.

It now occurred to MacGahan that Ak Mamatov might have reasons of his own for not wishing to succeed in his search. The thought that his own servant had deliberately made him waste two more precious days made MacGahan extremely angry. Before sending him out again, he gave him to understand in the most forcible terms that any further prevarication on his part would bring down on him instant retribution of the most violent kind.

This time Ak Mamatov returned with 'a kind of renegade Jew' who said that he knew every inch of the way to the mountains of Bukan Tau and would gladly serve as a guide. After prolonged discussion as to terms and as to the number of horses they would require, a mutually satisfactory bargain was finally concluded. Whereupon the Jew disappeared and never came back. Yet another day had been wasted.

The threatened retribution now overtook Ak Mamatov and he set out on his next morning's search much chastened, returning in a very short time with a Karakalpak called Mustruf who seemed to mean business and who announced that in return for a large sum of money he would act as guide, provided that the Russians gave him permission. After his experience at Kazala, MacGahan had intended to keep clear of the Russian authorities, but on calling on the District Governor he was surprised to find him as helpful as Vereschagin had been obstructive, and quite ready to issue permits for the whole party. Moreover, now that it had at last become known in the town that the American wanted to buy horses, the street round the inn where he was living suddenly filled with a seething crowd of horses and horse-dealers. From these he chose six, two for the baggage and the others for himself, Mamatov, Mustruf and a young Kirghiz named Tangerberkhen who had also joined the party.

It was three o'clock on the afternoon of April 30th when MacGahan, having bid farewell to his friend Schuyler, stepped into the boat which was to carry him across the Syr Daria. With him went Mustruf and three of the little Kirghiz horses, while Mamatov, the rest of the horses, the food and the party's modest baggage followed in a second boat. Over his shoulder MacGahan carried his Winchester repeating rifle. 'Being a man of peace,' he writes, 'I went but lightly armed. A heavy double-barrelled English hunting rifle, a double-barrelled shot-gun, both of which pieces were breech-loading, an eighteen-shooter Winchester rifle, three heavy revolvers, and one ordinary muzzle-loading shot gun throwing slugs, besides a few knives and sabres, formed a light and unpretentious equipment.'

Once across the river, MacGahan pushed on as fast as he could go, anxious to put as many miles as possible between himself and Fort

Perovski that night, in case the Commandant should change his mind and send after him to fetch him back. His plan was to follow the course of the Yani Daria, a tributary of the Syr Daria flowing in a south-westerly direction, until he reached Irkibai, the point at which the Grand Duke was reported to have built a fort. There he hoped to receive more recent news of the column's movements.

After riding all that afternoon through the tangled jungle of reeds and brushwood that fringed the river, the travellers came towards nightfall to a pleasant grassy glade, in which there were four or five *kibitkas*, round Kirghiz tents of felt stretched over a lightly constructed wooden framework. One of the Kirghiz nomads who lived in them was, it seemed, a friend of Mustruf and, after much exchanging of greetings and stroking of beards, invited his American guest to be seated on the gaily coloured rugs with which the floor of his tent was strewn. In the middle of the tent a cheerful fire was burning, its blue smoke curling up through a hole in the roof. That night the travellers and their hosts sat down together to a lavish supper of wild duck shot by MacGahan and white biscuits, an unheard-of luxury to the Kirghiz, to whom even black bread was a rarity. After which, the flap of the tent was let down and hosts and guests, wrapping themselves in sheep-skins, lay themselves down to sleep.

MacGahan was now beyond Russian jurisdiction, amongst the notorious Kirghiz of the Kizil Kum, famous murderers and bandits. 'When starting into the desert,' he writes, 'I knew I must adopt one of two systems in dealing with such a people. Either fight them, or throw myself entirely upon their hospi-tality and generosity; I chose the latter system.' From now onwards this was his rule. On entering a Kirghiz tent he would at once hand to his host his rifle, his revolvers and any other weapons that he

A KIRGHIZ

might be carrying, as a sign of complete confidence. He would then enter into the life of the family, romping with the children, kissing and flirting with the girls, and distributing cigars to the men. The Kirghiz, he found, just loved it, the children crowing with delight, the almond-eyed beauties responding enthusiastically to his advances and the bearded elders puffing away with gusto at their regalias.

For the next four days the travellers pushed on in a south-westerly direction, covering about fifty miles a day, sometimes through scrub and brushwood, sometimes over low sand dunes and sometimes across a bare, open plain. Although they did not follow the river itself, they remained close enough to it never to be seriously short of water.

On the fifth day they struck the desert track from Kazala which had been followed a month earlier by the Grand Duke and, a little farther on, arrived at the new fort which he had built at Irkibai. Having learnt from the officer in charge that nothing had been heard of General Kaufmann or of the Kazala column since the latter's departure a fortnight before, MacGahan announced his intention of pressing on across the desert next day, May 7th. The officer raised no objection, and, after a good night's rest, the little party set out again on the following afternoon.

MacGahan was now leaving behind him the relatively well watered region which fringed the Syr Daria and entering the desert proper. At first sight the prospect was a fair one: green, rolling country stretching away into the distance.

'But', wrote the special correspondent of the *New York Herald* in a notable descriptive passage, 'all this beauty is deceptive. These gentle hills are only sand, and the verdure which clothes them hides horrors as great as those covered by the roses that twine themselves over sepulchres. Blossoms shoot up, ripen, die, and rot, in the course of a few days. The verdure consists of but a rank soft weed that breaks out into an eruptive kind of flower, which, dropping off at the slightest touch, emits a most offensive odour. Beneath the broad leaves lurk scorpions, tarantulas, immense lizards, often five or six feet long, turtles and serpents, and the putrefying bodies of dead camels. Once lost in this desert ocean, without guide or water, you may wander for days, until you and your horse sink exhausted to die of thirst, with the noxious weed for bed, winding-sheet, and grave.'

Upon 'this world of desolate life', 'this plain of charnel-house vegetation', they entered, he tells us, 'with a sickening feeling of depression'. Sixty miles of desert lay between them and the next well at Kizil Kak and they had with them only two hogskins of water for themselves and their horses.

After marching far into the night, with only a brief rest before dawn, MacGahan pushed on all next day across a scorching expanse of desert under a blazing sun, arriving towards evening at the well of Kizil Kak. Here he halted to feed his horses and replenish his meagre supplies of water and then, a little before nightfall, set out once more.

He had not gone far when he encountered a caravan coming in the opposite direction. After the usual exchange of salutations, he inquired of the Caravan-bashi whether he had seen anything of the Russian army.

'Yes,' he answered, 'at Tamdy.'

'And where is Tamdy?'

'Ten days from here,' came the disheartening reply. And indeed a glance at the map showed Tamdy to be a hundred and sixty miles from Kizil Kak as the crow flies, probably two hundred by the caravan route.

'Which way were they going?'

'South.'

'South? Why, Kaufmann is coming north-west towards the mountains here.'

'No. He had just started for Aristan-Bel-Kuduk, which is two days south from Tamdy.'

This was a serious blow. Instead of continuing in a north-westerly direction as far as the Bukan-Tau Range and then turning south to the Oxus, Kaufmann had apparently turned south long before. The chances of overtaking him were now smaller than ever. What was MacGahan to do? To go back was as difficult as to go forward. With many misgivings, he decided to press on.

Having travelled nearly all night, he and his party found themselves at first light in sight of the Bukan Tau, a grey, forbidding mountain barrier, some twenty-five miles away across the desert. Several hours later they pitched their camp at its foot.

Next day, after a short rest, they were picking their way along the northern slopes of the Bukan Tau, when suddenly they saw a party of a dozen horsemen advancing towards them. They were armed and had no camels with them; the chances were that they were Turkoman marauders. As soon as they saw them, MacGahan and his companions got ready their arms and prepared for a fight. On closer investigation, however, the horsemen turned out to be not Turkomans but a number of Kirghiz who had gone with the Kazala column as guides and were now on their way back. Their news, too, was deeply discouraging. The Kazala column, it seemed, had effected their junction with Kaufmann ten whole days ago at Aristan-Bel-Kuduk and the two detachments had then set out together for Karak-Aty, a point some forty miles south of Tamdy. By now they must already have passed through Karak-Aty on their way to the Oxus. On examining his map, MacGahan now found a caravan route branching off to the south in the direction of Karak-Aty from a point not very far ahead of them. This he decided to take.

After travelling all day and most of the next night, he arrived at noon on the following day at a well where a number of Kirghiz had pitched their tents. As usual, his first demand was for news of General Kaufmann, and this the Kirghiz chief was able to supply. Kaufmann, he said, had left Karak-Aty and was now at Khala-Ata, another hundred miles farther south and a hundred miles from the Oxus. He himself had just come from there and had seen the Russian Army with his own eyes. The shortest way there would be straight across the desert towards the river a little west of south. But there was no road, not even a sheeptrack.

Realizing that if he were to take this route he would need another guide, MacGahan now asked his informant, by name Bii Tabuk, if he could find him one. He would, Bii Tabuk replied, have gone himself, but he had been commissioned to buy sheep for the Russians and did not like to return without any. All right, said MacGahan. If Bii Tabuk would act as guide, he would pay for the sheep, and in the end it was decided that the Kirghiz should accompany him and that someone else should be found to drive the sheep to Khala-Ata.

Next morning Bii Tabuk set off with Ak Mamatov to buy sheep, but returned at nightfall without any. There were, he explained, plenty of sheep to be found, but there was no one to drive them. Another whole day had been lost, owing, MacGahan surmised, to fresh machinations on the part of Ak Mamatov, whom he once more suspected of deliberately thwarting his plans.

Having reluctantly decided to stay where he was for one more night, he now asked Bii Tabuk if he could not find him another guide. In due course the latter returned with a young man who was ready to conduct him to Khala-Ata in return for twenty-five roubles, and it was agreed that they should start early next morning. But next morning Ak Mamatov announced that the guide was now not prepared to come unless he was provided with a horse or with the money to buy one. This was too much for MacGahan. Now certain that Ak Mamatov was deliberately doing everything in his power to prevent him from starting, he announced that if the guide would not come for the price agreed on, they would go without a guide.

At this there were loud protests from the whole party, but MacGahan had decided that he would no longer be trifled with. Drawing his revolver, he sternly ordered Ak Mamatov to mount and proceed. The response was immediate. Within an hour another guide had been found, an old man, this time, who turned out to be Bii Tabuk's brother and who invited them all to a mutton breakfast in his tent. After which, with the old man leading, they set off southwards across the trackless desert, sleeping that night in the sand where they halted.

Next day the going became very bad, the tired horses sinking knee-deep in the soft, powdery sand. The sun blazed down. At midday they reached a well of warm, brackish water. In the afternoon the going became worse and they encountered huge sand drifts through which they struggled with extreme difficulty. By now one of the horses was beginning to show serious signs of distress. In vain they removed its load and distributed it amongst the others. That night it suddenly stumbled and lay where it had fallen. Leaving it to die, they plodded wearily on.

The prospect that confronted MacGahan was far from cheerful. He had been fifteen days in the desert and was apparently as far as ever from his objective. For several days his horses had eaten nothing save what they could pick up in the desert. A small quantity of barley which he had obtained at Irkibai had been long since exhausted. It could now only be a matter of time before one after another of the poor brutes fell dead from hunger and exhaustion, leaving their riders to continue their journey on foot. And in any case, supposing that they did eventually catch up with General Kaufmann, how could they in their condition ever hope to evade the savage Turkomans, whose marauding cavalry, magnificently mounted, would be hovering on the flanks of the Russian Army. To MacGahan, tired and dispirited as he was, his horse's death seemed the beginning of the end, the harbinger of his own doom.

For the rest of that night, with one brief rest, they struggled painfully on, clambering up the steep slopes of soft, shifting sand and sliding down again into the hollows beyond. Under the pale light of the moon the bare expanse of the desert had a ghostly look and their own black shadows stood out grimly against the moonlit sand. Scarcely had the sun risen before its rays grew unbearably hot and soon, as they plodded along beneath its fiery glare, they again began to suffer the now all too familiar torments of unquenched thirst.

At noon they reached the summit of a range of black sandstone hills, barren and bare under the burning sun. From where they stood, they looked out over a vast tawny plain, stretching away to the south, beyond which, blue and misty on the horizon, rose another mountain range. Beyond it, said the guide, at a distance of twenty-five miles from where they stood, lay Khala-Ata.

For the remainder of that day and for a part of the following night, they pushed on, searching as they went for the smallest patch of grass on which to feed their famished horses. When at last they camped, they were careful to screen their fire in order not to attract the attention of the Turkomans. For MacGahan it was a time of intense anxiety. How much longer, he asked himself, could they last out?

Soon after sunrise they reached the top of the mountain range which they had seen in the distance. Advancing to the ridge and peering cautiously over, the guide beckoned to MacGahan. Joining him, the American found himself looking out over yet another arid plain stretching far away to the south. But in the middle of it, some eight miles from where they were, stood row upon row of tents, while here and there the bright morning sunlight caught the glitter of brass and bayonets and the dazzling white of summer uniforms. This, surely, he told himself, must be Kaufmann at last.

An hour or so later, at six o'clock on the morning of May 16th, MacGahan, dust-covered and weary after his long journey through the desert, rode into the Russian camp at Khala-Ata. Addressing himself to the first officer he met, he asked him where he could find General Kaufmann. But the answer dashed his hopes to the ground. General Kaufmann, he was told, had left Khala-Ata five days ago and had by now quite certainly reached the Oxus.

This was a bitter blow to MacGahan. There now seemed no hope whatever of attaining his objective. By the time he reached the river, Kaufmann would have crossed it and taken Khiva and his long and arduous journey would have been in vain. The disappointment was almost more than he could bear, especially when he reflected that he had been deliberately held up in the desert for three days while Ak Mamatov and Bii Tabuk pretended to look for sheep and for a guide. However, there was nothing for it but to make the best of a bad job. Explaining to the officer that he was an American on his way to see General Kaufmann, he asked him to inform the Commanding Officer of his arrival and to tell him that he would like to call and pay his respects.

On learning that MacGahan was an American, the Russian at once invited him into his tent and sent for tea. The Commanding Officer, he said, was still asleep, but would, he knew, be glad to see him as soon as he got up. It was his intention, he added, to move forward on the following day with two companies of infantry, two field guns and a hundred Cossacks, and he would certainly be glad to take MacGahan with him.

This was a little more encouraging. There seemed a chance that he might after all catch up with General Kaufmann and, with luck, see something of the fighting. Feeling rather more cheerful, he settled down to wait for the Commanding Officer, whose name was Colonel Weimarn, to send for him.

Gradually the morning went by. As the sun climbed higher, the heat became more intense. Having reached the meridian, it began to sink towards the west. Still there was no summons from Colonel Weimarn. In the end MacGahan, growing impatient, decided to take the initiative. Having had the Colonel pointed out to him, he went up to him, as he strolled about the camp, and introduced himself.

'I owe you an apology, Colonel,' he said, 'for not calling on you sooner to present my respects; but the fact is they told me you were asleep.'

'Well, what do you want?'

'As I said before, I wish to pay my respects.'

'I am much obliged; but I do not suppose you have come all the way from New York to pay me your respects.'

'Why, no, Colonel; my business here is with General Kaufmann.'

'Oh, you have business with General Kaufmann, have you? How are you going to get to him?'

'I'm going to ride.'

'What is your business with General Kaufmann?'

'That I can only tell to General Kaufmann himself.'

'Have you the written permission of General Kaufmann?'

'No, but I have the permission of ... '

'It makes no difference whose permission you have got; without the written permission of the Governor-General you can't go. And as to your papers, I won't look at them.'

'How can I obtain that permission?'

'I do not know. You may send on your papers if you wish, but I am almost sure you will not be able to obtain it without a personal interview. He is too busy to answer letters.'

'I beg your pardon, Colonel. His Excellency General Kaufmann seems to be very difficult of access. I cannot see him without his permission and I cannot get his permission without seeing him. How do people who have business with him usually proceed?'

'That', replied the Colonel, 'is no concern of mine' — '*Das geht mich nicht an.*' And, turning on his heel, he walked away, leaving MacGahan to decide what his next move should be.

The problem was not an easy one. To content himself with forwarding a letter to General Kaufmann and awaiting a reply would mean giving up all hope of achieving his aim. On the other hand, to try to break through the lines and escape would clearly be the height of folly. Even if he succeeded in getting away from the camp, how, he asked himself, could he hope to elude the vigilance of the savage and restless Turkomans, not to mention the squadron of Cossacks which Colonel Weimarn would probably send after him to bring him back?

And yet, what other hope had he of reaching Kaufmann in time? In the end, he decided that, however unlikely he was to succeed, he must try to make a dash for it.

Meanwhile there was the more immediate question of his own sustenance to be considered. He himself had been living for the last two days on sour milk. He was entirely without shelter or provisions for himself or his companions. He had no forage for his horses, and it seemed abundantly clear that Colonel Weimarn had no intention of providing him with any. He was just wondering how long it would be before they all starved to death, when, much to his relief, he was approached in the most friendly manner possible by two or three Russian officers who said that they had come to welcome him and offer him hospitality. Quite clearly they were seeking to make amends for the behaviour of their Commanding Officer, whose German origin did not endear him to them and to whom they referred quite openly as '*cette canaille d'Allemand*'. Soon he had had a badly needed square meal and was comfortably installed in one of the officers' tents.

It remained to decide how best he could make his escape from the camp. After some thought, he came to the conclusion that a favourable opportunity would present itself when Colonel Weimarn set out at two o'clock next morning at the head of his troops to join General Kaufmann. At that moment there was certain to be considerable confusion, under cover of which, and of darkness, it should be possible for himself and his little party to slip away unnoticed.

But at the last moment, when all was ready, it was announced that orders had been received from Kaufmann that Colonel Weimarn was not to march after all. Something had gone wrong. The General himself had not yet reached the Oxus and Colonel Weimarn's force were to postpone their advance. Slightly comforted by the news that Kaufmann had not yet crossed the river, MacGahan settled down to await further developments.

For the next five days nothing more was heard from General Kaufmann. MacGahan spent his time lying idly in his tent watching the heat haze dancing over the desert and cursing Colonel Weimarn, the flies, the dust and the heat. Then, just as he had decided that there was nothing for it but to attempt to escape without waiting for Weimarn to move, the latter decided to advance on his own initiative, leaving Khala-Ata in the early hours of the morning of May 24th.

A week of standing in the blazing sun with nothing to eat save dried up brushwood and a minute quantity of barley, procured for them clandestinely in direct defiance of Colonel Weimarn's instructions, had reduced MacGahan's five remaining horses to a more pitiable plight than ever. At least two of them looked as if they would never reach the Oxus. Nor were Ak Mamatov and the two Kirghiz any readier than before to undertake a journey which they had long regarded with grave misgivings. As always, they could find ten good reasons for staying where they were. Threats, which in the desert had proved so effective, were here of no avail. In the end a bribe of a hundred roubles all round was needed before they would even consider embarking on such a hazardous project.

For all this, when the time came to start and at one in the morning on the appointed day Colonel Weimarn's force began to file out of camp in the direction of the Oxus, MacGahan and his little party, having informed no one of their project and taken leave of no one, were ready waiting to slip out unobtrusively behind the Cossacks who led the advance. His intention was to leave the camp in the wake of the cavalry and, counting on the darkness and on his own superior speed, make a wide circuit in the hope of reaching the Oxus before they did. As for the Turkomans, at this moment undoubtedly hovering in swarms round the flanks and rear of General Kaufmann's army, he would just have to trust to luck.

*

In accordance with their plan, MacGahan and his followers now dropped silently in the rear of the Cossacks and, having climbed a low line of sandhills a mile from the camp, dropped as silently out again. After which, turning their horses' heads northwards, they set off alone into the darkness, in the hope that by daylight they would be out of sight of the advancing column. Their five remaining horses were loaded as lightly as possible. Their baggage had by now been reduced to forty pounds of black bread (which Ak Mamatov had bought surreptitiously from the soldiers, and which constituted the sole means of sustenance for themselves and their horses), to a single tin kettle and to MacGahan's 'light and unpretentious' collection of arms and ammunition. Almost everything else had been jettisoned.

Guided by the North Star, they made their way forward as fast as they could in the darkness, plodding through sand-dunes, struggling over broken and uneven ground, trampling through brushwood and occasionally stopping to reconnoitre, when they thought they saw something moving in the shadows ahead of them. As he urged his tired, hungry horse along, it occurred to MacGahan that this wild and foolhardy venture was almost bound to end tragically. But so great was his relief at being once more on the move that the dangers involved seemed of little importance and he felt almost cheerful as he stumbled along through the darkness.

At first light they paused and looked round to make sure that they were well out of Colonel Weimarn's clutches. Far away to the south-east they could see a dark speck moving slowly forward which they took to be his rearguard. After watching this disappear on the horizon they now turned westwards and headed directly for the Oxus across bare, rolling country.

At nine they stopped to make tea. No sooner had they halted than one of the horses threw itself down, too tired even to seek the scanty nourishment afforded by the thin, brown, dried up grass which its companions were eagerly cropping. It did not look as though it would go much farther. But an hour's rest and what was left of the barley seemed to revive it and after its load had been divided amongst the other four, it had recovered sufficiently to go on.

At two in the afternoon they came to some sand dunes fairly thickly covered with scrub. Climbing these, they found themselves looking out over some salt flats, two or three miles wide, beyond which were some more sand dunes. They had come to the sand sea, to Adam Kürülgan — the Destroyer of Men — traversed ten years before by Arminius Vambery. Somewhere in these sand dunes was the single well on which they were counting to replenish their now almost exhausted supply of water. But, on examining them through his field glasses, MacGahan was surprised to see amongst them the white uniforms of Russian troops. With a sinking heart he recognized, blocking his line of advance, the very Cossacks with whom he had started that morning from Khala-Ata and whom he had quitted so stealthily in the darkness.

For MacGahan this was a crushing blow, made all the harder to bear by the sly smile of triumph and relief which now spread over the features of Ak Mamatov and the two Kirghiz. Without water and with Colonel Weimarn's Cossacks in occupation of the well for which he was making, there could be no question of pushing on to the Oxus, a distance of at least another seventy-five miles. The choice lay between giving himself up to Colonel Weimarn or returning to Khala-Ata. Both involved the admission of defeat.

It was while he was pondering these two equally disagreeable alternatives that he suddenly recalled a conversation, overheard by chance at Khala-Ata, in the course of which mention had been made of another well lying somewhere between Adam Kürülgan and the Oxus. This, he had reason to believe, he would also find occupied by a detachment of Russian troops dispatched there by General Kaufmann. But at least they would not be under Colonel Weimarn's command and perhaps they would not try to stop him.

It was a gamble. Deciding to take it, he ordered his companions to remount. It was, he explained, his intention to push straight on to the next well, without stopping at Adam Kürülgan.

This announcement was greeted with a storm of protests by Ak Mamatov and the two Kirghiz. The horses, they said, were already exhausted and would never get across the intervening desert without rest and water. They would be left on foot in the middle of the sands and would all perish.

But MacGahan was now once again in a position to make effective use of the threats which he had been obliged to forgo at Khala-Ata. His followers had got three hundred roubles out of him the day before, when he had been in their power. Now it was his turn. 'In five minutes', he tells us, 'we were moving forward.'

Leaving Adam Kürülgan behind them, they plunged into the sand sea. Almost immediately they were in difficulties. The sand grew deeper and deeper. Piled up by the wind in huge drifts twenty or thirty feet high, it loomed menacingly above them as they plodded along. A single storm of wind would have sent it rolling over them, burying them without a trace. The unfortunate horses sank almost to their bellies and could only struggle forward in a series of desperate plunges. As soon as the riders dismounted, they, too, sank in up to their knees. Before they had gone many miles, the feeblest of the horses stumbled, staggered and then fell heavily to the ground with a groan. Jettisoning part of its load, they distributed the rest amongst the others and, taking off its saddle and bridle, left it to die.

That night they pushed on as far as they could until it became clear to MacGahan that, if he was not to lose his remaining horses, he must stop and camp. There was now nothing left to drink at all for either man or beast, and after the long day's ride under the scorching sun both they and their horses were too thirsty even to try to eat the hard, dry, black bread. Hungry and intolerably thirsty, uncertain of the whereabouts of the well for which they were looking, but certain that neither they nor their horses could hold out much longer, they lay gloomily down to sleep.

But next morning, after riding for two more hours, their eyes caught once again, far away on the horizon, the glitter of bayonets in the sunshine. Some way farther on they came to the first Russian outposts keeping watch from the top of a sandhill, and not long after that MacGahan and his three companions rode hopefully but also somewhat apprehensively into the camp which the Russians had pitched at Alty Kuduk or the Six Wells—'the sandiest, dreariest spot I have ever seen'.

As no officers were yet stirring, MacGahan sat down on a heap of baggage and waited for something to happen. He had not been there long when a head emerged from a near-by tent and shouted, *'Que diable faites-vous là? Entrez donc!'* Reassured, he did as he was told and was soon ravenously devouring a meal of dried beef, biscuit and tea. From the cheerful young officer who had befriended him he now learned that Kaufmann had already been gone six days and must by now be on the Oxus if he had not already crossed it. The detachment at Alty Kuduk were hoping to receive the order to march any day. If MacGahan would wait a day or two, he could accompany them. The road to the Oxus was infested with marauding Turkomans, and it would be extremely dangerous to attempt the journey alone.

But MacGahan would risk no more delays. After being hospitably entertained by the officers of the little garrison and provided with all the barley he wanted, he set out again next morning, May 27th, for the Oxus.

As it happened, his anxiety to be on the move again as soon as possible proved to be fully justified. He had, he learned afterwards, been gone only a few hours when an officer galloped into Alty Kuduk at the head of twenty-five Cossacks with orders to arrest and disarm him and take him back to Tashkent. He had been dispatched post-haste from Tashkent by some zealous official in pursuance of a standing order prohibiting all Europeans other than Russians from entering Turkestan. In accordance with his instructions this emissary had conscientiously pursued MacGahan across six hundred miles of desert; had had news of him from wandering Kirghiz; had got on to his trail, lost it, and found it again; had lost several horses; and had finally arrived at Alty Kuduk only to be laughed at by the officers of the garrison who assured him that his quarry was by now either with Kaufmann or the jackals — in either case, beyond his jurisdiction.

Meanwhile, in ignorance of his narrow escape, MacGahan was making his way westwards towards the Oxus. How far he still had to go, he was not certain — his guess was between thirty and fifty miles — but he hoped with luck to reach the river before nightfall. After two or three hours' ride he came to a place littered with dead Turkoman horses, evidently killed in an engagement with the Russians. Henceforward he advanced with ever greater caution, making sure that the country ahead of him was clear of Khivan troops before crossing it. In the late afternoon he emerged from the sandhills into a wide, level plain intersected to the north by a range of hills. Soon the sun had sunk below the horizon, and still there was no sign of the Oxus. Then, just as darkness was beginning to fall, he saw, far away in the distance, the glimmer of water.

They did not reach the water's edge until long after dark. Once there, having stealthily watered their horses amongst the rushes, they silently withdrew to the sand dunes to wait for daylight, not knowing whether it would reveal the white tunics of the Russians or the tall black caps of the Khivans.

At dawn they climbed out of the hollow in which they had spent the night and, ascending a sand dune, looked cautiously round them. There was no sign of anyone. The only living creature in sight was a loose horse which galloped off as soon as it saw them. What they had taken for the river the night before was in reality a reedy marsh situated at the foot of a range of low sandstone hills.

Slowly they climbed the nearest of these and, having reached the summit, again looked warily round. There, at last, stretching away below them to the north and south, broad and shining in the sunlight, flowed the Oxus. 'I forgot', wrote MacGahan, 'Kaufmann, the Turkomans, the object of my expedition, everything, in the one delight of beholding its swiftly running waters.' From where he stood, with his field glasses, he could see up and down the river for twenty miles and beyond it across the desert where the sands gleamed yellow and bare. But of friend or foe there was still no sign.

When MacGahan had first set out from Fort Perovski, he had hoped to catch up with Kaufmann in five days. He had now been pursuing him for a month and had still not found him. 'To my imagination,' he writes, 'Kaufmann began to appear like a phantom; I half expected to wake up in my hotel in Paris, and find the expedition against Khiva a myth and my own strange adventures a troubled dream.' 'A prey to a vague terror,' he hurried down to the water's edge. And there at last he found some trace of the passage of the Russian army: the tracks of cannon in the sand and the dead ashes of some burned-out camp fires. But that was all.

After stopping briefly to make tea, he now set out again along the river bank in the direction of Khiva, cautiously ascending every hillock and anxiously watching the far bank for any sign of movement. At one moment they were alarmed as a camel, falling suddenly from the cliff above them, landed with a broken neck at their feet. Thinking that the Turkomans were attacking them, they took up their arms, and prepared to sell their lives dearly; but nothing more followed. Once again they seized their arms when, rounding a bluff, they suddenly found themselves face to face with five horsemen. But the horsemen, dashing into the river, swam across it and scurried off in the direction of Khiva, hastened on their way by two or three shots from MacGahan's Winchester. Again, towards nightfall they saw some more horsemen who seemed to be watching them from across the river, but soon they and the far shore were lost from sight in the gathering darkness.

Pushing on until far into the night, the little party once more pitched camp. They had covered forty-five miles since dawn. They and their wretched horses were worn out and it was all that MacGahan could do to keep awake as, fearful of a surprise attack, he wearily stood guard above the prostrate forms of his slumbering followers. And still he had not found General Kaufmann.

At sunrise they again set out, passing at a distance of no more than a mile from their camp of the night before, the still smouldering ashes of a Khivan camp fire. Then, just as MacGahan was congratulating himself on yet another lucky escape, a sudden thundering fell on his ears, repeated again and again: the roar of cannon.

The river at this point took a sudden turn to the left; the noise of the cannonade came from directly in front of them. Leaving the river bank, MacGahan now rode straight on across the sand dunes to where the noise was coming from. A mile farther on, as he and his followers were slowly ascending a little hill, five native horsemen came suddenly galloping over the crest and then, seeing them, swerved off towards the river and disappeared. Clearly they were now close to the scene of events. Plodding on through the soft sand they continued to climb the hill as fast as their horses would carry them, hoping that what they saw from the summit would give them some indication of their position in relation to the contending forces.

In the event, the view from the hilltop was scarcely reassuring. At a distance of about two miles from where they stood, a hundred or so horses were scattered along a line a mile long. With them were a number of men who, from their clothes, were certainly not Russians. They seemed to have blundered right into the enemy lines. And now, as they watched, two horsemen suddenly detached themselves from the line and started towards them at full speed.

Escape was out of the question. Dismounting, MacGahan ordered his men to do the same and to get their arms ready. As he gave them these orders, it occurred to him forcibly that none of them was remotely likely to hit anything and that all three of them would probably run away. But it was too late to worry about that. Lying down in the scrub, he cocked his rifle. His intention was to allow the two Turkomans to approach to within ten yards, and then shoot them, and, if possible, seize their horses. With a good horse, he argued, he would at any rate have some chance of reaching the Russians.

When the two horsemen were not more than fifty yards away, MacGahan asked Mustruf if he still thought they were Turkomans. He replied that he did. At twenty-five yards the answer was the same. Then, just as MacGahan was about to press the trigger, his companion suddenly leaped up from beside him and threw his cap in the air with a shout of joy. He had recognized one of the advancing horsemen as a friend of his. They were, it transpired, not Turkomans after all, but Kirghiz guides in the Russian service. All the Khivans, they said, had been driven to the other side of the Oxus. The Russians were only three miles farther on, bombarding a fort across the river at Sheik-Arik. Remounting, they pushed on and in half an hour reached a sand dune on the river bank from which they had an extensive view of river and valley.

The Oxus was at this point about three-quarters of a mile wide, a broad, muddy stream. On the near bank, at a distance of about half a mile, were the Russians, watching while two of their six-pounders lobbed shells across the river. On the far bank, which was considerably higher, the Khivans had built at Sheik-Arik a fort to command the passage of the river. From in front of this, down at the water's edge, two pieces of cannon, firing not shells, but solid shot, were booming away with might and main, while the whole shore swarmed with

Khivan cavalry. Farther away still could be seen the gardens and orchards of the oasis. Suddenly, as they watched, a Russian shell burst right amongst the enemy's cavalry beyond the river. General panic ensued. Then horses were rushed down and the cannon at the water's edge hastily hauled away. In the space of a few minutes there was not a soul to be seen on the far shore.

MacGahan now set off towards the Russian lines. As he approached them, he was hailed by an officer.

'*Vui kto?*' he shouted. 'Who are you?'

'*Amerikanets,*' replied MacGahan.

'So you', said the officer, 'are the man who crossed the Kizil Kum alone. Come along and I will present you to the General.' And he led him up to a big, broad-shouldered, heavily bearded and whiskered man sitting on a gun smoking a cigarette.

Having shaken hands with MacGahan and congratulated him on his achievement, the General, whose name was Golovachov, asked him to breakfast: 'cold boiled beef, cold chicken, sardines and a little *vodka*, laid out on a clean cloth spread on the grass'. Avidly, he fell to, while the Russian officers, 'all spruce in their white coats and caps, and gold and silver buttons, as clean and starchy as though they were on parade in Isaac's Square, St Petersburg', clustered curiously round this dirty, hollow-eyed, hollow-cheeked, ragged figure and plied him with questions about the remarkable journey which he had just accomplished. 'They gave me', says MacGahan, 'such a lively account of the dangers I had escaped, that I really began to be frightened.'

General Golovachov, who had been entrusted with the task of reducing the fortress of Sheik-Arik, now set out to rejoin General Kaufmann at his camp some five miles farther down the river. MacGahan went with him. His first care on arrival was to pay his respects to the Governor-General. He found Kaufmann sitting in an open tent wearing a Bokharan *khalat*, drinking tea and smoking a cigarette. He was a man of between forty-five and fifty, bald, slightly built, with a long fair moustache and a kindly expression. Having in his turn congratulated MacGahan on his journey, he gave him some account of the campaign up to date.

*

General Kaufmann had set out from Tashkent on March 15th with a force of 2500 men, composed of eleven companies of infantry, six hundred Cossacks, a battery and a half of artillery, a battery and a half of rocket-launchers and a company of sappers and miners. His baggage train had consisted of between three and four thousand camels, hired from the Kirghiz.

After a successful and relatively uneventful march in bitterly cold weather, he had arrived a month later at the well of Aristan-Bel-Kuduk. Here he had abandoned his original intention of making for the Bukan Tau Range and had decided instead to march to Khala-Ata, at the same time sending instructions to the Kazala column, the strength of which was about 1400 men, to join him there.

The junction of the two columns had taken place on May 6th. On May 12th the combined force had advanced to Adam Kürülgan, where they had obtained a sufficient supply of water by digging wells. This was the last point at which they could count on finding water before they reached the Oxus. How long this would take them they did not then know, but they hoped to get there in two or at the outside three days and accordingly took with them supplies of water for three days.

On the morning of May 17th they had set out from Adam Kürülgan into the sand sea. The going was very bad. The camels were enfeebled by their long march from Tashkent. Many had to be abandoned on the way. At the end of the first day's march General Kaufmann found that, instead of thirty, he had covered only fifteen miles. His supplies of water were almost completely exhausted.

His position was now extremely critical. Between him and the Oxus lay not less than thirty and possibly as much as a hundred miles of unknown desert. To attempt to cross this without water would be folly. If, on the other hand, he were once to retreat, it might well be the signal for the whole population of Turkestan to rise against him. Either course spelt disaster.

After much heart-searching, he was about to give the order to withdraw when a nondescript-looking Kirghiz was brought before him in rags and tatters. He wished to offer his services against the Turkomans, who had murdered some of his relatives and made slaves of the rest. And now, while the fifty or sixty other guides accompanying the expedition were maintaining that there was no water nearer than the Oxus, he, it seemed, was claiming that he could find some in the immediate neighbourhood.

As a last resort, it was worth trying. Taking out his pocket flask, Kaufmann handed it to the Kirghiz. 'Bring me that back full of water', he said, 'and I will give you a hundred roubles.' The man was given a good horse and was off like the wind. A few hours later he came back with the flask full of water. He had found three wells at the place later to be known as Alty Kuduk, four miles north of the regular caravan route. At once Kaufmann gave the order to march and two hours later the advance guard reached the wells.

But even now his troubles were not over. The water in the wells was bad and there was not much of it. Even after three more wells had been dug, there was still only enough to allow each man a pint a day. As there was not enough water at Alty Kuduk for the camels, or indeed for the native guides, two or three of whom had already died of thirst, Kaufmann now decided to send the whole train back to Adam Kürülgan under a small escort to fetch fresh supplies.

This gave the enemy cavalry the opportunity they had been waiting for. Realizing that if they could cut off Kaufmann's camel train, the whole expedition would be doomed, they waited until the camels with their escort had reached Adam Kürülgan and then swooped down on them in strength. But, in a pitched battle, their superior equipment gave the Russians the advantage. With their breech-loaders, the Russian sharp-shooters took terrible toll of native horsemen armed only with sabres, and the attack, though vigorous, was successfully driven off. Another whole week, however, was lost before the camels, with their fresh supplies of water, eventually returned to Alty Kuduk and General Kaufmann was finally able to start on the last stage of his march to the Oxus.

By now large numbers of camels had perished and those remaining were only fit to carry greatly reduced loads. Abandoning everything except a bare minimum of food, forage, water and equipment, the expedition now set out, unsure as yet of the distance which still separated them from the river and sure only that, as far as they were concerned, the next few days must bring either victory, or failing that, total disaster.

The ensuing march to the Oxus had tried them severely. They suffered badly from heat and thirst and on the last day were continually harassed by Turkoman cavalry. But they had successfully fought off the enemy's attacks and had finally reached the Oxus. When they first came in sight of the great river, Kaufmann and his officers took off their caps and devoutly crossed themselves, while their men shouted out loud for joy.

On reaching the Oxus, Kaufmann at once passed from the defensive to the offensive. In a first engagement with the Khivans he put the enemy to flight and captured eleven native boats. Continuing his advance along the river bank, he shortly afterwards came under fire from the enemy's cannon at Sheik-Arik and decided that before he attempted to cross the river the fort would have to be reduced. It was during the ensuing battle on May 29th that MacGahan had joined him.

Next morning, Kaufmann began his crossing of the Oxus at Sheik-Arik. It was a fine morning. The broad stream sparkled in the sunlight and from where he lay on the grass in front of his tent MacGahan could make out through the haze which enveloped the far bank, the gardens and orchards, the mosques and farmsteads of the oasis. 'It lay', he writes, 'silent and lonely, without any moving figure to give it life, this strange, unknown land of Khiva; and seen, away over the water, bathed in a sleepy, glorious splendour, looked as beautiful and dreamy as the fabled land of the lotus-eaters. Idly I watched it, thinking of all the stories I had ever heard of it; of its cruel and despotic Khans; its wild fanatical Mohammedan population; its beautiful women; its strange mysterious character; and its isolation, which had rendered it as inaccessible to Europeans as the enchanted caves of the mountain. I was unable to realize the situation, and half expected to wake up and find myself some thousands of miles away in another hemisphere.'

Meanwhile on the near side of the river intense activity prevailed. Infantrymen and Cossacks, artillerymen and engineers splashed about in the water, climbed into the clumsy native boats, dragged in guns, baggage and horses to a deafening accompaniment of shouts, yells and curses, while General Kaufmann in person urged on his troops from a camp-stool by the water's edge. Before long, two companies of infantry and four small guns had reached the far side without encountering any opposition and had established themselves in the fort.

The passage of the Oxus was now assured. The crossing continued all that day and all the following day. On June 1st Kaufmann and his staff moved to the other side and MacGahan went with them. For weeks the Russians had been on short rations. Suddenly they found themselves in the midst of plenty. In response to a proclamation by General Kaufmann, the local population flocked down to the river, bringing with them whole cartloads of meat, fruit, chickens, fresh wheaten cakes, apricots, rice, sugar, tea, honey and mulberries. The Khivan merchants were lean, medium-sized, muscular men with long black beards and a slightly sinister cast of countenance. They wore dirty cotton shirts and trousers and striped *khalats* of a dingy yellowish brown, very unlike the gorgeous robes of the Bokharans, and, on their heads, high, black sheepskin hats. Busily they sold their wares to the Russians at three or four times the proper price. On this basis friendly relations were quickly established between conquerors and conquered.

But after three days these abundant supplies suddenly ceased. The Khan, it seemed, had let it be known that he would cut off the head of any of his subjects who sold food to the invaders. General Kaufmann accordingly now sent out into the oasis a column five or six hundred strong to forage and reconnoitre and MacGahan went with it. The way led between fertile fields of corn, rice and barley, pleasant gardens and well-stocked orchards. Elms and poplars lined the streams and watercourses. Over the road hung fruit trees laden with apricots, apples, cherries and mulberries. Through the trees they caught glimpses of the sun-baked walls of houses and farmsteads. To men who had spent so long in the glare and dust of the desert, the cool shade of the trees, the running water, the sudden greenness and luxuriance of the vegetation made the oasis, reached after so many hazards and hardships, seem like paradise.

After advancing for five or six miles, they got their first sight of the enemy. On either side Turkoman cavalry in their high sheepskin hats could be seen galloping through the trees in groups of fifteen or twenty, while the whole countryside resounded with their bloodcurdling yells. Advancing another three miles, the Russians now came to an open space on the far side of which several thousand Khivans were drawn up ready for battle. To the ineffective fire of the enemy's matchlocks the Russians replied by bringing up two field guns and lobbing a few shells into them. These caused the Khivans to disperse, but not to withdraw. The Russians were now at no great distance from the Khivan fortress of Hazar Asp. Finding himself, for all his advantage of armament, greatly outnumbered, their commander sent back to General Kaufmann for reinforcements. But by the time these arrived under command of the Grand Duke Nicholas, it was too late to attack the fortress before dark and they accordingly fell back to the river, harassed by the Khivans as they went.

Next morning at dawn the Russians marched in strength on Hazar Asp. On reaching the scene of the previous day's engagement, they were surprised to find no signs of the enemy and assumed that they must have withdrawn into the fortress, which was the key to the defence of Khiva itself. After advancing some way farther, however, they encountered two ambassadors, who, on meeting the advance-guard, dismounted from their richly caparisoned horses and humbly took off their high sheepskin hats. They had, they declared, been sent by the Governor of Hazar Asp to offer their submission and surrender the fortress.

Continuing their advance through the smiling gardens and orchards — 'the march', writes MacGahan, 'seemed more like a holiday excursion or picnic than the iron tread of grim-visaged war' — the Russians soon came in sight of the fortress with its moat and its high, battlemented walls and buttresses, which gave it, as it stood out above the trees, 'a noble appearance, not unlike that of Windsor Castle'. Followed by his staff and two companies of infantry, General Kaufmann now entered the fortress. To the Russian officers, longing for action, the campaign up to date had been frankly disappointing. They could only hope that the enemy might perhaps make a last desperate stand in Khiva itself.

Before making his final attack on the capital, it was General Kaufmann's intention to assemble his whole force, including the detachments left behind at Khala-Ata and Alty Kuduk. By June 8th, this had been done and by the evening of the 9th his advance-guard was within ten miles of Khiva. Since crossing the Oxus, Kaufmann had received a number of letters and messages from the Khan, expressing astonishment at the Russian invasion of his dominions, inquiring the reason for it, and inviting the invaders to withdraw immediately. Now, at nightfall on the 9th, a further letter was delivered. In it the Khan proffered his submission and announced his readiness to surrender unconditionally.

To do him justice, the Khan's position was by now well-nigh hopeless. Some days earlier General Kaufmann had at last succeeded in establishing communication with General Veryovkin, the commander of the combined Orenburg and Kinderly columns. Approaching Khiva from the north, Veryovkin had captured the fortress of Kungrad, and was now attacking the capital from the other side. Thus, of the five columns which had originally set out, four, starting from bases many hundreds of miles apart, had, after innumerable hazards and vicissitudes, finally arrived before Khiva within a day of each other. Only one column, that commanded by Colonel Markosov, had failed in its objective, having run out of water and been obliged after severe sufferings to turn back to the Caspian when still at a distance of one hundred and twenty miles from Khiva.

The dangers and difficulties overcome by the Orenburg and Kinderly columns had been no whit less formidable than those encountered by their comrades from Tashkent and Kazala. Setting out in February, the Orenburg column of some 3000 men commanded by General Veryovkin had at first suffered severely from cold. They had reached the last Russian outpost of Emba towards the end of March and, striking southwards across the desert, had arrived at the Aral Sea on May 2nd. Following its western shore they had, after an approach march of over a thousand miles, crossed the Khivan frontier on May 14th and some ten days later had occupied the Khivan fortress of Kungrad. There they had been joined by the Kinderly column of 1800 men under Colonel Lomakin, who, during their long march from the Caspian across waterless desert, had suffered torments of thirst and had only escaped disaster thanks to the fortuitous discovery, when they were at their last gasp, of a small well. Among the officers of the Kinderly column who particularly distinguished themselves during the arduous advance from the Caspian were two who were later to become famous in Russian military history, Colonel M. D. Skobelyov, and his friend, Captain N. I. Grodekov.

From Kungrad the united columns had advanced in the direction of Khiva, fighting several engagements on the way and inflicting one major defeat on the Khan's forces. Having reached the outskirts of the city on June 7th, General Veryovkin had waited for two days and then, being still without recent news of General Kaufmann, had attacked. But on the evening of June 9th, while an intensive bombardment of the city was in progress under the direction of Colonel Skobelyov, a messenger had arrived from General Kaufmann bringing news of the Khan's offer of surrender and orders for an immediate cease-fire. With these orders the troops of General Veryovkin, who, as it happened, had himself just been shot in the head, reluctantly complied. Shortly afterwards, however, the Turkomans in the garrison, disregarding the Khan's attempt at surrender, again opened fire on General Veryovkin's troops, who, glad of an excuse to resume their bombardment, once more began to shell the city and continued to do so throughout the night.

On the following morning, General Kaufmann, who, it will be recalled, was still at a distance of ten miles from the city on the other side, set out for Khiva, having first sent a message to the Khan, telling him to meet him outside the city gates in order that he might inform him of the terms of surrender. The Khan, meanwhile, scared by the bombardment, had fled from the city, leaving his uncle, Said Emir Ul-Umar, to surrender in his place. Said Emir now came out to meet the Russians, very old, very feeble and with 'a perfectly idiotic expression of face', due, it appeared, to opium eating, which had caused his jaw to sag and his mouth to hang permanently open. He wore a high black sheepskin hat, a bright green *khalat* and big boots with high heels and turned-up toes, and had, it seemed, always been in favour of giving the Russians anything they wanted.

Taking Said Emir Ul-Umar with him, General Kaufmann now entered Khiva in triumph with drums beating and colours flying while a band played the Imperial Anthem. Meanwhile, from the other side of the city, came the sound of firing. Colonel Skobelyov and a number of kindred spirits under General Veryovkin's command had chosen this moment to take Khiva by storm from the north and were even now fighting their way into the centre of the city, hotly opposed by some equally bellicose Turkomans. Just in time the order was given to withdraw and General Kaufmann, followed by the Grand Duke Nicholas and Prince Eugene of Leuchtenberg, was enabled to continue his dignified progress between bowing rows of bearded Khivans towards the Palace of the Khan, which Colonel Skobelyov, sword in hand, had only a few moments earlier taken by storm under a hail of bullets.

For J. A. MacGahan, as for General Kaufmann, this was a big moment. He had scooped the world. His first sight of Khiva had, it is true, been something of a disappointment to him. 'There are', he tells

KHIVA: INSIDE THE WALLS

us, 'points of view in Khiva which are *very* picturesque, but this was not one of them.' The dust, too, rising in dense clouds from beneath their horses' hooves, he found highly obnoxious. But, picturesque or not picturesque, dust or no dust, he had got there. And he had got there at a moment in history. Of this he was deeply conscious as he rode in triumph through the streets of the conquered city, past crowds of citizens as yet uncertain whether they would all be massacred or not. 'With what strange awe and dread', he wrote in a notable dispatch to his paper, 'they must have gazed upon us as we passed, dust-covered and grimy, after our march of six hundred miles over the desert, which they had considered impassable. Grim, stern, silent and invincible, we must have appeared to them like some strange, powerful beings of an unknown world.'

On reaching the Palace gate with its twin turrets, Kaufmann dismounted and made his way on foot through a series of passages and rooms to the Grand Court of the Palace. On its southern side was the Grand Hall of State, an open veranda thirty feet high, flanked on both hands by towers ornamented with blue and green tiles, its roof supported by slender pillars of carved wood. Here, where the Khan had been accustomed to dispense justice, Kaufmann and his suite now flung themselves down to rest, while the band struck up an air from Offenbach's *Belle Hélène* and one of the Khan's Ministers brought them iced water, wheaten cakes, cherries and apricots, 'with which', writes MacGahan, 'we merrily proceeded to refresh ourselves'.

Such was the fall of Khiva, which for more than two centuries had successfully resisted all Russian attempts to subdue it.

For the next day or two MacGahan occupied himself most enjoyably in 'rummaging', as he put it, about the Khan's Palace. Though a loyal citizen of the United States (he was later to explain to a bewildered Khan the workings of the American Constitution), he was not entirely proof against the glamour of monarchic institutions. Earlier, during the fighting, he had been much impressed to learn that a dashing young officer who gave him a drink of sherry out of his pocket flask was none other than Prince Eugene of Leuchtenberg and, in improving this acquaintance, had been agreeably surprised to find that, like the Grand Duke Nicholas, His Highness was simple and unassuming in his manners and on terms of good fellowship with everybody. Now he rummaged with relish amongst the barbaric and somewhat tawdry splendours of the labyrinthine tangle of towers, verandas, passages, courtyards, stables and mud buildings which together formed the Palace of the Khan of Khiva. The Throne Room, the Treasure Room, the Armoury, the Library — he inspected them all. In the Throne Room he found the Throne — 'quite a curiosity'; in the Treasure Rooms, a gold-plated saddle and bridle set with rubies, emeralds and turquoises of inferior quality; in the Library, three hundred books — all written by hand — some bows and arrows, some chain armour and half a dozen old telescopes; in the Armoury, pile upon pile of arms of the most varied description, swords, daggers, pistols and guns of every shape and size, some splendid old matchlocks inlaid with gold and a particularly fine new English sporting rifle. With the rifle was a letter from the Viceroy of India, Lord Northbrook, written in September 1872 in reply to an urgent request from the Khan for help against the Russians. The help which the Khan demanded had not been forthcoming. Instead, Lord Northbrook had sent him this rifle, a pair of field glasses and a musical-box. By the time these gifts reached him, the invading Russian armies were already assembling.

As he wandered through the Palace, MacGahan came at last to the gate of the Harem where two Russian sentries were posted. Behind them he could see a crowd of weeping girls and women. One of these immediately attracted his attention. 'She was', he writes, 'about eighteen, of medium size, had a clear rosy complexion, showing her Caucasian origin, broad low forehead, round face, black hair and large dark eyes. Her quiet firmness, tranquil air of authority and noble appearance, convinced me, in spite of the old ragged *khalat* she wore over head and shoulders, that she was the Sultana of the Harem. She turned her eyes towards me in a half-imploring way, as though she would have spoken to me.'

This was too much for MacGahan. 'I never in my life before', he tells us, 'so much regretted my ignorance of an unknown tongue ... The dark eyes of this woman haunted me after she had disappeared.

DR JOSEPH WOLFF

COLONEL CHARLES STODDART

CAPTAIN ARTHUR CONOLLY

THE EMIR NASRULLAH OF BOKHARA

THE NAYEB ABDUL SAMUT KHAN

ARMINIUS VAMBERY

BOKHARA: THE LIABI KHAUS

EDMUND O'DONOVAN

SAMARKAND: THE TOMB OF TAMERLANE

KHIVA: THE KHAN'S PALACE

FOUR INCARNATIONS OF JOSEPH KASTAMUNI

TURKOMANS

THE FOUR KHANS OF MERV

ENVER PASHA

'THE BOKHARANS STILL WEAR THEIR NATIONAL DRESS'

BOKHARA: FIRST LIGHT

I could not forget her calm, majestic figure ... I determined to communicate with her and help her.'

But this was easier said than done. The sentries on the gate of the Harem would admit no one, not even the correspondent of the *New York Herald*. The officer of the guard, if directly approached, might well misinterpret his romantic, though apparently honourable, intentions. Ak Mamatov, who might have had some ideas, was, as usual when he was needed, nowhere to be found. Thrown on his own resources, MacGahan decided to see if he could not somehow reach his objective without passing the sentries.

Setting out at about midnight, he made his way along the battlements of the palace to a point from which he could peer down into what he took to be the Harem. By night Khiva was transfigured. The silent, sleeping city lay bathed in a flood of glorious moonlight. To the romantically inclined young American, it seemed 'no longer a real city, but a leaf torn from the enchanted pages of the Arabian nights'. Then, suddenly, as he looked down, he saw a female figure flit across the moonlit court below and vanish into the shadows beyond. In a flash he was after her.

A locked door presented no difficulty. Wrenching it from its shaky hinges, he pushed boldly on, revolver in hand. Down a stone stairway. Along a passage, feeling his way in the pitch dark. Through another courtyard. Along another dark passage. Into a room with six doors. Through one of these, chosen at random in the darkness, into a veritable labyrinth of rooms and passages, all empty and all plunged in the most impenetrable darkness. Once, feeling the floor wet beneath his feet, he struck a light to find that he was standing at the brink of a well fifty feet deep. Lighting a candle he had brought with him, he hurried on, only to extinguish it hastily on finding that the next room was a powder magazine.

By now he was hopelessly lost and his enthusiasm had begun to wane. He had just decided 'to let the dark-eyed beauty of the Harem take care of herself' when all at once, as he was feeling his way along yet another dark passage, he came to a locked door from the other side of which came sounds of girlish laughter. A tentative knock was greeted by silence from the other side; another produced whispering and suppressed giggles; a third was answered by some incomprehensible words in Tartar, pronounced in an agreeable girlish voice.

'*Aman*', said MacGahan hopefully, exhausting at one blow practically his whole stock of Tartar — 'Peace be with you'. '*Aman?*' the voice queried. '*Aman*', replied MacGahan with all the assurance he could muster. At which there was more giggling, a rattle of bolts, and the door swung open, revealing the eighteen-year-old beauty of the day before, with six or eight girls and women round her, standing by the door holding a lamp above her head.

She was no longer wearing the ragged *khalat* in which he had first seen her, but was dressed in a short jacket of green silk, fastened on the throat with an emerald, slightly open on the bosom, and reaching below the knees, wide trousers, fastened at the ankles, and embroidered boots. She wore no turban, and her hair was wound about her well-shaped head in heavy glossy braids. Curious earrings, composed of many little pendants of pearls and turquoises, hung from her ears, and heavy, solid silver bracelets encircled her wrists.

The only difficulty was to know what to say. The young lady was looking at him intently with her great dark eyes and smiling gravely. Her companions, for their part, were convulsed with laughter. '*Salaam*', said MacGahan, feeling rather inadequate, and then, falling back on almost the only other Tartar word he knew, '*Chai*' — 'Tea'.

'Instantly', he tells us, 'they understood.' Taking his hand, the fair Caucasian at once led him out, through a moonlit courtyard, to a larger room which lay beyond and there motioned him to a pile of cushions, while she and her companions busied themselves with a teapot. Once again MacGahan was struck by her superior intelligence, her exquisite grace of movement and her indefinable air of superiority.

Returning with cups, sweetmeats and a steaming teapot, his fair hostess now knelt on the ground before him and watched him intently with her beautiful dark eyes, while he drank some tea and ate a large quantity of sweetmeats, and the others sat round waiting eagerly for one of them to say something. Again he was overcome by a feeling of inadequacy.

At this moment he had an idea. By a process of elimination he would find out her name. 'Fatima?' he said pointing at her inquiringly. But she shook her head and pointed at one of the other women. 'Zuleika', she said, indicating herself. Emboldened, he now embarked on more general topics. '*Urus ma yakshe?*' he asked. 'Are the Russians good?' '*Yoke! Yoke! Yoke!*' came the answer. 'No! No! No!' As they presumably took him for a Russian, this was scarcely encouraging. '*Min Urus yoke,*' he said hastily. 'I am not a Russian.' 'Yes, yes,' they chorused eagerly. 'We know, we know.'

At the time he could not understand what they meant. Only later did he discover that it was generally believed by the Khivans that he was an Englishman, sent by the British Government to help them in their hour of need, just as Shakespear, Abbott and Conolly had been sent at the time of General Perovski's expedition, and that this was the true explanation of the beseeching glances which Zuleika had cast on him and of the friendly reception she and her companions were now according him.

As it was, all that MacGahan could do was to try to explain, for the most part by signs, that they really had nothing to fear from the Russians and then give them a few little trinkets which he had brought with him. When, two hours later, he finally got up to go, Zuleika came with him as far as the foot of the stone stairway by which he had entered the Harem, then, as he turned at the top to look back, she kissed her hand to him and vanished into the shadows.

Next day, when the Russians as usual sent food to the Harem, they found that there was no one there. Every one of the women had escaped in the night. Inquiry showed that, in the absence of any more effectual rescuer, they had taken refuge with the Khan's idiotic old uncle, Said Emir Ul-Umar.

General Kaufmann, meanwhile, had sent a letter to the Khan, telling him that if he did not come back immediately he would make someone else Khan in his place. If, on the other hand, he came back and gave himself up, he would be accorded all the honours due to a sovereign. It was not, added Kaufmann, the intention of the Russians to occupy the country permanently.

Reassured by this message, the Khan, who had temporarily taken refuge in the desert with his faithful Turkomans, now returned to

Khiva and on June 14th was conducted into the presence of his conqueror, who received him under the elms in front of his tent. Dismounting while still some distance away, the monarch advanced down his own garden path on foot, tall sheepskin hat in hand, bowing low to Kaufmann as he approached. A big man, of about thirty, well over six feet tall and heavily built, with a rather crooked aquiline nose, a heavy sensual mouth and a thin black beard and moustache, he had a frightened look and, as he knelt on the ground before Kaufmann, a fair, slightly built figure on a camp stool, could scarcely look him in the face.

'Well, Khan,' said Kaufmann with a gentle smile which did not altogether disguise his satisfaction, 'you see, I have come to see you at last, as I wrote you I would, three years ago.'

'Yes; Allah has willed it.'

'No, Khan, there you are mistaken. Allah had very little to do with it. You have brought it upon yourself. If you had listened to my counsel three years ago, and acceded to my just demands, you would not have seen me here. In other words, if you had done as I advised you, Allah would not have willed it.'

'The pleasure of seeing the *Yarim-Padshah* is so great, that I could wish nothing changed.'

'The pleasure, I assure you, Khan, is mutual. But now let us proceed to business. What are you going to do? What do you wish to do?'

'That I leave to you to decide in your great wisdom. If I could wish for anything, it would be to become a subject of the Great White Tsar.'

'Very well. You shall not be his subject, but his friend, if you will. It only depends upon yourself. The Great White Tsar does not wish to deprive you of your throne. He only wishes to prove to you that he is too great a Tsar to be trifled with, which I hope he has shown to your satisfaction. The Great White Tsar is too great a Tsar to take revenge. Having shown you his might, he is ready to forgive you, and let you retain your throne under conditions, which you and I, Khan, will discuss another day.'

'I know I have done very wrong in not granting the just demands of the Russians, but I was ignorant and ill-advised; I will know better in the future. I thank the Great White Tsar and the illustrious *Yarim-Padshah* for their great kindness and forbearance to me, and will always be their friend.'

'You may return now, Khan, to your capital. Re-establish your government, administer justice, and preserve order. Tell your people to resume their occupations and their work, and they will not be molested. Tell them that the Russians are neither brigands nor robbers, but honest men; that they have not come to carry off their wealth, nor violate their women.'

Having been thus briefly apprised of what the future held in store for him and his subjects, the Khan now went off to start his life anew. Henceforward, like his neighbours the Emir of Bokhara and the Khan of Kokand, he would be no more than a Russian puppet. Some two months later, on August 23rd, 1873, he signed a treaty with Russia in which he expressly declared himself 'the humble servant of the Emperor of All the Russias', surrendered to Russia the conduct of his foreign policy, granted her far-reaching economic rights and agreed to pay her an enormous indemnity. Without bothering to annex or even occupy its territory, Russia had gained complete control of the Khanate of Khiva.

On August 24th, the day after the signing of the Treaty, General Kaufmann and his victorious troops left Khiva and set out on the long march back to the bases from which they had come. During recent weeks they had not been idle. From the Uzbeg population of the Khan's dominions, dwelling for the most part in the towns and villages of the oasis itself, the Russians had nothing more to fear. The Yomud Turkomans, on the other hand, who lived in the desert to the west of Khiva were quite a different proposition. A proud warlike people, they had always been impatient of authority — and this, in Russian eyes, was an unpardonable sin. Before setting out on his return journey, General Kaufmann decided to deal them a crushing blow. On the pretext that they had not paid their share of the indemnity quickly enough, he sent against them a strong force of infantry, cavalry and artillery with ten guns and a battery of rocket-launchers. For a fortnight these apostles of civilization massacred, ravaged and burnt, leaving behind them a trail of desolation and despair. By the time they returned to the oasis, the power of the Yomud Turkomans had been broken once and for all.

Having ridden with Kaufmann's Cossacks on their expedition against the Yomud Turkomans and assisted at the signing of the treaty of August 23rd, MacGahan, his mission accomplished, set out for home. This time he made the journey by boat with a party of wounded, travelling down the Oxus to its mouth in a native *kayuk*, then by steamer across the Sea of Aral and up the Syr Daria as far as Kazala, which he reached on September 12th. Three days later he was once more on the post road to Orenburg, *en route*, although he did not know it at the time, for Cuba.

WHITE GENERAL

CONSTANTINOPLE lay under the guns of an invading army. In December 1877 Osman Pasha had finally been forced to surrender at Plevna and the Sixteenth Russian Division, sweeping, under command of the now famous General M. D. Skobelyov, over the snowy Balkan passes and again defeating the Turks at Senova near Shipka, had established their lines before the Turkish capital.

From where they were, the Russians could see Constantinople in the distance, Tsargrad, as they called it, the City of the Eastern Emperors. 'Straight before us towards the north', wrote one of them, 'Byzantium revealed herself to our gaze, with its countless mosques and palaces: that Byzantium which had been the dream of Russia for so long, of Russia so cruelly hemmed in within her wide domains, so vainly seeking a southern outlet for her possessions and her wealth ... We could distinguish the marble walls of its kiosques, their tall, slender minarets, the splendid cupolas of Sophia, Izeddin, Omarah, Muhraddah and Bayazid. Tens of thousands of roofs and towers reared themselves on those hills and were lost in the dark shadows of cypress forests and green clouds of gardens. It looked like a beautiful dream, this Eastern Rome, this Rome of the Slavs, for which so many tears and so much blood had been shed ... At night our delighted eyes again turned towards it. Myriads of fires were kindled on those shores, as though some legendary leviathan were lying there, luxuriating in the caressing waves of the Bosphorus and watching it with many flaming eyes.'

Meanwhile, only a few miles away in the Sea of Marmara, lay the ironclads of the British Mediterranean Fleet at anchor off Ismid, silently menacing, and ready, should they be so instructed, to sail at short notice up the Bosphorus to the defence of the Sultan and his capital.

But while all over Europe diplomats and politicians sought frantically for a way out of this dangerous deadlock, in Constantinople itself life – especially night-life – went on as usual; and one evening in the early part of the year 1878 a visitor to the Café Concordia might have seen a tall, good-looking man of about thirty, in civilian clothes, with dark hair and fair, flowing beard and whiskers, and clear, rather cruel blue eyes, sitting at the roulette table, drinking champagne and idly slipping an occasional half-imperial to the pretty young French *chanteuse* next to him, who lost them as fast as he gave them to her.

'Do you know,' said this fine-looking fellow to a friend as the evening wore on, 'it's rather fun to go about like this and not be recognized, to be a *bon bourgeois*. It's a sort of relaxation. It's delightful to be no one in particular.' But in the end he tired of the pastime and got up to leave. As he was going down the stairs, there was a patter of feet behind him. It was the little *chanteuse*.

'I have a favour to ask,' she said.

'And what may that be?'

'Will you', she pleaded, 'allow our *troupe* to visit you and give you some concerts?'

'Where do you want to come to? Who do you take me for?'

'Oh,' came the answer, 'we all know *you*, you are General Skobelyov – *Akh-Pasha*, the White General!' And Skobelyov, it seems, was very much amused.

But, whereas there were times when General Skobelyov found these clandestine excursions behind the enemy's lines highly diverting, there were others – for he was a man of many moods – when his reactions to the situation in which he and his troops found themselves were entirely different. 'This', he would say, pointing angrily to his civilian suit, 'is how Russian generals have to show themselves in their conquered town! But I cannot believe it. I still have hopes. I think even *our* diplomatists must come to their senses soon. From day to day I am expecting to get orders to march on Constantinople.' And from sheer frustration he would burst into tears. 'I would hold a Congress here', he would shout, 'and I would preside myself, with three hundred thousand bayonets round me. Then we could talk to them!' 'The English', he would announce, after dining with Sir Henry Layard at the British Embassy, where he was a frequent visitor, 'are afraid. They are unprepared for war.'

But of this many of his more cautious compatriots were not so sure. The British ironclads were, after all, still lying off Ismid, and any Russian who cared to had only to stroll up into the tawny hills above the Sea of Marmara to be reminded of their silent, ever-present menace. Whether Skobelyov himself went to look at them is not recorded, but we know that, shortly before leaving on a special mission to Central Asia, his Chief of Staff and close friend, Colonel Grodekov, a bald, frail-looking officer with spectacles and a beard, did so, and stood for a while looking thoughtfully down on the formidable array of battleships spread out before him.

The British men-of-war at anchor in the narrow straits, the Russian staff officer gazing down at them, and, just round the corner, the great straggling city on the shores of the Bosphorus, lying helpless between the two, aptly symbolized the situation. If the Russians were to advance any farther, if they were to seek to give to the defeated Turks the *coup de grâce* which it was in their power to administer, there could in fact be little doubt that Great Britain would go to war.

Barely twenty years after the Crimea, relations between the two powers were once again dangerously strained. 'It is not', wrote Queen Victoria, 'a question of upholding Turkey. It is a question of Russian or British supremacy in the world.' And again: 'Oh, if the Queen were a man, she would like to go and give those Russians, whose word one cannot believe, such a beating! We shall never be friends again till we have it out. This the Queen feels sure of.' Disraeli, to whom these exhortations were addressed, though sympathetic, was, for his part, inclined to be rather more cautious. But, as so often, large numbers of the Queen's subjects were thinking along almost exactly the same lines as their sovereign.

We don't want to fight,' they sang, 'but by Jingo if we do,
We've got the ships, we've got the men, we've got the money too.
We've fought the Bear before and, while Britons shall be true,
The Russians shall not have Constantinople.

On the other side of the hill, meanwhile, these bellicose sentiments were no less enthusiastically echoed by Pan-Slav patriots in St Petersburg and, as we have seen, in the Russian camp before Constantinople, where General Skobelyov and those who thought like him were growing daily more impatient of the restraint imposed on them. But there was still one all-important question to be resolved. The Russians were threatening Constantinople with their army. The British, to the dismay, be it said, of the Sultan, were protecting it with their fleet. The Russian Army was powerless to attack the British Fleet and the British Fleet, when it came to the point, was equally powerless to attack the Russian Army. If the two great powers were, in Queen Victoria's words, to 'have it out', they would need to do so somewhere accessible to the armed forces of both countries. The question was: where?

General Skobelyov, for his part, had no doubts as to the answer. In his view, the ultimate solution to the Eastern Question must lie in Central Asia — in Afghanistan and in India. Two years earlier, in 1876, while himself serving in Central Asia, Skobelyov had worked out a plan for the invasion of India. This had met with approval in St Petersburg and Tashkent; the finishing touches had been put to it only a few weeks earlier; and now at this very moment, in Central Asia, preparations were actually in train for its implementation. It was to take part in these preparations that Skobelyov's Chief of Staff, Grodekov, after one last lingering look at the British men-of-war in the Marmara, was now leaving Turkey for Central Asia.

Neither General Skobelyov nor Colonel Grodekov are, as it happens, altogether strangers to us. We encountered them both seven years earlier, plodding together through the burning sands of the Kara Kum to Khiva, almost perishing in the attempt, and eventually fighting their way into the Khan's Palace under a hail of Turkoman bullets, while General Kaufmann and his Staff made their State entry from the other side.

Skobelyov and Grodekov were old friends. They had been to school together. They had also served together as subalterns in the Caucasus. But it was in Central Asia, where so many reputations were made or marred, that each had spent the bulk of his career. In the Khivan campaign Skobelyov had, as a cavalry commander, distinguished himself by a number of daring skirmishes and reconnaissances, while Grodekov had served with distinction on Colonel Lomakin's Staff. When two years later, in 1875, a rebellion had broken out in Kokand, Skobelyov, assisted by Grodekov, had taken a leading part in its suppression, again covering himself with glory by a series of successful cavalry actions. In 1876 the Khanate of Kokand had finally been turned into the Russian province of Ferghana, and Skobelyov, a major-general at thirty, had been appointed its first Governor.

In 1877, with Russia's declaration of war on Turkey, Skobelyov had left Central Asia for the Balkan front.[1] There, he achieved fresh fame by his spectacular cavalry actions and also by his open disregard for orders. 'Surprise', he would say, 'is the essence of victory.' And, as often as not, his military superiors were every bit as much surprised by his actions as was the enemy.

But, though he had his detractors, Skobelyov's brilliance could not but compel respect. It had been he who in April 1877 had seized the bridge over the Sereth at Barborchi. In June he had crossed the Danube with the Eighth Corps and had commanded the Caucasian Cossack Brigade at the Second Battle of Plevna. After capturing Lovcha, he had so distinguished himself in the desperate fighting which marked the Third Battle of Plevna that he had been promoted Lieutenant-General on the spot and given command of the Sixteenth Division. It was as Commander of the Sixteenth Division that, after taking part in the last battle of Plevna, he had in January 1878 crossed the Balkans in a snowstorm, heavily defeated the Turks at Senova, capturing at one stroke ninety guns and 36,000 prisoners, and finally arrived before Constantinople, flushed with victory and impatient for further conquests, only to find his further progress obstructed, by, as he saw it, the cowardice and indecision of the diplomats and politicians.

Coming on top of his successes in Central Asia, his spectacular victories in the Balkans had made of Skobelyov a national hero at thirty-five. *Akh-Pasha*, 'The White General', the Turks had called him, from the white uniform he always wore, and his own soldiers had taken over the nick-name from the enemy.

---

[1] He served at first as Chief of Staff to the Cossack Division commanded by his father, but in a few months had become his father's senior in rank, a fact of which he would constantly remind his somewhat peppery parent. 'You should treat your superior officers with more respect, father,' he would say, and then, for he was always short of cash, would set about trying to borrow some money from him.

LIEUTENANT-GENERAL M. D. SKOBELYOV

Startlingly handsome, a brilliant commander, Skobelyov was a man of extremes, of sudden, violent moods, who plunged abruptly from the heights of exaltation to the depths of depression. Now he was bold and arrogant, now querulous and morose, now wildly confident, now deeply despondent. His countenance and his physical condition changed as often as his moods. Sometimes, his contemporaries tell us, his expression was beautiful, at others hideous. At one moment he was full of vigour, at the next prostrated with exhaustion. Impatient of authority, he repeatedly disregarded the orders of his superiors and

204

even of the Tsar, while at the same time demanding implicit obedience from his own subordinates. Inspired on occasion by the most lofty motives, he would descend at times to the lowest tricks and stratagems in order to achieve his immediate ends, and more than once was found to be claiming credit for the success of military operations which were in fact a figment of his own imagination. His private life gave rise to constant scandals.

On all those with whom he came into contact the White General exercised a magnetic influence. 'Soldiers, civilians, women — everybody', writes a contemporary, 'was crazy about him.' For his associates he chose men as ruthless, as reckless and as headstrong as himself. On the field of battle the mere sight of his dazzling white uniform and splendid white charger excited his troops to a frenzy.

His courage was magnificent. He showed a complete disregard for danger. 'The bullet', he would declare, 'does not exist that can strike me down.' To a defeated enemy he was merciless. Utterly contemptuous of human life, he was possessed in battle by a physical excitement, by a lust for blood, which speedily communicated itself to his followers.

His exchanges with Madame Juliette Adam, a sympathetic, yet discerning, Frenchwoman, throw an interesting light on Skobelyov's character and personality.

'Am I really as brave as people say?' he once asked her.

'Very brave,' was the reply, 'but your courage, so virile in itself, has an element of feminine coquetry.' And in an aside to her reader: 'Skobelyov, asking if he was brave, was just like a beautiful woman who asks if she is looking pretty.'

'*Vous avez*', she went on, '*toutes les sensualités du courage personnel.*'

'That's it!' replied Skobelyov, delighted. 'The sensuality of courage ... You have found the definition I was looking for. I run after danger, just as I run after women. But my desire for danger is unappeasable. I never tire of it. Even if it were always identical, it would always bring me fresh delights. When I set out on an adventure in which I hope to encounter danger, my heart beats frantically. At one and the same time I dread it and long for it. A *frisson*, at once agonizing and delicious, runs through me. My whole nature carries me on irresistibly to meet it. And then, when the climax is over, I am at peace once more. I have taken my pleasure. I have mastered it and entered into possession of it ...'

'*Halte-là, mon général,*' hurriedly put in his companion. 'You have, perhaps involuntarily, answered questions which it would have been difficult for me to put to you. Let us leave it at that. Now I know that, unlike Don Juan, it is not the woman that you seek in your love affairs — *ce n'est pas la femme que vous cherchez dans les femmes* — but the conquest — *la conquête*. Now I know that the pleasures which both your admirers and your detractors accuse you of indulging in to excess, of indulging in to the point where you forget your true character, your mission and yourself, are merely a kind of intoxication that beguiles you and which in a sense replaces that other intoxication, the intoxication of danger.'

Once again the General was delighted. '*Il me prit les mains*', writes Madame Adam, '*avec une joie d'enfant.*'

A contemporary has vividly portrayed Skobelyov's appearance before battle. 'He rode to battle', he writes, 'clad in white, decked with orders, scented and curled, like a bridegroom to a wedding, his eyes gleaming with wild delight, his voice tremulous with joyous excitement.' A friend — J. A. MacGahan — has left us a companion portrait of him after an engagement. 'He was', he writes, 'in a fearful state of excitement and fury. His uniform was covered with mud and filth, his sword broken, his Cross of St George twisted round his shoulder, his face black with powder and smoke, his eyes haggard and bloodshot, and his voice quite gone. He spoke in a hoarse whisper. I never before saw such a picture of battle as he presented.' To Skobelyov, war was the highest expression of human force. The Turkomans, for their part, regarded him with superstitious terror. *Guenz Kanli*, they called him — 'Bloody Eyes'.

Skobelyov's plan for the overthrow of Britain in Asia was, as one would expect, nothing if not ambitious. As a first step, it provided that a Russian mission under a certain General Stolyetov should go to Kabul in order secretly to enlist the sympathies of the Emir, Shir Ali. When this had been done, General Kaufmann, setting out from his Headquarters in Turkestan would enter Afghanistan at the head of three columns of Russian troops and the combined Afghan and Russian forces would then march upon India, where, they had no doubt, they would be greeted by the Indians as liberators. Having once lost India, Great Britain would, in Skobelyov's view, rapidly sink to the status of a second-rate power and would be powerless to oppose Russia's policy of expansion in Europe. It was as simple as that. Meanwhile the necessary troops for the expedition were already assembling at Tashkent, and it was in order to join them that Skobelyov's friend and Chief of Staff, Grodekov, was now leaving the shores of the Bosphorus, with its frustrating array of British men-of-war.

On his arrival in Central Asia, Colonel Grodekov found intense excitement prevailing. All was ready for the expedition. A force of 20,000 had been assembled. One column was to march up the Oxus to Charjui. The second, under General Kaufmann himself, was to march by way of Djam on the Bokharan frontier to Karshi and the Oxus. The third, starting from Ferghana, was to scale the Pamirs and descend on India from Chitral or Kashmir.

At General Kaufmann's Headquarters in Tashkent everyone seemed certain enough that, with Afghan support and with the aid of a second Indian Mutiny, the Russians would succeed in ejecting the British from India. Buoyed up on this current of optimism, Colonel Grodekov set out in June 1878 with General Kaufmann on his march to the Bokharan frontier. It was here that, a month later in the little border town of Djam, they received the heart-rending news that a peaceful settlement had been reached by the powers assembled at Berlin and that their own expedition had therefore been cancelled.

But if the Russian plan to invade India had been temporarily discarded, the idea which lay behind it was as much alive as ever. Indeed it had gained new impetus from a desire to revenge the set-back which the Berlin settlement had inflicted on Russian prestige. Finding her progress blocked in Europe, Russia as usual turned with renewed energy towards Asia. In Kabul, General Stolyetov had without much difficulty managed to win the Emir Shir Ali over to the Russian side and, Berlin Treaty or no Berlin Treaty, was staying on to follow up his advantage. Colonel Grodekov, meanwhile, now unable to enter Afghanistan with General Kaufmann's column, had evolved a private plan for getting there on his own.

*

In the opinion of many strategists, both Russian and British, the key to India was the town of Herat in northern Afghanistan. Once Herat had fallen, they argued, the road to India would be open to invasion. Since Vambery had gone there fifteen years earlier disguised as a dervish, no European had entered Herat. On receiving orders to return to St Petersburg, Grodekov now asked the authorities for leave to travel there by way of Herat. This was granted and on October 9th, 1878, he set out from Samarkand, accompanied by an interpreter, a native servant and a groom.

Colonel Grodekov has left an entertaining account of his journey. He wore, characteristically enough, no disguise, but relied on Russian prestige and his own force of character to carry him through the inhospitable regions into which he was venturing. 'I travelled', he tells us, 'in my uniform, concealing neither my nationality nor my rank. Nor did I seek to hide the route which I intended to follow on my way to the Caspian.'

His ride through the satellite Kingdom of Bokhara as far as Patta Hissar on the Oxus was on the whole uneventful and on October 18th, nine days after leaving Samarkand, he crossed the Oxus into Afghanistan.

On the Afghan bank of the river he was met by a Chamberlain with a cavalry escort, who, he later discovered, had in fact been sent to meet someone else and who sought to delay him. But Grodekov had no intention of being delayed. 'I had already noticed', he writes, 'that the locality was a damp unwholesome place, covered with reeds and bushes and without any signs of a human habitation (one can hardly term the huts built by the Afghan fishermen human habitations); and had made up my mind ... that under no circumstances would I wait even an hour on the spot.'

The Chamberlain prevaricated as best he could. But it was of no avail. 'I put it to him', writes Grodekov, 'that if I stayed the night in such a marshy spot, I should be sure to catch ague.' Then, raising his voice, 'Is there to be an end of this or not?' he shouted. 'I am tired of this nonsense.' At which the Chamberlain, in despair, finally capitulated and half an hour later Grodekov was on his way southwards across the desert to the holy city of Mazar-i-Sherif.

For the rest of his journey Grodekov maintained the ascendancy which he had thus established. When his escort halted to drink, he rode on alone. When they shouted to him to stop, he pretended not to hear them. When they galloped after him, he stared at them severely through his steel-rimmed spectacles and asked them if they did not know who he was. The Chamberlain he took severely to task. Did he, he asked him, think that it was his intention to run away? At this, the Chamberlain protested that such a thought had never entered his head; he had only been concerned about the Colonel's safety. 'What nonsense you talk!' was the Colonel's reply. 'Put an end to this farce. You can see round you for miles. There is not a soul in sight. How could there be any danger? Accept it as an axiom from this moment that I am not compelled to conform myself to you, but you to me.'

When they halted for the night, a conversation which he overheard brought home to Grodekov the very real perils which surrounded him. 'If I had my way,' said one Afghan sentry to another, 'I would cut that Infidel to pieces.' 'Let us go', said another 'and kill the Infidel. What does it matter what happens afterwards? You know what awaits us in the life hereafter if we kill an Infidel.' And so on, until a less courageous man would have been convulsed with fear.

Next morning, while he was brushing his teeth in front of an inquisitive crowd of Afghans, he had another unpleasant moment. 'What', asked one of the onlookers, 'is that brush made of?' 'Pig's bristles,' replied the interpreter brightly. Whereupon the crowd of pious Moslems fell back in horror, spitting violently to express their disgust at anyone who used the bristles of an unclean beast to scrub his teeth, and Grodekov was obliged to withdraw hurriedly.

On reaching Mazar, Grodekov was brought before the Governor-General of the Province, Khosh Deel Khan, the Emir's brother-in-law, a handsome young man with a beard, wearing a double-breasted tunic with bone buttons, blue breeches, patent leather boots, a felt cap, white cotton gloves and a yellow silk handkerchief round his neck.

In Khosh Deel Khan, Grodekov soon discovered that he had met his match. He could not, said Khosh Deel, let him go on without express permission from the Emir, which it would take ten days or a fortnight to obtain. Nor, during this period, could he allow him to leave his quarters, in case 'something unpleasant' were to happen to him. He could equally not let him return to Bokhara. 'Why?' asked Grodekov. 'Because no one asked you to come here,' replied Khosh Deel. 'It seems then that I am your prisoner,' said Grodekov. 'You have your law; we, ours,' calmly replied the Governor-General, adding naively, as Grodekov rose angrily to take his leave, 'Do you find my company dull?'

A week passed. The guards on Grodekov's lodging were strengthened. A message came from Khosh Deel asking whether the Colonel would lend him his uniform; he thought it remarkably smart and wanted to have one made like it. A letter which he tried to send to General Kaufmann was handed back to him unsent. He discovered that Khosh Deel had bribed his interpreter. And still there was no news of his onward journey. In the end Grodekov lost patience. He ranted and raved and told the Governor-General's secretary to his face that he thought the Afghans were a lying, treacherous, fickle lot. After which the Governor-General's secretary kept away and sent a message to say that he was not feeling well.

Then, just as he was making plans to shoot his way out of Mazar and make a dash for the frontier, and had managed to bribe a blacksmith to smuggle in some weapons for the purpose, Grodekov received a fresh summons to appear before the Governor-General. This time Khosh Deel Khan was wearing a new black tunic, cut, in imitation of Grodekov's own uniform, after the Russian fashion, with gold lace on the collar and facings; white cotton gloves; white breeches; patent leather boots; and a small grey helmet. He had heard, he said, that Grodekov was finding it dull. Would he not like to hear a little Afghan music? Whereupon a band was brought in wearing scarlet uniforms and helmets and played a succession of slow, ordinary and quick marches, while a company of infantry marched up and down in time to the music. 'This audience', writes Grodekov, 'lasted until one o'clock in the morning and somewhat reassured me.'

Finding time still hanging heavy on his hands, Grodekov tried to devise new ways of amusing himself. But he was unlucky. When he asked for dancing girls, he was told that they had all gone to a wedding in the mountains. When he called for performing serpents, he was informed that at that time of the year the serpents were in a dormant condition. In the end he was reduced to exchanging stories with his companions and taking a spade and clearing out the drain in the court-yard of his lodgings.

At last, the long-awaited courier arrived from Kabul with a personal message from the Emir Shir Ali. Colonel Grodekov, said the Emir, was to be treated as an honoured guest, sent on his way with an escort of three hundred men, and in general treated 'as though he were the apple of his eye'. Shir Ali knew — or thought he knew — on which side his bread was buttered.

Before finally leaving, Grodekov asked to see Khosh Deel Khan. He was informed that Khosh Deel Khan was ill and was in any case too busy counting his money to receive any visitors.

Grodekov's onward journey from Mazar, though arduous and instructive, was marked by no untoward incidents. Leaving on October 29th, he and his escort reached Maimene on November 6th and Herat on the 16th. At Herat, on the orders of Shir Ali, he was treated with the greatest respect, lodged in a palace, waited upon by fifteen servants and given a ride on an elephant. Setting out again on November 19th, he arrived at the Persian frontier three days later and finally reached St Petersburg in January 1879, the bearer of much valuable information concerning the regions through which he had travelled.

In the capital, he was greeted as a hero, granted a high decoration, received in audience by the Tsar, and subsequently given a key appoint-ment on the General Staff. In St Petersburg there had clearly been no falling off in the general interest in Central Asia.

Afghanistan, in particular, was in the news. General Stolyetov's mission had by now begun to bear fruit. Reaching Kabul on July 22nd, 1878, nine days after the signature of the Treaty of Berlin, Stolyetov had left again at the end of September, taking with him the secret treaty which he had been sent to conclude and leaving behind him the bulk of his mission, under General Razgonov, to carry on the good work. 'Be as a serpent,' was Razgonov's advice to Shir Ali, 'make peace openly with England, but in secret prepare for war.'

A crisis followed quickly. In November the Government of India, disturbed by the increasingly hostile attitude of the Emir, and by his intrigues with the Russians, had delivered an ultimatum in Kabul and, on its expiry, had invaded Afghanistan in force. Fort Ali Musjid in the Khyber Pass was captured on November 22nd, the very day on which Grodekov crossed the frontier into Persia, and on December 2nd General Roberts carried the Peiwar Kotal by storm.

Ten days later, Shir Ali fled northwards from Kabul with what was left of the Russian Mission. 'Treat the English with deceit and fraud,' General Kaufmann wrote to him from Tashkent, 'until the present cold season passes away, when the will of the Almighty shall be made manifest to you; that is to say, the Russian Government having repeated the *Bismillah*, the *Bismillah* will come to your assistance.' But long before the cold season had come to an end or there had been any sign of the *Bismillah* or of help from Russia, Shir Ali's forces had been scattered and he himself was dead.

For all this, the peace which was signed in the spring of 1879 between the British and the Afghans was of short duration. The Third Afghan War followed the Second, and for the next two years British troops were almost continually in action in Afghanistan.

The Russians, meanwhile, had their own problems in Central Asia. Bokhara, Khiva and Kokand, it is true, were secure under their domination. But, north of the Afghan frontier, the turbulent Tekke Turkomans still remained unconquered. Moreover, if Herat, recently reconnoitred by Grodekov, was the key to India, the Tekke stronghold of Merv was pronounced by many the key to Herat and, for British and Russians alike, a strategic position of considerable importance. In September 1879 a Russian force was sent out under General Lomakin to subdue the Tekkes. It was, however, cut to pieces before the fortress of Gök Tepe, and the Tekkes, intoxicated by their triumph, became more turbulent and more troublesome than ever.

Following, as it did, a number of other set-backs in Central Asia, the news of General Lomakin's disastrous defeat provoked a strong and unfavourable reaction in St Petersburg. The conduct of the campaign was sharply criticized and drastic changes were demanded. Measures were clearly called for of a kind calculated to catch the public imagination, and early in 1880 it was announced that General Lomakin had been disgraced and General Skobelyov, 'Akh-Pasha', the heroic White General, appointed in his place as Commander-in-Chief of the Trans-caspian Military District with a free hand for the conduct of operations against the Turkomans.

For Skobelyov, the long-awaited opportunity had arrived. All eyes were upon him. He was back in Central Asia. He had an independent command and a vital and challenging task. It might lead him anywhere. Perhaps, in the long run, if he got his way, even to India.

His first care on assuming command was to make a personal recon-naissance of the Turkoman position. The key to this, he found, was the Tekke fortress of Gök Tepe, the Blue Hill, where Lomakin's force had been annihilated the year before. The fortress was situated in the Turko-man desert, half way between Merv and the Caspian, some ten or twelve miles from the foot of the range of mountains which marked the Persian border. Inside its high mud walls clustered many thousands of kibitkas which housed most of the population of the oasis. For water the garrison depended on two streams and numerous cisterns and reservoirs. Adequate supplies of food had also been accumulated. The walls, some four miles in circuit, were pierced with nine gates. Opposite each gate was a large traverse, to protect it against artillery fire. Within their mud fortifications, solid enough to withstand any artillery short of a regular siege train, and high enough to make an assault an extremely hazardous undertaking, the Tekkes confidently awaited the Russian advance.

Returning towards the end of the summer to his base at Krasnovodsk on the Caspian, Skobelyov completed his preparations there and in December 1880 set out once more across the desert for Gök Tepe, taking with him this time a force of 7000 men and 60 guns and a baggage train of over 12,000 camels. With him went once again the faithful Grodekov, promoted to General, as his Chief of Staff.

Having reached his destination without mishap, Skobelyov pitched his own camp at a distance of about a mile from the main Turkoman position. In this were now assembled under the command of their ruler, Makdum Kuli Khan, and of his general, Tokme Serdar, the flower of the Akhal Tekkes with their wives and families, amounting in all to some 35,000 people together with a force of 10,000 cavalry.

Warned by the example of Lomakin, Skobelyov had decided against an immediate assault on the Tekke stronghold. He would, he determined, reduce it by siege. Under the care of Grodekov, thousands of tons of stores were brought in from Persia, and, during the next three weeks, from January 1st to the 24th, 1881, the Russians laid a first, a second and finally a third parallel of siege works, and at the same time sited enfilading batteries so as to command the interior of the fortress. Steadily the Russian lines were pushed forward, until at last their advanced redoubt was barely seventy yards from the fortress. From where they stood, the Russian sentries could hear the Turkomans talking on the ramparts, and Skobelyov's officers were greeted with a hail of bullets as they made their way to and from the conference tent. Characteristically, the Commander-in-Chief had caused his own tent to be pitched amongst the troops in the forward trenches. He found that he ate better under fire, he said. In general, he himself courted every danger and liked others to do the same. Indeed, it was known to give him particular pleasure to hear from his officers that they had been shot at.

The Turkomans, meanwhile, though under heavy and continuous shellfire from the Russian batteries outside the walls, continued to fight back undismayed. For the Russians the outlook was not as encouraging as it had at first seemed. Skobelyov's troops were separated from their base by two hundred miles of waterless desert. Time was not on their side. A serious attempt by the neighbouring Turkomans of Merv to relieve the beleaguered garrison was by no means out of the question. It became increasingly clear that to continue the siege was not enough. If Gök Tepe was to be reduced, it would, after all, have to be taken by storm.

On January 20th, breaching operations were begun. Part of the wall of the fortress was demolished by artillery fire, but the damage was at once repaired by the defenders. Two mines were then dug, one on the eastern and one on the western flank, and the former charged with over a ton of gunpowder. The proceeding greatly mystified the Turkomans, who could be heard speculating as to what the Russians were doing, 'poking their snouts like pigs into the ground'.

They were to find out soon enough. By the night of January 23rd all was ready for the final assault. At 1 a.m. on the 24th, under heavy fire, two volunteers, Lieutenant Osipov and a Naval Cadet of German origin called Meyer, carried a powerful charge of gun-cotton up to the very walls and successfully exploded it in the western breach which had already been battered open by the cannon fire. At six the attacking force was in position. It was divided into three columns, two to the south and one to the west. At seven the breaching battery again opened fire with thirty-six guns, breaking down the wall where the Turkomans had repaired it and firing through the gap into the densely crowded interior of the fortress, where the bursting shells wrought terrible destruction. At eleven-twenty the mine on the south-east face of the fortress was exploded. An immense pillar of smoke and dust rose into the air and then fell back to the ground disclosing a gap in the wall fifty yards wide.

Simultaneously, with a great shout, the two main Russian storming columns rushed forward into the breach, where soon a tremendous hand-to-hand battle was raging. The attack was supported by reserves who advanced from the rear with bands playing, drums beating and colours flying. At the same time, the third column, with scaling ladders, launched an assault against the western face of the fortress. The Turkoman resistance, though desperate, was soon crushed. Only isolated groups still held out here and there. By midday the three columns had driven back the defenders and joined ranks within the fort. Thence they advanced in close formation with massed bands to the hill of Denghil Tepe, where at 1 p.m. the two-headed eagle, fluttering in the breeze, proclaimed a Russian victory.

The most appalling massacre now followed. In the words of Grodekov, 'all who had not succeeded in escaping were killed to a man by the Russian soldiers'. Soon the interior of the fortress was littered with thousand of corpses. Not content with this, Skobelyov now gave his troops the order to pursue the retreating enemy and give no quarter. His commands were carried out with merciless precision by six companies of infantry, a division of cavalry and four *sotnias* of Cossacks, with a battery of horse artillery in support. For eleven miles the Russians, with horse, foot and cannon, hunted and harried the panic-stricken throng of fugitives, killing another eight thousand men, women and children. 'They lay', wrote an eyewitness, 'in rows like freshly mown hay, as they had been swept down by the *mitrailleuses* and cannon.' In all, no less than 20,000 Turkomans were killed, for the loss of fewer than 300 Russians. 'I hold it', wrote Skobelyov, 'as a principle that in Asia the duration of peace is in direct proportion to the

slaughter you inflict upon the enemy. The harder you hit them, the longer they will be quiet afterwards.'

But for Skobelyov himself, life, now that the fighting was over, had lost its zest. 'How unutterably bored I am,' he remarked, when the fortress had fallen and the last fugitive had been slaughtered. 'There is nothing left to do.'

*

Not many weeks after his victory at Gök Tepe, the White General, with truly Russian suddenness, was disavowed, recalled, and posted to the town of Minsk.

Deprived of a fighting command, he now directed his exuberant energy to politics and in particular to Pan-Slavism, of which he became a leading exponent. Leaving his post at will, he delivered in Moscow and later in Paris a series of fiery and highly provocative speeches demanding a militant Pan-Slav policy in the Balkans and predicting, indeed advocating, a struggle to the death between Teuton and Slav. In his eyes, the Germany of Prince Bismarck had now become the enemy to be destroyed at all costs and he made no secret of his views. He spoke of the pleasure it would give him to meet the German Chancellor in single combat before the assembled armies of the two countries. He even came to believe that Bismarck had somehow been responsible for his mother's murder. Soon indignant protests were pouring in from half the Chancelleries of Europe, and it was not long before an embarrassed Government had ordered the errant General to take the next train back to Minsk.

But already the end of his strange, meteor-like career was approaching. Of late Skobelyov, though still in his thirties, had more and more been troubled by gloomy forebodings and had devoted more and more time to thoughts of death. 'I have not long to live,' he would say, 'I shall not survive this year. I don't want to die in the least. I should like to have a European war, to disperse Russia's enemies and annihilate them all. After that you could take my name off the books. But it is not to be. It is not to be.' He was, he would tell his friends, 'haunted by the idea of dying stupidly', of making an unworthy exit. 'Je voudrais mourir très bien,' he would say. His wish was not to be granted.

One fine July morning in 1882 Skobelyov's friend, Grodekov, was sitting in his apartment in St Petersburg working at an official history of the Turkoman campaign. Almost everything in the room recalled the White General. On the floor lay a splendid Turkoman carpet, part of the spoils of Gök Tepe. By the window was the easy chair in which Skobelyov, when he came to visit him, would sit reading the partly finished manuscript of his history. All round the room on chairs and tables were large piles of manuscript celebrating his victories. Near the door a table was entirely covered with military maps and plans of his campaigns.

Suddenly, as Grodekov sat writing, there was a knock at the door and his servant came in with a telegram. It was from Skobelyov's aide-de-camp, Abadzayev, and it brought to Grodekov an appalling piece of news. It announced that Skobelyov, his commanding general, his oldest friend, his closest associate, Skobelyov, whom he had seen only a day or two before, and who he had every reason to believe was at this moment at Minsk and in the best of health, had been found dead that very morning in a bedroom of the Hôtel Duseaux in Moscow. Death, it seemed, had been due to a heart attack. As to the immediate cause of the heart attack and the circumstances in which it had taken place, the less said the better. It was only later that the somewhat unsavoury details of Skobelyov's demise became more widely known.

Such was the end of the White General. 'A General at thirty, and a popular idol when he succumbed to a discreditable end at the age of thirty-eight, it is impossible', wrote a contemporary, 'to say if he had lived what he might not have done or become.'

KHAN OF MERV

EARLY on the morning of January 24th, 1881, that fateful day in the history of Central Asia, while General Skobelyov was assembling his forces for the final assault on the Turkoman stronghold of Gök Tepe, a small party of native horsemen led by a solitary European, might have been seen slowly making its way to the top of the mountain range which rose abruptly to a height of six thousand feet above the plain ten or twelve miles away to the south. On reaching the summit, their leader, a tall, good-looking Irishman of about thirty-six with a fair beard and an enormous sheepskin hat, pulled out his field-glasses and turned them in the direction of the great Turkoman fortress twelve miles away across the plain.

From where he stood he could clearly see both the fortress and the Russian forces besieging it. As he watched, the smoke of the guns and the movements of the combatants showed that an attack had begun against the southern wall and soon a desperate battle was in progress. Fascinated, he saw the attackers overcome the defenders and force their way through the breach into the interior of the fortress. For a time all was confusion. Then there issued from the far side of the fortress a stream of horsemen who scattered in flight across the dusty plain. They were followed immediately by a great crowd of fugitives, men, women and children, fleeing as best they might before the fury of the invaders. Gök Tepe had fallen. All was over with the Akhal Tekkes.

For Edmund O'Donovan, special correspondent of the London *Daily News*, the dramatic events which he had just witnessed necessitated a rapid change of plan. After long months of waiting about in the little towns and villages on the Persian side of the frontier, after endless frustrating interviews with equivocating Persian officials, headmen and tribal chieftains, after laboriously circumventing, as he thought, the wiles of the innumerable Russian agents who haunted the border regions and who had done everything they could think of to impede his progress, he had a few days earlier finally completed his arrangements for entering Gök Tepe.

Originally his purpose had been to observe and report on the Turkoman campaign. With this object he had applied to General Skobelyov for permission to accompany his forces on their march from Krasnovodsk and had met with an uncompromising refusal. Undeterred, he had decided to observe the campaign from the Turkoman side and, making his way to the Turkoman-Persian border, had, from Persia, finally succeeded in establishing communication with Makdum Kuli Khan, the commander of the Turkoman forces, who, anxious to obtain British support and not distinguishing very clearly between a newspaper correspondent and an official envoy, had responded with a cordial invitation to visit Gök Tepe.

And, now that all the obstacles had been overcome and all the arrangements finally made, he had arrived just in time to witness the fall of the fortress through field-glasses from a mountain-top twelve miles away and to see what was left of Makdum Kuli's army streaming in confusion from the stricken field. In short, material for one brief, dramatic dispatch; and that was all.

Another might in the circumstances have felt that he had done all that was required of him. But not Edmund O'Donovan. He was not so easily put off. His was an enthusiastic nature which invariably led him to press on regardless of the consequences. His father, a well-known Irish antiquary and scholar, had at one time hoped that he might make a career in the Royal Irish Constabulary. But in his early twenties young Edmund had become, not an upholder of law and order, but a notorious Fenian agitator. In 1866 he had been arrested and spent twelve months in Mountjoy Prison. Released on condition that he went to America, he had paid a flying visit to the United States, and had then come back to Ireland to resume his subversive activities. Once more he was arrested, this time for the illegal possession of arms and spent ten months in Limerick Gaol.

On his release he betook himself to the north of England where he at once set to work to organize an underground Irish revolutionary movement. Before long he was in trouble again. One of his associates was caught and sentenced to fifteen years' penal servitude. But, before the police could arrest him for the third time, O'Donovan fled across the Channel to France. There he joined the Foreign Legion and fought as a volunteer in the Franco-Prussian war, being taken prisoner by the Germans at the battle of Orleans. From France he went to Spain where he became involved in the Carlist war and was again thrown into prison. Moving gradually eastwards, he next visited the Balkans, where he reported on the Bosnian and Montenegrin insurrection of 1876 and then went on to cover the Russo-Turkish war of 1877, ending up in Armenia. From Armenia he had in 1879 made his way through Persia to Central Asia and had, as we have already seen, spent the next two years hovering on the Persian-Turkoman frontier in the hope of seeing something of the impending campaign, if not from the Russian, then from the Turkoman side.

Having through no fault of his own missed the battle of Gök Tepe, O'Donovan was determined to be present at the next major engagement in the campaign. That, he calculated, would in all probability be the siege of Merv, the last remaining Turkoman position of any importance and, in the view of many well-qualified observers, the key, strategically, to Herat and to the British position in India. For Merv, accordingly, he now set out, in the hope of arriving at the oasis in advance of General Skobelyov's army. Were he to reach that ancient city, he would be the first European to do so since Dr Wolff.

During the days that followed, the immediate neighbourhood of Gök Tepe offered little security for man or beast. The whole countryside was in a state of turmoil. Leaving their homes, the panic-stricken inhabitants of the surrounding villages were fleeing in confusion for the Persian frontier. The Tekke warriors who had escaped from the fortress were everywhere, robbing and murdering all and sundry. The Russian pursuing parties were no less active and, from O'Donovan's point of view, every bit as dangerous. To make things worse, hordes of moss-troopers from Derguez and of Kurds from Kuchan, scenting booty, had come swooping down from the surrounding hills to join in the looting.

Riding eastwards along the Persian border, skirting the foothills of the main frontier range, O'Donovan reached Askabad only a few hours ahead of a Russian scouting party, paused briefly at Lutfabad, and then, turning southwards into the mountains, pushed on through precipitous country to the secluded valley of Kelat-i-Nadri, on the Persian side of the frontier. Here, while planning his next move, he would, he calculated, be able to watch the movements of the Russians without himself attracting undue attention, and would at the same time be able to maintain contact with Makdum Kuli Khan, the defender of Gök Tepe, who, it seemed, had now retreated with what was left of his forces into the impenetrable swamps of the Tejend river.

Even before Skobelyov's victory at Gök Tepe, the Persian authorities had shown themselves highly susceptible to Russian pressure. Now, after so striking a demonstration of Russian ruthlessness and strength, they were more anxious than ever not to offend their formidable neighbour, and O'Donovan soon found that he was being kept under strict surveillance by his host, the Khan of Kelat.

The choice of Kelat as a jumping-off place from which to reach Merv soon began to seem less fortunate. Meanwhile, from Makdum Kuli Khan there came a message to say that he and his troops were now leaving the Tejend swamps and falling back on Merv for the purpose of digging in there. This intelligence, coupled with news of continuing Russian activity throughout the area, seemed to betoken an early trial of strength and made a quick start for Merv more necessary than ever, f he was not once again to be too late.

There was another thing. O'Donovan had been disagreeably surprised to see riding past his gate a renegade Russian nihilist named Dufour, whom he had encountered earlier and who he had reason to believe, was now acting as an agent of the Imperial Russian Government. Clearly there was no time to be wasted. Taking advantage of Dufour's temporary absence from Kelat, he made hasty application to the Khan for permission to visit Kaka, a village on the edge of the plain not far from the head of the Tejend swamp. Somewhat to his surprise permission was given, and, accompanied by an escort which was clearly also a guard he set out on February 25th, back through the mountains on what he hoped would be the first stage of his journey to Merv.

O'Donovan had scarcely arrived at Kaka when he was told that there was someone to see him, and Dufour was shown in. He had come to try and dissuade him from his enterprise. Having failed in this task, the Russian became so offensive that O'Donovan was obliged to order him out of the house. But next morning he was back and had soon so terrified the Persian escort with his talk of advancing Cossacks that they refused to move a step farther.

By ridding O'Donovan of his official escort, Dufour had unwittingly rendered him a considerable service. To neither Dufour nor the Persians had it for one moment occurred that anyone in his senses would attempt to cross the Merv desert unescorted. But such in fact was O'Donovan's intention. Aware that he was being closely watched from the ramparts of Kaka, he now set out with his two servants along the road leading back to the mountains, as though returning to Kelat. But no sooner had he reached the foothills and was hidden from sight amongst their spurs and ravines than he immediately changed his course, and, turning his horse's head towards the desert, started as fast as he could go in the direction of Merv.

At first his way lay through broken country, intersected by mountain streams and deep ravines filled with thickets of reed and cane. Pheasants got up from under his feet by the dozen. Wild boar crashed through the reed beds and now and again he caught sight of a leopard or a lynx stealing away into the jungle. After a time the ground underfoot became dangerously swampy and, making his way to a near-by hill top, he paused to survey the scene around him and take his bearings for his future line of march.

From where he stood, the plain stretched away northwards and eastwards into the blue distance. Over its surface were scattered the crumbling walls and towers of countless deserted towns and villages, quivering and dancing in the midday haze. After a prolonged but not particularly fruitful survey of this desolate panorama, he finally decided to make straight for the only inhabited place within reach — Dushakh, which lay at a distance of some twenty-five miles across the plain and which, although on Persian territory, was inhabited for part of the year by Turkomans from Merv, who came there to sow and later to reap the harvest.

All day long he travelled across that dreary plain. As he arrived at Dushakh, the sun was setting. On an ancient mound a long low wall enclosed an irregular space a hundred yards square. Uncouth forms showed themselves upon the ramparts and curious eyes watched the approach of the three strangers. Then the rickety gate of unhewn tree trunks was unbarred and O'Donovan found himself in a rectangular open space dotted with reed huts resembling giant stacks of corn. A couple of hundred horses stood tethered around. Some camels grunted and groaned. Women with wild eyes and dishevelled hair, clad in purple trousers and flowing red tunics, peered at him from round corners. At his entry, fifty or sixty men in colossal black sheepskin hats and deep red robes with carbines on their backs and swords at their belts advanced towards him. It was his first encounter with the Merv Tekkes.

Clearly possessing no idea who he was or what he wanted, the headman of the encampment now conducted O'Donovan to a low room at the foot of the ramparts, which at once filled to suffocation with as many Turkomans as could squeeze their way into it. These showed their curiosity by getting as close as they could to the newcomer and then peering into his face. Although the majority on inspection expressed the view that he was a Russian spy and should be dealt with accordingly, an active minority appeared to be in his favour, and, after a supper of greasy rice eaten with his fingers from a communal bowl and a few hours' sleep with huge black fleas springing and dancing all around him, he was allowed to set out again in the angry red dawn accompanied by an escort of four armed Tekkes and a musician who twanged briskly on a two-stringed guitar. But these, on learning that he was bound for Merv, soon took leave of him and left him to continue his journey with no other escort than his two servants.

One of these was a Turkoman from Gök Tepe, who now had nothing to lose but his horse and the ragged clothes he stood up in and who looked on the desert as his own country and the nomads his own people. The other was a somewhat bombastic Kurd, with an entirely fictitious reputation for courage, who had hitherto engaged in a good deal of vapouring and boasting, but soon began to grow uneasy as the wilderness opened out before them. As the little party continued their progress eastwards, the mountains of Persia gradually faded away until they were no more than a faint blue line on the southern horizon.

More than once during their journey they experienced false alarms, for in the trembling, heated air it was hard to tell at a distance of three or four miles whether what you saw was a horseman or a ruined watchtower. At each alarm the Kurd became more afraid and it was all that O'Donovan could do to stop him from turning back towards the mountains. It was, he kept saying, utter madness to venture into the desert without an escort. Why, the Khan of Kelat, or anyone else in his senses, would never have dreamed of setting out across such country with less than five hundred men.

At last came a real alarm. An hour or so before sundown, O'Donovan, topping a slight rise, caught sight of two horses grazing some three miles away. Then, as he approached, two men rose suddenly from the ground where they had been lying, mounted, and rode towards him. At a distance of four hundred yards they unslung their muskets and laid them across their saddle bows ready for action — a gesture which O'Donovan promptly imitated. At fifty yards, they halted. '*Salaam aleikum*', they said, 'Peace be with you' — an indication that, for the moment at any rate, they did not want to fight. The two parties then approached to within half a dozen paces of each other, muskets at the ready and each eyeing the other intently for a good minute before breaking silence.

The horsemen, it appeared, were Merv Tekkes from a Turkoman encampment at Meneh, a ruined town some forty miles east of Dushakh and were at the moment roaming the desert in search of plunder. But on learning who O'Donovan was and whither bound, they turned back and escorted him towards their encampment. It was some time after sunset when they finally saw some lights glimmering through the darkness and came to another ruinous old mud fort, crammed, like that at Dushakh, with men, women, children, cattle and horses and stinking to high heaven. Here, in a reed hut shared with fifteen Turkomans, O'Donovan spent another uneasy night.

It had been his intention to start for Merv next morning, but the day wore on, the sun sank lower towards the horizon, and still there were no signs of the escort he had been promised. Towards sundown he could bear it no longer and asked why no preparations for his departure had been made. Because, came the answer, it was not safe to travel by daylight. Since the fall of Gök Tepe the journey to Merv had become doubly dangerous. The country was filled with marauding bands who, if they caught sight of them from a distance, would waylay them.

Finally, sometime after sunset, an escort of four Turkomans assembled, 'each', in O'Donovan's words, 'as truculent-looking a fellow as I ever met with in any part of the world'. When they were all in the saddle, there was a further delay of half an hour while his escort smoked their *kalioun* or water-pipe. Then they started. The chief of the encampment came a short distance with them to ensure that nothing happened to his guests while they were still on his territory. It was his hope, he said, that they might meet again in Merv — 'If', he added, 'you ever get there.'

The night was dark. For the first three hours a slender moon shone fitfully from behind drifting clouds, and in its faint light they caught glimpses here and there of the remains of old buildings. Then the plain widened out before them and in pitch darkness they came to the naked Turkoman desert.

They were now travelling due north. After riding all night, they arrived just after dawn on the banks of the Tejend river. Fording it, they emerged from the belt of vegetation which marked its course and set out once more under a blazing sun across a dreary plain varied only by patches of gnarled and twisted tamarisk. Towards evening these assumed the proportions of a forest. It was, said the escort, a likely place for an ambush.

After midnight it became pitch-dark. They had now been riding at a brisk pace for a day and the best part of two nights. The horses, who had suffered severely from thirst during the day, seemed at the end of their strength. From time to time O'Donovan, who had eaten nothing all this time except a crust of bread and a piece of particularly nasty cheese, suggested a halt, only to be told, in a dramatic whisper, that it was not safe to stop: there was no knowing when *ogri*, robbers, might not appear. At last, having found an open space in the tamarisk, he finally induced his indefatigable companions to make a brief halt, and wrapping himself in a leopard-skin, a horse-cloth and an old ulster, lay down and from sheer exhaustion fell asleep.

It was still dark when voices round him told him that a fresh move was impending. Torrents of rain were falling. He was soaked through and aching in every limb. Extricating himself from his sodden leopard-skin and brushing from his hair and clothes the collection of insects, varying from tarantulas to stag-beetles, which had taken refuge there, he slowly and stiffly started to put himself in marching order. As he did so, he noticed that even the hardbitten Turkomans, having failed to get their beloved water-pipe to light, looked ineffably cross, as they busied themselves with the horses. The horses, for their part, stood around dismally with ears and tails drooping beneath the downpour and, as O'Donovan tried to climb into the saddle, his own mount subsided under him from sheer weakness and wretchedness. When they had got it to its feet again, they set out once more across the plain in the leaden dawn of a rainy morning.

They were, or so the Turkomans said, about sixteen miles from Merv. The nearer they got to their destination, the gloomier became the prognostications of O'Donovan's Kurdish servant. They would, he kept saying, all be murdered on arrival. Nor was his master in a much better humour as the hours went by and the rain poured down and there was still no sign of any human habitation.

At length they came to some marshes and then to a sodden, dun-coloured patch of land, traversed by narrow, deep-cut trenches from which vapour was rising in the fitful morning sunlight. Some spectral camels and a few lean cows stood dismally about and some sheepskin-clad youths rose from their smoky fires to stare at them as they passed. One of O'Donovan's servants had put up an umbrella to keep the rain off, thus attracting more spectators. From what he could understand of the remarks of these onlookers, O'Donovan gathered that the view generally held was that his companions were returning from a success-ful raid and that he was the principal captive.

Not long after this, O'Donovan, as he peered through the mist, made out the first beehive huts of the oasis. He had reached Merv — Merv, the most ancient of all cities, known once as *Merou Shahou Jehan*, Merv, Queen of the World. It was — or should have been — a big moment. 'After all I had heard of Merv,' he said, when recounting his experiences later, 'I was not quite sure whether I should not see domes and spires flashing in the amber sunset; but instead of this I found some wretched hovels, sheepskin-clothed people and wretched cattle feeding in a bog.'

His companions now halted and started an animated discussion. Some of them, it seemed, had suddenly conceived doubts as to his nationality and the reasons for his journey. 'How', they asked each other, 'can anyone tell that he is not a Russian?' 'What will our friends say when we bring him among them?' 'What is his business here?' And, perhaps more kindly meant, but scarcely reassuring: 'Who knows they won't kill him at the first village?'

For another two interminable hours they sat on their horses in the driving rain, discussing the problem from every angle. Some scowled ferociously at the subject of their discussion and seemed in favour of finishing him off there and then, but in the end less bloodthirsty counsels prevailed and one of them rode over to tell him not to be afraid — all, he hoped, would yet be right. And if, he added consolingly, all were by any chance not to turn out right, he would at least have only himself to blame for coming there in the first place. After which, they all set off once more in the direction of the nearby *kibitkas*.

There were about a hundred and fifty of these. Jujube, apple and willow trees grew all around them with here and there occasional patches of melons and vines. At the approach of O'Donovan's little party, the villagers left their work to stare at him. All quite clearly took it for granted that he was a prisoner and, as he entered the door of the hut to which his horse had been somewhat peremptorily led, he suddenly realized for the first time the full extent of the dangers which confronted him. And yet, however precarious his prospects, he had achieved his object: he had reached Merv. The future, he told himself, could look after itself.

But he was allowed little leisure for these reflections. The hut which had been allotted to him was immediately filled to suffocation with a milling crowd of Turkomans, all falling over each other in their eagerness to get a view of him. Nor can it be denied that his appearance was, by any standards, most unusual. 'I wore', he tells us, 'an enormous tiara of greyish-black sheepskin, eighteen inches in height. Over my

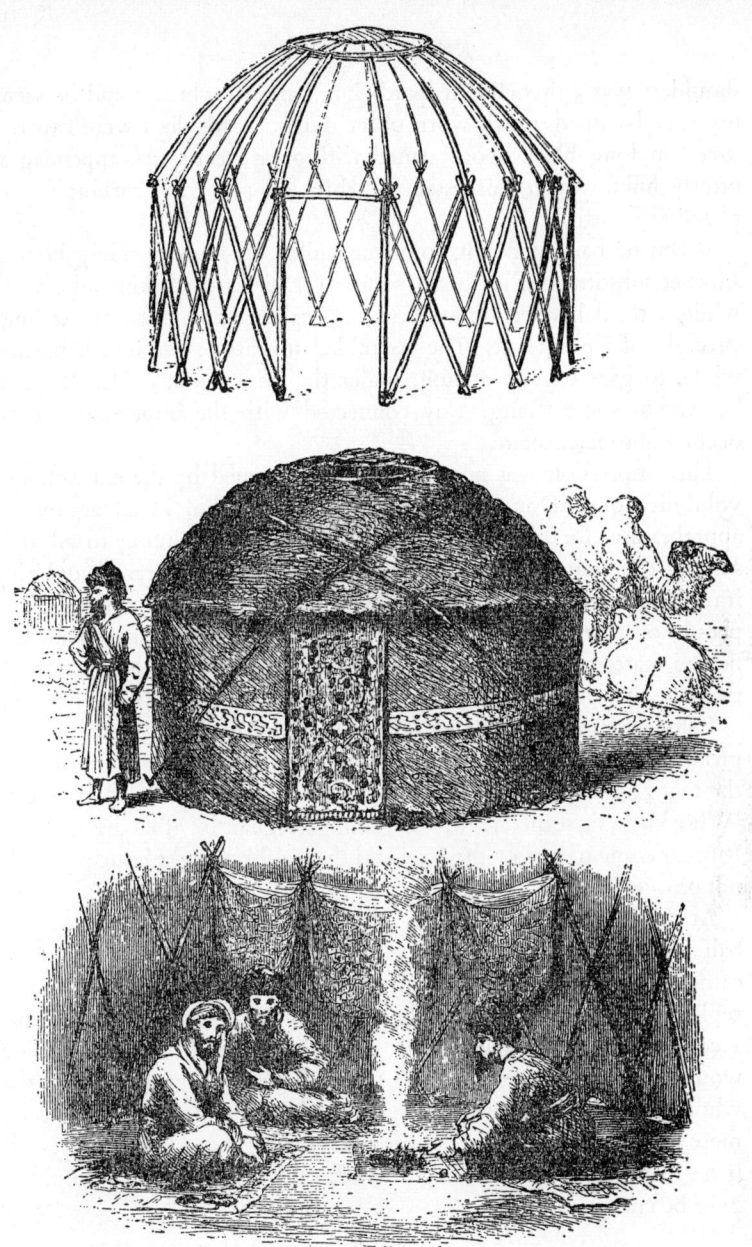

A KIBITKA

shoulders was a drenched leopard-skin, beneath which could be seen my travel-stained, much-worn ulster overcoat. My legs were caparisoned in long black boots, armed with great steel spurs, appendages utterly unknown in Turkestan. A sabre and revolving carbine completed my outfit.'

When he had sat down, someone pulled off his wet riding boots; another substituted a lambskin mantle for his leopard-skin and ulster, while a third handed him a bowl of scalding-hot green tea tasting strongly of Epsom salts. The assembled multitude continued, meanwhile, to gaze eagerly at him, under the impression, evidently, that he was in some strange way connected with the important events occurring so near them.

This impression was now further strengthened by the extravagant volubility of O'Donovan's Kurdish servant, who, in an agony of apprehension for his own safety, was loudly proclaiming to all and sundry the tremendous importance of his master's arrival and the immense benefits which, if given the chance, he would confer on the people of Merv. At the same time some of his late escort had not helped matters by announcing that he had come from the direction of the Russian camp, while others said straight out that he was a spy.

Before long it became clear to O'Donovan that he was losing ground. The crowd in his hut began to edge away, while from outside the tent he could hear snatches of conversation which boded no good. 'Who knows', someone was shouting indignantly, 'that he is not a Russian come to survey the road and that in forty-eight hours we shall not be overrun?'

At this stage a great fat man with an expression half ruffianly and half humorous, who clearly occupied a position of some authority, came in and asked O'Donovan straight out who and what he was. In reply he did his best to explain the functions of a foreign correspondent, a concept completely unfamiliar to his audience. If, he added, they would only let him send a letter to the British Agent at Meshed, the whole question of his identity could quickly be cleared up. But at the mere mention of a letter there came a warning shout from all present. If he so much as wrote a single word, they said, his throat would at once be cut.

Nor was this an empty threat. Some time later, having momentarily forgotten the warning he had received, and feeling, as a trained journalist, the urge to record his impressions while they were still fresh in his mind, O'Donovan reached without thinking for his notebook and pencil. Immediately, an excited Turkoman darted out of the hut with the news that the *Ferenghi* was writing, at which an appalling hubbub broke out and from all sides came the suggestion that he should be finished off at once. Fortunately, however, milder counsels eventually prevailed. The big, humorous-looking ruffian, whose name, it seemed, was Beg Murad Khan, reappeared and admonished him in the most vehement tones for his foolhardy behaviour. The hut was then cleared and a strong guard placed on the door, after which some boiled rice was brought and O'Donovan was left to himself. But, though tired after his arduous journey, the correspondent of the *Daily News* did not lie down to sleep until, with due precautions to avoid being seen by the many curious eyes which peered at him through cracks in the walls of the *kibitka*, he had under cover of his sheepskin robe duly recorded in writing his first impressions of life with the Turkomans.

At ten o'clock next morning O'Donovan was told to mount his horse and proceed to Merv itself, to the centre of government. With him went the fat Beg Murad Khan and an escort of twenty horsemen. A crowd of over a hundred accompanied them. It was still raining as they started, and the flat country looked dismal and depressing. They rode in a northwesterly direction, making their way across irrigation channels and floundering about in flooded fields under the beating rain. Then the weather began to clear and O'Donovan was able to obtain a better view of his surroundings. An immense plain stretched away on all sides, broken here and there by plantations of trees and villages of beehive-shaped huts. Everywhere the ground was tilled, cornfields alternating with melon-beds.

After another hour or so they reached the Murgab river and, crossing it by a rickety bridge, came to a group of some two hundred huts. In front of one of these a small red banner was flying from a lance-shaft. This was the residence of Kadjar Khan, the *Ichthyar* or Supreme Chief. Six hundred yards to the north rose a great earth rampart a mile and a half long, which formed part of the new Turkoman stronghold of Kouchid Khan Kala. A few yards from Kadjar Khan's hut was a sky-blue pavilion tent into which O'Donovan was now shown. Inside it was a thick felt mat covered by a Turkoman carpet. A charcoal fire burned at one end. Here he was politely received by a decent-looking, white-bearded old man, a *mullah*, the brother of Kadjar Khan, who, he explained, was away on a journey. But, though civil, the old man was extremely reserved in manner. He doubtless did not, writes O'Donovan, 'care to be too cordial with a person whose throat might have to be cut within the next twenty-four hours'.

For the rest of that day O'Donovan was left in comparative peace. On waking next morning from a heavy sleep and sitting up and rubbing his eyes and looking round, he was momentarily bewildered to find his tent completely filled with Turkomans. In their long loose robes and gigantic sheepskin busbies they squatted in serried ranks all round him and gazed and gazed at him 'with the ludicrous eagerness which may be observed in baboons and apes when some unfamiliar object meets their eyes'. Outside the tent an immense crowd, flocking in from the bazaar and from the *chai khanas*, had gathered in the hope of catching a glimpse of its inmate. Scores of eyes peeped through every crack and crevice and sometimes the throng was so terrific that the whole tent reeled and swayed. '*Oroos!*' he could hear them murmuring, '*Oroos!*' 'A Russian!' 'A Russian!'

Finally, a number of spectators, who had failed to get within reach of a peephole, attempted simultaneously to lift up the edges of the tent and push their heads underneath, with the result that all the pegs were pulled out at the same time and the tent subsided, almost smothering O'Donovan and the rest of the party inside. There followed a rush of *yassauls*[1] or police, hitting out left and right with their sticks and cursing the too persistent sightseers for their bad manners. But no sooner had the tent been re-erected than the crowd re-assembled and from now onwards, day and night, sleeping or waking, the unfortunate Irishman was never left alone for a moment. A great crowd of spectators watched —and commented on— his every movement, coming back again and again to stare at his tunic and breeches and breaking into loud exclama-

[1] From *yass* and *aul*, 'Beat' and 'Village'.

tions at the way in which he washed his face and hands and combed his hair.

When, at the end of his tether, he asked the old *mullah* if there was no way of getting rid of his tormentors, the latter only replied that it surely did not do him any harm to be looked at. In the end he got used to it. 'It was', he tells us, 'like living in the interior of a much-patronized peep-show ... At first the effect was maddening, but I afterwards fell into a kind of comatic stupor.'

On the following day, as he sat there being stared at, there was a sudden commotion amongst the crowd outside the tent and a general making way amongst those within, whereupon three personages made their entry and, saluting O'Donovan with great ceremony, took their places beside him. These were the three hereditary Khans, Baba Khan, Aman Niaz Khan and Yussuf Khan, who, with Kadjar Khan, the Supreme Ruler or *Ichthyar*, together formed the Government of Merv.

Baba Khan, the Chief of the Toktamish group of Turkoman clans, who lived in the eastern part of the oasis, was a small, cunning-looking man in sombre attire. One of his eyes was completely destroyed by disease. That which remained was jet-black and sparkled with vivacity and penetration. His attitude was not particularly friendly. While ostensibly talking to O'Donovan, he was in reality quite clearly addressing himself to the crowd in the tent, sneering at the visitor's assertion that he was not a Russian and hinting that he could quite easily tell his true nationality by the cut of his long boots. He also referred rather pointedly to the relative positions of the British and Russian troops, the former so far away from Merv, the latter so near.

Aman Niaz Khan, the Chief of the Otamish or Western division, was, in O'Donovan's words 'evidently more of a natural gentleman'. Over his long, sash-girt robe of striped crimson silk he wore a second, outer robe of white silk brilliantly splashed all over with red, blue, yellow and purple, giving from a distance the impression that he was wrapped up in a large Union Jack. His features were regular, but wasted, his eyes feeble and watery. He affected an extreme humility of manner and had the sallow, downcast air which comes from the excessive use of opium. His health, he told O'Donovan, was very delicate owing to the amount of opium he took. This was gradually ruining his constitution, but he had smoked it ever since he was a child and could not give it up.

Yussuf Khan, the third chieftain, was a lad of not more than fifteen or sixteen with grey eyes, a flat Tartar nose and high cheek-bones. He was, it seemed, half-brother to the famous Makdum Kuli Khan, supreme Chief of the Akhal Tekkes and defender of Gök Tepe. Out of reverence for his elders Yussuf scarcely said a word, but squatted on his heels, wearing a robe of amber-coloured camel hair and gazing fixedly before him, as though lost in contemplation. His companions, however, more than made up for Yussuf's silence, and for hours on end O'Donovan was obliged to repeat his answers to the same wearisome questions.

Towards evening, after the three chiefs had taken their leave, he was visited by one of the few Jews still living in Merv, a merchant named Matthi. He wore a long robe of red-and-white-striped cotton and a dome-shaped hat of yellowish brown leather bordered with astrakhan. His beard, which was tinged with grey, was immensely long and he carried a staff some five feet in length, but no arms. With him he brought a bottle of arrack and a bottle of sweet, sticky brown wine from Bokhara. There were, he said, seven families of Jews in Merv. They had been there from time immemorial. No one interfered with them and, largely owing to the indifference of the Turkomans in religious matters, they were allowed to practise their religion in peace.

It was not until after sunset that O'Donovan realized that for the past hour or more Kadjar Khan, the *Ichtiyar*, the fourth and nominally highest ranking member of the quadrumvirate that governed Merv, had been quietly sitting quite near him amongst the crowd in his tent without giving any indication of his presence and without any notice being taken of him by those round him. A tall, gaunt man of over sixty, he wore plain, dark brown robes with no external symbols of rank. His fine aquiline features, somewhat resembling those of Julius Caesar, were spoiled by an uneasy, vulturine look. He had no beard save for a few scarcely perceptible hairs on his chin and upper lip. The pupils of his eyes was entirely surrounded by the white, his jaw muscles twitched and worked convulsively as though he were under the influence of some strong emotion.

Having finally introduced himself, Kadjar Khan still said but little, watching O'Donovan closely and adding '*Inshallah*' — 'Please God', at the end of each of his sentences. He gave the impression of a man not altogether at his ease. After a time he suddenly got up and left and did not come back.

During the days that followed O'Donovan continued to be the object of unflagging curiosity. People came from far and wide to stare at him and he was allowed not a moment's privacy. He was kept closely confined to his tent, and whenever he tried to leave it was at once urged to return to it on the grounds that 'the dogs might bite him' if he sought to wander too far afield. The heat in the tent was stifling and matters were made worse by the fine dust of the desert which blew about and finally found its way into everything. If he tried to read, he was immediately pestered with demands to know what he was reading. He could not even think without someone putting a question to him. 'It was', he tells us, 'wearisome work, sitting there all day to be stared at, with absolutely nothing to do.'

At last, after a whole week had gone by, came the news that a *Medjlis*, or general council of the chiefs and elders of Merv, was meeting to decide whether or not he was a Russian and what should be done with him. At this, his Kurdish servant, who had long expressed the view that neither of them had the slightest chance of escaping with their lives, finally gave way to despair and was soon lying prone in a corner of the tent stupefied by the fumes of the opium he had smoked in order to deaden his terror of what was coming next.

The council of elders had been sitting for over an hour when O'Donovan was finally summoned to appear before them. It was not without trepidation that he obeyed the summons. From his tent he was led through a surging crowd to a large open space. Here some two hundred chiefs and elders were seated on the ground in a circle twenty yards in diameter. Round them pressed an immense throng of Turkomans of both sexes and of all ages and conditions. Within the circle and rather to one side of it was spread a large felt rug. On this

he was invited to sit. There was dead silence while the whole crowd
looked at him. Their general expression of countenance was far from
reassuring.

There now followed a general whispering, when all of a sudden
O'Donovan was addressed in thundering bass tones from the other
side of the circle. The speaker was a man of colossal proportions and
advanced age, with a long white beard, known, it seemed, as *Killidge
Aksakal* or the Old Man of the Sword. 'Who and what are you?'
asked this formidable veteran, in tones accustomed to soar above the
din of battle. 'And what brings you here?'

Feeling that a comprehensive answer was called for, O'Donovan
replied at some length. He was, he said, a native of that part of
Ferengistan called England. His present occupation was to observe and
report on the progress of the Russian arms and he had come to Merv
while fleeing before the advancing Russian armies.

This provoked a general discussion, after which the Old Man of the
Sword addressed him once more. 'What proof', he asked, 'can you
give of the truth of your statement?' At this, O'Donovan took out his
pocket-book and handed to the Old Man such personal documents as
he possessed, some in English and others in Persian. These evidently
made a favourable impression and a murmur of approval ran through
the crowd. 'But', asked the old man half jokingly, 'how can anyone
tell that you are not a Russian who has murdered some Englishman
and taken his papers?' If, replied O'Donovan, they would only let him
communicate with his friends in Persia, he could easily prove to them
who he was.

There followed a variety of questions from different members of
the assembly. How long was it since he had left England? What was
his rank? Where was Hindustan, and where was England? Could it
be true that the *Padishah* of England was a lady? Who and what was
Coompani?[1] For in their minds Hindustan and England, *Padishah* and
Coompani were all inextricably confused and mixed up.

After an hour of this, O'Donovan was told that he might withdraw
and was led back to his tent whence he could hear the loud and eager
debate which ensued. These were anxious moments. For all he could

---

[1] The East India Company.

tell, sentence of immediate death might be passed on him and he did his best to steel his mind against the worst.

After half an hour he was called back. He was not, said the Old Man of the Sword, to be killed. But he would remain a prisoner until more information could be obtained about him from Abbas Khan, the British Consular Agent in Meshed.

Weeks went by, weeks of sitting in a hot, stuffy tent, being stared at and asked questions. In due course couriers were dispatched to Meshed and in due course they returned bearing, much to O'Donovan's relief, a letter from Abbas Khan testifying to his British nationality and declaring that he had no connection whatever with the Russians. From that moment, his position improved. Though still subject to surveillance, he enjoyed comparative liberty. He now had his own *kibitka* and wore Turkoman clothes in place of his European suit: a long crimson tunic of coarse silk from Bokhara with a slender black and yellow stripe and over this an outer robe of the finest camel hair; an embroidered skull-cap; a great shaggy sheepskin hat; a shirt; a sash; wide white cotton trousers; and red leather slippers. Thus equipped, he found that he attracted considerably less attention than before and could walk abroad without being followed by a crowd of more than two hundred people.

Better still, he was now allowed, in fact encouraged, to move about the oasis and see things for himself. Kadjar Khan, for instance, took him to see the defences of the oasis. In anticipation of a Russian attack an immense quadrangular fortress was being built on the lines of Gök Tepe, surrounded by a forty-foot mud wall, within which it was intended that the whole population should take refuge. Seven or eight thousand men were at work on the half-finished terraces and parapets, toiling, like ants, up the specially built ramps with great sacks of earth on their backs. It was all too clear that the Merv Tekkes had learnt nothing from the disaster of Gök Tepe and still did not realize how useless their mud-built fortifications would be against modern Russian howitzers.

Nor was the state of their artillery any more reassuring. Proudly they showed O'Donovan a mixed lot of two or three dozen bronze cannon captured from the Persians at the time of their unsuccessful attack on

Merv a quarter of a century before, and which constituted the entire armament of the oasis. Some of these were still on their ponderous field carriages; others lay on the ground, with the broken woodwork of their supports rotting all around them. How was it, asked O'Donovan, that in view of the possibility of an early Russian attack no one had bothered to mount the disabled pieces? 'Oh,' replied Kadjar Khan, 'there are plenty of people who could do that in a couple of weeks and there is an abundance of wood growing in the gardens.' 'I myself know', he added reminiscently, 'where the tyre of one wheel is. It fell off as we were bringing the gun across the river.'

An inquiry about ammunition produced a similar reaction. The merchants in the bazaar, said the Khan, had any number of cannon-balls which they used as weights when selling corn. 'Besides,' he went on, 'the Persians fired off a great many. The old men who were there at the time could easily point out where they fell, and we could dig them up as and when we needed them.' As for gun-powder, there were thought to be several people in Merv who knew the ingredients and, failing that, the Emir of Bokhara could probably be induced to supply some in return for a good 'present'.

Clearly certain aspects of the Merv defence programme had hitherto been sadly neglected. But now, stimulated by O'Donovan's arrival and by his interest in these matters, the Khans conceived a new and sensational idea. The time, they decided, had come to convert the captured Persian muzzle-loaders into breech-loading artillery like that possessed by the Russians or, as they called it, *susanna thob*. On returning to his tent, the Irishman found waiting for him the *usta adam* or 'artist', a general handyman who worked in silver and gold, shod horses, mended guns and did any other odd jobs that came his way. Could O'Donovan, he asked, provide him with the design for a *susanna thob* and also help him to make one? On O'Donovan's inquiring what tools were available, he eventually produced from beneath his robe an old rasp, used for finishing off the hooves of newly shod horses and a home-made handsaw, each tooth of which pointed in a different direction. Thinking it preferable in the circumstances not to disillusion him, O'Donovan simply nodded his head, looked very knowing and adopted 'such other tricks as are usual when one desires to pass for

being exceeding wise'. Soon there was talk of building a large arma-
ments factory of which he and the *usta adam* would be in charge, and
he was officially informed that he personally would command the
artillery in battle, an announcement which he received by solemnly
rising to his feet and bowing profoundly.

Though the idea that he was a Russian spy still lingered in some
quarters, O'Donovan's standing had by now greatly improved and he
felt that he was fairly firmly established in his hosts' good graces; but
time was passing and it was clearly necessary to make plans for the
future. His purpose, as he now defined it, was 'to make as perfect a
survey as possible of the Merv district, to become fairly acquainted
with the manners, customs and government of the people and their
general tone of mind and then to get out of the place as quickly as
possible' — a plan of which the first part now seemed likely to prove
far easier of fulfilment than the last.

As a first step, he wrote in the following terms to Mr Thomson, Her
Majesty's Minister at Teheran.

Merv: March 19, 1881.

Dear Sir,

I find myself rather in a scrape here, owing to the persistent suspicion of the *medjlis* that I am a Russian spy. My only
chance of getting away is that a letter in Turkish or Persian, bearing
unmistakable signs of its coming from an English source, should
summon me to Meshed immediately, as it were, on business with
Abass Khan. By the same messenger who takes this I write to
Abass Khan asking him to summon me to Meshed; but as he does
not understand English, and will have to apply to Daoud Mirza,
the Chief of Telegraphs, to interpret my letter, I am in serious
doubts as to the result.

The Merv chiefs want me to mount the old guns they took
from the Persians, and whose carriages have rotted, and to do a
number of things quite out of my power; among them to make
extensive presents of money. As, however, they are all quite in
favour of England, a letter with as many stamps and marks as
possible, indicating its origin at a British source, would be invaluable. Kadjar Khan, the chief of the Merv deputation last year

to Teheran, is the person to whom communications should be addressed. He is the most influential of the whole of them. He says he saw you four times at the Embassy, and remembers Dr Dixon. I must be brief, as I am narrowly watched, and write this in bed under the cover of my quilt, pretending to read a book.

I remain,

Sincerely yours

E. O'DONOVAN

This letter he eventually dispatched to Meshed by his Kurdish servant, Gholam Riza. This was an arrangement that suited everyone. Despairing of ever getting out of the hands of the Tekkes, Gholam Riza had for some time past done nothing but drift aimlessly about 'in a state bordering on distraction, engendered partly by fear but to no small extent by excessive indulgence in arrack and opium'. On learning that he was to leave with the next caravan he was overjoyed. As for O'Donovan, he was only too glad to see the last of him. He had shown himself worse than useless as a servant and ever since their arrival had embarrassed him acutely by deliberately spreading the story that he was an immensely important emissary of the British Government on a tremendously important mission. The Turkomans, for their part, readily gave permission for the Kurd to go. As Kadjar Khan put it, 'he goes round to all the *evs* at mealtimes, a thing highly improper in itself, for the people of Merv have not too much to eat and cannot afford to support a stranger'. Perhaps, too, they calculated that without Gholam Riza, who possessed an intimate knowledge of the country, O'Donovan would be less likely to escape, which was something they were particularly anxious to prevent.

At the end of March, having heard no more, O'Donovan, now entirely alone among the Turkomans, wrote another letter to Mr Thomson:

My own position is somewhat singular. Owing to the pressure of circumstances, especially the opposition offered by the Persian authorities to my going among the Turkomans, I was obliged to make a rush for this place, unprovided with credentials, which would duly weigh with the authorities here, whose name is legion.

I have with me the British passport, the Sipah Salar's pass, the letter in Persian of the former British Consul at Asterabad (Mr Churchill), the pass of the Persian Foreign Minister's Agent at the same place, and another from the Persian Governor of Meshed. I had nothing specially addressed to Kadjar Khan; still, thanks to Abass Khan of Meshed, I have succeeded more or less in proving that I am not a Russian. But I can't prove, unfortunately, that I am unconnected with diplomacy, and a cowardly servant, trembling in his skin for himself, fostered the belief that I was a political agent by saying that I had come to hoist the British standard here. This illusion I of course did my best in broken Turkish to dispel. Still, I am looked on as the proper channel through which to transmit the accompanying document. At the same time, while treated as a friend, I am evidently a prisoner. These people think that by holding me they can guarantee some supplies.

I wish it to be distinctly understood that I neither claim nor ask any kind of official interference on my behalf. I don't think it at all necessary. But it would be satisfactory to the minds of the people here if I left them under circumstances that allowed no doubt as to my nationality. As in my former letter, I would ask you as a favour to send a letter through Abass Khan, ordering me to come to Meshed immediately, and certified by as many imposing stamps and seals, both on letter and envelope, as might to the utmost impress the minds of the people here with an impression of its undoubted emanence from the proper source. Another, sent to Kadjar Khan, telling him that I am wanted at Meshed, would also be necessary.

April went by and still his hosts showed no inclination to let O'Donovan go. Meanwhile he had every opportunity of studying 'the manners, customs and government of the people and their general tone of mind'. At the beginning of May he was taken by Baba Khan on a three days' expedition to inspect the all-important waterworks and irrigation system of the oasis. He was by now thoroughly familiar with all the niceties of local manners and behaviour. On arriving in a Turkoman hut he would at once squat down on his heels and, together with his companions, mutter the prescribed compliments which preceded any serious talk. Confronted with food of any kind whatever, whether sour milk, leathery unleavened bread, or gamy, grey-green coagulated mutton fat, he would throw himself on it voraciously and gorge himself till he could eat no more. He would then join assiduously in saying grace, concluding in subdued tones with the phrase, '*El Hamd Lillah*', 'Praise be to God'. After this he would stroke his beard first with the right hand and then with the left, look cautiously over both shoulders to make sure that the Devil was not lurking anywhere near, and then emit a deep sigh followed by the resounding eructations, natural or forced, which in the East are taken as denoting polite recognition of hospitality.

All this redounded greatly to his credit. 'He is a good man; he is an excellent man', his hosts would exclaim admiringly as they watched him avidly shovelling down one enormous dish of sour milk after another. Nor, with his natural inventiveness, was he now ever at a loss for an answer. Noticing that he kept glancing at a small prismatic compass with which he was surreptitiously taking his bearings, and thinking that it must be a watch, Baba Khan asked him why he was always looking at the time. 'A *Ferenghi*', he replied without a moment's hesitation, 'is required to pray much oftener than a Mussulman and cannot allow the proper hour to pass without committing a grievous offence against his religion.' 'But', retorted the Khan, 'you never seem to pray at all.' 'I pray always,' replied O'Donovan sanctimoniously. 'That is the difference between the *Ferenghis* and you of the Eastern plains. You snatch a few minutes from your occupations to pray to your Creator. Our life is one continual prayer.'

On May 7th, two days after his excursion to the water-works, O'Donovan was sitting alone in his tent when a tall, slender young man came in. He had very regular features, large hazel eyes and a faint moustache. His expression was one of extreme mildness and he looked permanently as if he was on the point of sneezing. He wore a long, striped crimson tunic, girt with a voluminous white sash knotted in front and a long-sleeved camel hair robe. In his sash was a long dagger with a handle of embossed gold set with turquoises. Having gravely saluted, he knelt down and there followed the exchange of formalities required by Turkoman politeness. It then dawned on O'Donovan that his visitor was none other than the redoubtable Makdum Kuli Khan, who for so long had held the Russians at bay before the ramparts of Gök Tepe and who, after spending some time in the swamps of the Tejend river, had now moved to Merv and established himself on the territory of his brother, Yussuf Khan.

At first, Makdum Kuli explained, a large number of his Akhal Tekke followers had remained loyal to him. But, on learning of the favourable terms offered by the Russians, more and more were now leaving him and going back to their old camping grounds. He reckoned, however, that he still had three thousand horsemen who would stand by him to the last. He himself had been offered the most favourable conditions by the Russians if he would return to Gök Tepe, but he had steadily refused to accept them. If Merv were invaded, he intended to fight to the last, and, if defeated, to withdraw with his remaining followers into Afghanistan. If not well received there, they would then seek asylum in British India.

Makdum Kuli did not stay long. He had, he said, had considerable difficulty in obtaining permission to come. Kadjar Khan did not like anyone to visit O'Donovan except himself and he did not want to arouse his suspicions by remaining too long. They would meet again. There was just one thing he would like to say before he went. In one of his letters from Persia, O'Donovan had kindly promised to make him a present of some field-glasses, a revolver and a signet ring. Had he by any chance these articles with him now?

This inquiry placed O'Donovan in something of a dilemma. As his Smith and Wesson revolver and field-glasses were at that very moment lying there in full view of his visitor, he could scarcely deny that he had them with him. On the other hand he had originally offered them to Makdum Kuli as an inducement to let him enter Gök Tepe, since when circumstances had changed considerably. Both, moreover, were now essential items of his own equipment. However, on second thoughts, he felt that it was perhaps better to gratify his visitor's desires, especially as his brother's territory adjoined the ruins of Old Merv which he particularly wanted to see. And so, putting a cheerful face on it, he now handed them over to Makdum Kuli together with a heavy gold ring which he had had especially made in Persia. Where-upon Makdum Kuli, clearly delighted, took his leave.

No sooner had Makdum Kuli departed than O'Donovan's hut at once filled with visitors, all eager to learn what had passed between them. But this was not all. Something else was clearly afoot — something of no ordinary importance. A change, some of his visitors implied, was about to take place, a change in the position of Kadjar Khan, the *Ichthyar*. Others, evidently supporters of Kadjar, hotly denied that there was any question of such a change and feelings soon ran high. There was much talk, too, of a newly captured Russian officer. Some, on O'Donovan's advice, were disposed to release the Russian and so avoid giving Skobelyov a pretext for attacking the oasis. Others, led by Kadjar, loudly insisted on holding him to ransom.

From the ensuing discussion O'Donovan was able to glean some interesting and important information. He had hitherto regarded Kadjar Khan as being of right *Ichthyar* or Supreme Ruler of Merv. He now discovered that this was not so. Some months earlier, the Shah of Persia had sent a messenger inviting the Khans of Merv to visit him in Teheran in order to discuss how Merv could best be placed under the protection of Persia. Rightly dubious as to the Shah's motives, and half suspecting that his intention was to hold any emissaries who might visit him as hostages, but for all that not wishing to reject his approach out of hand, the two hereditary Khans, Baba and Aman Niaz, had hit upon an ingenious compromise. Temporarily retiring from their hereditary office, they had induced the notables of Merv to elect as *Ichthyar* Kadjar Khan, a deserving and fairly distinguished public figure, with no claim to hereditary rank. They had then declined the Shah's invitation on their own behalf and dispatched Kadjar in their place, nominally Supreme Ruler of Merv, but in fact a man of straw. In the event the Shah had not held Kadjar as a hostage, but it had equally not been possible to arrive at any agreement and, after some months of inconclusive negotiations, Kadjar had returned to Merv. The Russians, meanwhile, had invested Gök Tepe; circumstances were threatening; no one could quite foresee what would happen; and the hereditary Khans, deeming that the moment had not arrived to reassert their natural supremacy, had accordingly left their man of straw to act as scapegoat in any awkward situation that might arise.

Now, however, things were changing. O'Donovan had arrived. Bit by bit his conduct, their own perceptions of his character and the assurances they had now received about him from the British Minister at Teheran had helped them to overcome their original suspicion that he was a Russian spy. Once satisfied on this score, they had run at once to the other extreme — and had attributed to him and to his mission immense importance and significance. They were, they told themselves, no longer isolated. They were at last in touch with the West, with the celebrated and mysterious *Coompani*. The British were at Kandahar. They would soon reach Herat and Merv. They would bring in their train untold wealth and prosperity. Quite clearly, the moment had come for them to reconsider their own position — and that of Kadjar Khan.

The discussion in O'Donovan's hut lasted on and off all day. Towards evening Kadjar Khan himself made his appearance. His manner, O'Donovan soon noticed, was more conciliatory than before. Clearly he, too, was concerned to enlist O'Donovan's support. Having once savoured supreme power, he was not unnaturally reluctant to let it slip from his hands. After first ordering the hut to be cleared, he proceeded to deliver to O'Donovan a solemn warning. He had, he announced, discovered that Baba and Aman Niaz were plotting to deliver Merv into the hands of the Russians. He begged him to have nothing to do with them. He alone was the ruler of Merv. For O'Donovan to lend the authority of his approval to others was to invite disaster and seal the fate of the oasis and its population.

To this O'Donovan, feeling that in the face of such universal crookedness brutal frankness was probably the best policy, replied that he for his part had been informed of the circumstances in which Kadjar had attained power and understood that he was not in fact the legitimate *Ichthyar*.

At these words, the old man flew into a furious rage. His eyes flashed and, rising to his feet, he stamped round and round the hut, cursing and swearing. Then, growing calmer, he sat down next to O'Donovan and assured him in urgent tones that if the other good-for-nothing Khans came into power, it would be the worse for him. His life would not be worth a moment's purchase. A great council had been called for the following day. A crisis was approaching. He begged him to stand by him, by his old friend Kadjar, who at any rate recognized that he was not a Russian. After which he abruptly left the hut.

Not long after this there was a tremendous uproar and horsemen could be heard galloping off in all directions. Just as O'Donovan was wondering what had happened, the curtain before his door was roughly thrust aside and Kadjar Khan again burst into his tent, once more beside himself with rage. The Russian prisoner, he said, had escaped. The pro-Russians had deliberately let him go. It was a plot. And he again rushed furiously from the tent. It was only later that O'Donovan discovered that the Russian had in fact been helped to escape by Kadjar's own son, who at that very moment was being publicly punished for his treachery, having been bound hand and foot to the flagpole from which floated the crimson banner of Merv.

O'Donovan's next visitor was Kadjar Khan's brother, the white-bearded old *mullah* who had looked after him when he first arrived. He, too, spoke of the plot against his brother and sought to enlist O'Donovan's support for him. 'The moment', he said, 'is a critical one for you. It is probable that you have no friend here except my brother.' After which, he went on to speak of the need to give *zat*, or presents, to people of importance. 'I would beg to remind you', he said, 'that you have omitted an indispensable ceremony as a stranger visiting Merv. You have not presented any *zat* to the Chief.' To this O'Donovan, who had come well supplied with jewellery and other suitable articles, replied that he was by no means forgetful of his obligations in respect of *zat* and was only awaiting a proper occasion to hand over the presents. 'You may give them to me', said the *mullah*, 'or, if you like, you can send them by your servant to the Khan's house.' To which O'Donovan replied that he would rather send them by his servant.

As it happened, O'Donovan had with him a silver casket, richly engraved and embossed and set with turquoises and rubies for which he had paid about six hundred *krans*, or twenty-five pounds sterling. Placing inside it some ruby and turquoise rings, he now wrapped it up, sealed it, and sent it round to Kadjar Khan's residence. No sooner had he done so than Aman Niaz Khan arrived, accompanied by his uncle and several of his followers, for the manifest purpose of informing him of the latest developments.

But he had scarcely sat down, when Kadjar Khan again appeared, and, after a time, produced the casket which O'Donovan had sent him. 'What', asked Kadjar, 'is this?' 'As you see, Khan,' replied O'Donovan, 'it is a jewelled silver casket.' 'What is it for?' 'To keep as a tribute of my respect.' 'What is it worth?' 'Six hundred *krans.*' '*Ouallah Billah!* Six hundred *krans!* Why, I would not give you two for it!' And throwing the casket contemptuously on the carpet, 'Take back your box', he exclaimed, 'and give me the money!'

O'Donovan had, he tells us, gained 'at a bound' an enormous insight into the mental temperament of Turkoman chiefs. 'Certainly, Khan, if you wish,' he replied: 'I thought you might be offended if I merely offered you money,' and with these words took out of his pocket twenty-five pounds in gold and handed it to him. But Kadjar Khan remained unabashed; 'By God!' he said, pocketing the money, 'that is right! I am satisfied,' and walked out.

No sooner was Kadjar gone than Aman Niaz, who had been watching the scene through opium-bleared eyes, raised both his hands and then spread them out behind his ears, to denote amazement at Kadjar's behaviour. '*Sahib,*' he said, 'you can see that Kadjar is no Khan. Had a statesman, a *dowlet adam*, offered *me* such a present, I would not have parted with it for four times its value, not even if ten horses were offered to me in return.'

This was too broad a hint to be ignored. 'Aman Niaz Khan,' said O'Donovan, 'there are Khans and Khans. You I recognize as a true Khan. Will you accept this casket as a token of my regard?' Whereupon Aman Niaz again raised both hands behind his ears, bowed low and, stretching out both his palms, received the much coveted gift amid loud applause from all present. Before they dispersed, Aman Niaz Khan's uncle gave O'Donovan the assurance that all that his nephew possessed and all his clansmen were at his service. 'Not', he added, 'because of the present but because I can at once perceive that you really are a *dowlet adam.*' His stock, quite clearly, was going up.

Events were now moving fast, and in a direction seemingly

favourable to O'Donovan. After Aman Niaz had gone, a leading
Turkoman cavalry commander arrived with a soda-water bottle full of
arrack as a present from Baba Khan, while Beg Murad Khan, the fat,
humorous-looking ruffian whom he had met on his first day in the
oasis, sent him a shaggy, big-tailed sheep. Kadjar Khan's supporters, for
their part, tried unceasingly to extract from him an assurance that he
would acknowledge no one else as *Ichthyar* and, having failed to do
this, asked him, with engaging frankness, to lend them small sums of
money against the day when their faction went out of power. Not long
after midnight, Kadjar Khan himself came back and stayed until a
little before sunrise.

Between one and two o'clock the following afternoon, as
O'Donovan lay dozing on his carpet, a message was brought to him,
summoning him to attend a meeting of the Council of Khans.
Rousing himself somewhat unwillingly, he followed the messenger to
the Council Chamber, a large round tent, the walls and floor of which
were covered with rich carpets. Here were assembled some twenty-five
notables, including Baba and Aman Niaz Khan. Kadjar Khan and his
supporters were, he noticed, not present.

The *Medjlis*, it appeared, had met earlier in the day and had entrusted
the Council of Khans with the task of forming a new and vigorous
executive capable of dealing with the critical situation occasioned by
the Russian advance. O'Donovan, feeling thoroughly tired and sleepy
after his all-night interview with Kadjar Khan, had no sooner appeared
in the Council Chamber than he became the target for a regular
barrage of questions as to the way in which he thought the situation
was likely to develop.

'Are the Russians', he was asked, 'coming to Merv, or are they not?'
'Where are the English troops now?' 'Are *they* coming here?' 'What
would you recommend us to do?' 'Would the English *Padishah* receive
the people of Merv as her subjects?' 'If we are received as subjects by
England, shall we be required to pay taxes?' 'Will the English *Padishah*
provide us with cannon, and breach-loading rifles, and ammunition
and the money for two thousand cavalrymen?'

To these and other questions O'Donovan replied as best he could, urging the Khans to embody their views on the future of Merv in a document bearing all their seals which could be sent to Meshed for onward transmission to London. The notables, apparently well satisfied with his answers, then fell to debating amongst themselves what course of action they should adopt, and O'Donovan, who was suffering from lack of sleep and was in any case not anxious to become involved in the domestic crisis that was clearly brewing, took the opportunity to withdraw.

It was only after he had gone some way that he noticed that, instead of taking him back to his tent, the half dozen Turkomans who escorted him were leading him in the direction of an open space at some distance from the other dwelling-places. Here about a hundred work-men were busy building a formidable redoubt seventy or eighty yards square in the middle of which was being constructed a large round hut. Following his companions over the narrow causeway which served as entrance to the redoubt, he found that a carpet had been laid and that his saddles, arms, bedding and other belongings had been piled inside the half-completed hut.

He was by now 'too accustomed to the vicissitudes of fortune and the unforeseen whims of the Turkomans to be surprised at anything'. Could this, he wondered wearily, be a kind of State prison in which he was henceforth to be lodged for greater security? He decided to ask his escort outright. 'Why', he inquired, 'have you moved my tent from the place where it stood. And what is the meaning of this breastwork you have thrown up around it?'

'This', they replied solemnly, 'is your residence as a Khan.' 'The *Medjlis*', they added, 'has decided that you are to be recognized as the representative of the English *Padishah*.'

Coming on top of everything else, this announcement was almost too much for O'Donovan. 'But,' he tells us, 'retaining my self-possession, I simply bowed, as if all this were only a matter of course, and, sitting upon the carpet prepared for me, made note of the circumstances.'

After an hour or two's badly needed sleep, he woke to find that the Council had broken up and that a number of its members were now sitting round waiting for an opportunity to speak to him. Several of these, he noticed, belonged to the faction who had most loudly and persistently declared that he was a Russian spy and should be dealt with accordingly. Now they were falling over each other to ingratiate themselves with him. It was, said one, a shame that he had ever been treated as a prisoner. How brave he was, said another, to have come among the Tekkes unaccompanied. He had, they chorused, come, not as a raider, but as a friend to visit friends, bringing his saddle-bags with him. He was a *bahadur adam*, a great and glorious man.

O'Donovan took all this with a grain of salt. But at the same time he noticed something which struck him as significant. In speaking to him, his visitors no longer addressed him as *sahib* as they had done hitherto, but as *Khan* or *Bahadur Khan*, a form of address never in any circumstances applied save to those entitled to it by right, hereditary or otherwise. It looked very much as though there had indeed been a revolutionary change in his status, although exactly what that status now was, was still far from clear. After enduring an hour of adulation, he asked his visitors to leave him alone. He had, he said, much to think of.

The present moment, he reflected, was quite clearly a critical one for the Tekkes. They would shortly be called upon to decide whether to throw in their lot with England or with Russia, whose respective forces, they believed, would shortly encounter each other somewhere in the neighbourhood of Merv. Their hatred of Russia was of long standing and had recently been further inflamed by what had happened at Gök Tepe. Even though the Russians were much closer to them than the English, they still inclined to England, or rather, as they themselves put it, to '*Coompani*'.

Earlier attempts on their part to establish contact with the British having failed, it was only natural that, despite his own repeated asseverations to the contrary, they should attach considerable political importance to his arrival. Such, it seemed to him, was the logic of his own sudden and unforeseen advancement. It only remained to acquit himself as best he could in the position in which fate, his own adventurous character and the indiscretions of his Kurdish servant had together placed him.

*

The revolution was by now far advanced. Although no public announcement had been made, Kadjar Khan had, in fact, been eliminated from the direction of affairs, and control had passed back into the hands of Baba Khan and Aman Niaz Khan, each of whom for the time being ruled over his own clansmen separately on a basis of mutual equality. To O'Donovan, exhausted by the events of the last few days, this seemed a convenient moment to do something he had long wanted to do, namely visit the Old Cities of Merv and also to look in on Makdum Kuli Khan and his half-brother, young Yussuf Khan, in whose territory they lay.

The expedition, which lasted two days, was undertaken in company with Aman Niaz Khan. Enveloped as usual in his coat of many colours and carrying, in addition to two formidable horse pistols, a double-barrelled English fowling-piece, an antiquated Colt revolver and a cavalry sabre, the latter, on arrival at the rendezvous, presented a more sickly appearance than ever. Sallow and worn, with red-rimmed, bloodshot eyes, he looked a complete wreck. He had, he explained, smoked even more opium and drunk even more arrack than usual the night before and now felt very far from well. But, once in the saddle, the Chief of the Otamish showed that, when it came to endurance, he could outlast the best of his men.

Having ridden all day across the plain in an easterly direction they came at sunset to the residence of Yussuf Khan, which stood in an open space in the middle of a pleasant grove of fruit trees. It consisted of a massive tower of unbaked brick some thirty or forty feet high, some outbuildings, and half a dozen of the usual circular tents. It was here on his half-brother's territory that Makdum Kuli Khan was for the time being installed, not in the tower but in a tent, having, like all Turkomans, a strong prejudice against any more solidly constructed form of dwelling.

On arrival the travellers were made hospitably welcome by Yussuf and Makdum Kuli, who, though strict abstainers themselves, had laid in a good supply of arrack in anticipation of their visit. Next morning, after a copious breakfast of green tea and boiled mutton, they set out again, accompanied by their hosts. Leaving the cultivation behind them, they soon came to higher ground and, reaching the top of a little hill, suddenly saw spread out before them and stretching away into the dim distance, an immense wilderness of ruined buildings — all that now remained of the three once-splendid cities which in turn had won for Merv the proud title of 'Queen of the World'. Snakes abounded on every side and here and there a hawk or vulture hovered above the ruins, but of human inhabitants there was now no sign.

Immediately in front of them, on the far side of a great belt of nondescript ruins, stood Bairam Ali, the youngest of the three cities of Merv, laid waste barely a century before by the Emir of Bokhara — a high embattled wall, flanked by circular towers and pierced by two great gateways, surrounded the ruins of mosques, palaces, houses and baths. In one corner stood what was left of the Ark or Citadel. Beyond Bairam Ali to the east, on rising ground across a shallow valley, rose the great ramparts of Giaour Kala, the oldest of the three cities, destroyed by the Arabs a thousand years earlier. To the north of Bairam Ali stood Sultan Sanjar, the second of the three, sacked by Genghiz Khan's son Tului in 1221. Within its walls nothing remained of the city save the massive domed mausoleum of its founder, now a shrine and a place of pilgrimage. Of all its other buildings not one stone was left upon another. But at a distance of about a hundred and fifty yards from the Sultan's mausoleum were two large piles of broken brick and tile. These, O'Donovan's companions solemnly informed him, were the Tombs of Sultan Sanjar's enemies. Having halted about fifty yards short of them, each horseman then proceeded to gallop past them in turn, discharging his musket at them as he went and calling down the most appalling curses on their occupants. But who Sultan Sanjar had been or what he and his enemies had done or when they had lived, not one of them could say. Nor were they any better informed concerning the history of two other handsome tombs at which they prayed devoutly. These, they said, were the Tombs of the Beheaded Gentlemen, *Sahaba Bouridal*, men of great sanctity who at one time or another had died for their faith.

While his companions were praying, which they did frequently and with the most varied and elaborate ritual at a number of different shrines, O'Donovan was in some doubt as to how he should behave. If he joined in their devotions, he was afraid that they might suppose that he did so in mockery; if he did not, he feared that they might equally take it as a slight. In the end, he decided that it was best to dismount from his horse and stand quietly by, doing nothing. It was, however, while inspecting an ancient monument which, so far as he knew, had nothing to do with the Mohammedan religion, that he came nearest to causing serious offence. This was *Iskender Kala*, a rectangular space, surrounded by the barely visible traces of some ancient earthworks, where, or so he was informed by one of the party, a *mullah*, Alexander the Great had camped on his way to India. Alexander, the *mullah* added, had been a great *pihamber* or prophet and had foretold the destruction of Merv. Being naturally argumentative, O'Donovan was unwise enough to question this. Whereupon his informant flew into a violent rage, declaring that it was easy enough to see that O'Donovan was an unbeliever and an ignorant one at that. Alexander, he kept repeating, was a *pihamber*, second only to Solomon himself, and it was only when O'Donovan climbed down and pleaded ignorance of such matters that he could finally be appeased.

After a long day spent inspecting ruins and tombs, with frequent intervals for prayer, O'Donovan was glad enough when the time came to turn homewards. But the ride back from the ruins was anything but restful. One or other of his companions was for ever starting off at full gallop with a wild whoop, letting off his rifle as he went, or racing up with drawn sword to exchange passes and flourishes with the rider nearest to him. Occasionally, much to O'Donovan's delight, a hidden trench or mudhole would intervene and he would have the pleasure of seeing a gallant Khan crash headlong to the ground, horse, armament and all. But his companions' favourite amusement of all was to charge straight at a party of villagers coming back heavily laden from market, sending men, women and donkeys flying in every direction and knocking senseless any who were too old or infirm to get out of the way. Having seen the way in which they treated their own tribesmen out of mere high spirits, O'Donovan had little difficulty in picturing their ferocity on a foray against a real enemy.

The sun was setting by the time they arrived back at Yussuf Khan's tower. Yussuf and Makdum Kuli had ridden on ahead and, as O'Donovan dismounted, came forward to greet him. A supper of mutton broth and bread was now served in the upper chamber of the tower and, after it had been cleared away, the company sat in the gathering darkness looking out across the dim plain and listening to the flocks and herds bleating and lowing as they made their way homewards.

For some time past his companions' conversation, which consisted in the main of highly improbable stories about *pihambers*, *djinns*, *dirs* and other supernatural beings, had begun to pall on O'Donovan and he was glad of this momentary respite. His thoughts far away, he started whistling some snatches of tunes, but at once those nearest to him began to shift uneasily in their seats and at length Makdum Kuli lent across and touched him on the shoulder. 'For God's sake', he whispered in urgent tones, 'don't whistle!'

Fearing that he had committed some enormity, O'Donovan hastily stopped. 'What objection', he asked a little later on, 'was there to my whistling?' 'Is it possible', came the answer, 'that you don't know that at this hour the ghouls and *djinns* are wandering to and fro? If they hear you whistle, they will suppose that you are calling them; and, *Bismillah*, we have no wish for *their* company.'

Not long afterwards Yussuf and Makdum Kuli retired to their wig-wams, leaving O'Donovan alone with Aman Niaz Khan and his followers. Taking off their tunics and their immense sheepskin hats, the Turkomans quickly disposed themselves to sleep. But, try as he would, O'Donovan, tormented by myriads of sand-flies, could not find any rest. Nor was his humour improved by a whispered conversation which he chanced to overhear between Aman Niaz and one of his attendants, a scribe.

'Did you see the English gentleman today, while we were praying at the tombs of the Sheikhs?' asked Aman Niaz. 'He was leaning on his sword and looking on as if he didn't care a fig for our prayers.'

'After all, he is only an unbeliever,' came the reply.

'What are we to do tomorrow? We can't stop here any longer.'

'But a Mussulman has a right to nine days' hospitality.'

'Mussulmans — yes, but a wicked unbeliever like that! We couldn't share hospitality with him for more than three days. He gives presents to scoundrels, but he gives nothing to Khans.'

Reflecting that his companions were only enjoying Makdum Kuli's hospitality at all because of his own presence there, and recalling the generous presents he had given to Aman Niaz, O'Donovan's anger redoubled at the thought of such double-faced ingratitude; the sand-flies kept up their attacks; and the saffron light of dawn coming up behind the black dome of Sultan Sanjar found him still awake and seething with unkind thoughts on the subject of Aman Niaz. Setting out after the usual breakfast of green tea and boiled mutton, they reached the round tents of Kouchid Khan Kala about an hour after sunset.

During O'Donovan's absence, the revolution which had begun before his departure had been carried several stages further. This much he gathered from the conversation of the crowd of distinguished visitors who, whether he liked it or not, now sat in his tent from early morning until far into the night, arguing, intriguing and speculating as to the future.

The climax came on May 15th, two days after his return. Waking early, he at once realized that something unusual was afoot. All round his tent could be heard the trampling and muttering and shouting of a great multitude. Throwing a sheepskin robe round his shoulders, he ran to the door. Everyone was astir. A vast, excited concourse, on horseback and on foot, thronged the main avenue of Merv. Baba and Aman Niaz were, it seemed, about to make a triumphal entry into the capital and the people of Merv had turned out in their thousands to welcome them.

From the western end of the ramparts a column of four or five hundred horsemen was now seen approaching. In front and on either side armed outriders galloped to and fro, their sabres gleaming in the early morning light. Every now and then there was a burst of firing as one or other of them discharged his musket in full career and his companions responded with an answering fusillade. At the head of the cavalcade rode the sombre figure of Baba Khan. Around him clustered his kinsmen and the chieftains of his tribe, all arrayed in their finest robes. At his side was carried a great red and white standard on a high pole and from the lances of his bodyguard fluttered red and white pennants.

Feeling that the occasion demanded it, O'Donovan now mounted his own horse and rode out to meet the Khan of the Toktamish, while a great crowd of excited citizens surged around him as he went. When he was within fifty yards of the approaching cavalcade, he dismounted and awaited Baba's approach. At this, Baba also dismounted and came forward on foot to greet him. Holding hands, the two then slowly advanced together to where a large felt carpet had been spread. Here the *Medjlis* was assembled, the morning light slanting down on the circle of swarthy notables in their great sheepskin hats, as they awaited the approach of the gaily attired cavalcade with its glinting bannerets and flashing sabres and, at its head, the Irishman and the one-eyed Tekke, walking together with their hands clasped in friendship.

From the other side, meanwhile, swirling clouds of dust announced the approach of a second cavalcade with at its head Aman Niaz Khan, as sickly looking and as brightly garbed as ever. As the Chief of the Otamish drew near, Baba Khan and O'Donovan went forward together to meet him and, after the usual greetings, all three marched solemnly towards the carpet of honour which had been laid down for them at one end of the expanse of felt matting provided for the members of the *Medjlis*. Aman Niaz Khan's pure white standard and the red and white standard of Baba Khan were then run up, the cannon boomed from the ramparts, a richly jewelled water-pipe was handed round, new arrivals were welcomed, and the usual courtesies exchanged. '*Nemeh Khaber var?*' the members of this distinguished company inquired of each other every few minutes, 'What's new?'

After half an hour of these preliminaries the whole company was assembled, and Baba and Aman Niaz now each took one of O'Donovan's hands and led him back through the entrance of the redoubt to his tent. There he found, lashed to his doorpost, a bright crimson banner of silk, about three feet square. It was, they told him, the emblem of his office as Khan, as representative of *Coompani* and of the British *Padishah*, as a member, in fact as President, of the newly established Triumvirate, in short, as *Ichthyar* of Merv. In this manner and almost without realizing what was happening, Mr Edmund

O'Donovan, correspondent of the London *Daily News* and former inmate of Limerick Jail and Mountjoy Prison, was formally installed as Supreme Ruler of Merv and the Mervli.

A large number of rich carpets had been spread upon the ground in front of the door of the Irishman's tent. Upon these he and his fellow Khans now took their seats. 'It was', he writes, 'a curious sight that I gazed upon from my door. The Murgab flowed sluggishly by; the huge mass of nearly completed ramparts rose against the morning sky, covered with thousands of spectators, who availed themselves of every coign of vantage to catch a sight of the doings within my re-doubt. From moment to moment the guns thundered out, their echoes rolling away across these historic plains, the snow-white smoke clouds from each gun sailing glidingly in procession through the still air until they were lost to view in the far distance. The crimson flag flapped and fluttered above our heads; and the warriors and chiefs of Merv, in their best and brightest apparel, grouped around; some sitting, some standing, presented a spectacle the theatrical effect of which was only surpassed by its political interest.'

For a time the three Khans sat in silence, each waiting for one of the others to say something, ostensibly out of politeness but in fact in order to gain time and find out what the other two were thinking. Large quantities of scalding hot green tea were brought and consumed, still without a word being said.

At length O'Donovan could stand it no longer. Was there, he asked, any matter of pressing interest to be discussed? At this Baba Khan nodded to Aman Niaz Khan and Aman Niaz nodded back to Baba. The latter, addressing O'Donovan, then said that the Council would like to hear something about the actual state of affairs between Russia and Great Britain. They would also welcome his advice as to the best course to be pursued under the present difficult circumstances. The Mervli, Baba went on, had now accepted British rule. They looked to him, as British representative, for instruction and direction. They were all, Chiefs, Chieftains and people of Merv, O'Donovan's subjects. He had but to command and they would obey. After which, taking from his own finger the ring which he wore as Senior Khan, he placed it upon O'Donovan's, thus solemnly inaugurating him as ruler of the oasis. The entire assembly then looked eagerly and expectantly at their new and rather bewildered monarch.

In coming to Merv, O'Donovan had had two objects: to find out as much as he could about the situation there and, having done that, to leave again as expeditiously as possible. He had at no time claimed to represent the British or any other government. Indeed he had repeatedly and vehemently denied this. But his denials had been unavailing. His Kurdish servant's romancing and the fact that his arrival at Merv had exactly coincided with the cessation of the Russian advance had convinced the Mervli not only that he was the representative of Great Britain but that, as such, he was destined to be their saviour. In the circumstances it seemed to him pointless to go on protesting. 'I began', he tells us, 'to perceive that by passively accepting the situation I might doubtless have greater facilities for the investigations which were the object of my journey, and, subsequently, for leaving the oasis with greater ease than could otherwise be the case.' Such was the background against which he now opened his discourse to his assembled subjects.

It was, he began by telling them, of little use to put themselves under British protection unless they so informed the British *Padishah*. But if they would draw up a formal document stating their intentions and desires, he would gladly send it to the Ambassador at Teheran for transmission to England. Their next care must be to avoid giving the Russians any pretext for attacking them. Their raids along the Russian border must cease. Neither should they attack Persia or Bokhara. 'You ask', he continued, 'for alliance with England. Do you think that the English or any other *Padishah* will unite with thieves or support them in their action?'

Here he was angrily interrupted by a member of the assembly, who asked how in the name of Allah he thought they were going to live if they did not make raids on someone. But O'Donovan, after pointing out that, since Russia had extinguished the slave-markets of Khiva and Bokhara, their national occupation was in any case gone and that the reform he advocated was therefore an unavoidable necessity, went on unperturbed to draw as attractive a picture as he could of a peaceful and prosperous Merv becoming again the centre of commerce and civilization which had once rejoiced in the proud title of Queen of the World.

Robbery, he said, must cease and all prisoners, Russians and others, must be set free. (Here he was again indignantly interrupted, this time by the Chief of Police, who said that it was a poor compliment to the Mervli to insinuate that they were robbers.) If, he went on, ignoring this remark also, they would adopt the policy he proposed, Merv would gain the support not only of England, but of other civilized countries, who would not look idly on and see her territory overrun and her people conquered in the interests of mere aggrandisement. For the moment, he concluded, the Russians had halted at Askabad and, in view of this, the British had done likewise at Kandahar. For the present, therefore, they need have no fear of invasion.

A general discussion ensued which showed that most of those present agreed with the policy he had propounded. The assembly then broke up and the remainder of the day was given over to festivities. There were races and wrestling. Prizes were given and presents exchanged. Baba Khan sent O'Donovan a magnificent pale pink silk mantle, striped with crimson and dark emerald green with a pattern of embroidered flowers. Aman Niaz sent him a rainbow-hued robe like the one which he wore himself, with irregular splashes of vermilion, yellow, purple and many other colours. He also sent him a finely embroidered skull-cap and a handsome quilt of dark red-purple silk, heavily embroidered with gold and silver.

O'Donovan had by now run out of presents. He accordingly gave to each of his fellow Khans an order on Meshed for twenty-five pounds. To Baba Khan he also gave a prismatic compass so that he might tell the exact direction in which to turn when praying. But this was not all. Further presents had to be given to the messengers who brought the presents, to a succession of poets who composed and recited complimentary odes in honour of the three Khans, and finally to the Public Crier who made the necessary proclamations. To all these the new ruler distributed silver *krans* by the handful from a bag which he kept by him for the purpose, while the Public Crier, encouraged by the present he had received, stood at the door and proclaimed in a voice that could be heard half a mile away, 'Dower! Dower! Dower! Bahadur Sahib Khan gives so much money to the poets!'

Towards evening O'Donovan had a sheep killed in order to regale his own immediate retinue, which by now had assumed the most alarming proportions, and there was general rejoicing inside the redoubt. Relays of mounted messengers were kept plying backwards and forwards with fresh supplies of *arrack* from the shop of Matthi the Jew and an endless succession of allegedly celebrated commanders were brought up to be presented — hook-nosed ruffians with buff leather boots like stage brigands, who told long stories of their own exploits and drank immense quantities of *arrack* at O'Donovan's expense.

After sunset Aman Niaz Khan, having doubtless heard that there was *arrack* to be had, appeared with his chief of staff, his maternal uncle and a whole regiment of hangers on. It was at once apparent from his expression that he had some tremendous surprise in reserve for his host. But it was not until a good deal later, when the *arrack* had done its work and the whole company were boisterously hilarious, that he finally revealed what it was. Then, from under his robes, he produced with infinite pride a toy concertina made of stamped gold paper and imported from somewhere by Matthi the Jew. On this he now proceeded to perform with great energy, but without any idea whatever of how it should be played, to the delighted amazement of his audience who clustered spellbound round this miraculous instrument, while the Khan, enchanted at the effect he was producing, sawed away unceasingly, grinning and giggling with exultation as he played.

O'Donovan meanwhile squatted wearily on his bed watching the proceedings and longing for them to end. But more and more dishes of mutton fat and bread were brought in, the toy concertina was passed from one notable to another, the *arrack* flowed freely, and it was not until well after daybreak that the festivities celebrating his elevation to the dignity of *Ichthyar* finally came to an end.

The last to leave was Aman Niaz. His brightly coloured robes awry, his complexion more bilious and his eyes more bleary than ever, supported on one side by his maternal uncle and on the other by his chief of staff, he was with difficulty conducted home, whooping, hiccuping and hallooing as he went.

O'Donovan had hoped that, as Khan, he would at least enjoy a little more privacy than hitherto. But he was doomed to disappointment. On his announcing that he would in future be at home only to his two fellow-Khans or to other leading members of the community, he was told that there could be no question of this. 'A Khan's door,' said his major-domo, 'is always open. He must receive and entertain anyone who calls on him.' With a feeling of despair he realized that he had become a public personage in every sense of the word.

At about this time, considerable embarrassment was occasioned him by some seemingly harmless parcels of newspapers which had been sent to him from Teheran. Nothing of the kind had ever been seen before in the oasis and that evening there took place a regular gathering of the clans to watch them being opened.

As it happened, the Mervli, while raiding the Russian lines of communication near Gök Tepe, had captured not long before a large batch of rouble notes. These had been quickly bought up by Matthi the Jew at the ridiculously low rate of two silver *krans* for a ten rouble note. That a flimsy piece of paper should be worth even two *krans* had been a source of wonder to the Turkomans, but, as they received value for it, they had concluded that printed paper must possess some mysterious virtue of its own.

Watching O'Donovan carefully unfolding his newspapers, they now assumed that these too were currency, only, being much larger than rouble notes, of infinitely greater value, and the news soon spread that the first remittance of public funds had arrived from the English *Padishah*. His denials that this was so provoked dangerously intense disappointment on the part of some, while others merely assumed that his purpose was to throw dust in their eyes and so secure possession of the treasure for himself. It was only when they observed the use to which O'Donovan put the newspapers after he had read them that the people of Merv finally accepted his assurance that they were not in fact gigantic bank notes.

Nor was this his only worry. Having placed themselves under British rule, his loyal subjects now decided that they must duly hoist the British flag. Pieces of red, blue and white cloth were procured and he was invited to draw a design from which an *usta adam* could manufacture the necessary ensign. But at this stage it occurred to him that by hoisting the British flag without authority he might, as he put it, 'get himself into some scrape'. It was, he tried to explain to his associates, not enough for the *Medjlis* to want to hoist the Union Jack. The sanction of the British Government must also be obtained. If, as he had already suggested, they would write to the British Government and secure their permission, he, for his part, would at once arrange for a Union Jack to be manufactured or even sent out from England. Meanwhile, the crimson banner already flying over his house would meet all immediate requirements and adequately express the feelings of amity entertained by the Government of Merv for that of Great Britain. In this way he succeeded in evading for the time being an awkward issue.

At once he was faced with another. All the horses in Merv, announced Baba Khan, must now be branded with the mark used on British Army horses. This would not only emphasize the link with Great Britain, but would also save the horses from confiscation if the Russians were to overrun Merv. What mark, he inquired, did the British Army use to brand their horses? Not knowing the answer to this question, but equally not wishing to offend Baba Khan, O'Donovan on the chance roughly sketched for him a V.R. surmounted by a crown. That very evening Baba was back with a specially made branding-iron bearing the royal cypher, which, to the accompaniment of much squealing and kicking, was at once applied to the rump of his own charger and of a number of other valuable horses. It was only then that O'Donovan observed that, the *usta adam* having exactly copied his design and then applied it upside down, the mark on the horse was reversed as well as inverted.

Such, meanwhile, was the effect produced on the minds of the population by the events of the last few days that from all over the oasis and from far beyond its borders travellers now began to arrive seeking from the new Khan documents bearing his seal and certifying their desire to become British subjects. In return for these they brought him presents: water-pipes, saddlery, tea-bags, slippers, knitted gun-slings and, in the case of one remote chieftain, three silver watches.

The latter were, it seemed, the first watches ever seen in Merv. Soon a crowd had collected and it was not long before Baba Khan sent one of his cavalry commanders to say that he, too, would like to see a *sahat nameh* or 'hour indicator'. From where he sat, in front of his tent, O'Donovan could see Baba and his suite curiously examining the wonderful machine and half an hour later the cavalry commander returned, but without the watch. The Khan, he said, was most grateful for the kind present. Enraged at this piece of effrontery and knowing the natural cupidity of the Turkomans, O'Donovan revenged himself as best he could on the spur of the moment by sending back a message to say that it had been his intention to present the Khan with a gold watch, but that, as he had now provided himself with a silver one, he was cancelling the order for the more costly present.

Of more interest to O'Donovan than the strange assortment of presents which piled up in his tent were some cases of champagne and a quantity of hams, destined no doubt for some Russian officers' mess and captured together with their owner, a Georgian sutler, by a raiding party operating between Gök Tepe and Askabad. Not having now tasted such things for years, the new *Ichthyar* made a determined effort to obtain one of the hams for his own use. But the pious raiders, having discovered that they were pigs' flesh, immediately buried every single one. Over the champagne they were more lenient, but most of it, needless to say, found its way to the residence of Aman Niaz Khan, one of whose clansmen happened to have made the capture. As for the unfortunate sutler, he was, on O'Donovan's intervention and after payment of a ransom, set free, but only after he had been stripped of his gorgeous national dress: red silk tunic; silver-laced cloth coat; enamelled cartridge cases, silver belt, decorated *hanjar* and lambskin hat.

For the rest, O'Donovan's meals followed the same frugal pattern as those of the other inhabitants of Merv — hot griddled bread, fruit, cheese, sour milk, green tea and, of course, mutton: mutton fat, mutton broth, mutton stew, mutton *pilaf* and mutton pies. Finding the latter, which were known as *sumsa*, more palatable than the rest, he took to ordering them by the dozen from Matthi the Jew. But as soon as this became generally known, his tent filled towards mealtimes with crowds of hungry visitors, all hoping to be asked to partake of this particular delicacy. Foremost among these was Beg Murad, the 'fat, humorous-looking ruffian' whom he had encountered on first arriving in the oasis, who was extravagantly fond of meat pies and, like all his countrymen, always ready for a meal at someone else's expense.

'It was', O'Donovan tells us, 'hateful to eat with these people.' The snatching, gobbling crowd of intruders, who often left him hardly anything to eat himself, got more and more on his nerves. Sometimes he would deliberately fast all day, simply for the pleasure of disappointing them. For, if he did not himself, he was, under local rules of hospitality, under no obligation to provide food for them. Then, tiring of this method, he took to concealing a supply of mutton pies in his saddle-bags. But soon someone betrayed their hiding place to Beg Murad who, more rapacious than the rest, would creep into the tent before dawn while O'Donovan was still asleep, and polish off a whole day's supply before breakfast, then adding insult to injury by waking his involuntary host and asking him if he would not make tea for him, until finally the latter, losing patience, called him a thief to his face and drove him headlong out of his tent — to the vast amusement and delight of all present.

O'Donovan was by now firmly established as a member of Merv society. It was known that he now accepted Alexander the Great as a prophet in addition to Adam, Noah, Moses and David, his intimate knowledge of whose histories stood him in excellent stead. His conversion to Islam was believed to be imminent. Any reluctance he still showed to settle down in Merv for good was attributed to the lack of a wife and he was freely assured that nothing could be easier than to provide him with as many as four should he so desire.

The suspicion that he might be a Russian agent had by now entirely vanished and the conviction had taken firm root that he was a friend and a very valuable friend. Indeed, the mere fact of his presence in the oasis was believed to have checked the Russian advance. But in many ways his position had become more precarious than ever. It was clearly inadvisable for him to appear to be trifling with his hosts' religious or matrimonial proposals. On the other hand, to reject them out of hand might easily produce a crisis. It might equally be the worse for him if the extravagant hopes which his arrival had raised should in the event be disappointed. It was, therefore, with some trepidation that he learned from a news bulletin which had reached him at the beginning of June from Teheran that the British troops at Kandahar, far from advancing to Herat and Merv, as the inhabitants of the oasis now confidently expected, were in all probability to be finally withdrawn from Afghanistan, thus removing the last effective deterrent to a further Russian advance in Central Asia. Should this happen while he was still in the oasis, the ensuing reaction might, he calculated, well prove fatal to him. He accordingly decided to leave at the earliest possible opportunity.

This was easier said than done. At his request, the British Minister at Teheran had duly directed Abbas Khan, the British Agent at Meshed, to write to him in Persian stating that his presence was required at Meshed. On the arrival of the letter, O'Donovan had shown it to the Khans, explaining that he only wanted to pay a short visit to Meshed and would come back as soon as his business there was completed. But their reaction was most unfavourable. His business, they said, could be equally well transacted by letter. To this he replied that he did not know Persian well enough to be able to say all he wanted in a letter. He must go himself. Otherwise there would be endless delays and misunderstandings. Indeed, if he did not go, the British authorities might well gain the impression that he was being detained against his will and that the Mervli were not as sincere in their professions of loyalty and friendship as they would have it believed.

These arguments carried more weight, but there was still a marked reluctance on the part of his fellow rulers to let him go. They seemed to consider his continued presence in Merv as being in some way a guarantee of the success of their plans, to regard him as something between a hostage and a talisman, to be clung to at all costs. 'If once he gets within sight of the gates of Meshed,' he heard one chieftain saying to another, 'depend upon it, we shall have seen the last of him.' 'I could not', is O'Donovan's comment, 'help inwardly complimenting the speaker upon the extreme justness of his ideas; however, I held my tongue.'

Shortly after this an event took place which might well have had the most unfortunate consequences. One day a messenger arrived from Meshed, bearing three letters from Abbas Khan, the British Agent. Of these one was to O'Donovan, summoning him once more to Meshed, and one to the Khans, lending encouragement to their idea of a British alliance. The third, on the other hand, was addressed to a private agent of Abbas, a certain Khodja Kouli, instructing him to do everything in his power to secure the acceptance by the Mervli, not of British, but of Persian sovereignty. All three letters, as it happened, were delivered to Beg Murad, the *sumsa*-stealer, who gleefully handed them over to Baba Khan.

No sooner had Baba read them than, seething with indignation, he rushed round to O'Donovan's tent and threw the letters on the carpet. 'The British agent at Meshed is a traitor,' he shouted, his single eye flashing angrily. 'You must have no dealings whatever with him. See what he writes to me and how differently he writes to Khodja Kouli! He is evidently in the pay of the Persians and we can attach no credit to anything that he says. He summons you to Meshed. I do not believe that the British Minister asked you to go there. It is simply a plot on the part of Abbas Khan to take you away from Merv in order that he may pursue his own machinations the more freely. In future we will pay no attention to letters from Meshed, but only to those which come from the Minister at Teheran or the British Government in England.'

O'Donovan now found himself in a most disturbing situation. There could be no doubt about Abbas's double dealing. And it was on Abbas's testimony that his own allegiance to Great Britain had originally been recognized, and on Abbas's invitation to visit Meshed that he was ultimately counting to get away from Merv. Now all this was once more in question. Even the good faith of the British Government themselves might seem in doubt. Some quick thinking was clearly called for.

With the incriminating letters lying in front of them, there was manifestly no denying Abbas's treachery. The only thing was to play down his importance. O'Donovan therefore asked Baba Khan to recollect that Abbas was only a subordinate who might well be under Persian influence, but whose views were in any case of no importance. Baba, he went on, gamely seeking to recover the initiative, was quite right in saying that they would in future only pay attention to direct communications from the Minister in Teheran or the Government in

London. Had they, by the way, ever forwarded to Teheran the formal application for British protection, which he had suggested they should send? No, replied Baba, a little guiltily, as a matter of fact, they had not, but they would do so immediately.

The initiative had been regained. There would, it was true, be further delay in getting away, while a reply came from Teheran. But at least no irretrievable harm had been done.

Next morning there appeared at Kouchid Khan Kala a *khodja* or scribe, a man of Arab descent, with a great reputation for learning, who was always employed when important documents had to be drawn up. He brought with him in a long cylindrical tin box a roll of documents signed by the Sherif of Mecca, the Khans of Khiva and Bokhara, and other oriental potentates, testifying to his direct descent from Ali and to his right to the title of *Seyd*. He was received with great ceremony and lodged in considerable luxury at the house of Beg Murad, the mutton-pie fancier. It was only that evening, on receiving a bill from Beg Murad for four *krans*, for a portion of snuff, a portion of tea and a portion of opium, that O'Donovan realized that he was to share in the honour of entertaining the *Seyd*. Next day a further bill was presented for the same sum. 'What!' exclaimed O'Donovan, 'has the *Khodja* not yet written the simple document which it is necessary to send to Teheran?' 'No,' came the reply, 'it is a matter of much weight and requires grave deliberation.' 'Well,' replied O'Donovan, 'I will give three *krans* on this occasion. And if necessary I will give two *krans* tomorrow. And if the document is not prepared on the following day, I will give nothing at all.' And with this he waved his hand, 'as a sign that further discussion was needless and useless'.

In the end the document was drawn up and, when the seals of the Chiefs and Chieftains had been affixed, six horsemen set out with it for Persia. With it, O'Donovan dispatched yet another personal letter to Mr Thomson, the British Minister, asking him to send a letter to the Khans saying they it was absolutely necessary for him to visit Persia and bearing the most impressive-looking seals and signatures that he could muster. After which he settled down as patiently as he could to wait for the answer to arrive.

★

The next three or four weeks were a trying time for O'Donovan. He travelled about the oasis, went, in company with Aman Niaz Khan on an *arrack*-drinking and opium-smoking expedition to the square mud castle which Matthi the Jew had built himself outside Kouchid Khan Kala, and, in his own words, 'devoted himself as assiduously as possible to still further studying the characteristics of the Turkomans'. But the truth of the matter was that the Turkomans were beginning to get badly on his nerves. Since arriving in Merv he had gained a considerable reputation as a physician and now to the throngs of visitors who came to his tent in search of free food and political gossip were added vast crowds of would-be patients, recounting at length the most improbable-sounding symptoms and begging for medicine of one kind or another. At first he sought to rid himself of them by dosing them indiscriminately with colossal quantities of croton oil. But the harder he dosed them, the faster they came, until at last his supplies not only of croton oil, but of all other medicaments were completely exhausted. in despair, he now prescribed dandelion juice all round and the whole oasis resounded with the rhythmic pounding of dandelions.

For a while he managed to secure a little more privacy by retiring inside a kind of muslin tabernacle which he had had erected inside his tent and pretending to be asleep. But soon the bolder spirits took to lifting up one side of his Ark, as they called it, and peering underneath, and then he was at their mercy once more. From the moment when the smoke of his fire showed that his morning tea was being brewed, right through the day until late into the night, he was never alone; there was always a crowd of voracious visitors prowling round his redoubt, ready to pounce on any food or drink that might come their way.

His diary gives some indication of his frame of mind. 'These Merv Turkomans', he wrote, 'seem to have nothing to do but loafing about all day from hut to hut to see if they cannot surprise some eatables. They gorge themselves to excess on every possible occasion with greasy food, and are continually ill from indigestion. They throng my house, partly to satisfy their curiosity by staring at me, and partly to devour the greater portion of any food I may have prepared for my own use. In this way, unless one is prepared to feed a dozen persons on each occasion, he has no chance of getting a mouthful from his meal. It is of no use saying that what you are eating is pig, for they eat pork readily. Covetous rapacity seems to be their leading characteristic. They appear to think the whole world bound to contribute to their support, they to give nothing in return.

'To say that both temper and patience have been severely tried during my stay at Merv would be to convey but a very inadequate idea of the physical and moral annoyance I have undergone from the crooked-mindedness and rudeness of these wretched Turkomans. Their craving after the smallest sums of money and their general greed surpass my worst experiences in other parts of the world. I would rather live in a remote Chinese province, or among the dwarf savages of the Malay Archipelago, than at Merv. Their power to inflict annoyance, and their obtuseness to any sense of delicacy, make them a most undesirable race to live among.

'No one who has not suffered as I have among the Merv Turkomans by being constantly intruded upon and persecuted in every way by their abominable presence could appreciate the exquisite luxury of being left in quiet solitude.

'A daily administration of half glasses of *arrack* to patients who require *arrack derman* (spirituous medicine) for internal ailments, aches in their stomachs, and the like. This is all a pretence. It is simply a method of getting half-intoxicated at my expense ... I give replies to the various consultants — on foreign policy, improvements in the fortifications, pains in their joints and stomachs, and soreness in their eyes. I indiscriminately order dandelion juice, and scores of people are to be seen dotting the plain culling that useful plant ... I have stated over and over again that my stock of medicines is at an end; but all in vain. The daily crowd of applicants for remedies for their various bodily ills remains undiminished. Many whose legs and arms have been badly injured by Russian projectiles feel quite scandalized that I cannot restore the use of their limbs, and leave with the profound conviction that I could cure them if I would. If I only had a hundred-weight of antibilious pills, a stone or two of Epsom salts, and a quart of croton oil, I could get on famously, and be first favourite here.

'Relay after relay of these vile beasts of Turkomans render life insupportable during the day and the night, too. One would think they imagined I derived intense pleasure from their uncouth, unfeeling, treacherous presences. The constancy of their intrusion passes all belief. Medical advice about their *kessels* (livers) is the pretence, and each passer-by eyes the door longingly, for he imagines there is a never-ending feast of fat mutton, rice, and *arrack* progressing within. They are like the pestilent flies who vie with them to render life miserable. Ten an hour is a minimum allowance.'

And, on top of all this, there weighed on O'Donovan's mind the knowledge that at any moment a crisis might occur in the affairs of Merv or of Central Asia which would lead to his execution, or, at best, to years of dreary captivity amongst these very Tekkes whom he had come to dislike so much and 'whose conically-formed crania, swelling at the base, and tapering almost to a point backwards, indicated egotism, firmness and ferocity'. 'It is worth while', he wrote at this time, 'to have suffered toothache, to know the enjoyment which accompanies its cessation; and it is well worth while to have lived among the Tekkes, to know the ecstatic delight of parting company with them.'

But if O'Donovan had come to detest the Turkomans, the Turkomans' delight in O'Donovan grew from week to week. Sitting quietly in his tent one day, he was startled by the sudden entry of the Town Crier, followed by six other Turkomans, each carrying in his arms a newly born child. These were then presented to him with a good deal of formality. Though he could not catch the exact words, he gathered that one of the infants was O'Donovan Beg, another O'Donovan Khan, a third O'Donovan Bahadur, and so on. Alarmed, he asked why these babies had been brought to him. Because, came the reply, it was the custom in Merv to give to new-born babies the name of any distinguished stranger who happened to be in the oasis at the time of their birth. 'I felt', he tells us, 'relieved by the explanation, even though I had to give a *peshkesh* of five *krans* for each of my youthful namesakes.'

Still there was no word from Teheran. Then, one sweltering day towards the end of June, as O'Donovan was lying in his tent, disconsolately wondering what fortune held in store for him, his servants announced that Baba and Aman Niaz Khan were without. As they were but rarely seen together, it was clear that something of importance had happened. The curtain at the door was pulled aside and the two Khans entered. Baba was holding a portentous-looking document and wearing an expression of displeasure. 'The British Minister', he said, as he entered the tent, 'is evidently in error. He has addressed his letter to "The Khans of the Otamish and the Toktamish". As Khan of the Toktamish, I am the senior. I cannot understand why this slight has been inflicted on me.'

After O'Donovan had apologized for Mr Thomson's ignorance of precedence and soothed down Baba as best he could, he finally succeeded in getting a sight of the document on which for him so much depended. In it the Minister acknowledged receipt of the Khans' letter proffering allegiance to the Queen of England, which, he said, he had duly transmitted to Her Majesty's Government. He was, he continued, glad to hear that the tribes of Merv were animated by kindly sentiments towards the British Government. He must, however, make it clear that the proposal that the people of Merv should become British subjects was one which, for various reasons, physical as well as political, could not be entertained. Mr O'Donovan, he added, was not an emissary of the British Government, but an agent of the British public, whose duty it was to keep the latter informed of events in the oasis, and it was now 'both desirable and expedient' that they should send him to Persia without delay in order that he might make a personal report.

Having perused the Minister's letter, which was on exactly the lines indicated by O'Donovan, Baba Khan told O'Donovan that he was free to go. 'But', he added, 'before you leave us there must be a general *Medjlis*.' 'Then call it immediately,' replied O'Donovan, knowing all too well what 'immediately' was likely to mean.

And, indeed, the days dragged wearily by and still there were no signs of a *Medjlis*. Every day O'Donovan asked when it was to be called, and every day some reason was found why this was impossible. When one Khan was available, the other had gone on a tour of inspection. By the time the second had returned from his tour, the first was ill. When both were present and in good health, the waters of the dam had risen to such a height that the members of the *Medjlis* were all too busy to attend a meeting.

In the end, O'Donovan could stand it no more. Summoning the

leading chiefs and chieftains to his tent, he issued them with an ultimatum. 'I am going', he said, 'to leave Merv for Meshed in three days.'
And, when there was an outcry, 'I will hear of no objection,' he continued. 'You have told me that since the arrival of the British Minister's
letter I am free to go where I please. If within three days I am not in the
saddle for my destination, I shall haul down my flag as a declaration of
war ... I shall mount and ride away. Prevent me at your peril. It will be
a declaration of war with England if you do, and I shall haul down my
flag.'

'This,' O'Donovan reports, 'fell like a thunderbolt among them.'
But the three days went by and still he had not left the oasis. Nor was
there any sign that his hosts intended to let him go. The ladies of Merv,
announced one chieftain, notorious for his own gallantry with the fair
sex, could not bear to think of his going away — surely he did not want
to distress them.

In the end, however, fortune favoured him. Reports were received
that Russian Cossacks had been seen acting as an escort to men bearing
mysterious machines, presumably engineers with theodolites surveying
the frontier. This was his chance. Taking advantage of the alarm caused
by these signs of renewed Russian activity, he invented, on the spur
of the moment, a meeting of the European Ambassadors to be held at
Meshed, for the purpose of determining the new frontier. The fate of
Merv, he declared, depended on this meeting. Would they not send
him to it as their representative? Surprisingly enough, his stratagem
worked and the *Medjlis* was summoned for July 19th.

It was not yet light when the notables began to assemble, seating
themselves on the sloping shore of the Murgab River, the usual place
of assembly being too small to contain them. Having taken the wise
precaution of first distributing large sums of money amongst those
most likely to influence the outcome of the discussion, O'Donovan
waited impatiently for the summons to join the gathering; waited all
through the morning until finally at two in the afternoon an emissary
with an escort of fifty horsemen arrived to fetch him.

He found the principal chiefs and chieftains seated in a circle by the
water's edge, surrounded by a crowd of many thousands more on foot

and on horse. Above them towered the ramparts of the newly completed fortress. In the centre of the circle was laid a large carpet and on this O'Donovan with due solemnity took his place. Behind him sat Baba Khan with the Old Man of the Sword near by. Aman Niaz, he noticed, was absent and so was Kadjar Khan, his predecessor as *Ichthyar*. Near where the Councillors were sitting a fire was burning at which from time to time one or other of them would light his water-pipe.

On the appearance of the Irishman a sudden hush fell on the crowd. Then Baba Khan asked him if he would address the assembly, before they reached a final decision.

O'Donovan spoke at some length. He recapitulated the arguments which he had used in his earlier speeches and laid particular stress on the imaginary Conference of Ambassadors at Meshed. After he had finished speaking there was silence once more. Only Baba Khan and his councillors whispered together. Then there rang out the tremendous bass voice of the Old Man of the Sword as he called the roll of the chiefs and chieftains.

Aman Niaz and Kadjar alone were absent. 'Where is Kadjar?' asked the Old Man. 'He is absent,' came the answer. 'Why is he absent?' 'He does not admit the jurisdiction of the Council.' 'Where is Aman Niaz Khan?' 'His eyes are sore.' 'How many eyes has he got?' 'Two.' 'He has two eyes, and he is not here. And yet Baba Khan has come, who has but one eye.'

At this rough and ready sally, Baba Khan, his solitary eye aflame, made a ghastly attempt at a grin, and then, raising his voice, asked if any one could say why the Bahadur Khan should not start for Meshed. After some whispering, an ugly-looking man with narrow eyes and high cheekbones said that he did not think that adequate presents had been given to all concerned. Baba retorted that he thought the presents given had been perfectly adequate. 'Oh yes,' said the ugly man, 'I know that yesterday you received a bag of six hundred *krans*. You are all right. But what about those of us who have had nothing?'

Fortunately at this stage, the Old Man of the Sword intervened. 'The Bahadur Khan', he thundered imperiously, rising to his full height, 'came here to serve us and he is going to Meshed to do the same. We Mervli may rob our enemies, but we do not rob our friends.'

Though the meeting dragged on until after sunset, the main issue had now been settled and, in theory at any rate, O'Donovan was free to go. In practice, needless to say, all kinds of reasons were found to delay his departure. Aman Niaz Khan's eyes were still sore. Baba Khan had sprained his ankle. The Russian surveyors made travelling unsafe. At last, however, on July 28th, it was agreed that he should leave on the following day. That night 'a sumptuous banquet' was given in his honour, at which sheep's tail fat flowed in unlimited quantities, and the guests were each served with boiled eggs. After dinner he paid a farewell call on his old enemy Beg Murad, the *sumsa*-stealer, whom he found 'dreadfully ill from having eaten an excessive greasy food', and to whom he gave, as a parting gift, his bedstead and an enormous bottle of pepsin.

At six o'clock next morning O'Donovan was waiting, ready to start. 'July 29th, 1881, six o'clock a.m.,' he wrote in his diary, 'I have put on my boots with the resolution of not taking them off till I reach Meshed.' At ten o'clock he was still waiting. 'There is', he wrote, 'among these people some ineradicable objection to do anything at once. It is now three hours after sunrise and I sit here waiting. Last night I delivered strict orders about being in the saddle at sunrise. I gave out the horse-shoes, even the nails. Now it seems that the "artist", the *usta*, as they are pleased to call him, has lent his hammer to someone who lives sixteen miles off. I am in a violent rage: but what can I do?'

It was midday before his escort finally assembled, each man with his hand on the bridle, awaiting the order to mount. But now there arrived a succession of visitors, bearing gifts. First came Baba and Aman Niaz, with fine Turkoman carpets, then Kadjar Khan with a large copper jug for making tea, and Matthi the Jew with a brass-mounted, iron-headed pipe, while Murad Beg brought a suit of chain armour and a great steel helmet like a dish cover, and someone else a porcelain tea-bowl in a leather case. When all these presents had been duly acknowledged and stowed away on the already over-loaded pack horses, the order to mount was again given.

But now someone remembered O'Donovan's standard, the symbolic crimson banner which floated over his tent. What was to be done with this, now that he was going away? It should remain there, he replied, until his return. And once again he climbed into the saddle. But there was yet another question to be resolved. Who, they asked, was to have charge of his pets? With due care and consideration he distributed them: his tame antelope, his gerfalcon, his jackal, his wolf-cubs and, last but not least, his black kitten, which he sent, with his compliments, to 'the ladies of Merv', who had been so distressed at the prospect of his departure.

At last, at two in the afternoon, the cavalcade set out: O'Donovan and his escort of fifty horsemen, Baba, Aman Niaz, Makdum Kuli, Kadjar and two or three hundred of their followers. Thus accompanied, O'Donovan passed for the last time through the entrance to his redoubt and, with a momentary, but only a momentary, twinge of regret, rode away across the rickety bridge over the Murgab which he had crossed under such different circumstances six months before.

Along the route, the people of Merv were gathered in their thousands to watch him leave and had to be restrained by force from accompanying him across the river. As he rode on his way, he could hear them expressing grave misgivings at his departure and saying that, once he had left, the Russians would come in. But he, for his part, was heartily glad to be going. 'To say', he wrote in his diary, 'that I am delighted to be on the road would be to convey a very slight idea of my satisfaction at leaving Merv. D —— the place!'

At the first halt, Baba, Aman Niaz and the other chiefs and chieftains took leave of him and turned back to Merv, while he, with his escort, continued on his way to Meshed, wondering right up to the last whether it was really the Turkomans' intention to let him go, or whether they would not in the end find some pretext for bringing him back. But his journey, as things turned out, proved uneventful. Following for the most part the same route across the desert as he had taken on his journey to Merv, he and his escort came six days later to the first Persian outposts and, having crossed the mountains, arrived at sunset on August 6th before the gates of Meshed, much to the astonishment of the Persian guards, who were amazed to see so large a body of Turkomans, fully armed and accoutred, boldly demanding admission. 'I have arrived here', he cabled to the *Daily News*, 'after a seven days' weary march across the desert and mountains.' In London, where for months past grave concern had been felt for his safety, the news was received with acclamation.

On reaching Meshed, O'Donovan sent his escort back to Merv, having first provided them with suitable presents for themselves and for their chiefs. The 'Conference of Ambassadors', he told them, had been transferred to Teheran and they, in their innocence, believed him. He himself spent a month in Meshed recuperating and then, at the beginning of September, set out for Teheran on his way to Constantinople and London.

Before leaving Meshed he received from Merv a letter dated August 8th and bearing the seals of Baba Khan, Aman Niaz Khan and seventeen other notables:

May it be known to his honoured mind, *they wrote*, that after Your Excellency's departure Tokme Serdar[1] on the ninth of the present month Ramazan came to Merv; he it was who formerly went to the Emperor of Russia with several Akhal horsemen. No one of the chiefs or elders of the Merv tribe went to him to enquire as to his news or designs. As soon as he appeared they sent you this letter. It is most probable that the purpose of his arrival is to secure in any way that may be possible the submission of the tribes of Merv to Russia, and to incite and stir them up in favour of that Power. In this respect he will spread sedition and commotion amongst the Merv people, either with or without money. The tribes of Merv, after you came to Merv, firmly grasped the skirt of submission to the Queen of England. Now you must issue instructions in what way we should deal in this matter with Tokme Serdar. Assuredly send us a letter, for we will all do as you bid us. As for the rest, Kurban Nazr Bahadur and Kuli Murad Bahadur will represent matters to you by word of mouth; you must accept it as true. Dated twelfth of the month Ramazan 1298 [August 8, 1881]. Salaam. Peace be on him who follows the right guidance.

This letter, in O'Donovan's words, 'will speak for itself'. But, he

[1] The defender of Gök Tepe. He had made his peace with the Russians some months earlier.

tells us, after the answer returned by the British Government, he, for his part, had nothing to say and so left it unanswered.

Two or three weeks later, as he was riding out of Meshed on his way to Teheran, he encountered some Turkoman couriers, who were entering the city as he was leaving it. They were the bearers of another letter from Merv, dated August 26th, 1881. This also 'spoke for itself'. It was addressed to 'His Excellency the Associate of Majesty and Pomp, the Seat of Hope, Mr O'Donovan' and bore the seals of twenty-five notables of Merv.

May this be known [it began] to his illustrious mind. After you went to Meshed, Tokme Serdar came to Merv from the capital of the Russian Government, and incited the people in favour of that Power, desirous of stirring up strife among the tribes. And on the last day of the month of Ramazan an Envoy, by name Khuyuk, came to Merv on the part of Russia, desirous with money and goods to make the tribe of Merv work effectually and strive jealously on behalf of the Russian Government. In the Kingdom of Tejend also, two persons have arrived from the Russians, and they are at the present time there. It is heard, also, that an Envoy from Bokhara, on behalf of the Russians, is about to arrive; so the people of Merv are very distressed and perplexed in their affairs through fear of the Russians. The men, too, from these parts who accompanied you to Meshed, not having met with any specific instructions at your hands, returned to this locality.

Oh, Sir! after your stay at Merv the people thereof all submitted to the British Government. Now that there is a strong probability that the Russian army is on its way to the regions of Merv, we send this letter to your Excellency in the hope that you will devise a remedy in any way you can against the Russian army, and if you cannot do so, send us an explicit reply, so that we may follow our own devices in this matter. We are surprised in this respect, that, so many monarchs having scattered to the winds their money and their force to take Merv, and not having succeeded, yet now that all the people of Merv are willing and ready to submit to and obey the English Government, the latter are not very eager. Dowlet

Bai and Muhammed Murad are sent to your Excellency, so now let us know as quickly as possible how you mean to deal with the Russian army; and should you not think of the Russians, or postpone the matter, do not put the blame on us. The rest will be represented by word of mouth by the two aforesaid persons. Be it accepted as true.

But this letter, too, was left unanswered and its recipient, having read it, continued on his way.

For a time after O'Donovan's departure the chiefs of Merv still clung to the hope that the British might somehow come to their rescue, until the British evacuation of Kandahar finally left them alone and face to face with the Russians. For a few more months the Mervli remained aloof from the conquerors of Gök Tepe. Then, finding that no immediate advance was made towards their oasis and encouraged by the tales of Russian generosity brought back to them by Tokme Serdar and others, gradually a few of them began to appear in the bazaar at Askabad. There they found new and attractive European wares for sale and a ready market for their own produce. Before long they became regular visitors to the Russian outpost. In due course there followed an invitation to the Russian merchants in Askabad from Baba Khan to bring their wares to Merv itself and to sell them there in the bazaar.

To Colonel Baron Aminov, Chief of Staff of the Transcaspian Military District, this was an opportunity to be seized with both hands. From the hills behind Askabad he could look out for twenty miles across the desert in the direction of Merv. What lay beyond, he knew only from guess-work and hearsay. But sooner or later, he calculated, the Russians were bound to continue their advance and, both on military and geographical grounds (for he happened to be an ardent geographer), it seemed to him most desirable to obtain a regular survey of the oasis and its approaches. At the present time, everything, as it happened, favoured such an enterprise. The Governor of Transcaspia, General Röhrberg, had gone to St Petersburg and left him in charge. There was at Askabad a Russian caravan, the owner of which,

Gospodin Kosikh of the firm of Konshin & Company of Moscow, was on the look out for new markets in which to sell his goods. Finally, he had on his own staff the very man for the job: Lieutenant Alikhanov.

Alikhanov was by origin a Moslem from the Caucasus, his name being simply a Russianized form of Ali Khan. His father was a Lesghian chief from Daghestan, who had first fought against the Russians in the Caucasus campaign, but had later become reconciled with them and risen to be a general in the Russian Army. Ten years earlier the young Alikhanov had served under Skobelyov in the Khivan Campaign and for his bravery in the war had been promoted to Major and appointed Aide-de-Camp to the Grand Duke Michael, Viceroy of the Caucasus. In 1875 he had, for fighting a duel with a brother officer, been court-martialled and reduced to the ranks. After this, he had fought as a private soldier in the Russo–Turkish War of 1878 and in 1879 had been sent to Transcaspia, there to join the many officers of broken fortunes who, relegated to Russia's Asiatic frontiers, formed some of the finest fighting material in Kaufmann's and Skobelyov's armies. There, by his courage and other soldierly qualities, he had in due course regained a commission and was now eagerly awaiting some further opportunity of restoring his reputation.

As a Moslem, it was easier for Alikhanov than for a Russian to mix with the Tekkes in disguise though, with his tall stature, ruddy complexion, fair hair and prodigious auburn beard, he looked more like a Scotsman than an Asiatic. On his own responsibility and without reference to St Petersburg, Colonel Aminov now entrusted him with the task of making a survey of Merv, using Kosikh's caravan as a cover. To prepare the way, a Russianized Khivan named Fazil Beg was sent ahead to obtain guides and arrange for the caravan's reception at the Tejend and Merv. The actual party, it was decided, would consist of Kosikh, the merchant, nominally in charge of the caravan, Alikhanov, disguised as his clerk and interpreter, Ensign Sokolyov of the Cossacks, also disguised as a clerk, and an escort of half a dozen well-armed native horsemen.

Starting from Askabad in February 1882, the caravan made its way to Kaka and thence across the desert to Merv. They reached the oasis in the middle of the night in a state of some uncertainty as to the reception likely to await them. But, thanks to the arrangements made on their behalf by Fazil Beg, they were well received by influential friends. Next morning, when it became generally known that a number of Russians had arrived in the oasis, there was considerable excitement in Merv and a Council of Chiefs was held. To these Alikhanov, having first distributed suitable presents, explained that his mission was purely commercial in character and in the end, by a judicious mixture of threats and persuasion, secured permission to stay in the oasis for a number of weeks.

During this period, he himself managed to make a complete reconnaissance of the area, slipping out of his quarters in the early morning disguised as a Turkoman. How far he succeeded in deceiving the inhabitants of Merv as to his true intentions is a matter for conjecture. Certainly they never ceased from voicing their suspicions and setting traps for the Russians the whole time they were there. 'If you are a mere trader, how do you *know* all these things?' they would ask Alikhanov suddenly, after first encouraging him to discourse on the most abstruse subjects. 'Oh, we pick them up at school,' he would hastily reply. 'In Russia the schools are open to everybody.' In the end, however, the rumours of plots to murder them grew so alarming and so persistent that Kosikh, the merchant, refused to stay any longer and they were obliged to leave the oasis.

But Merv was already doomed. Early in 1883 the Mervli, after prolonged negotiations, accepted the suzerainty of Khiva, itself by now a Russian protectorate. Then, a year later, without any provocation from the Tekkes, the Russians suddenly dispatched to the Tejend a force from which a detachment under Alikhanov's command swooped down on Merv. On reaching the oasis, Alikhanov assembled the chiefs and, after telling them that the Tejend force was the advanced guard of a great army, finally induced them to go to Askabad and there offer their submission to the Russians.

'I am happy', telegraphed the Russian Governor of Transcaspia early in February 1884, 'to inform Your Majesty that an assembly held this day at Askabad of the Khans of the four Turkoman tribes of Merv, each one of them representing two thousand tents, declared themselves unconditionally subjects of Your Majesty, confirming the same upon solemn oath taken on behalf of their ownselves and on behalf of all the people of Merv. This decision, according to the statement of the Khans and the delegates, was arrived at by the Turkomans of Merv because they were assured of their inability to govern themselves and were convinced that Your Majesty's powerful Government could alone establish and maintain order in Merv and assure its prosperity.' The Russian conquest of Central Asia was complete.

In Great Britain the attention of the Government and public was focused at the time on the no less disturbing events which were then taking place in the Sudan. It is conceivable that their reaction to Russia's annexation of what had so long been regarded as a vital political and strategical position might otherwise have been stronger and more rapid. As it was, nothing was done for a fortnight. Then, on February 29th, 1884, a long historical memorandum was dispatched by the Foreign Office to St Petersburg, recapitulating the correspondence which had passed between the two Governments on this subject and sadly recalling how often the Russians had assured Her Majesty's Government that they had no intention of occupying Merv. It seemed, therefore, wrote Lord Granville, 'entirely inconsistent with the whole tenor of the mutual explanations between the two Governments that one of them should take a step which appears to be in contradiction with the assurances which have on so many occasions been received both from the Emperor and his Government without any previous communication of their change of views'.

The tone of the Russian reply, when it arrived, was scarcely forthcoming. Russia, wrote M. de Giers, having abstained from observations concerning the transactions by which England, at different periods, had extended her sphere of action along the Indian frontier, had a right to expect the same consideration for the freedom of the decisions demanded by the interests of Russia. And there the matter rested. Meanwhile, for his part in this successful *coup de main*, the red-bearded Alikhanov was duly restored to the rank of major. He was later to become a full colonel and the first Russian Governor of Merv.

Whether or not O'Donovan ever intended to fulfil his promise to return to Merv, he in fact never did so. Not long after his return from Central Asia, he set out once more in pursuit of adventure. His travels took him this time to the Sudan, where, during those same summer months of 1881 which he had spent as Khan of Merv, a new prophet had arisen, Sheik Mohammad Ahmed of Dongola, otherwise known as El Mahdi, the Messenger of God. Thus it was that, when two years later Hicks Pasha's ill-starred expedition set out against the Mahdi, O'Donovan accompanied it as a special correspondent, and, with Hicks and several thousand others, lost his life in the terrible slaughter that ensued.

SUPERIOR PERSON

URING the half century that followed Charles Stoddart's departure for Bokhara, practically the whole of Turkestan had, bit by bit, been brought under Russian domination. With the annexation of Merv the last remaining centre of resistance to Russian encroachment had been removed. Khiva and Bokhara were already Russian protectorates, while the rest of the territories which lay to the north of Persia and Afghanistan, from the Caspian on the west to the Chinese border on the east, were now all directly ruled by Russia. Only here and there in the frontier regions did the ownership of isolated scraps of territory remain in doubt, giving rise every now and then to a border incident such as that which occurred in March 1885, when a clash between Russian and Afghan troops at Penjdeh so stirred public opinion in Great Britain as to bring the two great powers to the brink of war.

Meanwhile, all over Transcaspia and Turkestan Russian garrison towns were springing up and Russian officials and merchants moving in, telegraph lines were being laid and post roads built, while the Transcaspian Railway, begun in 1880 as a military line for use in Skobelyov's Turkoman campaign, had, by the spring of 1888, been carried from the railhead on the shores of the Caspian right through to Samarkand. Thus, in a surprisingly short time, a comprehensive system of communications had been set up and effective military, political and economic ascendancy established throughout the whole area. To many observers, it seemed as though Russia, with new bases established and new lines of communication assured, was now gathering her strength for a fresh advance, an advance through Persia and Afghanistan down into the rich plains of British India.

For the time being, at any rate, the heroic days of Central Asian travel were over. All that the would-be traveller now needed was a Russian travel permit and a railway ticket. Once these had been obtained — and the travel permit was not always easy to secure — he had only to sit quietly in his railway carriage to be rapidly and comfortably conveyed to Samarkand, Bokhara or the Oasis of Merv, unlikely to encounter any worse misfortune than a missed connection, a bout of fever or the loss of a suitcase in regions where ten or twenty years before his very life would have been constantly in danger.

To choose, in these circumstances, between one traveller and another, or, should we say, between one tourist and another, may seem at first sight invidious or indeed superfluous. But of the relatively few Englishmen who in those early days of Russian rule were admitted to Turkestan, none was better equipped to observe or, for that matter, more worthy of study for his own sake, than the Honourable George Nathaniel Curzon, Fellow of All Souls College, Oxford, and Member of Parliament for Southport. Indeed it would have been hard to find a better informed, a more enthusiastic, or a more painstaking traveller than this promising young Tory politician, with the pink cheeks, sleek hair and somewhat rigid manner, whose 'air of ineffable superiority' had led the *Observer* to remark not long after his election to Parliament that 'he had always the same appearance of being a distinguished historical personage sitting for his portrait'.

In pursuance of what he liked to call his 'middle-class method', George Curzon would carefully read up his subject before setting out on his travels, note down during the journey every scrap of information that came his way and, on his return, carry his investigations yet a stage further by the 'subsequent study of every available authority'. Only then would he commit the results to paper in the grandiose, if at times somewhat pretentious, prose of which he was master. On this occasion his subject was one that fascinated him. For him the East possessed a spell that throughout his life was to hold him enthralled, that was linked in his mind with his passionate belief in Britain's Imperial Destiny. 'Asia', he wrote to a friend, 'looms before me, vast, magnificent, inspiring.' And now in the summer recess of 1888 he was setting out for Bokhara, almost the first Englishman to make the journey since Dr Wolff.[1] It was an undertaking in every way calculated to appeal to him.

[1] He had, in fact, been preceded that summer by Mr Dobson, the correspondent of *The Times* newspaper and in 1882 by the Rev. Dr Lansdell, a Russophile clergyman.

With those earlier travellers who 'pursued their explorations slowly and laboriously, either disguised or armed to the teeth, amid suspicious and fanatical peoples, over burning deserts and through intolerable sands', George Curzon did not 'presume to enter into the most remote competition'. As a politician, he approached a problem 'almost exclusively political, from a political point of view'. His journey, 'taken under circumstances of exceptional advantage and ease', lay through a region of which the interest 'consisted no longer in its physical remoteness and impenetrability, but rather in the fact that those conditions have just been superseded by a new order of things capable at any moment of bringing it under the stern and immediate notice of Englishmen, as the theatre of imperial diplomacy; possibly — *quod di avertant omen* — as the threshold of international war'. What he tells us of his travels and of the impressions he brought back from them carries our story a stage farther. It allows us to observe the initial phases of a new process, a process which, with interruption, has gone on ever since. 'Before our eyes', in the traveller's own characteristically grandiloquent words, 'the sands of an expiring epoch are fast running out; and the hour-glass of destiny is once again being turned on its base.'

On a fine September afternoon in 1888, barely four months after the official opening of the Transcaspian Railway, Mr Curzon, having arrived the afternoon before from Tiflis, embarked at Baku in the paddle-steamer *Prince Bariatinski*, a no longer very new craft belonging to the Caucasus and Mercury Company. Renouncing for this September the country house parties he enjoyed so much — 'a large slice out of the happiness of the year. But I think I am right' — he had travelled out from England two or three weeks earlier by way of St Petersburg and Moscow. Before leaving London he had been assured by the representatives of the Wagon-Lits Company that all arrangements for his journey to Central Asia had been made and a special permit, an *autorisation spéciale*, obtained for him to visit Transcaspia.

On his arrival at St Petersburg, however, he had found that this was not so. For the issue of the permit in question, without which the journey could not be undertaken, it was, it seemed, necessary to obtain the agreement of no less than five different independent or semi-independent authorities: the Governor-General of Turkestan; the Governor-General of Transcaspia; the Head of the Asiatic Department of the Foreign Office; the Minister for Foreign Affairs; and the Minister of War. So far, not one of these had signified his assent. Nor did they seem very likely to do so. The Minister for War was on tour with the Tsar. The Ministry for Foreign Affairs were dubious. The Governors of Turkestan and Transcaspia had not answered the telegrams that had been sent to them. There were rumours of a breakdown on the line and of trouble on the Afghan border, while General Annenkov, who had built the railway and had promised to arrange everything, was believed, for his part, to be in Nice.

By the time George Curzon left St Petersburg, the permit had still not been granted. On reaching Moscow, he had been advised on the highest authority not to persist in the attempt. The Minister for War was, he learned, refusing his consent in order to annoy the Ministry for Foreign Affairs, a department which he cordially disliked. For all this, Curzon, after waiting in Moscow for a week, had pushed on to the Caucasus, and there, three days later, had received the unexpected news that permission had after all been granted. Casting about as usual for new methods of annoying the Minister of Foreign Affairs, the Minister for War had, it appeared, finally decided to vent his spite on his colleague by suddenly granting the Englishman the permission he was seeking on his own authority without so much as informing him. And so, profiting by this interdepartmental feud rather than suffering from it, Curzon had hurried on to Baku to book his passage before any of the authorities concerned could change their minds.

The sun was setting behind the pink cliffs of the Apsheron Peninsula as the *Prince Bariatinski* put out from Baku harbour into the Caspian, and for a long way out to sea the surface of the water gleamed dully under the metallic lustre of the floating oil. In the sky above the Baku refineries hung a leaden canopy of smoke and the cloying stench of petroleum pervaded everything.

At sunrise next morning a row of rocky peaks could be seen to the north-east. These were the mountains behind Krasnovodsk, the first Russian settlement on the eastern shore of the Caspian. As the ship

came nearer, low sandhills came into view, clean, yellow and ubiquitous, fringing the shore or distributed in melancholy islets over the
bright blue surface of the bay. They now entered a narrow channel,
at the end of which a collection of masts and funnels and several piers
and wharves seemed to indicate considerable activity, and at half past
two in the afternoon the *Prince Bariatinski* was moored to the landing
stage of Üzün Ada, where the entire population of the settlement had
gathered to watch her arrival.

The town of Üzün Ada, or Long Island, was at that time the starting
point of the Transcaspian Railway. It lay under the brassy glare of the
Central Asian sun, a nondescript collection of wooden shacks and shops
and sheds built on a long, low, straggling island of dazzling yellow
sand, midway between the dazzling blues of sky and sea. On the piers
and wharves were bales of cotton and other merchandise. The population, Curzon discovered, numbered eight hundred, and from the fact
that during the four hours he spent there he discovered a toy-shop he
concluded that children must actually 'be born and exist in this God-
forsaken place'. Eventually the time came to start. Trudging through
ankle-deep sand to the railway station, which, they noted, possessed no
platform, the passengers clambered up into their comfortable new
second-class carriages and the train, having steamed at a leisurely pace
across the causeway which linked the island to the mainland, 'plunged',
in our traveller's vivid phrase, 'into the sullen dunes of the desert'.

Passing between the peaks of the Greater and Lesser Balkan Ranges,
round which Arminius Vambery and his fellow pilgrims had skirted
so painfully a quarter of a century before, the train emerged three or
four hours later into the utter desolation of the Kara Kum. At nightfall
the temperature in the railway carriage dropped sharply, as it always
does in the desert, and Curzon was glad of the blankets, coverlets and
rugs which he had prudently brought with him.

All next day they travelled at a speed of twelve miles an hour across
that tawny and interminable plain. To the north, nothing was now
visible save the dreary waste of the desert, stretching away with
depressing uniformity to a blurred and distant horizon. To the south,
for mile upon mile, splendid and remote above the haze, rose the
amethyst barrier of the Persian mountains.

At two-thirty in the afternoon the train stopped at a station: Gök Tepe. Only a few yards from where the railway line now ran rose the massive ruins of the great Tekke stronghold. In the centre stood the main gate of the fortress, from which only seven years before the defenders had four times swept down on the besieging force like a tornado and four times been repulsed. Near by, great gaps marked the breaches made by the two Russian mines and the crumbling walls were still pitted with old shell holes. Clambering up the ruined bank to the ramparts, Curzon, who possessed a vivid imagination and was accompanied by an actual eye-witness of the siege, stood and looked down on the desolate enclosure, where, seven years after the great massacre the scattered bones of the vanquished still lay bleaching in the sun.

The country now became more fertile and from the train window could be seen the local Turkomans in their dilapidated cotton dressing gowns and big brown sheepskin bonnets, cultivating the land, tending their flocks or riding quietly along on their donkeys, father and son as often as not bestriding the same animal. 'Who', asks our traveller, 'would divine in these peaceful and unimposing rustics the erewhile scourge and man-hunter of the desert?'

An hour or two after leaving Gök Tepe the train reached Askabad, now the capital of Transcaspia and residence of the Governor and Commander-in-Chief. The platform of the large and well-appointed station was crowded and a number of droshkies awaited the arrival of the train. A respectable meal could be had at the buffet and a samovar dispensed excellent tea. The town itself, now the seat of a considerable garrison, had a flourishing appearance, boasting a printing press, a photographic establishment and European shops and hotels. It was at this time still almost entirely a Russian settlement, the Turkomans, for their part, preferring the freedom of the desert. The houses were for the most part one-storied and freely bedaubed with white. A small fort recalled the not so far distant days when this was an outpost surrounded by hostile territory, and in the centre of the town an obelisk commemorated the Russians killed at Gök Tepe.

From Askabad, Curzon was told, the Russians had built a broad military road running straight to the Persian frontier. Nor, in the

political climate then prevailing, was he particularly reassured to hear
Russian officers talk openly of the Shah as a vassal and of Persia as
another Khiva or Bokhara. Northern Persia and Khorasan were, he
observed, now entirely at Russia's mercy. The Transcaspian Railway
'commanded along its entire length the northern flank of Khorasan',
'a sword of Damocles' perpetually suspended above the Shah's head.
Here was yet another cause for uneasiness. 'At any moment', he wrote,
'we may find that the centre of interest has shifted from the Afghan to
the Persian frontier.' And, in a letter to a friend, 'this railway makes
them prodigiously strong. And they mean business'.

A hundred miles farther on, at Dushak, the line reached the point
where it came closest to Afghanistan and also, incidentally to Chaman,
the nearest railhead in British India. How soon would it be before the
gap between the two systems was bridged and it became possible to
travel right through to Quetta and the Bolan Pass? And what would be
the military, political and economic implications of such a development? How far, he wondered, was Skobelyov's famous plan for the
invasion of India still a reality? All these made fascinating subjects for
speculation.

At Dushak, where the line takes a turn to the north-east, the train
left the Persian mountains behind it and was soon passing through the
jungle-covered swamps and marshes of the Tejend Oasis, where
Makdum Kuli and his followers had taken refuge after Gök Tepe.
Then there was sand again for another fifty miles, then more vegetation, and then, on the early morning of the following day, the
second after leaving the Caspian, they glided gently into a station
which bore, displayed for all to see, the historic and once mysterious
name of Merv.

A visitor who had expected some signs of the former splendour of
the Queen of the World to have clung to the modern Merv would
have been sadly disillusioned. Curzon, who had read the dispatches of
Edmund O'Donovan, knew better, but even so he was disappointed
by what he saw: some station buildings, two or three streets of irregular wooden houses and that was all. In the evenings the main saloon of
the mud-built Grand Hotel served as a *café-chantant*. A few hundred
yards away, beyond the muddy stream of the Murghab, rose the

crumbling walls of the great fortress of Kouchid Khan Khala inside which had now been built a house for the Governor, a little Russian church and a few other whitewashed European buildings.

But if Curzon could see in Merv no trace of that city's ancient glories, he found there fresh proof of Russian military strength and also of the Russian talent for winning over former enemies. In addition to two battalions of the line, a regiment of Cossacks and a company of sappers, the Merv garrison now numbered three squadrons of the newly raised Turkoman Horse, a native force calculated to provide a congenial occupation for the more dangerous and turbulent elements of the local population. Volunteers, it seemed, had poured in, including a number of officers and men who had fought against Skobelyov at Gök Tepe, and who, clad in their national dress but bearing Russian arms, had already greatly distinguished themselves in the frontier clash of 1885, charging down with gusto on their hereditary enemies the Afghans. Curzon had, he tells us, hoped to find at Merv, the Governor, the famous red-bearded Colonel Alikhanov, for whom he had brought a letter of introduction. But on arrival he learned that the Colonel had left shortly before for the frontier with a Russian infantry battalion and a squadron of Turkoman cavalry for the purpose of making one of those periodic military demonstrations against the Afghans which at that time had such a disturbing effect on British public opinion.

Of the ease with which the Russians assimilated their former opponents George Curzon was to find further evidence on his return to Baku, where, drawn up on the landing stage, ready to greet the Governor-General, were a number of gorgeously clad Turkomans, robed in magnificent velvet or embroidered *khalats*, their breasts ablaze with decorations. At the head of the line was a dignified-looking personage with an immense pair of silver epaulettes. This, it seemed, was none other than O'Donovan's friend Makdum Kuli Khan, the heroic defender of Gök Tepe. Reconciled to Russia at an early date, he had gone to Moscow to attend the Tsar's coronation in 1883 and was now a full colonel in the Russian Army and Governor of the Tejend Oasis, where only a few years before he and his followers had taken refuge from the Russians after the siege. Next to him came his brother Yussuf Khan and two or three more hereditary chieftains, and finally the one-eyed Baba Khan, now a Russian major. Aman Niaz, Curzon was told, was now also an officer in the Russian service. 'I do not think', he wrote afterwards, 'that any sight could have impressed me more profoundly with the completeness of Russia's conquest, than the spectacle of these men, only eight years ago the bitter and determined enemies of Russia on the battlefield, but now wearing her uniform, standing high in her service, and crossing to Europe in order to salute as their sovereign the Great White Czar.'

There was, however, one notable absentee. Kadjar Khan, the old *Ichthyar*, whom O'Donovan had displaced, was not at Baku. He, it seemed, had resisted the Russians to the last and was now held as a political prisoner in St Petersburg.

Continuing his journey, Curzon caught from the window of his railway carriage a passing glimpse of all that was now left of the ancient cities of Merv. 'The spectacle', he writes, 'of walls, towers, ramparts and domes, stretching in bewildering confusion to the horizon, reminds us that we are in the centre of bygone greatness ... very decrepit and sorrowful looked these wasting walls of sun-dried clay, these broken arches and tottering towers; but there is magnificence in their very extent, and a voice in the sorrowful squalor of their ruin.' Then, giving free rein to his literary gifts: 'In these solitudes', he continues, 'the traveller may realize in all its sweep the mingled gloom and grandeur of Central Asian scenery. Throughout the still night the fire-horse, as the natives have sometimes christened it, races onward, panting audibly, gutturally, and shaking a mane of sparks and smoke. Itself and its riders are all alone. No token or sound of life greets eye or ear; no outline redeems the level sameness of the dim horizon; no shadows fall upon the staring plain. The moon shines with dreary coldness from the hollow dome, and a profound and tearful solitude seems to brood over the desert. The returning sunlight scarcely dissipates the impression of sadness, of desolate and hopeless decay, of a continent and life sunk in a mortal swoon. The traveller feels like a wanderer at night in some desecrated graveyard, amid crumbling tombstones and half-obliterated mounds. A cemetery, not of hundreds of years but of thousands, not of families or tribes but of nations and empires, lies outspread around him; and ever and anon, in falling tower or shattered arch, he stumbles upon some poor unearthed skeleton of the past.'

The oasis, with its irrigation ditches and cultivated fields, continued for another thirty or forty miles, after which the desert began again. 'The sorriest waste', Curzon calls it, 'that ever met the human eye. East and west, north and south, stretches a troubled sea of sand, each billow clearly defined and arrested as it were in mid career, like an ocean wave curving to fall. I never saw anything more melancholy than the appearance of this wilderness, and its sickle-shaped dome-like ridges of driven sand with smoky summits, succeeding each other with the regularity of infantry files.'

Finally, after a whole day of this desolation, our travellers once again emerged from the desert and, after crossing six miles of orchards and gardens, came late that night to the banks of the River Oxus, 'rolling its stately burden down from a hoar antiquity through the legends and annals of the East. There in the moonlight gleaming before us is the broad bosom of the mighty river that from the glaciers of the Pamir rolls its 1500 miles of current down to the Aral Sea'. In George Curzon's ears, the words of the poet Arnold were, he tells us, continually ringing:

> But the majestic river floated on
> Out of the mist and hum of that low land
> Into the frosty twilight, and there moved
> Rejoicing through the hushed Chorasmian waste
> Under the solitary moon.

But already the train was cautiously feeling its way across the temporary wooden bridge which the Russian engineers had built over the river, and Curzon, a conscientious traveller if ever there was one, was making his usual searching inquiries into the character and composition of this 'inelegant structure'. It was, he soon discovered, 2000 yards long, had cost £30,000 to build, rested on 3000 piles, had been put up in 103 days and took fifteen minutes to cross. Beneath the bridge could be seen some of the boats of the much-vaunted Oxus Flotilla, which, in the heated imagination of some Russian patriots, would provide an alternative line of advance on Afghanistan. For the moment, however, its resources consisted of two small paddle steamers and two large barges and did not seem to constitute a very serious threat to anybody.

Five or six miles before reaching the Oxus, the railway had entered Bokharan territory and they were now not more than a hundred miles from the capital. As they continued their journey next day, a new country spread before them, no mere oasis in the desert, but a region long and habitually fertile. 'Great clumps of timber', writes Curzon, 'afforded a spectacle unseen since the Caucasus; and large walled enclosures, over-topped with fruit-trees, marked the country residences of Bokhariot squires.' Finally, in the early afternoon there appeared above the trees to the north of the line a tall, graceful minaret and two large domes, and they knew that they had reached *Bokhara es Sherif*, the famous city of Bokhara.

The station, they found when they reached it, was at a distance of ten or twelve miles from the town. The inhabitants, it appeared, had at first viewed the advent of the railway with grave misgivings, calling it the Devil's Wagon, and had asked that it should be kept well away from the city. This suited the Russians, who seized the opportunity to start building a rival Russian town round the station with a Russian garrison to guard it, a firm foothold in the very centre of the Emir's dominions. Then, no sooner was the railway working, than the apprehension of the inhabitants turned to ecstasy and the trains were boarded as they came in by struggling crowds of native passengers who waited patiently under the blazing sun or the drenching rain for the engine to puff and the train to move.

At the railway station, the travellers were met by an open carriage drawn by a *troika* or team of three horses which had been sent from the Russian Embassy. Blinding clouds of white dust rolled along the road to the city which was thronged by a jostling crowd of horses, donkeys, camels and high-wheeled native carts. Passing between vineyards, cornfields, melon plantations and orchards of mulberries, apricots, peaches and figs, with here and there a cluster of clay-built farmsteads, they came at last to the massive walls of the city with their lofty buttresses and towers and, entering one of the great gates, made their way through a bewildering labyrinth of streets and alleys to the house of the Russian Resident, the only foreign representative in Bokhara.

By the time they reached their destination, the sun was sinking. As its last rays lit up the horizon, throwing the outline of domes and towers into sharp relief, the cool evening air resounded to a chorus of piercing cries, as the muezzins called the people to prayer from a hundred minarets. For a minute or two there was a babel of sound. Then all sank into silence. The shadows descended. And soon nothing could be heard save the melancholy beat of the night watchman's drum as he patrolled the dark, empty streets.

The Embassy was a large native house, placed at the disposal of the Russians by the Emir, who on this pretext had confiscated it from its former owners. It possessed an extensive fruit garden surrounded by a high clay wall. In the outer court sat the Emir's Master of the Horse, whose duty it was to keep the Resident supplied with servants, horses, groceries and food and who spent the day smoking his pipe and tranquilly surveying operations. In another court were picketed the horses of the Embassy Guard, consisting of twenty Cossacks of the Ural. In the next were several rooms for visitors, each furnished with a carpet, a table and a rope bedstead; and in a fourth were the offices and reception rooms of the Embassy, all in the same unpretentious style. Washing, the visitors found, was a problem. All that could be produced was a brass ewer, about the size of a teapot, from which water was poured into a small bowl. Curzon, however, being an experienced traveller, had brought with him an india-rubber bath with which, he tells us, he created a great sensation.

Each day attendants would bring to the Embassy mutton, chickens and fruit. Doubt as to their time of arrival and the quantities they would bring rendered the hours of meals rather uncertain. But every morning a strange collection of sugar plums, sweetmeats, little cakes, dried raisins and a huge flat slab of brown bread would also appear as a token of the traditional hospitality of the Emir — rather to the embarrassment of the recipients, who did not find these delicacies altogether to their taste and could not think what to do with them.

In the Resident's absence from Bokhara the travellers were made welcome by the *chargé d'affaires*, a much occupied official, who, in addition to his other duties, was constantly obliged to attend to deputations of the Emir's Ministers and other gorgeously robed visitors. The importance of the Russian Embassy was universally realized and, if lost in the intricate maze of narrow, winding streets, it was only necessary to ask for *Elchi Kaneh*, 'the Embassy', to be shown the way there at once.

Having climbed to the highest point of one of Bokhara's many cemeteries, George Curzon could see the city spread out all round him: the Ark or Citadel, the Registan, the Great Minaret, crowned by an enormous stork's nest, the Covered Bazaar, the ruined *pishtaks* of the *medressehs* and the blue-green domes of the mosques, and, all around them, a sea of flat clay roofs broken here and there by courtyards and gardens. From where he stood he could distinguish the single turquoise dome of the Great Mosque, the Musjid Kalian, where each Friday the Emir worshipped in the presence, theoretically, of the entire population and, opposite it, the twin domes of the Mir Arab, the largest of all the *medressehs*. It was, he was told, the boast of a devout Moslem that in Bokhara he could worship Allah in a different mosque every day of the year — a claim which, with characteristic regard for accuracy, he tells us that he considered to be in all probability exaggerated. But, even allowing for exaggeration, there must, he admitted, be at least a hundred and eighty mosques and seventy or eighty *medressehs*.

In the streets, Curzon admired the dignified passers-by with their fine beards and their large snow-white turbans and brilliantly coloured robes. 'A statelier urban population', he writes, 'I never saw.' The women, their features hidden behind thick black horsehair veils, their figures wrapped in loose blue cotton dressing-gowns, their feet encased in big leather boots, he found considerably less ornamental than the men. 'Bokhara', he remarks, 'may have its Poole, but it certainly lacks a Worth.'

He himself, needless to say, was easily distinguishable as a foreigner. 'For an Englishman,' he tells us, 'a pith helmet, similar to those worn in India, is a useful protection, but does not seem to be affected by the Russians. The latter wear the universal flat white cap, with cotton crown. It ... is the most serviceable and least conspicuous headpiece that can be worn, the more so as the calico covering is removable and can be washed.'

On some of his walks abroad Curzon was accompanied by a knowledgeable young Bokharan who went by the name of Captain Haider Khoja Mirbadalev and proved an agreeable companion and an excellent guide. Taken from Bokhara as a boy, he had been educated and half-Russianized at Orenburg and had subsequently been commissioned in the Imperial Russian Army. He had now returned to his native city, where, thanks to his knowledge of foreign parts, he occupied a position of some importance.

But even when he ventured out alone, Curzon was relieved to find little or no evidence of the spontaneous hostility to Europeans which he had been led to expect. The fanaticism of the Bokharans had either vanished on closer contact with civilization or else was now prudently disguised. What a few years before had been a haunt of zealots was now a city of merchants. Everyone, he found, was ready to help him in his untiring quest for information, and acquaintances of the day before would salute him as he passed by placing their hands on their breasts and stroking their beards — a form of salutation which embarrassed the meticulous Englishman who had no beard to stroke and feared that it might be thought undignified or contrary to etiquette to finger the empty air.

The bazaar, in particular, provided endless opportunities for contact with the local population. Bargaining, Curzon discovered, was only to be pursued with great patience and much cajolery. If he tried to buy anything, a crowd would at once collect round him, following each stage of the transaction with keen interest and loudly applauding the rival strategy. The object in question would be passed from hand to hand and each onlooker would give his own opinion. A middleman would then usually detach himself from the crowd and with a great show of disinterestedness affect to conciliate the owner and complete the bargain — all this to the accompaniment of a great deal of gesticulation and elaborate, leisurely calculations on the abacus. Most Bokharan merchants, he found, proved particularly amenable to personal attention. They liked to be whispered to and patted on the back and if, after a series of encounters lasting sometimes several days, you could finally get hold of them by the hand and give it a hearty shake, the purchase was as good as yours.

In 1888, the Great Bazaar or *Char Su* still possessed much of its medieval magnificence. Covering an enormous area of ground, it consisted of thirty or forty different bazaars, of twenty-four caravan-serais for the storage of goods and accommodation of merchants and of six vaulted *ronds-points*, from which radiated the principal alleyways, shaded with mats from the sun and crowded with human beings on donkey-back, on horse-back and on foot. On either side of these narrow lanes squatted the merchants in their small cupboard-like shops. In one part, the armourers still forged their intricately decorated weapons of war. In another, the saddlers offered for sale ivory-inlaid saddles and gold-embroidered velvet saddle-cloths. In yet others were the bazaars for harness, carpets, rope, iron and hardware. Elsewhere, the jewellers, the gold and silver smiths, the brass and copper workers, the lambskin sellers, the boat-makers, the snuff-sellers, the druggists, the silk-merchants and the vendors of cosmetics, all plied their trades and sold their wares.

But already more and more goods from Russia were beginning to make their appearance. Mass-produced Russian calicoes and cottons were sucessfully competing with the more beautiful native materials, while hideous brocades from Moscow debauched the instinctive good taste of the East. Russian samovars were everywhere. Russian iron, hardware and porcelain had supplanted the local products and Russian ink, pens, writing-paper and note-books were now exposed for sale. Kerosene lamps were taking the place of mutton-grease candles and sewing-machines buzzed in the cotton-seller's shop. In 1873 there had only been one Russian merchant in Bokhara. As lately as 1885 only one Russian commercial firm had been represented there. Now, with the advent of the railway, a score of enterprises had opened branches in Bokhara and were already doing profitable business amounting annually to many millions of roubles.

In some respects, however, foreign influence in Bokhara was less immediately noticeable. The Bokharan Court was still surrounded by all its old pomp and mystery. The Emir, Seid Abdul Ahad, a young man

of twenty-eight or twenty-nine who had succeeded his father Mozaffur-
ed-Din in 1885, was still treated as a sort of demi-god whom inferior
beings might only admire from a distance. Once Curzon encountered
him, tall, black-bearded and dignified, clad in magnificent robes,
riding through the bazaar at the head of a long cavalcade. No glimpse,
the travellers were told, was ever caught of the royal harem and they
were shocked to learn that *batchas* or dancing-boys 'were still among the
inseparable accessories of the palace'.

Nor had there so far been any radical change in the country's
judicial system. Criminals were still thrown headlong from the top of
the Great Minaret or Tower of Death, to be dashed to pieces in the
street below, and the visitors were told that shortly before their arrival
at least one condemned murderer had been disposed of in an even less
enlightened way. After first being beaten with sticks and cut about with
knives by his victims' relations, his eyelids had been cut off or, according to another account, his eyes gouged out. He had then been
tied to the tail of an ass and dragged through the streets of the market
place where his body was quartered and thrown to the dogs.

Sauntering out early one morning in search of first-hand information,
Curzon tried to gain access to the Ark or Citadel, where Stoddart and
Conolly had endured so much, but was stopped and sent back by the
significant frowns and gesticulations of a crowd of natives sitting in the
doorway. One of his companions, however, who managed somehow
to penetrate into the interior of the State Prison, came upon a hundred
or more prisoners huddled together in one low cell, chained to each
other by the necks and wearing manacles on their hands and fetters on
their feet so that they could neither stand nor turn nor move. All of
which seemed to show that the Russians, while doing everything to
strengthen their own military, political and economic hold on Bokhara,
had so far been careful not to interfere more than was strictly necessary
with long-established local customs and traditions.

Under the Treaty of 1873 the Emir retained the right to maintain his
own army which now numbered some 12,000 men and was rumoured
to include two squadrons of cavalry and ten pieces of artillery. The
uniform worn by his troops consisted of a black sheep-skin shako, a
scarlet tunic with a leather belt and a cartridge pouch, abundant

pantaloons and big leather boots. Each soldier carried a sword as well as some kind of musket.

Paramount importance was attached to precision in drill. The words of command, originally framed by a Cossack deserter named Popov, were delivered in a mixture of Russian, Tartar and English. They were supplemented and to some extent replaced by one hundred and fifty different bugle-calls which were said to take several years to learn. Not all the movements executed were strictly orthodox. Thus, where a British soldier would have stood at ease, the Bokharan sat smartly down on the ground. At yet another bugle-call, the soldiers of the Emir would lie on their backs and kick their heels vigorously in the air. This movement, it seemed, had been copied from the Russians who, after crossing a river in the course of a battle against the Bokharans, had been ordered to lie down and shake the water out of their boots — a manœuvre to which the retreating Bokharans attributed a magical share in the eventual Russian victory.

Of the officers Curzon tells us only that their uniform was fantastic and their appearance contemptible. Asked for his opinion of the Bokharan Army as a whole, a Russian general replied with an indulgent smile that they were 'possibly better than the Persians'.

For his own part, Curzon left Bokhara with a feeling of satisfaction that he had seen it still in the twilight of its glory. 'Already', he writes, 'the mist of ages is beginning to rise and dissolve. The lineaments are losing their beautiful vague mystery of outline. It is something in the short interval between the old order and the new, to have seen Bokhara, while it may still be called the Noble, and before it has ceased to be the most interesting city in the world.'

From Bokhara to Samarkand, a distance of about a hundred and fifty miles, the railway followed the valley of the River Zerafshan or Gold Strewer, perhaps the most fertile region of Central Asia. A network of side-streams and irrigation canals, their course marked by lines of willows and osiers, criss-crossed the countryside and on either side of the line a succession of well-stocked orchards and vineyards stretched away as far as the eye could reach. At Katta Kurgan the train entered what was now Russian territory, having been annexed from Bokhara after the war of 1868, and four or five hours later drew into Samarkand railway station.

As lately as 1870, Curzon recalled, Prince Gorchakov had assured Sir Andrew Buchanan, the British Ambassador in St Petersburg of the Tsar's desire to restore Samarkand to Bokhara, an undertaking which, says Curzon, only a Russian diplomat could have given and in which only a British diplomat could have believed. Certainly by 1888 it was clear enough that the Russians had come to stay. From the station a broad avenue of poplars led to the new Russian town, where low, white houses stood out against a background of trees and rivulets of running water bordered broad boulevards planted with poplars and acacias. Embowered here and there amid these agreeable surroundings were some larger buildings: the Governor's residence, standing in a fine park; the Orthodox Church, with its blue, star-spangled domes; and the Officers' Club. There were also some public gardens containing a lake. Only the hotel was disappointing — 'the humble lodgment', Curzon calls it, 'which presumed at the period of my visit to call itself a *Gastinitsa*'.

The new Russian town was separated from the native city by a bare, stony hill, once the site of the fortress and palace of the sovereign and now occupied by the trim outline and modern fortifications of the new Russian citadel. Beyond this, on the other side of a slight valley, stood the ancient city of Tamerlane, with its flat clay roofs, its mosques and *medressehs*, its soaring, glittering arches and enamelled domes, much as it had appeared twenty-five years earlier to Arminius Vambery, though here and there a Russian shell, fired during the siege, had helped on the work of time and finally demolished some tottering minaret or blown a fresh breach in an already crumbling wall. On the right, from where Curzon stood surveying the scene, the turquoise dome of Tamerlane's burial place, the Gur Emir, emerged from a cluster of fruit trees. In the centre stood the three *medressehs* that frame the Registan: Ulug Beg, Shir Dar and Tillah Kari. On the left rose the gigantic ruins of the mosque and *medresseh* of Bibi Khanum, the Chinese princess who became Tamerlane's wife, while farther away on a hillside were clustered the terraced cupolas of Shakh Zindeh, the Living King.

George Curzon, for his part, carefully inspected each monument in turn; deriving at the tomb of Tamerlane melancholy inspiration from the thought that he stood above the dust of one who was a king among statesmen and a statesmen among kings; reaching the conclusion in the Registan that nothing in the East, or indeed in Europe, approached the massive simplicity and grandeur of its three great *medressehs*, noting that their minarets seemed slightly out of the perpendicular, noting also the influence on architecture of country, climate and natural resources; 'briefly dismissing' the 'remaining ruins'; and finally witnessing, from the hill above the tomb of Shakh Zindeh, one of those Eastern sunsets which 'though they cannot compete with the troubled grandeur of our Western skies, are yet incomparable in their tranquil glory'.

It was not until he had left Samarkand and the terminus of the railway far behind him and was on his way to Tashkent across the Hungry Steppe that Curzon fully realized the relative advantages of second-class railway travel. The journey of 190 miles by *tarantass* occupied thirty hours. The air-cushion with which he had prudently provided himself proved 'invaluable', it is true. But what was one air-cushion in 'a kind of ramshackle wooden boat, resting on long wooden poles, which themselves repose on the wooden axles of wooden wheels'? 'Tossed about like a cork on troubled water', it was not long before he had taken a strong dislike to this 'sorrowful and springless vehicle'. Nor was he any better pleased with the post-houses, with their wooden tables and uncovered settees, 'whose culinary resources', he sadly observed, 'do not rise above the meagre level of a cup of tea and a boiled egg', and where, as everywhere else in Central Asia, 'familiar precautions' had to be taken against 'small but familiar pests'. In the end, however, the barren wastes of the Hungry Steppe were at length left behind and the Syr Daria crossed; tall snow-capped mountains appeared in the distance; and amid the sound of running water, and under the shade of broad avenues of trees, our traveller found himself approaching the capital of Turkestan.

In Tashkent Curzon was the guest of the Governor-General, General Rosenbach. The latter did not keep up the same state as his predecessor, General Kaufmann, who never went out without a mounted escort of a hundred Cossacks and whose return to Tashkent was always marked by the erection of triumphal arches and the firing of cannon. Indeed, life at Government House struck the visitor as simple and the furniture and appointments as 'almost jejune in their modesty'. The Governor-General's smoking-room, it is true, was 'entirely carved and painted in oriental style and upholstered with divans of parti-coloured Bokharan velvet' and his coachman wore a black velvet cap with peacock feathers stuck in the brim, but there was 'no throne-room or daïs' and the only two large rooms were 'practically unfurnished'. 'I cannot', wrote the future Viceroy of India, 'imagine a greater contrast to the state observed by the Indian Viceroy.'

Behind Government House was a garden in which a band played. It contained an artificial waterfall and a bear-pit, empty since one of the bears had bitten off his keeper's leg. Near by, among the leafy avenues and gardens of the Russian town, were the other principal public buildings: a new Orthodox Cathedral; an Officers' Club in which dances were held every Sunday night; an observatory; a museum; and a military hospital. Along the broad, poplar-lined avenues, each in its own garden, were the villas of the senior officers and high officials. But everywhere the soldier predominated over the civilian. Uniforms, parade-grounds and barracks abounded and the administration itself was essentially military in character. Nor was this confined to the capital. 'Russian Central Asia', wrote Curzon on his return, 'is one vast armed camp.'

Separated by a valley from the new Russian quarter lay the old city, with its flat mud roofs, its bazaar and its vast, tightly packed native population, leading their own lives, completely cut off from the Russians on the other side of the valley.

From Tashkent George Curzon made his way back to England by the same route that he had followed on his outward journey. He was well pleased with all that he had seen and learned. 'The thing', he wrote to a friend, 'has been a marvellous success.' With him he took first and foremost the conviction that in Central Asia the Russians had come to stay. 'A sense of utter powerlessness against the Russians', he wrote on his return, 'has been diffused abroad amongst the Central Asian peoples.' For this he saw three main reasons: the savage ferocity of the original Russian onslaught; the obvious futility of any attempt at resistance to such overwhelming and ever-present military power; and the certainty, based on past experience, that Russia would never retreat. 'No return tickets', he observes, 'are issued to a punitive foray of Cossacks.'

But, while under no illusions as to Russian aims and methods, Curzon was also prepared to admit that the change had on the whole not been for the worse and that the Russians had conferred undoubted benefits on the races which they had brought under their sway. 'The Russian eagle', he wrote, 'may at first have alighted on the Eastern shores of the Caspian with murderous beak and sharpened talons, but her appetite once satisfied, she has shown that she also came with healing in her wings.' Nor could it be denied that Russia's rule seemed acceptable to, as well as accepted by, the majority of her Asiatic subjects. 'Russia', he tells us, 'unquestionably possesses a remarkable gift for enlisting the allegiance and attracting even the friendship of those whom she has subdued by force of arms ... The Russian fraternizes in the true sense of the word.'

But, while entertaining no doubts as to the permanence of Russia's rule in her existing dominions in Transcaspia and Turkestan, Curzon found it harder to fathom her future intentions with regard to her immediate neighbours. The Transcaspian Railway, along which he had just travelled, had clearly revolutionized the strategic position. Russia could now, without undue difficulty, assemble and maintain a force of 100,000 men on the northern frontiers of Afghanistan. Herat, the gateway to India, was now at her mercy. From Askabad she commanded northern Persia. The question was: would she now make use of these newly acquired strategic advantages to embark on the grand design canvassed by Russian statesmen for a hundred years or more, namely the invasion of British India?

The possibility of invading India was, Curzon felt sure, periodically examined by Russian statesmen and generals. Of that there was, after all, abundant proof. But now, as it had been ten years earlier, the project was linked in Russian minds with other aspects of national policy. Russia's primary aim was not Calcutta, but Constantinople. 'To keep England quiet in Europe by keeping her employed in Asia, that', wrote Curzon, 'is the sum and substance of Russian policy.' 'Without a serious demonstration in the direction of India,' Skobelyov had written, 'a war for the Balkan Peninsula is not to be thought of.' And again: 'The stronger Russia is in Central Asia, the weaker England is in India and the more conciliatory she will be in Europe.'

Despite the autocratic and oppressive nature of their own regime, the Russians, oddly enough, persisted in regarding themselves as natural liberators. 'The sufferings under which the population of India groans,' the Emperor Paul I had written in 1800, 'have inspired France and Russia with the liveliest interest; and the two governments have resolved to unite their forces to liberate India from the tyrannical and barbarous yoke of the English.' 'The might of Russia, God be praised', wrote Skobelyov eighty years later, in terms which today have a strangely contemporary ring, 'brings with it in Asia peace, equality and freedom of person and property; it is based, not on privileged classes, but on the struggling multitudes.'

In Curzon's view, it would have been a mistake to suppose that during the past century or half-century, Russian policy had been continuously and consistently directed to the overthrow of British rule in India. 'So far from regarding the foreign policy of Russia as consistent, or remorseless, or profound,' he wrote, 'I believe it to be a hand-to-mouth policy, a policy of waiting upon events, or profiting by the blunders of others, and as often of committing the like herself.' 'Whilst, however,' he concluded, 'I have confessed that, in entering upon her Central Asian career, I believe Russia to have been actuated by no far-seeing policy, and in pursuing it to have been driven largely by the impulse of natural forces, I am not the less convinced that her presence there is a serious menace to India, and that she is prepared to turn it for her own purposes to the most profitable account. She is like a man who has tumbled quite naturally, but very much to his own surprise, into the inheritance of a wealthy relative, of whom he never heard, but of whom he was the unknowing heir; and who is not deterred by the adventitious source of his fortune from turning it to the most selfish advantage.'

Such were the absorbing thoughts which arranged themselves in George Curzon's lucid, well-disciplined mind, as he sat in his railway compartment, travelling rapidly and comfortably homewards to his parliamentary and other duties in the late autumn of 1888 — thoughts which seventy years later still have their bearing on our problems.

Already, although he did not realize it, the danger of a clash between England and Russia in Central Asia had, for the time being, begun to recede. The period of greatest tension between the two powers had in fact been reached some three or four years earlier at the time of the Russian annexation of Merv and the ensuing Penjdeh incident. Since then, the final delimitation of the Afghan-Russian frontier, following the establishment of what amounted to a British protectorate over Afghanistan, had by the creation of clearly defined zones of influence done much to stabilize the situation and so reduce the risk of war.

At times during the next two decades there were to be fresh danger-periods, but any remaining rivalry between Great Britain and Russia was to vanish in the long run before the ever-increasing menace of German Imperialism. The alliances concluded between France and Russia on the one hand and Great Britain and France on the other prepared the way for the Anglo-Russian Convention of 1907, which, by expressly eliminating any remaining causes of friction in Persia, Tibet and Afghanistan, laid the foundations for a firm understanding between the two countries — an understanding which the outbreak of war in 1914 was to convert into an alliance.

Curzon himself viewed these developments without enthusiasm. For him, Russia remained 'the mammon of unrighteousness'. Both as Under-Secretary for Foreign Affairs from 1895 to 1898 and later as Viceroy of India he retained in unalleviated form the suspicion of Russian motives and intentions which he had brought back from his early travels, and there was no sharper critic than he of the Convention of 1907, which, he declared, had thrown away a hundred years of diplomacy and trade.

As for the future of Turkestan, the consolidation of Russian power which George Curzon had in 1888 so confidently foretold was to continue uninterrupted for close on three decades. That towards the end of the third decade this process would be brusquely interrupted and the whole region plunged once more into chaos and confusion, was something which neither he nor anyone else could at that date have reasonably been expected to foresee.

ALL IS KNOWN TO FINKELSTEIN

As it swayed and rattled through the chilly night air of the desert, the goods wagon, temporarily converted into a passenger coach, was quite full; there were even people clinging to the roof. Inside, in the stuffy half darkness, the passengers were an oddly assorted crowd. There was a party of teachers; and a party of actors — Russians for the most part. There were three Afghan soldiers and three Afghan merchants who had joined the train at Samarkand. And in a corner of the wagon, with their belongings piled all about them, were a young married couple from Tashkent accompanied by a nondescript-looking man of about thirty-six with a short brown beard, dressed in a suit of coarse native cloth and wearing in his hat a hammer-and-sickle badge.

The Hammer and Sickle were very much in evidence in Central Asia that autumn. Two years before, in October 1917, while Europe was still in the throes of the Great War, the Bolshevik Revolution had broken out in Russia and now, a year after the end of the European War, the civil war which had followed the Revolution was still raging in Turkestan. In various parts of the country fighting was in progress. Here and there, the anti-Bolsheviks, with British backing, were still holding out. But in Tashkent, where fifty years before General Kaufmann had hoisted the Imperial flag, a Bolshevik Government now held sway and the flag that flew over the Viceroy's palace was red and instead of the Imperial Eagle bore the workman's hammer and the peasant's sickle.

From time to time the train, as it rattled across Turkestan, would stop at a wayside station, a group of low white-washed buildings with, beyond them, sometimes a grove of poplars and a village street of flat-roofed mud houses and sometimes simply the desert stretching away under the brilliant starlight of Central Asia. And each time, whatever the hour, there would be a rush to fill kettles with boiling water at the station samovars and to buy food from the peasant women waiting on the platforms.

Russian railway coaches have always been convivial places, and, even in that troubled autumn of 1919, the passengers were soon all talking and shouting and arguing amongst themselves. To amuse their fellow-travellers, the actors gave one or two little sketches from their repertory. The Afghan soldiers, in broken Russian, described the victories they had won in their recent war against the British — how they had captured Peshawar, Lahore and Delhi, though not, it seemed, Calcutta or Bombay. Every now and then one of the teachers, a woman of advanced political views, would launch into a long diatribe about the misdeeds of the *bourjoui* and the terrible fate which she personally would mete out to any she met. 'Why,' she cried, as the train jolted along, 'every sleeper on the line has cost the life of a workman, sent to toil here by the Tsarist slave-drivers!'

The young married couple did not take much part in the general conversation, but whispered to each other in Serbian, the clear-cut syllables contrasting strangely with the soft slurring Russian that was being spoken all round them. From their behaviour, it was evident that they had not been married long. Their wedding had, in fact, taken place in Tashkent less than a week before. The husband, it seemed, was a person of some consequence, for when a Red Army soldier tried to force his way into the wagon, saying that he had just come back from the front and could do what he liked, he at once jumped up and called out that he was a representative of the General Staff, and the soldier, a tired-looking Jew, immediately changed his tune and disappeared into the darkness.

The man with them — he of the hammer-and-sickle — also talked less than the rest and when he spoke Russian it was haltingly and with some kind of a foreign accent. But it was evident from the deference with which he was treated by the Bolshevik officials at Samarkand and at the other stations at which they stopped that he, too, held an important appointment of some kind.

As far as the ordinary railway officials were concerned, the exact nature of this appointment quite properly remained a mystery. All that they were shown, when they asked for his papers, was an open permit to travel, issued a few days before by the proper authorities in Tashkent and made out in the name of Joseph Kastamuni. Had this not been enough for them (and it always was), they would have further been shown a passport from which it appeared that Joseph Kastamuni was an Albanian who had been sent to Russia by the Serbian military authorities in 1915 to help with the organization of the Serbian Volunteer Corps which the Russians had raised from Serbian or Croat deserters from the Austrian Army and in which, incidentally, Kastamuni's companion, whose name was Mandić, had also served. Since his discharge, quite soon after the Revolution, he had, it seemed, wandered about European Russia, Siberia and Turkestan until he had finally reached Tashkent.

Though a member of the Serbian Volunteer Corps, Kastamuni, being an Albanian, did not speak Serb and was accordingly obliged to converse with Mandić and his bride in broken Russian or German. On the whole, it seemed unlikely that the poor fellow would find many opportunities of speaking his native Albanian in Turkestan. But in these troublous times he had retained at least one hobby to remind him of happier years. Anyone who took the trouble to go through the solitary bundle, which constituted his entire luggage, would have found in it a tin cigarette box containing a carefully packed collection of butterflies. There was *Lycaena thersamon*, caught on June 22nd; and *Polyommatus gigantea*, caught on July 8th; and *Satyrus dissoluta*, taken on July 11th; and a number of other species, all neatly ticketed.

At first sight, an Albanian naturalist, quietly pursuing his vocation, butterfly-net in hand, in wartime Turkestan, may seem a somewhat surprising phenomenon; but by then most people in those parts had long since ceased to be surprised by anything. The tide of war and revolution had caught up in its swirl the most fantastic collection of human flotsam and jetsam and sent them drifting haphazard over the whole of Central Asia. There was the Englishman on his way to Kashgar with his troupe of performing elephants. And the immensely old Serbian whose parrot told fortunes, picking from a packet of similar envelopes an envelope containing your fortune, inscribed on a scrap of paper, and handing it to you. Then there was the Chinese dentist who worked in the streets of Tashkent. His diagnosis was always the same: maggots. Poking a pair of chopsticks into his patient's mouth, he would extract, ostensibly from the offending tooth, a maggot or caterpillar, alive and squirming. This he would throw to the ground and stamp on, hand the patient an opium pill, and the treatment was complete. There was also the Orthodox prelate who had once been Bishop of San Francisco. And Miss Houston, the Irish governess, now obliged to teach in a Soviet school. And Josip Broz, one day to become famous as Marshal Tito of Jugoslavia, but now employed as motor-mechanic and general handy-man by the hereditary chieftain of a tribe of Kirghiz nomads. And the morganatic wife of the Grand Duke Nikolai Konstantinovich, who was working as caretaker in her husband's former residence. Why not, then, an Albanian lepidopterist?

But there was more to Joseph Kastamuni than met the eye. In addition to their passports and their travel permits, he and his companion, Mandić, carried another document which they only displayed to officials of the Cheka, or Secret Police. This was signed by a certain Dunkov and showed both to be members of the Bolshevik Military Control Department or counter-espionage service. Mandić, it seemed, was to take charge of the Military Control Department at Kagan, the nearest station to Bokhara on the Transcaspian Railway. Kastamuni for his part had been entrusted by the department with a highly secret and extremely delicate mission in Bokhara, for which ancient city he was now bound. When they had read the documents, the Cheka officials looked at the Albanian with curiosity. He must, they felt, be a brave man. Or else a very foolish one.

Before leaving Tashkent, Kastamuni had been given his instructions by Dunkov, who was head of the Bolshevik Military Control Department there. The Bolsheviks, Dunkov told him, were disturbed by persistent rumours that there were British officers in Bokhara, training and organizing the Emir's forces. They wanted to find out what truth there was in these stories. With this object, fifteen agents had already been sent to Bokhara. Not one had returned. All had been caught by the Emir's secret police and strangled. Fresh volunteers were hard to find. It was with gratification that he had learnt from Mandić of Kastamuni's readiness to undertake the task.

Such was the immediate background of Joseph Kastamuni's journey to Bokhara.

★

Much had happened in the world at large during the thirty years which had elapsed since George Curzon had visited Bokhara in 1888. Amongst other things, Curzon himself, now first Marquess Curzon of Kedleston, had in 1919, after a long period of comparative frustration, become His Majesty's Principal Secretary of State for Foreign Affairs and was pursuing a policy which in Central Asia and elsewhere clearly reflected his long-standing distrust and dislike of Russia, now further intensified by the Revolution of 1917. But until quite lately Bokhara and its Emir had remained remote and secluded from the main current of affairs. Even the Great War had scarcely ruffled their serenity. Heedless of the clash of vast opposing forces on land and sea and in the air, the soldiers of the Emir, resplendent in scarlet and blue, had continued to perform the complicated manœuvres of their anti-quated drill. Indeed it was not until 1918 that the first repercussions of the world-shaking events which were happening elsewhere had begun to make themselves felt in Bokhara.

Then, all of a sudden, something wildly improbable had occurred. Russian suzerainty, which for close on half a century had isolated Bokhara from the rest of the world, had vanished overnight. With the Russian Revolution, the sovereign power of the Tsar had melted away in chaos and civil war. And, so far as Bokhara was concerned, nothing had yet taken its place. Through no effort of his own, the Emir had regained his independence – independence as complete as it had been eighty years before, when Bokhara had stood poised between the British and Russian Empires, courted by both and able to play one off against the other.

A passing phase, it might be said. No doubt. But, when in March 1918, the Bolsheviks from Tashkent under Kolesov had attacked Bok-hara, they had after five days of fighting been soundly defeated by the Emir's comic-opera army. An armistice had subsequently been signed by that same Haider Khoja Mirbadalev, who, thirty years before, as a young man of twenty or so, had been Curzon's guide to the anti-quities of Bokhara and was now a high functionary in the service of the Emir. On March 25th the Tashkent Bolsheviks had signed a treaty with the Emir, recognizing Bokhara as an independent state. And now, at the frontier-post at Kagan on the Transcaspian Railway, in full view of the Red Army sentries across the border, the troops of Bokhara could be seen, marching boldly up and down, their tunics lavishly bedecked with medals, loudly singing patriotic songs. 'The Emir', they chanted nasally, 'is our father.' And again: 'Our General is a brave man who does not fear the Bolsheviks.' Occasionally their General would himself come and inspect them, a magnificent figure, preceded by men who rode in front of him carrying white wands.

Nor was this all. Now that all restraining influence had been removed, any appearance of humane or constitutional government that had been assumed during the past fifty years was rapidly cast aside and Bokhara reverted once more to the barbaric despotism for which it had long been famous. Once again the Tower of Death was restored to the use which had given it its name and from its summit the writhing bodies of its victims were sent hurtling to destruction at its foot. It was quite like old times.

But the Emir was nevertheless fully alive to the need for caution. For the time being, the might of Russia was, it seemed, in eclipse. His own army had defeated and driven off the Bolshevik invaders. But it was too much to hope that this happy state of affairs would last indefinitely. A Soviet Government, thirsting for revenge, still held sway in Tashkent. Invasion was not the only danger that threatened the Emir. Revolution was contagious and, in his own domains, for all his repressive measures, a new spirit of rebellion was abroad. Of recent months there had been talk of a Young Bokharan Party, reputed to be infected with the new revolutionary, anti-monarchical, anti-capitalist ideas from across the border and led, strangely enough, by the nineteen-year-old son of one of the biggest capitalists in Bokhara, young Faisullah Khojaev.

Nor was Russia the only factor to be considered. Once again England had come into the picture – England, that remote fog-bound island, which somehow dominated half Asia. Even now, there were British troops in Persia and Afghanistan, British troops in the Caucasus, and until quite recently British troops only a few miles away on the Transcaspian Railway. British troops whose avowed intention was to destroy the Bolsheviks and who might be disposed to leave him at any rate nominal independence.

And so in many ways the Emir's position had come to resemble that of his predecessor Nasrullah eighty years earlier. Like him, he found himself poised uneasily between two contending colossi, not wishing to commit himself too far with either, but equally anxious to avoid an irreparable breach with either one or the other — a baffling situation for a ruler long accustomed to have his mind made up for him by a Russian Resident, especially accredited to him for the purpose. He found it all very puzzling. But of one thing he was quite certain: of the absolute necessity of liquidating without delay any Bolshevik secret agents — as opposed to official representatives — he might catch on his territory. There, at any rate, he was on safe ground.

At half past eight on the morning of October 18th the train from Tashkent and Samarkand jolted to a stop at Kagan, the nearest station to Bokhara on the Transcaspian Railway. This was a cluster of modern buildings which had sprung into existence since the railway had been built and was, like the railway itself, Russian territory. The city of Bokhara lay ten or twelve miles away across the cotton fields. Joseph Kastamuni had reached his jumping-off place.

On arriving at Kagan, he and Mandić at once got into touch with the proper authorities and were allotted a room at the inn reserved for Soviet officials. On its whitewashed walls hung pictures of Karl Marx with his flowing white beard and Lenin with his little brown pointed one.

When they were told of his mission, the Cheka officials at Kagan regarded Kastamuni with interest. They knew of the fate of his fifteen predecessors. How, they inquired, did he propose to get into Bokhara? The gates and walls of the city were heavily guarded and all who entered, especially Europeans, were thoroughly searched and questioned. But Kastamuni was giving nothing away. His plans, he replied, were his own business and no one else's.

He had, in fact, made all arrangements before leaving Tashkent. There, with the help of friends and in return for an easily given assurance that he was no Bolshevik, but simply a foreigner who wanted to go to Bokhara to buy some goods which were unobtainable in Tashkent and which on his return he would be able to sell for a profit, he had succeeded in obtaining from the Bokharan Consul, Mir Baba, a letter of recommendation to his colleague at Kagan. Now, without telling anyone except Mandić, he made his way to the Bokharan Consulate.

A richly dressed Bokharan, in a gaily striped *khalat* and large white turban, was sitting in an archway looking out on to the street, as though profoundly conscious of being the representative of an ancient civilization among barbarian upstarts: the Consul in person. But just as Kastamuni, in his rough suit, with the hammer and sickle badge on his peaked cap, was approaching to hand to him his letter of recommendation, a man sprang out and, pulling him roughly away, told him to stand back and take off his cap while he presented the letter to the Bey. The Bey, for his part, did not seem to have noticed this incident. When the letter was handed to him, he read it. Then he gave an order. A note was brought to him. He sealed it, and it was handed to Kastamuni, who had stood waiting, cap in hand. It was a permit to enter Bokhara.

Mandić meanwhile, treated by all with the deference due to so important an official, had taken up his duties as Head of the Military Control Department at Kagan. The plan was that he should remain at Kagan and act as Kastamuni's rear link while the latter was in Bokhara. Such work was familiar to him. He had been employed by the Bolsheviks on special duties of this kind ever since the Revolution.

Soon after taking over, he was handed a telegram. It was addressed to him by name and was signed by the Chief of the Bolshevik General Staff at Tashkent. It was partly in plain language and partly in cypher. 'Please transmit', it began, 'all information in your possession regarding 19922 05692 12506 65696 15506 82066 86015 69260 27659 62066.' The cypher-books were brought out and the second part of the message which indicated the subject of the inquiry duly decyphered. ' ... Anglo-Indian Service Colonel Bailey', it read. The signal was marked Urgent.

With Kastamuni to help him, Mandić sat down at once to draft a reply. It was known from secret sources, they wrote, that in December of the previous year Colonel Bailey had been in Ferghana. In January he had been in the old town of Tashkent. Quite recently, in September, three Europeans, one of whom corresponded to the description given of him, had left Patta Kessar on the Afghan frontier for Shirabad in

Eastern Bokhara. Thence it was thought that he was either returning to Ferghana or else heading for the Pamirs.

When they had finished, Mandić and Kastamuni read through what they had written and were not displeased with their work. It just needed something to round it off. Mandić added one more sentence. 'All', he wrote, 'is known to Finkelstein.' Then they looked at each other and smiled.

In order to understand why they smiled, it is necessary to go back some way.

In the first place, Finkelstein was dead. He had, as it happened, been shot at Tashkent during the 'Events', as they were euphemistically called, of the previous January. Nor was it likely that he had, even when alive, in fact possessed quite such a complete grasp of the case under reference as their telegram suggested. For that, he would have had to keep track of the movements of 'the Anglo-Indian Service Colonel Bailey' from the moment when that gallant officer had first entered Russian Turkestan in the late summer of 1918. And the chances are that, had he attempted to do this, Finkelstein would sooner or later have arrived at a dead end.

For the first couple of months after his arrival from India Colonel Bailey, a placid, mild-mannered officer in the Indian Political Service who had never before visited Turkestan, had done nothing to complicate the task of the various Bolshevik agents detailed to keep a check on his movements. On reaching Tashkent on August 14th, 1918, he had hastened to call officially on the Soviet authorities and to explain to them the purpose of his mission. Briefly, this was to ensure that the Central Powers, with whom the Allies were still at war, did not exploit the disturbed situation in Russian Turkestan and, in particular, to try to ensure that some control was kept over the large numbers of German and Austrian prisoners-of-war who had been sent there by the Russians earlier in the war.

Unfortunately, Colonel Bailey's arrival was anything but well timed. As it happened, it coincided almost exactly with the first clash between British and Bolshevik troops farther west, along the Trans-caspian Railway, where the British, under General Malleson, were from their base in Persia supporting the anti-Bolshevik Government of Transcaspia and were for a time in actual occupation of the oasis of Merv. During his two months' journey from India through Chinese Turkestan, Colonel Bailey had been completely out of touch with current events. Now, at his first interview with the Foreign Commissar of the Soviet Government of Turkestan, he found himself unexpectedly confronted with this awkward fact and invited to explain how it was that his Government had sent him on an allegedly friendly mission to the Soviet authorities at a time when their troops were actually fighting against the Red Army only a few miles away on Russian territory. Nor did his reply that it must surely all be a mistake make much impression on the Turkestan Government, at that time fighting for their lives on four fronts simultaneously, and possessing irrefutable evidence of the presence of British troops amongst their opponents. Bailey, a transparently honest man, did his best to reassure them. But it could not be said that his Mission had got off to a good start.

During the weeks that followed, Bailey had led an uneasy, frustrating existence, regarded with profound suspicion by the Bolshevik Government, out of touch with his own Government, cut off from all reliable news of the outside world, surrounded on all sides by spies and *agents provocateurs*.

Time hung heavy on his hands. He went to the Opera where they were giving *Rigoletto*. He visited the Natural History Museum which contained a fair collection of birds and butterflies. At the cinematograph he sat through the same films over and over again: *Sherlock Holmes* and *The Prisoner of Zenda*. He went to cafés where the music was provided by Austrian prisoners-of-war, still wearing the Imperial uniform. He read Bolshevik newspapers, roughly printed on paper that was sometimes pink and sometimes brown, and which hardly mentioned the war in the West, but concentrated rather on highly coloured prophesies of early World Revolution. From time to time he would call on the Foreign Commissar, Damgatski, and they would resume their argument as to what was really happening farther up the line. Meanwhile, all round him suspected enemies of the Bolshevik regime were being led off daily to imprisonment or execution. Sooner or later his own turn seemed bound to come.

And come it did. On October 15th, 1918, he was arrested by two members of the secret police. But the Tashkent Bolsheviks lacked assurance. Their prisoner's warning that such high-handed action would not only upset the House of Commons but also infuriate the House of Lords, a notoriously irritable and unaccountable body of men, was enough to sow serious doubts in their minds. A day or two later Bailey was released. But it could only be a matter of time before the secret police called for him again, and next time, he suspected, the outcome might be less agreeable.

His suspicions that more trouble was brewing was confirmed by an anonymous message that was handed to him a few days later while he was lunching with some friends. It was written in red ink and ended with the following sentence: 'For Bailey the position is especially dangerous and shooting is not out of the question.' The time had clearly come for him to make a move.

That evening — it was October 29th — the six police spies charged with watching his movements saw him start out for a stroll after dinner. As usual, they followed him. After going some way, he turned down one of the poplar-lined avenues of the New Town and entered a house standing in a row. As usual, the spies settled down on the opposite side of the street to watch the house, which, they noted, was one he had never before visited.

Time passed. People came and went. An Austrian prisoner emerged from one of the houses farther down the road and walked away. It grew late. The colonel, it seemed, was staying to supper. Spying was thirsty work and there was a *chai-khana* just round the corner. After a quick drink of tea, they returned to their post. Hours went by. Still there was no sign of Bailey. He must, they decided, have gone home while they were drinking their tea. At any rate, that was what they reported when they went off duty.

But when inquiries were made at his house next day, it was discovered that he was not there. And that was the last that had been seen or heard of Colonel Bailey in Tashkent. From the moment he entered the little house in the row and its door closed upon him, he had vanished as surely as if he had stepped out of this world, and the Bolshevik agents engaged in tracing his movements found themselves up against a blank wall.

Not that there was anything very surprising or unusual about this. There were a few judicious blanks in most people's lives in Central Asia in those troubled times. For one reason or another, a great many people had at one time or another found it convenient to disappear: to change, or at any rate to modify their identity in such a way as to throw possible pursuers off their trail.

Take Joseph Kastamuni, for example, even now preparing to follow his fifteen ill-fated predecessors into the walled city of Bokhara. If he was to escape their fate, he would have to remove the hammer and sickle badge from his cap and take greater pains to enter into the character of a small trader entirely without sympathy for the new rulers of Turkestan. Otherwise his chances of survival would be small.

For the time being, he would have to undergo a transformation. All traces of his immediate past, of the events of the last few days, of the days spent in the train and at Kagan, of his connection with the Soviet authorities, would have to be obliterated. He would have to become someone else, someone completely different.

As a matter of fact, it was not the first time that Kastamuni had found himself under such a necessity. Despite all the visas on his passport, tracing his movements step by step, month by month, year by year back to his native Albania, anyone endeavouring to follow those movements by other more direct means would soon have found himself in difficulties, in difficulties no less formidable than those confronting the Chief of the Soviet General Staff at Tashkent in his search for Colonel Bailey. Indeed, it would not have been easy to find many people who had known this particular Albanian for much more than a week. Dunkov, for example, the head of the Military Control Department at Tashkent, who, on Mandić's recommendation, had sent him on his present mission, had known him for exactly that length of time and no longer.

More people might have been found who knew a certain Roumanian coachman called Joseph Lazar, who strangely enough bore a strong resemblance to Joseph Kastamuni and, who, stranger still, had, after spending some months in and about Tashkent, vanished completely at just about the time that the Albanian first made his appearance there.

As for Joseph Lazar, anyone who took the trouble to trace his antecedents would, if he had been lucky, have found that in the previous March his personality merged mysteriously into that of a seventy-five-year-old Lett called Justus, who, according to his papers had lived in Tashkent for the past fourteen years but, who, only a few days earlier had been going under the name of Georgi Chuka, an officer of Roumanian extraction serving in the Austrian Army. The strange thing about Georgi Chuka (apart from the fact that like Lazar and Justus he, too, bore a strong family likeness to Joseph Kastamuni) was that there were two of him: one who lived quietly in the country, while the other, seriously inconvenienced by the temporary loss of his passport, earned his living as best he could in Tashkent.

Georgi Chuka was not the only person in Tashkent who had lost his passport. A few months before, the same misfortune had overtaken a Hungarian prisoner of war, a cook called Andrew Kekeshi. For a time he, too, had had a double, a double who bore not the slightest resemblance to him and who, incidentally, could not speak a word of Hungarian, but who had somehow obtained possession of his passport and, on the strength of it, had lived discreetly at a bee farm in the hills outside the town keeping as far as possible out of the way of the authorities. Then, after some months, this double had disappeared and his passport had been restored to the true Andrew Kekeshi. Simultaneously Georgi Chuka the Second had made his appearance.

Anyone possessing the patience to carry his investigation thus far would at this stage have made an interesting discovery. He would have found that the first appearance of the second Andrew Kekeshi almost exactly coincided in time and place with the disappearance of Colonel Bailey. He might, with luck, even have succeeded in identifying Kekeshi as that same Austrian prisoner of war who on that memorable evening of October 20th, 1918, had been seen to emerge from a gate several houses away from that which Colonel Bailey had entered, and walk unconcernedly away. He might also have found that the back gardens of the row of houses in question were only separated from one another by a low wooden fence, and that earlier the same evening, a complete Austrian uniform had been laid out in readiness in the house which Colonel Bailey had entered. And, having got thus far, our hypothetical investigator would probably no longer have had any difficulty in understanding the sudden merriment which had seized Kastamuni and Mandić on deciphering the Chief of Staff's telegram instructing them to investigate the movements of Colonel Bailey.

And what of Joseph Kastamuni's companion, Mandić? Mandić strangely enough, was Mandić, and had always been Mandić. But although he had clung with such unusual tenacity to one name, he had shown himself considerably more versatile in the matter of his allegiance. A Serb from Sarajevo in Bosnia, he had started the war as a lieutenant in the Imperial Austro-Hungarian Army. As a member of an underprivileged and disgruntled minority, he felt no loyalty to the Habsburgs and so took an early opportunity of deserting to the Russians. The Imperial Russian authorities, recognizing him as a man of ability, had employed him in their Intelligence Service. On the outbreak of the Revolution he had gone over to the Bolsheviks, who had employed him in the same capacity. But, before long, he had begun to doubt the wisdom of remaining indefinitely in Bolshevik employment or indeed on Russian territory.

These doubts had coincided with Colonel Bailey's appearance in Tashkent. Shortly after Bailey's arrival, Mandić had called on him privately at dead of night and offered him his services. Scenting an *agent provocateur*, Bailey had at first, not unnaturally, felt somewhat suspicious of his intentions. But in fact Mandić had proved useful to him in a number of ways and in particular had warned him in advance of his impending arrest.

This, and a feeling that the time had come for him to get out of Russian Turkestan, had, in the late summer of 1919 when, after a variety of adventures, he was passing as Joseph Lazar, the Roumanian coachman, led Bailey once again to resume contact with Mandić. Clearly, in so doing, he was taking a considerable risk. But by now he had been in hiding for nearly a year; conditions were steadily deteriorating; and his position was daily becoming more precarious. He decided to chance it. Once again Mandić turned up trumps. He announced that he would be only too glad to help Bailey to get out of Turkestan if Bailey, for his part, would help him and his bride (for he was about to get married) to get back to Sarajevo. Together they sat down to make a plan.

It was now that Bailey conceived the audacious project of joining the Bolshevik Secret Service. Here, Mandić, a trusted employee of that organization, could be of the greatest service to him, and, while, as a Roumanian coachman, an Austrian officer or a Hungarian cook, his hopes of getting out of the country were extremely poor, there was a good chance that, as a Soviet official, he might even be sent abroad by the Soviet authorities themselves.

The first step was to create the character of Joseph Kastamuni. They chose an Albanian, because in his new role Bailey would probably be subjected to much closer scrutiny than hitherto and, as an Albanian, the risk of being confronted with a compatriot or even an Albanian speaker would be comparatively small. His passport they fabricated with a typewriter, a sheet of paper and some rubber stamps produced by Mandić. The photograph on it showed its owner in what appeared to be the uniform of the Serbian Volunteer Corps. This effect had been achieved by cutting the shoulder straps off Bailey's old Austrian uniform, turning the képi back to front and sticking a paper cockade to it with the help of some apricot jam, the only substitute for glue available in Tashkent at the time. The photograph had then been taken with Bailey's own Kodak and duly attached to the passport.

Thus equipped, Bailey had been presented by Mandić to the redoubtable Dunkov, the head of the Bolshevik Counter Espionage Department in Tashkent, and had at once been given the task of investigating alleged British activities in Bokhara. In the event, Dunkov had never even bothered to look at Kastamuni's carefully prepared passport but, relying on Mandić's recommendation, had issued him with a complete set of Soviet papers, including a special secret pass.

On the morning of October 19th, 1919, Mandić and Kastamuni-Bailey hired a *tarantass* and in it set out along the dusty, deeply rutted road which led from Kagan to Bokhara. It was a fine bright autumn day and in the fields on either side of the road the fruit trees were laden with apricots and apples.

Before leaving Tashkent, Bailey had provided himself with secret letters from a friend in Tashkent to a certain Tisyachnikov, a Russian living in Bokhara, through whom he hoped to get into touch with the Emir. His aim was to spend some time in Bokhara, while still maintaining his connection with the Soviet authorities in Kagan through Mandić. Then, when he had fully exploited his position as a Bolshevik agent, he would make his way to the nearest British Headquarters, taking Mandić and Madame Mandić with him. In order to carry out this plan, it was vital that as few people as possible in Bokhara should know who he really was and that they should observe the strictest secrecy, as otherwise the news of his identity would almost certainly leak out and eventually reach the Bolsheviks in Kagan.

On reaching the city gates, Bailey sent Mandić, who knew Bokhara, into the city to find Tisyachnikov, while he himself waited anxiously at the guard post outside. As all arrivals from Bolshevik territory were regarded with extreme suspicion, and as Bailey and Mandić had only one permit between them, the attitude of the guard on the gate was not very friendly. Half an hour went by, and then an hour. Still there was no sign of Mandić. Then, just as his companion was beginning to wonder whether disaster had not overtaken him, he reappeared. But the news he brought was bad. He had, it seemed, found Tisyachnikov, but Tisyachnikov had flatly refused to have anything to do with him.

Bailey now decided that he must go into Bokhara himself. Having with difficulty overcome the guard's objections to admitting two strangers on one pass, he and Mandić set out on foot through the winding streets to Nazarov Passage, the business centre of the city, where they knew Tisyachnikov to be.

Finding Tisyachnikov outside in the street, Bailey accosted him and told him that he had a letter for him and mentioned the name of the writer, a certain Noyev. 'Show me the letter,' Tisyachnikov replied. At this Bailey produced what appeared to be a blank sheet of paper, explaining that the writing on it was in invisible ink and needed developing. 'Then develop it,' said Tisyachnikov testily. Bailey explained that he could not do this in the street in public. At length Tisyachnikov reluctantly agreed to take him indoors, but still insisted on his developing the writing in the presence of a Russian friend of his.

Almost immediately they were joined by several more people, including two Jews, who Tisyachnikov explained reassuringly were quite 'safe'. Then, just as Bailey had finished developing the letter, there was a knock and in came the Karshi Beg, a high Bokharan official whose business it was to investigate the affairs of all strangers arriving in Bokhara and submit reports on them. By now what had been intended as a private interview had become a public gathering.

Mandić, meanwhile, had remained outside in the courtyard of the house where they were. Suddenly from the courtyard there now came the sound of shouting and cursing. 'You are a brave man,' somebody was yelling, 'but you won't get back this time.' Alarmed, Bailey rushed out to see what was going on. Outside he found that the noise was proceeding from an angry little Tartar gentleman of about fifty-five to sixty with a big moustache, nattily dressed, and wearing a black lambskin hat jauntily set over one eye, who proceeded to introduce himself as Haider Khoja Mirbadalev, of the service of His Highness the Emir. On being told by Bailey that Mandić had come with him, Haider Khoja became angrier still and left post-haste for the nearest telephone, announcing that he would have him arrested immediately.

This clearly had to be stopped at all costs. Bailey rushed back into the house and got Tisyachnikov, who, running after Haider Khoja, explained to him what had happened and eventually succeeded in calming him down. All present then proceeded to a general review of the situation.

From this it emerged that both Tisyachnikov and Haider Khoja had at once recognized Mandić as a well-known Bolshevik agent. This accounted for their mistrustful attitude. Producing from his pocket a pistol, Tisyachnikov explained that he had kept Bailey covered with it throughout their conversation. Bailey, for his part, now explained that Mandić, though to all appearances a Bolshevik agent, was in fact his agent and that he, though apparently an Albanian, was in fact a British officer.

The atmosphere now gradually became calmer. The secret letters were passed from hand to hand and carefully examined by all present. Even the irascible Haider Khoja was reassured. In the end they decided that Bailey had better go and get his luggage, which he had left outside the city gate, and that after that room should be found for him in the women's hospital.

The immediate problem of Bailey's admission to the city and of his accommodation there had been solved. But at least half a dozen people were now intimately acquainted with his affairs. His hopes of carrying out his original plan had greatly diminished. Moreover, it would now be extremely dangerous for Mandić or his wife to remain at Kagan. Both must move to Bokhara without delay. While Bailey settled into his new quarters at the women's hospital, Mandić hurried back to Kagan to fetch his bride, with whom he returned to Bokhara the following day.

After the vicissitudes of the past year, Bailey found life in Bokhara agreeable enough. He slept in the women's hospital, but had his meals in the house of Haider Khoja, who told him how thirty years before he had acted as guide to Lord Curzon and who soon became a firm friend.

In Bokhara there were no signs of Bolshevism. On the contrary, capitalism was rampant. In the maze of covered bazaars, the finest in Central Asia, trade was brisker than ever. The money-changers still sat at the crossways with piles of different coins and notes in front of them. From the coppersmiths' bazaar came the sound of hammering. And in their bazaar the goldsmiths and silversmiths were hard at work in-laying and engraving and setting precious stones. Then there were the snuff-sellers, their piles of bright green snuff flanked by gourd snuff bottles of the most varied colours. If you had the money, you could buy yourself anything: fine carpets, or jewels or silk robes or even a packet of Lipton's tea. Food was plentiful and delicious. In the shops of the *shashlik*-sellers were piled hundreds of skewers on which tender lumps of lamb alternated with slices of onion. At the arrival of a customer, these were put to grill over a charcoal fire and then eaten with flat round loaves of bread. Near by, in other booths there was *kaimak* for sale, a sort of curdled cream, and in the *chai-khanas* turbaned old men sat endlessly smoking their pipes and drinking little cups of weak tea. Then there was the fruit bazaar, heaped at this time of year with great piles of peaches and apricots and melons. Sometimes on his walks abroad, Bailey would encounter the high officers of state riding forth, clad in their gorgeous robes and accompanied by a glittering staff, the Prime Minister or *Khush Begi*, the Finance Minister or *Kaznachei*, and the Chief Justice or *Kazi Kalan*, carrying in his hand a little inlaid axe. When he met these dignitaries he would stand aside and take off his hat and bow, as was customary.

Not long after his arrival in Bokhara, Bailey came by chance upon the origin of the stories of British machinations in Bokhara which had so disturbed the Bolshevik authorities in Tashkent. 'Do you know a man called Awal Nur?' Haider Khoja asked him one day. After a moment's thought, he remembered that Awal Nur was a *Havildar* in the Indian Army who the year before had accompanied him as far as Kashgar on his way to Tashkent. Yes, he said, he knew him. 'Well', said Haider Khoja to Bailey's amazement, 'he's here', and later that evening, as they were all sitting round the family *samovar*, the door opened and in came two men dressed in turbans and splendid silk Bokharan *khalats*. They were Awal Nur and another Indian Army non-commissioned officer named Kalbi Mohammed. They had, it seemed, returned from Kashgar to India and thence been sent to join the British Forces in Transcaspia. There they had been entrusted with the task of conveying a hundred camel loads of supplies across the desert to Bokhara, and this, after numerous adventures, they had done, skilfully evading the attempts of the Bolsheviks to intercept them. On arrival they had been rewarded with some fine silk robes and the blue enamel star of a high Bokharan order. They were now living in state at the Emir's Palace. When they saw their Colonel, sitting there in his old homespun Bolshevik suit, they came smartly to attention and saluted. He, for his part, now grasped that it was their presence in Bokhara that had given rise to all the rumours of British plots which had so alarmed the Bolsheviks and to which, indirectly, he owed his own presence there.

Despite the disturbance which had attended their arrival and the possibility that the Bolsheviks were by now fully alive to their true character and intentions, Bailey and Mandić thought it advisable to maintain contact with the Soviet authorities in Kagan. Immediately after their arrival they had dispatched to Kagan a letter announcing that they were engaged on very dangerous work, had already obtained important information and urgently needed forty thousand roubles. In reply to this they had received no roubles, it is true, but an answer which seemed to show that, so far at any rate, their employers' suspicions had not been aroused. After that they had sent in one or two routine intelligence reports and a report to say that Mandić was ill. Then, after an interval, they received an urgent message from Bugayev, their immediate superior at Kagan, asking them to meet him on very important business. To this they replied that Mandić was too ill to come but that Kastamuni would meet him at a *chai-khana* a few yards outside the city gate.

When Bailey, who was on the look out for trouble, reached the appointed place, there was no sign of Bugayev. But a further message was delivered to him by a man dressed as a cab driver, urging him to return to Kagan at once. From the terms of the message and from the knowledge of his movements which the messenger apparently possessed it seemed clear enough that the Bolsheviks had learned the truth and were aiming at kidnapping him.

This finally convinced Bailey that it was time to leave. He had, whenever the opportunity offered, dispatched various messages to the British Headquarters at Meshed in northern Persia, but so far he had received no reply and had no reason to believe that any of his messages had in fact reached their destination. He now decided to go to Meshed himself, taking with him Mandić and his wife and the two Indian N.C.O.s.

It was December. He had been in Bokhara for nearly two months. During this time he had not succeeded in seeing the Emir, who was becoming increasingly nervous of doing anything that could possibly offend the Bolsheviks. Nor did he find the Bokharan authorities very helpful when it came to preparing for his departure. In the end, however, he succeeded in obtaining six horses, three rifles, some food and two large pieces of felt for bedding. By the middle of the month he and his little party were ready to start on the hazardous journey which lay before them.

The route which they proposed to follow lay in the first place almost due south to Burdalik, on the near side of the Oxus. After that their intention was to cross the Oxus and make their way south-westwards across the strip of desert which lay between the Oxus and Murghab Rivers. The second part of their journey was the more dangerous. The wells were few and far between. The Bolsheviks held the strip of country along the Murghab. The rest of the area was infested by their patrols and by brigands. There was thus always a good chance that the travellers would find any given well in hostile hands and would be obliged either to fight for it or to die of thirst in the desert. In such circumstances nothing could be easier for anyone who so desired than to intercept a party of travellers.

During the last few days before their departure, Colonel Bailey's party had grown considerably in size. They had been joined first by four White Russian Officers, including a certain Captain Iskander, the son by a morganatic marriage of the Grand Duke Nikolai Konstantinovich, and then, at the last moment, by seven unknown Russians, one of whom turned out later to be a Roumanian and any or all of whom might be Bolshevik agents.

In the end they left Bokhara on the evening of December 18th. In order that from a distance they might present the appearance of a native caravan, they all wore *khalats* and big sheepskin Turkoman busbies. It had been raining all day and the roads were muddy. Just as they were starting, they found that their guide had forgotten the password and they had to wait while he went and found out what it was. Then one of the ponies got lost in the dark and there was further delay. It was after eight in the evening when they finally started on their way. They did not cover more than ten miles that night.

The first stage of their journey, as far as Burdalik, took three days. It lay for the most part through desert and waterless steppe and gave them a foretaste of what was to come. The weather was miserably cold and wet, the water in many of the wells was too salt to drink, and the arrangements they had made for supplies of food and fodder to be dumped at intervals along their route seemed somehow to have gone wrong. At Burdalik, where they spent three more days recuperating, they were hospitably entertained by the local Governor or *Beg*, a merry ruffian, who roasted a whole sheep for them, proudly showed them the rows of prisoners he kept with their legs in the stocks and a chain round their necks, organized a hawking expedition for them and on their departure sent them in a bill for five thousand roubles.

They left Burdalik and the *Beg* on Christmas Eve and, after travelling for some miles through cultivated land dotted with villages and farmhouses, came in the late afternoon to the reedy flats which fringe the Oxus. It was too late to cross the river before dark and, as they had control of the only available boat, there was no danger that news of their arrival would get ahead to their enemies. They decided to spend the night where they were and cross on Christmas Day.

The crossing next morning was made in three journeys and took nearly four hours. When at length they and their ponies were all across, they set out afresh across the undulating sand-dunes which lay on the far side of the wide, muddy stream. With enemies probably on the look out for them, time was precious and they pushed on as fast as they could. By the shores of the Oxus they abandoned a portmanteau belonging to Madame Mandić which had proved too cumbrous for the ponies to carry. For four days there was no grass for the ponies, only the small quantity of grain they carried with them. The water at the wells was brackish. The weather was dry and cold and a bitter wind blew the dust into their faces as they rode along.

After they had watered the horses, the Turkomans would gallop them round furiously in the desert. This, they said, was good for them. By Colonel Bailey's side trotted his fox terrier Zep, a dog that had had almost as many adventures as his master and, while living on his own in Tashkent, had long been the object of special attention from the secret police. When he felt tired, Zep would jump up in front of his master. Colonel Bailey's companions, who were not dog-lovers, regarded him without affection.

On December 28th Mandić announced that he was in pain and could go no farther. He urged his companions to go on and leave him to die. Some members of the party seemed to consider his suggestion a sound one. 'Leave him,' they said. 'We must go on. We have no food or water and will all die if we delay.' At this, Mandić's wife burst into tears. Colonel Bailey now intervened, soothing and sensible. In the end Mandić was given a pony with easier paces. This relieved the pain and the party set out once more.

Next morning the guides admitted that they were completely lost. This was a serious matter. The horses had had no water for twenty-four hours and were exhausted after their long marches on little or no food. They were, Bailey calculated, at least fifty miles from the Murghab River, the approaches to which were in any case held by the Bolsheviks. If they simply marched on a compass bearing, their chances of finding a well were slender and it seemed doubtful if the horses would survive for this distance without water. Even if they eventually reached the Murghab, they would be at their last gasp and in no condition for an encounter with the Bolsheviks who would doubtless be waiting for them there.

For three hours they drifted disconsolately along trying to find a landmark. Then, just as Bailey was beginning to give up hope, they suddenly came on a well with a hut and a flock of sheep. The well water was deliciously fresh and clear and with mutton bought from the shepherds they cooked large *shashliks* skewered on the cleaning rods of their rifles. There was even bread, big flat round loaves two inches thick and two feet across, freshly baked for them by the Turkomans. They spent the rest of that day and half of the next at the well, eating, resting and tending their ponies. At one o'clock on December 30th, they set off again, spending the night at another well some twenty miles farther on. That night it snowed and it was bitterly cold as they huddled together fully clothed between the two big strips of felt.

On New Year's Day, 1920, some twenty miles on from where they had spent the night, they espied a single horseman a great way off travelling very fast. Soon after, they came to a well. As they approached it they saw that it was held by armed men who were clearly preparing to defend it. The Russian officers were in favour of attacking at once, but Bailey, realizing that with their seven antiquated Bokharan rifles they would not stand a chance against men firing from a building, decided against this and himself went forward to parley with the occupying force. This consisted of half a dozen local robbers, who, he found much to his relief, were no more anxious for a fight than he was. In the end an amicable arrangement was arrived at, under which the two-roomed hut at the well was jointly occupied by both parties, each posting sentries to watch the others, while the rest slept. A solitary traveller, who, Bailey thought, might have been a Bolshevik spy, was taken into custody as a precaution and carried off with them when they left, his feet tied firmly together under his horse's belly. What might have been a awkward situation had passed off surprisingly well.

By January 3rd they were only a short distance from the Murghab River. From where they were on the edge of the desert they could see the river and some houses. They were now in Bolshevik territory and it was necessary to proceed with great caution. Approaching the river after dark, they found a man who in return for a large sum of money agreed to ferry them across in his boat. Beyond the river was the Transcaspian Railway which was regularly patrolled by the Reds. Any noise would have been fatal. Although the Murghab at this point was no more than twenty yards wide, it was an hour and half before the whole party had reached the other side. Two miles farther on, by bright moonlight, they came to the railway line and somehow managed to slip across unnoticed between two Bolshevik patrols. Then they pushed on as fast as they could into the desert beyond, determined to put as many miles as possible between them and the enemy before daylight.

Next day it was foggy. After they had gone some distance, they came on the tracks of a large party and only then realized that they had been going round in a circle and that the tracks were their own. The guides were lost again. Next day they had still not found the way. By now they were once more short of food and reduced to eating the horses' grain. That evening, as it was getting dark, they came on some men sitting round a camp fire and begged them for food, but all the men said was, 'Go away or we will shoot'. And there was nothing for it but to wander off again, still hungry, into the darkness. Soon they were lost again, but next morning they came to a Turkoman encampment and were able to gorge themselves once more with bread and mutton.

It was now January 6th and they were no longer far from the Persian border. Another long day's journey across bleak, waterless desert brought them in sight of a range of snow-capped mountains. These, they calculated, must be in Persia. Soon after, they topped a little ridge in the desert from which they could see below them, less than a mile away, the river which marked the actual frontier. There was a wide belt of green rushes on the side of the river nearest to them and a narrower belt on the Persian side. At the same time they saw something else. A mile away, on a hill overlooking the river were some men who, as they approached, made off rapidly.

Colonel Bailey's first impulse was to make a dash for the river in the hope of getting across before anyone could stop them. Then he reflected that he did not know whether it was fordable or, if so, where. He accordingly decided to send the two Indian N.C.O.s on ahead to make a preliminary reconnaissance. Before long the Indians returned, having found a well-marked ford and the whole party set out for the frontier at a brisk trot.

As they reached the belt of rushes, which at this point was some five hundred yards wide, a shot rang out, followed by another and another. The Bolsheviks had seen them. At once the horses broke into a gallop and went plunging headlong down the steep bank towards the river. Soon Madame Mandić, who was a poor horsewoman, was in difficulties. Her hat was off, her hair was down and her pony was out of control. A minute later she had fallen off and was lying on the ground, while her pony plunged on riderless down the bank into the river. Immediately, Captain Iskander, the morganatic son of the Grand Duke, rushed to her aid, urging her to jump up behind him. At first she demurred, refusing to leave her saddle-bags which had also fallen to the ground and which she said were full of beautiful silk dresses. Then a Bolshevik bullet hit the ground a couple of feet behind her. This made up her mind. After one unsuccessful attempt, she managed to clamber up behind her rescuer, and soon they were both safely across the river.

As soon as Bailey and Awal Nur had reached the other side, they and two Russian officers had started to return the enemy's fire, thus covering the retreat of the rest of the party. The Russians fired rather wildly from the saddle, while Bailey and Awal Nur lay down and took steady shots at the Bolsheviks whose big sheepskin busbies they could see bobbing up and down in the rushes. Then, once all the others were safely across, they stopped firing and struck out for a Persian village which they could see not far from where they were. The Bolsheviks also desisted and the skirmish came to an end.

The Persian villagers, meanwhile, hearing the noise of battle, had come to the conclusion that they were being invaded by the Bolsheviks and rushed out, rifle in hand, to defend their lives and liberty. 'Are you aware', said one of them indignantly to Bailey, 'that this is Persia?' 'Yes, indeed,' said Bailey imperturbably, 'a pleasant land, which I have been trying to reach for a long time. I am a British officer on my way to Meshed.'

A week later, on January 14th, Colonel Bailey and his friends reached Meshed. The golden dome of the great mosque of Imam Reza had been visible for an hour before they came to the outskirts of the city. As they entered the city itself, they caught sight of the Union Jack flying over the barracks. Riding up to the gate, Bailey, still dressed in Joseph Kastamuni's Bolshevik suit, said that he wished to see the General Officer Commanding, General Malleson. After convincing the Indian sentry on guard that he was not a Russian, he was allowed in and soon after, for the first time for two years, he was sitting down to luncheon in a British mess.

The Bolsheviks in Tashkent gave the story a different ending. The notorious Colonel Bailey, they reported, had been killed in his clash with their frontier patrol. But, bearing him no ill will, they had given him a military funeral and accorded him the honours which would have been due to a Russian officer.

A RENDEZVOUS WITH DEATH

THE year: 1922, five years after the Bolshevik Revolution. The season, summer, the blazing mid-summer of Central Asia. The time, early morning. The scene, once again, a railway coach, fitted with the three closely packed tiers of wooden shelves which give the Russian *zhyostki vagon* or 'hard carriage' its well-deserved name. Stretched out on their respective shelves, two itinerant merchants. On the shelves below them, a case packed with a varied assortment of groceries and a bag containing more groceries and some clothes and personal belongings.

Having left Bokhara, or rather Kagan, the night before, the train in which the two merchants were travelling, after covering no more than four versts, had, as is the way with Russian trains, come to an unexpected standstill in the little station of Emirabad. The delay, it seemed, was due to the necessity of taking in sufficient supplies of water to distribute to all stations along the line as far as Karshi. Water, that summer, was a serious problem, for during the recent disorders the insurgents had destroyed the water towers and in the villages along the railway water supplies were painfully short.

Waking at first light, one of the merchants, a young man of about five and twenty with a Tartar cast of countenance, felt the need for some refreshment. 'Let's have breakfast, Sasha,' he said to his companion. 'You go and fetch some boiling water and I'll get out the sausages and bread.' And while Sasha, a robust, stolid young man of about the same age, shuffled into his sandals and set out with his teapot in search of the *samovar* of boiling water which is to be found somewhere in every Russian station, he himself remained in the carriage. He could see all he wanted to see of the station through the carriage window, and he had at that moment a good deal to think about, though his thoughts, as it happened, were in no way concerned with the assortment of merchandise which lay just below his head.

From his bunk, Sasha's companion could see the ruined dome of the station building. It bore in golden letters an inscription to the effect that this was a stopping-place for the private train of His Highness, the Emir of Bokhara, in whose honour the station had been named Emirabad. But now, in 1922, the Emir, Abdul Said Mir Alim Khan, no longer lived in his summer Palace outside Bokhara. His sojourn there had been brought to an abrupt end some two years earlier in the summer of 1920, when, snatching up as much of the national treasure as he could conveniently carry with him, he had fled headlong from his capital before the advancing Red Army, and a revolutionary government had been installed there in his stead. Pursued by the Red Cavalry, His Highness had taken refuge in the mountains of Eastern Bokhara, dropping favourite dancing boy after favourite dancing boy in his flight, in the hope, it was said, of delaying his pursuers, to whom he rightly or wrongly attributed his own deplorable tastes. At about the same time a similar fate had overtaken the Khan of Khiva whose domains had been transformed into the Soviet Republic of Khorezm and who, like his neighbour, had been driven into exile.

Once in the mountains, the Emir had established contact with the *Basmachis*, the native insurgents, half-patriots and half-bandits, now waging a vigorous war of resistance to the Bolsheviks. For some months his followers had held their own, but, early in 1921, the pressure of the Red forces had become too great and in March he had been obliged to withdraw with several thousands of his followers across the frontier into Afghanistan.

Following up their success with more vigour than intelligence, the Bolsheviks, from their base at Tashkent, at once proceeded to wreak their vengeance on the civilian population. The result was a fresh insurrection. Once again armed bands of *Basmachis* sprang up everywhere. Those in the Karshi and Husar area linked up with their fellow-insurgents in the neighbourhood of Ferghana and Samarkand and by their combined efforts the Bolsheviks were once again driven back into the plain.

From his observation-post in Afghanistan the Emir of Bokhara followed these developments with interest and did what he could to make more trouble for the revolutionary regime which held sway in his former kingdom. The Nationalists, meanwhile, in order to gain the widest measure of support, sought to give their movement a popular character and to make of it a movement of national liberation. A great deal was said about the early abolition of taxes and less and less about the eventual return of the Emir, never a much beloved monarch.

By September 1921 the *Basmachis* had gained control of large areas of Eastern Bokhara and had also begun to penetrate into the western and central parts of the country. More and more malcontents – dispossessed peasants, former soldiers of the Emir's army, deserters from the Red Army and other inflammable elements – flocked to their standards. Their raids grew more and more daring. They rose up in the rear of the Soviet forces, attacking isolated garrisons, disrupting communications, burning villages, carrying off arms and supplies, cattle and horses. At the same time there were serious defections among those on whose support the Bolsheviks had thought they could most surely count, and finally, in the late autumn of 1921, it became known that a number of prominent members of the revolutionary puppet government of Bokhara, including the President of the Central Executive Committee, the Minister of the Interior and other prominent members of the powerful Young Bokharan Party had left their posts and joined the insurgents in the hills.

It was at this stage that the Moscow Government, by now thoroughly alarmed, had recourse to the services of a man whose dramatic career entitles him to a place of his own in history. At the beginning of November 1921, Enver Pasha was dispatched by Lenin to Bokhara with the task, apparently, of mediating between the Bolsheviks and the various dissident elements and of reconciling as many as possible of the latter to Soviet rule.

Enver had been born just forty years earlier at Apana, on the Black Sea coast of Turkey, where his father, a Turk by race, was a bridge-keeper, while his mother, an Albanian, followed the despised profession of laying out the dead. As for his grandmother, she was generally believed to have been a Circassian.

Entering the Turkish Army as a subaltern without money or influence, he soon, by sheer brains and will-power, gained admission to the Staff College at Constantinople. Thence he went to Salonika, at that time the chief centre of the Young Turk Movement, a revolutionary group committed to the radical reform of the Ottoman regime. In 1908, while still in his twenties, he played, as President of the so-called Committee of Union and Progress, a leading part in a successful *coup d'état* which in the following year culminated in the abdication of Sultan Abdul Hamid.

At twenty-six Enver was a popular hero. Realizing, however, that his time had not yet come, he arranged to spend the next two or three years as Military Attaché in Germany. There he pursued his military studies, made powerful friends in the German High Command, and in his spare time gained a considerable reputation by his successes with the ladies of Berlin. In appearance, he was a perky little cock-sparrow of a man with carefully brushed up moustaches and a high uniform collar. '*Ein jugendlicher Elegant*', wrote General von Seeckt four or five years later, '*dem man Energie und Leistungen nicht ansieht.*' And again, '*Sehr liebenswürdig, sehr selbstbewusst.*' But the Germans were also impressed by his '*bemerkenswerte Intelligenz*' and by the underlying streak of ruthless ferocity which in a very few years was to carry the bridge-keeper's son to supreme power.

After fighting in the Italo-Turkish war of 1912, Enver returned to Constantinople at the end of the year to find Turkey in the middle of the disastrous First Balkan War. During the December Armistice, he was made, or made himself, Chief of Staff of the Turkish Tenth Army Corps. In the following January, disliking the course which the peace negotiations were taking, he arrived with a group of friends in front of the Sublime Porte, shot the Minister of War, turned out the Grand Vizir, forced himself upon the Sultan and filled all possible Government appointments with Young Turks. After the new Vizir, their friend Mahmud Shevket, had been assassinated by their political opponents in June 1913, Enver and his group carried out a further and more drastic purge of all elements hostile to their movement. More than 1200 officers, including 153 generals and colonels, were dismissed in one day. Enver then put himself at the head of the Turkish Army in the field and, turning on the Bulgarians, drove them from Adrianople, which they had but recently occupied. In January 1914, at the age of

32, having first promoted himself Major-General, he assumed the office of Minister of War.

Enver now occupied a position of great strength. As War Minister, he controlled the army. With his friends Talaat and Djemal, he also controlled the all-powerful Committee of Union and Progress. He had, moreover, married the daughter of the Sultan, thus becoming the son-in-law of the Caliph. Finally, he possessed many powerful friends in Germany, on whose side Turkey, thanks largely to his influence, entered the First World War in October 1914.

During the War, Enver did not shine as a strategist. In the winter of 1914 to 1915 he personally led an entire Turkish Army to disaster in the snow-covered mountains on the Russo-Turkish border. Although he sought to take all the credit for the successful defence of the Dardanelles, he had in fact no share in it. For all this, he became by degrees the absolute ruler of the country, a tyrant to whom no one dared offer a word of advice or restraint. But the defeat of Turkey in 1918 signified Enver's downfall. He could not hope to make terms with the Allies, who knew him to be their bitter enemy. When the Turkish collapse came, he fled to Germany where he still had powerful friends. Not long after he was condemned to death in his absence by a Turkish court.

But what, in a sense, was to be the most dramatic phase of Enver's career was still to come. While he was in Germany he persuaded his former comrades at arms in the German High Command to put him into touch with representatives of the Russian Bolsheviks. Such a meeting, he hinted, might have consequences which would be to the advantage of all concerned. An interview was accordingly arranged for him with Karl Radek, at that time officially a prisoner in the Moabit Jail in Berlin, where, however, he was allowed almost unlimited contact with the outside world.

Enver and the Bolsheviks soon found common ground. Both, though for different reasons, desired the overthrow of the existing Turkish Government. Both cordially detested the British. Each felt that they could make use of the other. When in September 1919, he received, through Radek, an invitation to visit Moscow in order to discuss plans for a Soviet-Muslim alliance — a pact between Russian Bolshevism and Turkish nationalism — Enver accepted with alacrity.

Early in October 1919, arrangements were made through General Koestring, an officer on von Seeckt's staff with numerous contacts in Russia, for Enver, travelling under an assumed name as a delegate of the Turkish Red Crescent, to fly to Moscow in a new Junkers aircraft. The aircraft, however, made a forced landing near Kovno in Lithuania, and, although its passenger's true identity was not discovered, he was arrested on suspicion of being a spy and detained for two precious months. It was not until the end of December that he was finally able to return to Berlin. But even now his troubles were not over. His next attempt to reach Moscow was no more fortunate. He was again arrested, this time in Riga, and again thrown into prison.

But this time Enver did not stay in prison for long. He was, as it happened, an accomplished artist and, when the Governor of the prison saw the excellent sketches he had made of his fellow prisoners, he at once commissioned a portrait of his wife. Here Enver's knowledge of human nature came into play. The Governor's wife, he told him, was so exceptionally beautiful that he would need a great many sittings if he was to do her justice. Daily, accompanied by two guards, he would repair to the Governor's house, work for a time at the portrait and in due course return to the prison. It became a regular routine and, as part of the routine, the two guards fell into the habit of waiting for him, not in the Governor's house, but in a near-by inn where they could the better refresh themselves. This was what Enver had hoped for. Choosing a moment when his guards were thus happily occupied, he gave them the slip and, successfully eluding pursuit, crossed the frontier into Soviet Russia. It was by now the early summer of 1920.

In Moscow Enver was allotted quarters in a vast yellow mansion on the Sofiiskaya Naberezhnaya, across the river from the Kremlin, which had once belonged to a rich sugar merchant named Kharitonenko and which the Soviet authorities now used as a guest house for visiting foreigners. Its palatial rooms were lavishly decorated in a variety of styles ranging wildly from Early Russian to Louis Quinze, with sudden and alarming excursions into Tudor and Scottish Baronial. But Enver was interested in quite a different aspect of the architecture. His first care on arrival had been to locate the back stairs and, having located them, to secure the key of the door that led to them. Experience had taught him that for anyone who led his kind of life an alternative line of retreat was essential.

Enver's fellow guests were a strangely assorted crowd. There were the members of a diplomatic mission from Afghanistan. And Mr Vanderlip, an American mining engineer on the look-out for concessions, whom the Bolsheviks mistakenly believed to be a millionaire banker of the same name. And the correspondent of the *Manchester Guardian*, Mr Arthur Ransome. And a number of others. They all ate together, with Mr Vanderlip sitting, as befitted a putative millionaire, at the head of the table.

There were, it seems, times when they found Enver a disconcerting if stimulating table-companion. Thus once, as they were eating, he brought out pencil and paper and started to sketch Mr Vanderlip. As he was vigorously shading in his sitter's heavy black eyebrows, his pencil broke. At this stage his fellow guests were appalled to see him suddenly unsheathe, with a loud exclamation of rage, a large and deadly looking dagger. While his neighbours shrank back in horror, the son-in-law of the Caliph neatly sharpened his pencil and then, returning the lethal weapon to its scabbard, quietly resumed his task.

But all the while fresh plans were forming in his active, resilient mind, plans for his own aggrandizement and for the elimination of those who stood in his way. Sometimes in Moscow he would go driving in a sledge with the correspondent of the *Manchester Guardian*. The seat of the sledge was narrow and its two passengers would clutch wildly at each other as they turned the corners at high speed. 'And quite right too,' Enver would say to Mr Arthur Ransome, as they careered along the frozen streets thus involuntarily embraced; 'you and I are the only two imperialists in Russia. We must cling together!' For the sake of an argument, a pastime which he dearly loved, Mr Ransome would sometimes reproach the Turks for massacring the Armenians. 'But what else could you do with *lice*?' Enver would reply, accompanying his words with an annihilating gesture of the thumb. He was not, Mr Ransome concluded, a man who was unduly worried by moral scruples.

If the Russians believed that they could make use of Enver, he, for his part, was quite certain that he could make use of them. He was nothing if not plausible. It was not long before he was received by Lenin himself and on August 26th, 1920, we find him writing as follows to his old friend General von Seeckt: 'The day before yesterday we concluded a Turkish-Russian treaty of friendship: under this the Russians will support us with gold and by all means.' A few days later he was on his way to the First Congress of Peoples of the East which opened under Bolshevik auspices at Baku on September 1st.

For the purposes of the Baku Congress, Enver's credentials were not ideal. Though his social origins were sufficiently proletarian, his subsequent military and political career left, from a Marxist point of view, much to be desired. Though a revolutionary, he was the wrong kind of revolutionary. But no one could cast doubts on his hatred of the British. And the chief purpose of the Congress, as it happened, was to launch an anti-British crusade. 'Comrades! Brothers!' cried Zinoviev in his opening speech, 'the time has come when you can start to organize a true and holy people's war against the robbers and oppressors. The Communist International turns today to the peoples of the East and says to them: "Brothers, we summon you to a holy war, in the first place against British imperialism."' (Stormy applause. Prolonged Hurrahs. The members of the Congress rise from their seats and brandish their weapons. The orator is unable for a long time to continue his speech. The delegates stand and clap. The cry rings out: 'We swear it.')

Even so, Enver was not admitted to full membership of the Congress. In the end it was decided that he should not appear in the Congress hall in person. Instead, a declaration was read out on his behalf from the platform in which he expressed regret that he had been 'compelled to fight on the side of German imperialism', argued that 'if present-day Russia had then existed and had been fighting for her present aims', he would have been wholeheartedly on her side, and wound up by claiming to represent an entirely imaginary 'Union of the Revolutionary Organizations of Morocco, Algeria, Tunis, Tripoli, Egypt, Arabia and Hindustan'. His declaration, we are told, was received with 'noises' and 'protests' from certain sections of the audience, which, it must be remembered, included no less than 157 delegates from Armenia, every one of whom was certainly well aware of the prominent part played by Enver in the notorious Armenian mas-

sacres and of his consistently savage treatment of 'oppressed nationalities' in general.

But for Enver a far more disquieting phenomenon than any Armenian delegation was the presence at Baku of a representative of the
revolutionary Turkish government which had been established at
Ankara some months earlier by his old rival Mustapha Kemal Pasha.
During the last year Kemal had done what Enver himself had wanted
to do. He had defied the subservient Constantinople Government; he
had defied the victorious Western Allies, in particular the British; and he
had finally set up a revolutionary government of his own at Ankara.
Now, badly in need of outside support, he was using every endeavour
to establish satisfactory working relations with Soviet Russia, and
meeting with considerable success. Enough, indeed, to warrant his representative at Baku speaking in his address to the Congress of the
'close friendship' which existed between the 'national and revolutionary government' of Turkey and that of revolutionary Russia. And close
friendship between his Bolshevik protectors and any Turks except
himself was the last thing that Enver wanted.

From Baku, Enver next transferred the scene of his activities to
Batum where the Russians, while continuing their negotiations with
Kemal, seem to have allowed him to form, only a few miles from the
Turkish border, some kind of Soviet-sponsored free revolutionary
Turkish Government in exile, designed, should it prove desirable, to
replace that of Mustapha Kemal. But in March 1921 a formal treaty
was finally concluded between the Ankara Government and Moscow,
and, not long after, the Russians, either of their own accord or at
Kemal's request, put an end to Enver's activities in the Caucasus. His
free Turkish Government was arbitrarily dissolved and he himself
recalled from Transcaucasia.

Enver's hopes of re-entering Turkey under Bolshevik auspices had
been temporarily dashed. The Russians had put their money on what
seemed to them a more likely horse. But he remained no less determined to return to his own country and to return as its ruler. If anything, his purpose had been strengthened by the rise of Kemal, whom
he personally detested and whom it became his firm resolve to overthrow.

His ambitions now assumed a wider scope; his thoughts ranged farther afield, turning to Turkestan, the cradle of the Turkish race, and beyond Turkestan to India and Afghanistan. It became his fixed purpose to establish a vast Pan-Turanian empire, an empire stretching from Constantinople to the Caucasus and from the Caucasus, across the Caspian, to the confines of China, an empire such as had not been seen since the days of Genghiz Khan and Tamerlane, an empire over which he, Enver, would hold supreme sway, and which would include, as one of its provinces, his own Turkish fatherland, purged for ever of the upstart Kemal and of all that he stood for.

It only remained to find a starting point. To Enver it seemed that he had found such a starting point when at Lenin's behest he set out in the autumn of 1921 for Bokhara. In the confused state of Turkestan it should, he calculated, surely be possible for a man of his character and experience somehow to seize supreme power. And once that had been done, the rest would follow. From Turkestan he would, like Genghiz and Tamerlane before him, extend his empire to include every other people and nation of Turanian race. Such were the intoxicating thoughts which seethed through his restless brain as at the beginning of November 1921 he set out for Turkestan, charged by an unsuspecting Soviet Government with the task of restoring order in that sorely troubled region.

Enver reached the city of Bokhara on November 8th, 1921. Three days later, on the early morning of November 11th, he left with a few friends, ostensibly on a shooting expedition. Shortly afterwards the Soviet authorities were surprised and pained to learn that he had joined the *Basmachis* near Shirabad in the hill-country of Eastern Bokhara.

An eye-witness has left a dramatic description of Enver on his last night in the city, sitting cross-legged on the floor in his old Turkish uniform, deeply conscious of being in the cradle of the Turkish race, taking, with tears in his eyes, the decision to launch a holy war. 'I have decided', he is reported as saying, 'that I must go to Eastern Bokhara. If we succeed, we shall be victors for the faith. If not, we shall fall as martyrs on the field of battle. We must fight for Turkestan. If we fear the death which fate has ordained and prefer to live as dogs, we shall deserve the curses of our forebears and of our descendants alike. But if we have the courage to die for freedom, we shall ensure the freedom and happiness of those who follow us.'

It seems probable, however, that Enver's decision was not taken on any sudden impulse, that his mind had in fact long been made up and his plans carefully laid in advance. Within a few days of leaving Bokhara he had established contact with a number of neighbouring resistance leaders and soon his emissaries were on their way to Khiva, Ferghana and Samarkand to make contact with the *Basmachi* leaders in these regions. At the same time he dispatched messengers to the Emir, who responded by appointing him Commander-in-Chief of all the forces of resistance in his former kingdom and, more important still, put at his disposal a proportion of the considerable treasure which he had managed to carry off with him.

Arms and supplies now reached Enver from a variety of sources. Round him he collected a group of personal adherents who had served with him in Turkey and elsewhere. Before long he had a considerable force, built up under the overall control of a unified General Staff on German lines and bearing some resemblance to a national army, a national army of liberation from the Russians. At the same time, he issued a number of proclamations, announcing that it was his intention to form a new independent Moslem state in Central Asia, re-establishing the Caliphate, and declaring himself 'Emir of Turkestan'. He also caused a golden seal to be prepared which he used on official documents and which described him as 'Commander-in-Chief of all the Armies of Islam, Son-in-Law of the Caliph and Representative of the Prophet'. By his insistence on the Moslem character of his new state he won the support of the *mullahs* whose influence with the population was still considerable.

Enver's leadership and personal prestige, the disturbed state of the country and the prevalent dislike of the Soviet regime and of the Russians as such, all contributed to the success of his arms. He proved far more successful as a guerrilla leader than he had ever been in command of regular troops. His first victory against the Bolsheviks was a daring raid on Bokhara itself. After inflicting heavy casualties on the enemy and doing much damage, he withdrew again to the hills. From now onwards, each successive defeat which he inflicted on the Red Army brought fresh volunteers flocking to his banners, bringing with them more arms and more supplies. Of these, some were *Basmachis*, others former members of the Emir's forces and others deserters from the Red Army. The initiative passed into his hands. Most of the territory of Bokhara was under his control. Soon the whole of Turkestan was once more aflame.

For the Bolsheviks, the situation in Central Asia, long disquieting, was by the spring of 1922 deeply disturbing. Their troops, mostly European Russians, were at a serious disadvantage. In wild, unfamiliar, mountainous country, suffering from the heat, the sweltering, unbearable heat of Central Asia, from lack of food, from lack of water, from dysentery and malaria, surrounded by a hostile native population, constantly exposed to surprise attacks, unable to relax or rest, unable to move without fear of ambush, they were obliged to contend with a well-led, well-equipped and highly mobile enemy, who, knowing every inch of the country and enjoying the support of its inhabitants, could attack them at will from the front, from the flank, from the rear and then fade back into the mountains, or alternatively transform themselves into civilians, leaving no target whatever at which their opponents could strike back. When in May 1922 the Moscow Government received from their former protégé, Enver, now writing as supreme Commander of the Armies of Bokhara, Khiva and Turkestan, a letter offering peace and friendship in return for recognition and the withdrawal of their troops, it must have seemed to some of those who read it that there was a case for accepting this offer and making terms with its author, at any rate for the time being. But sterner councils prevailed. Enver's offer was rejected out of hand. And preparations were made to crush the rebellion once and for all.

For Enver, as for other leaders of irregular troops, it was no easy task to preserve unity and concord in his own forces. Not everyone shared his views of the future of Central Asia, nor was his past record of double-dealing calculated to inspire confidence in those who for the time being happened for one reason or another to find themselves on his side of the fence. Not long after taking command, he had made a bitter enemy of the one-armed Ibrahim Beg, chief of the warlike Lakai tribe, who after starting his career as a favourite of the Emir, had later become an officer in the Bokharan Army and, more recently, the commander of several bands of *Basmachis* operating between Samarkand and Karshi. Ibrahim Beg had resented Enver's appointment as Supreme Commander of the nationalist forces and in the summer of 1922 we find Enver writing to his 'dear brother' the Emir, complaining of Ibrahim's treachery and of the clashes which had taken place between the Lakai and his other troops, and asking him to dispatch additional men, arms and ammunition, for the purpose, apparently, of putting down this revolt in his own forces. 'The Russians', he added confidently, 'will soon cease to be any obstacle to me.'

But events were shortly to show that he was being unduly optimistic. Having rejected Enver's offer of peace, the Russians now dispatched strong reinforcements to Turkestan and launched an all-out offensive against his positions in the hills. From now onwards things began to go badly for Enver. Following the example of Ibrahim Beg and the Lakai, many of the hill-tribes either abandoned him or actually turned against him. The supplies and reinforcements for which he had asked the Emir never reached him. While the Russians advanced from the direction of Husar, Ibrahim Beg pressed forward from Sharshan in the north, and Tugai Sherif, another *Basmachi* leader, who had turned against him, attacked him treacherously from Shirabad in the south. Having shifted his headquarters to the village of Kafirnigan, he was suddenly attacked by two regiments of Red Cavalry who took him by surprise and forced him to fly headlong leaving everything behind him.

But still Enver did not despair. Moving to the gorges of the Yurchi, he again took the offensive, raiding the Red Army's camel-trains and playing havoc with their lines of communication. Every time the enemy sought to pin him down, he would slip through their fingers and strike again where they least expected it. Though the forces under his command were scattered and diminished and he himself a fugitive in the mountains, he still in a sense retained the initiative and still remained a serious menace to the Soviet position in Central Asia.

For the Red Army, the burning problem at the end of July 1922 was to find Enver Pasha: to find him and to eliminate him. So long as he remained alive and at liberty, neither the High Command of the Red Army in Turkestan nor, for that matter, their masters in Moscow would be able to sleep easy in their beds. The question was how to find him, how to discover the exact place in all that wild tangle of mountain ranges where he was lurking, ready to spring, and, having found him, how to pin him down and bring him to battle.

It was, as it happened, to this very problem that Sasha's companion was addressing himself as he lay on his hard wooden shelf in the train in Emirabad station, waiting for Sasha to come back with the hot water for the tea. It was, moreover, this problem rather than the case of assorted groceries which lay on the shelf below him that had caused him and Sasha to set out on their present journey.

In those disturbed and dislocated times itinerant pedlars were welcomed with open arms by the inhabitants of any part of Turkestan: there could be no better disguise for anyone whose wish it was to travel freely and unmolested from one part of the country to another — from, let us say, the areas under Soviet control to the areas under the control of the *Basmachis*. And it was for this reason that Comrades G. Agabekov and Alexander Osipov of the Cheka, at present serving with the Intelligence Branch of the Red Army in Turkestan, had assumed this particular cover before embarking on the difficult and dangerous mission with which they had been entrusted, namely to locate Enver Pasha and report his position back to their Headquarters in Tashkent.

Comrade Agabekov had joined the Cheka several months earlier after spending some time in the Red Army. As his name showed, he was of Central Asian origin. Having served his apprenticeship as a secret agent in Siberia, he had been posted to Bokhara where, in the course of blackmailing a beautiful Bokharan Jewess, he had made the important discovery that the recent revolt against the Bokharan Government had been inspired and organized by the Bokharan Government themselves and carried out by their own agents — a discovery that had led to the hasty intervention of Moscow and the rapid transformation of the 'People's Republic of Bokhara' into a 'Socialist Republic of Bokhara' of different composition and with considerably reduced powers. As a reward for his services in this connection Comrade Agabekov had now been given this fresh opportunity of still further distinguishing himself or at any rate of dying in the attempt. Of his companion, Comrade Osipov, who had been attached to him for liaison purposes and whose role was a subordinate one, we only know that he was a sturdy, phlegmatic young man who was apt to rely on his fists rather than his brains to get him out of trouble.

While the two travellers sat brewing the green tea which is drunk in the summer months in Bokhara and eating their sausages and bread, the train, which had remained stationary since the night before, gave a sudden jerk backward, then one forward, and then steamed slowly out of the station — slowly for the very good reason that at any point of their journey it might come to a place where the track had been torn up.

Soon they had reached the desert, stretching monotonously away under the brazen glare of the sun and broken only by occasional low hills and dunes with here and there a patch of greyish scrub. At long intervals the train would pass an oasis containing a few houses of sun-baked mud bricks, but these were for the most part crumbling into ruin and there was no sign of any inhabitants. When they had drunk their tea and had tired of looking out of the window, they played game after game of cards together, until they tired of that, too. All day they travelled and all the following night and in the early morning arrived at Karshi, where, hoisting their belongings on to their backs, they climbed down from their carriage on to the station platform. This was as far as the train would take them. From now onwards they must find some other form of transport or, failing that, walk.

Karshi station was at a distance of eight versts from the town. As they set out, they were watched by a number of dignified-looking Uzbeks who sat in the shade in their turbans and striped *khalats* drinking tea under the awning of a *chai-khana*. The white, dusty road ran between gardens and orchards fenced with mud walls. Although it was still early morning, the sun beat down on them unmercifully as they trudged along under their heavy loads. There was not a breath of wind. Every time one of the high-wheeled native carts went by, it threw up a dense cloud of fine white dust, which remained hanging in the air. It was with feelings of profound relief that, after they had covered less than a verst, they looked round and saw a convoy of empty Red Army waggons coming up behind them.

'Give us a lift to the town, Comrade,' said Osipov, stopping the first waggon.

'What have you got in that bag?' asked the driver.

'Do you want a hundred cigarettes?' asked Osipov.

'All right, get in,' said the driver.

'Thank you,' said Osipov, handing over the cigarettes as they both got in. 'And where are you going?'

'We are going into the town to our Depot to collect supplies and take them to Husar,' answered the soldier.

'Ah, there's a bit of luck. We are going to Husar, too. What about our going with you, Comrade?' said Osipov.

'And who might you be?' asked the soldier, looking at them suspiciously.

'Now, how should I put it? We are soldiers too and now that we have been demobilized we thought that we would do a little trading.'

'In other words you are speculators,' said the soldier with a laugh.

'We should be quite ready to pay,' put in Agabekov.

'I have got nothing against you, but my officers might not feel the same way about it. How much will you pay? Can you give me a million? I am taking a risk in giving you a lift even now.'

Soon agreement was reached and they were smoking another cigarette together like old friends.

'This is what we'll do,' said the soldier. 'You wait about somewhere or other in a *chai-khana*. When I've loaded up and come out of the Depot, then you get in.'

Not far from the town of Karshi they came to a two-storeyed building. This was the caravanserai. Near the gate was a tea-house, a *chai-khana*. Right in the doorway stood a gigantic yellow *samovar*, constantly on the boil. Next to it was a brazier on which a number of battered metal tea-pots were cooking. In front of the *chai-khana* there was a little stream and in the water an ancient tree which threw its wide shade over most of the *chai-khana*. Round the tree there were wide seats covered with carpets, on which a number of Uzbeks were sitting or lying, each with his pot of tea beside him. The two travellers walked over towards the assembled company.

'*Salaam aleikum,*' they said.

'*Aleikum salaam,*' replied the Uzbeks. And Agabekov and Osipov, throwing down their burdens, took their place amongst them. While they were waiting for the wagon to come back they drank tea and ate freshly baked cakes and rejoiced in the shade and cool.

In the end, the convoy made its appearance and Agabekov and Osipov climbed in and went bumping and jolting off over the rough road which led out of the town.

'Now, Sasha, keep a sharp look out. You must get to know the way perfectly. You are going to be my rear link,' said Agabekov.

'Don't worry,' replied Sasha, putting a handkerchief over his head to keep the sun off.

Life in Husar centred round the little bazaar. Under an awning, a lane led between cool, dark, mysterious shops. At the entrances to these, on benches covered with carpets, squatted merchants calmly contemplating the crowd as it pushed and swayed through the bazaar. At the inevitable *chai-khana* the travellers paid for their journey and the soldiers went on their way. A little boy brought them some water for washing in a copper pitcher.

After they had washed off some of the dust and dirt they settled down to drink tea. The Uzbeks in the *chai-khana* asked them who they were, where they had come from and what they were doing. But, instead of answering, Agabekov simply opened his bags and spread out his goods. This was their best passport. Everybody started looking at the goods and soon a lively conversation began about the price of things in Bokhara. The travellers, meanwhile, made inquiries about the markets in Dennau and Yurchi where, they said, they were hoping to sell their wares.

While they were talking, a poorly dressed Uzbek with a thin, vital, yellow face and clever eyes sat down next to Agabekov. He looked about thirty-five. 'Listen,' he said to Agabekov, 'I am called Abdurachman. For the last fifteen years I have been a commission agent in Eastern Bokhara. In the old days all the rich Russian merchants used to sell their goods through me. But now business is bad and there is no trade.

The goods are no longer coming through from Russia and I have got nothing to do. Would you like me to help you trade? I know the standing of every merchant here. I know the best market for any range of goods. Why' — he added solemnly, as though making a tremendous sacrifice — 'I will even accompany you to Dennau and Yurchi.'

Here was someone who might be of use. 'Very good, Abdurachman,' said Agabekov cautiously. 'We are going to be here for two days. Let us try working together and then we will see. If you help us to do good business, then we will continue to trade with you after we get back to Bokhara.' From now onwards, Abdurachman took them under his wing. He introduced them to all his friends and an ever closer relationship grew up between them. He was anxious that they should do well because he hoped to get his share of the profits. Under his guidance they went round buying a selection of goods which they would be able to sell profitably in the Dennau area.

'Listen,' Abdurachman whispered in Agabekov's ear one day. 'We must buy some goods from old Rachmatullah and drink tea with him.'

'Why particularly with Rachmatullah?' asked Agabekov.

'You will have heard that in Dennau and Yurchi there are a lot of *Basmachis*,' explained Abdurachman. 'You have got to be careful of your goods. There are robbers on the roads. But if we have a letter from Rachmatullah to his brother in Dennau we need not worry. Take it from old Abdurachman. He knows what he's talking about.'

Together they went to Rachmatullah's shop. It was a narrow, deep tunnel hung with goods of every kind from boots and galoshes to chintz and Kerosene lamps. In the doorway sat Rachmatullah himself wearing a white *khalat*. His big belly was wound round with brilliantly coloured silk Bokharan sashes. His brown, greasy face with its high cheekbones was thickly bearded. His narrow Mongolian eyes twinkled beneath heavy white brows. As he talked, he fingered a long rosary of black wooden beads.

'*Salaam aleikum*, Rachmatullah Bey,' said Abdurachman with a low bow. And the two travellers bowed low also. 'I have brought you some fine merchants from Bokhara,' he went on, taking off his shoes and squatting on one corner of the carpet.

'It is a pleasure,' answered Rachmatullah, calmly looking them up and down. 'Be seated. You are my guests'; and, stopping a passing boy from the *chai-khana*, 'Two pots of tea,' he said. Over the tea he started by asking what sort of journey they had had, but did not say a word about the goods they needed. In the East undue haste is frowned upon.

At long last, Abdurachman came to the point. 'You will understand, Rachmatullah,' he said, 'that these gentlemen have arrived from Bokhara and have brought a large quantity of goods with them. More goods will follow. But I have advised them to buy something here to sell in Dennau and Yurchi, where, if Allah is willing, we will go together. And so I have brought them to you, for who knows better than you what is needed for Dennau, where your brother, Djuma Bey, is head man?'

They talked and talked. Then they chose some goods. And then, after many exchanges of compliments, they started to bargain. There was a quarrel. The two travellers made as if to walk out, saying that Rachmatullah's prices were too high. They swore to each other by all the saints that the one was selling and the others buying at a loss to themselves. But in the end they reached agreement.

'Well, Rachmatullah Bey,' said Abdurachman after they had shaken hands, 'now you can see for yourself that these gentlemen are rich merchants and good men. They have bought a quantity of your goods. But you know that at the present time things are very unsettled in the Dennau area to which we are going. My friends do not come from this part of the country. Write them a letter to your elder brother, Djuma Bey, the head man, to say that you know them and that you are placing them under his protection. With such a letter, and with the will of Allah, they will sell their goods successfully and come back to you for more.'

'Good!' replied Rachmatullah, quietly telling his beads. 'Call in a writer and I will send greetings to my brother.' A writer was called in from the street. Having sat down on the carpet and laid out his pens and ink, he started to write at Rachmatullah's dictation. When he had finished, he read back what he had written and handed the letter to Rachmatullah. Opening his *khalat*, Rachmatullah disclosed a chain with a gold watch at one end and his personal seal on the other. Dipping his seal into the ink he applied it to the letter. Then he wished them a good journey and good trade. 'My greetings to my brother, the head man,' he added as he handed over the letter and took leave of them.

First light found the travellers on their way to Dennau. They had bought three small donkeys. Agabekov and Osipov each rode one, while the third was loaded with goods. Abdurachman walked most of the way and when he was tired took a ride on the third donkey. At the moment he was walking immediately behind it, prodding it with a stick.

Agabekov felt bored. 'Life has become difficult, has it not, Abdurachman?' he said. 'There is no trade at all.'

'None,' Abdurachman replied with a groan. 'The Revolution has ruined everything. If it hadn't been for the Revolution, I should be a rich man.'

'The *Basmachis* are against the Revolution. Why are you not with them?' asked Agabekov.

'The *Basmachis* want the Emir,' replied Abdurachman, looking all round as though somebody might be listening to him even in the middle of that howling wilderness, 'and I know what the Emir is like. Under the old Emir the Bey of Husar raped my sister. And his Secretary forced my younger brother to sleep with him. But what could one do? If you said a word they cut off your head. No, the Russians were better. Better than the Emir. And now Enver Pasha wants to make himself Emir. They chased him out of Turkey and now he has come to us. They fight, they rob and they stop us from making our living. Yes, it is a bad business.' And he started to beat the donkey savagely with his stick as though to vent his wrath on its innocent rump.

'Why don't you go to Bokhara and trade there?' asked Agabekov.

'But how should I get there? I have three children. To trade you need money. I should like to live in Bokhara. I have been there twice already,' he added thoughtfully.

This gave Agabekov an idea.

'Money is a great force and nowadays it is very hard to come by,' he said. 'Do you know, Abdurachman Bey, that the Russians are offering a big reward for anyone who finds Enver Pasha and tells the authorities where he is hiding?'

'It is not possible! And what are they offering?' he asked quickly.

'A hundred millions,' Agabekov replied. 'I myself read the notice in Bokhara before I left.'

'Wow! That is a lot of money. But why are they offering so much when every child knows that Enver is living in a hamlet in Dennau?' he went on dubiously.

'If that is true, would you be prepared to follow this up?' asked Agabekov.

'For half, for a quarter of that sum, I would sell Enver and all those Turks. It was they who brought the war into our part of the country.'

'Yes. Then you would be a very rich merchant,' said Agabekov and changed the subject. He felt that it was better to leave time for this thought to sink in. And so he started to talk to Sasha about matters of no account. And Sasha, who saw what was in his mind, did his best to help keep the conversation going.

That evening they had their evening meal in a *chai-khana* by the side of the road — a greasy pilaf and more tea. When they had eaten, they lay down to rest on a carpet on the floor.

'You are a good man, Abdurachman, and I should very much like to see you become a rich merchant,' said Agabekov before they went to sleep. 'Then we could do business together.'

'That would not be a bad idea,' he replied.

'You said today that Enver was in Dennau. Is it not dangerous to go there with our goods?' said Agabekov, bringing the conversation back to Enver.

'With a letter to Djuma Bey we have nothing to fear. He himself is a big *Basmachi*. He provides the *Basmachis* with all their supplies. Anyhow, by the time we get there the Russians may have caught Enver and it will all be over,' said Abdurachman.

'But, do you know, I should like you to be the man to help the Russians to catch him. Then you would make a lot of money.'

'I should like that, too. A hundred millions is a lot of money. But how am I to do it? I don't even know Russian.'

'If you like, we'll go to Dennau together to the Russian Commandant,' chipped in Osipov. 'He is a good friend of mine. You can

M   353

tell him your story and I will translate. He will probably give you the money straight away.'

'Splendid!' said Abdurachman. 'We'll go together.' After that they went to sleep where they lay, on the carpet.

When they reached Dennau, Agabekov and Osipov went to see the garrison commander. Some horses, ready saddled, were tied up in the courtyard near the gate. At the far end of the courtyard there was a little house. On a piece of paper on the door someone had written up laboriously in pencil: GARRISON COMMANDER DENNAU. They went in. A man was sitting at a plain kitchen table with a grey army blanket spread over it. His breeches and boots showed him to be a soldier. Above the waist he wore nothing at all. The heat was intense.

'Are you the Comrade Garrison Commander?' asked Agabekov.

'Yes. What can I do for you citizens?' he replied looking at them inquiringly.

'I am a plenipotentiary from the Revolutionary Military Soviet of Headquarters, Turkestan,' said Agabekov, by way of introduction, and taking a knife out of his pocket started to rip open the lining of his jacket. He then took out of the lining a document printed on a piece of silk and handed it to him.

'The bearer of this', Agabekov read out, 'has been entrusted with the active pursuit of the struggle with the counter-revolutionary insurgents. It is the duty of all military and civil authorities and individuals to afford Comrade Agabekov their full co-operation in carrying out his task. Signed: Voronin, Member of the Revolutionary Military Soviet of the Soviet Headquarters, Turkestan. Countersigned: Chief of Security Services, Ippolitov.' 'And this', he added, 'is Comrade Osipov, my liaison comrade.'

'Sit down, comrades,' said the Garrison Commander, offering them the chair on which he himself was sitting.

'Tonight', said Agabekov, 'we are going to pay a visit to the *Basmachis* at Enver Pasha's Headquarters. You are to keep in close touch with Divisional Headquarters and await a message from us.' After which they walked out of the office.

That night they set out for the *Basmachi* country. All preparations had been made. Agabekov and Osipov carried a letter from Djuma

Bey, describing them as peaceable merchants. Abdurachman, who had been given ten million roubles by the Garrison Commander, was radiant.

It was evening, their second evening amongst the *Basmachis*. They had already sold a great part of their goods. They had also made friends with a great many *Basmachis* and had come to be regarded as part of the community. They were now sitting in a *chai-khana* with *Basmachis* all round them. The *Basmachis* seemed depressed. They dared not show themselves anywhere. The Red Army was closing in on them from all sides.

'You wait,' said a *Basmachi* of terrifying appearance with a scar on his cheek. 'The Pasha has sent emissaries to every country in the world. Soon the Afghans will come to our help and then the British, and then we shall chase out the Russians.'

'We shall have a long time to wait,' said another who worked in Enver's kitchen. 'When they were having dinner yesterday, I heard the Pasha say that we should be staying here for at least three weeks.'

'Now would be the time to make an attack on some station,' said a third *Basmachi*, a man of about forty with a big nose — 'I particularly want to get myself a Russian wife.'

'You would do better to find out what your present wife is up to,' said a fourth, and everyone laughed. The company now grew more animated, the conversation became general and everyone started telling stories about remarkable episodes in their lives. Agabekov and Sasha, for their part, lay quietly listening to what was said.

'Tomorrow', whispered Agabekov to Sasha later that night, 'you must go to Dennau and arrange for our troops to surround this village at once. Did you hear that man say that they are going to stay here for three weeks?'

'All right, and what about you?' asked Sasha.

'I will stay here and await results.'

'They will do for you, if you stay here by yourself,' said Sasha, after a short silence. 'You had better come with us.'

'Don't talk nonsense, but do what you are told,' replied Agabekov.

'Your excuse will be that you have gone to get a new supply of goods.'
'All right,' said Sasha, and, turning over, lighted a cigarette.

Agabekov had now been living amongst the *Basmachis* for four days.
His goods were all sold. He had absolutely nothing to do. He spent
most of his time in the *chai-khana*. Occasionally he went and had a look
to see if anything was happening in the small mud-built house in which
Enver was living. Once he saw Enver himself, walking with one of his
officers. He was of medium height, handsome, with a short, brushed-up
moustache. He still wore the uniform of a Turkish officer with a white
turban in place of a uniform cap. His expression was thoughtful.
Something was clearly weighing on his mind.

Agabekov, now all alone, also had a good deal on his mind. The
more he thought about it, the more frightened he became. He was
young, he told himself, and he wanted to stay alive. And there he was,
all by himself, in the lair of the *Basmachis*. He put these thoughts out of
his head. He tried to think about the success of his undertaking and
how nice it would be, when he had fulfilled his task, to return to
Tashkent, to a town, where there was plenty going on and where
there were no *Basmachis* and no danger. Something might go wrong in
Dennau. Or they might be late. But no, Osipov was a trustworthy and
intelligent fellow. He would not slip up and would not let anyone else
slip up. He must take a grip on himself and wait.

Next morning Abdurachman arrived on a donkey with a fresh
supply of merchandise. When he had unloaded the donkey he slipped
a scrap of paper into Agabekov's hand. On the piece of paper was
written, 'The troops are on their way. Keep in touch. In case of any
change in the enemy's plans, let us know urgently.'

Agabekov rolled the piece of paper into a cigarette, put a match to it
and smoked it. Soon the *Basmachis* were haggling over the goods which
Abdurachman had brought. Once again time seemed to pass faster.

Late that evening Sasha arrived. When he saw Agabekov a smile
spread over his broad, stolid face.

'We have got to get out of here,' he said when they were alone.
'Why?' asked Agabekov.

'A squadron of cavalry has arrived at Dennau and will be here by dawn tomorrow.'

'Good! Tell Abdurachman to get ready'

An hour or so later, each of them came out of the *chai-khana* separately and made his way out of the village as though he were going for a walk. After dark they met at an agreed rendezvous and continued their journey together. They walked faster and faster until they finally broke into a run. Sasha carried a dagger which he had picked up on his last expedition. They ran and they walked. They walked and they ran. Their hearts were beating fit to burst, but they were afraid of being overtaken, afraid of being killed. Finally, in the distance, they heard the noise of horses. They flung themselves into the ditch and waited. Six cavalrymen came riding along the road and after them the whole squadron.

They rushed out to meet them and received a warm welcome from the squadron commander and the garrison commander. After providing them with some horses and with an escort, the troops continued their way in the darkness.

What we know of the end of this story is drawn from several different sources. At five o'clock on the morning of August 4th, 1922, having first dispersed his troops so as to cut off his enemy's possible lines of withdrawal, the Red Commander gave orders for the attack on the village to begin. The *Basmachis* were not, however, entirely taken by surprise. Their sentries gave the alarm and a fierce battle developed. In the end, finding his retreat cut off, many of his troops gone and the remainder heavily outnumbered by the enemy, Enver, according to one account, made up his mind to die gloriously. Mounting their horses, he and his Adjutant charged straight at the oncoming enemy. When the Bolsheviks later examined the enemy dead, they found amongst all the bodies dressed in turbans and *khalats* one that was clad in breeches and boots and a tightly buttoned blue tunic. The head had been completely severed from the body by a tremendous sabre cut. On one finger was a valuable signet ring. In a pocket were some papers — operation orders written in Turkish and three letters from Berlin in a woman's handwriting. These showed the dead man to be

Enver Pasha. Near him lay a pocket Koran which he had been holding in his hand as he charged, and which, with his papers, eventually found its way into the archives of the Soviet Secret Police.

According to another account, Enver and his Adjutant succeeded in escaping from the battle and in making their way to a neighbouring village. At the village fountain three men were resting — three itinerant merchants. As Enver bent over the fountain to drink, one of the merchants — it was our old friend Agabekov — drew an enormous sword from under his *khalat* and cut his head off.

EPILOGUE

THERE can be very few places in the world whose names possess a greater power over the imagination than Bokhara. Its romantic history, the remoteness of its situation, the atmosphere of mystery which surrounds it, all contribute to the fascination which it exerts over us. More surely than Chimborazo or Cotopaxi, more surely even than the spell of far Arabia, it conspires to steal our wits away. Such, at any rate, was my own experience. As a young man, the more I read about Bokhara, the more obsessed I became with the idea of going there.

The question, of course, was how. Like their Imperial predecessors, like the Emirs before them, the Soviet Government did their best to make Central Asia impossible of access to foreigners. It was not particularly easy to get into the Soviet Union itself; and, within the frontiers of the Soviet Union, Turkestan was a forbidden zone for which no permits were issued.

I was serving at the time at our Embassy in Paris. I have always enjoyed contrasts, and what greater contrast could there be after Paris than Moscow? I applied for a transfer. Moscow, it seemed to me, might somehow serve as a jumping-off place for a trip to the forbidden cities of Turkestan. Full of romantic projects, I boarded the Nord-Express on a bleak afternoon in February 1937.

But when I reached Moscow, I could not help being a little disconcerted by the mild amusement with which my plans were received by my more experienced diplomatic colleagues. Other people, they said, had had the same idea. Other people had thought it would be interesting to see Samarkand and Bokhara. But to go to Central Asia, you needed a permit. And the Russians just did not issue permits.

'What happens if you go without one?' I asked. 'Try and see,' they said. Partly from a spirit of contradiction and partly from plain obstinacy, I decided that I would.

I got the contrast I was looking for soon enough. Within a couple of months of leaving my comfortable flat in Paris, I had boarded an ancient paddle-steamer in the docks of Baku and was now in Southern Azerbaijan, riding through sub-tropical jungle a few miles from the Soviet-Persian frontier, accompanied by a solitary, rather anxious Tartar. The great thing, it seemed to me, was not to attract attention, to merge into the landscape, and then somehow, perhaps in a fishing boat, to slip across the Caspian and on to Bokhara.

So far everything had gone surprisingly well, I was beginning to enjoy myself. A snake slipped from the bushes and slid across our path; a brightly coloured bird flew out of a tree, its wings flashing in the sunlight. I felt I had left Europe far behind. Then, after my companion and I had been jogging quietly along for some hours, I became aware all at once of a troop of cavalry riding across country at full gallop. I looked at them with interest. They were well mounted and wore the uniform of the Special Troops of the N.K.V.D. or Commissariat for Internal Affairs. They would be something to tell the Military Attaché about when I got back to Moscow. It was only then that I noticed that they seemed to be heading in my direction. Then, suddenly, a broad circling movement brought them face to face with us, and, before I had taken in what was happening, I was staring down the barrels of a pistol and half a dozen rifles. 'Hands up!' said an officer, and up went my hands. A few moments later I was being led away to what my captors, a disagreeable-looking band of Tartar soldiery, assured me was immediate execution. I was not, they said, the first frontier-jumper they'd caught.

After riding for two or three miles with my hands still above my head, I decided that it was time to produce the diplomatic pass I was carrying. But this was no easy matter. Every time I tried to get at my pocket, I was rewarded by a sharp dig in the ribs from my neighbour's pistol. In the end he grudgingly consented to take it out for me himself, and, having taken it out, to look at it. But it did not produce the effect I had hoped for. Indeed it produced no effect at all. Then, to my dismay, I noticed he was holding it upside down and, after a little hedging, he finally admitted that he could read no Russian. 'But wait and see,' he said; 'at headquarters there are many people who can read Russian.' And we continued our dismal progress back to the nearest town.

At N.K.V.D. headquarters the entire force was paraded and each man inspected my card in turn. But without success. Some looked at it from one angle and some from another, but none could make head or tail of it. This gave me my cue. Taking advantage of their obvious embarrassment, I said that, as I seemed to be the only person present who could read Russian, perhaps I'd better read it for them. A little guilelessly they agreed, and I proceeded to read out, with considerable expression and such improvements as occurred to me as I went along, what my pass said about the treatment to be accorded to the representatives of friendly Powers. 'Signed,' I concluded, 'Maxim Litvinov, People's Commissar for Foreign Affairs of the Union of Soviet Socialist Republics.' Then I looked up to see what effect this had had on my captors.

It had made a considerable impression. As if by magic, they became amiable and apologetic. I was at once released and, after shaking hands with a roomful of Tartar militiamen, I took my leave and set out on my return journey to Baku, where, I soon found, my fame had preceded me.

Thus ended my first attempt to reach Central Asia. It had not been successful: I had not reached my destination; I had nearly been shot; and I had attracted a very great deal of attention; but I had learned much that was of value. Subsequent journeys taught me more and, as time went on, were attended by a greater measure of success. Drifting by gradual stages across Siberia and Asiatic Russia by whatever means of transport presented itself and in as unobtrusive a manner as possible, I penetrated in due course to Samarkand and Tashkent and to the borders of Chinese Turkestan. I visited the Tomb of Tamerlane and wandered in the foothills of the Tien Shan. Only Bokhara still eluded me.

The process of trial and error had been a lengthy and often frustrating one. But I had kept my ultimate objective firmly in view, and finally, in the autumn of 1938, the day came when I set out from Moscow, bound, as I very much hoped, for Bokhara.

The train I had taken had as its destination the town of Askabad in Turkmenistan, and, if pressed to state my business, it was my intention to say that I was in transit to Afghanistan. But to me the most interesting thing about this particular train was that it passed through Kagan.

And Kagan was the nearest point to Bokhara on the Transcaspian Railway.

Three or four days out from Moscow the landscape underwent a change, the gradual, but none the less dramatic change that in those parts marks the traveller's passage from Europe into Asia. In place of the birch forests and rolling green countryside of European Russia, varied here and there by groups of little wooden houses clustering round the whitewashed tower and onion dome of the village church, I found myself looking out on a howling wilderness stretching away on all sides as far as the eye could reach: the Kara Kum, or Black Sands. Only an occasional patch of scrub or a low range of sand hills broke the monotony of the desert. At sundown it grew suddenly cold after the blazing heat of the day. After another night and another day we came to the Aral Sea, storm-swept and dreary and fringed with bleak mud flats. Then the desert again — this time, the Kizil Kum, the Red Sands.

Here and there we passed encampments of native Kazakhs and Kirghiz: dark-skinned nomads with round moonlike faces, narrow eyes and high Mongoloid cheekbones, riding along beside the line on their sturdy little Tartar ponies or emerging from their round tents to stare at the train. The men wore padded coats or sheepskin robes and on their heads round fur hats or strange helmet-shaped hats of thick white felt with sharply upturned brims. The women were garbed in high medieval-looking headdresses and long coats of dirty velvet, from the innermost folds of which they would, at the stopping-places along the line, produce a varied assortment of goods for the delectation of the passengers: hard-boiled eggs and bits of roast chicken, black with age and dirt; flat round loaves of unleavened bread; small yellow melons; bottles of *kumiss*, fermented mare's milk; skeins of camel hair; dried fish and necklaces of cockle-shells from the Aral Sea. And the passengers, crowding eagerly round them, would, after much preliminary bargaining in Turki or pidgin-Russian, pay their money and take their choice.

In the middle of the fifth night from Moscow we passed through Tashkent, now the capital of the Soviet Socialist Republic of Uzbekistan, and awoke next morning to find ourselves approaching the oasis of Samarkand. It was a different world. After the desert, the oasis, in the bright Central Asian sunlight, was startlingly, exuberantly, green. Avenues of tall poplars lined the white dusty roads. Clumps of willows sprang up beside streams and watercourses. Fields of melons or Indian corn alternated with orchards and vineyards. At the wayside stations, olive-skinned Uzbeks with oval faces and regular features, wearing gaily striped *khalats* and on their heads turbans or finely enbroidered skull-caps had taken the place of the sheepskin-clad nomads of the desert. Down the poplar-lined village streets strings of heavily laden camels and donkeys made their way, while every now and then I caught sight of a bearded and turbaned village elder mounted magnificently on an ox. Far away to the south on the horizon rose the blue mountains of Kirghisia, barely visible above the haze.

For a moment I was tempted to leave the train at Samarkand and re-visit the glittering domes of Shakh Zinda and the Gur Emir. But I had already seen Samarkand and I reflected that by stopping there again I should only increase the risk of being intercepted and thus prejudice my chances of reaching Bokhara. And Bokhara, after all, was the place I wanted to get to most of all. And so I contented myself with buying on the station platform a bunch of delicious white grapes which I ate as the train carried me on my way along the fertile valley of the Zerafshan, towards Bokhara.

We reached Kagan in the afternoon. It looked very much like any other small Soviet railway station. The critical stage of my journey had now arrived. As soon as the train stopped, I shouldered my belongings and slipped unobtrusively into the crowd on the platform. Two alert-looking young men, whom I had already noticed on the train, followed my example. I deposited my luggage in the luggage office. They did the same. I strolled into the station buffet. They came too, stopping whenever I stopped. There was no doubt who they were: agents of the N.K.V.D. or People's Commissariat for Internal Affairs, in other words the secret police, sent from Moscow to keep track of me.

So long, however, as my escort did not seek to interfere with my movements, I had no objection to being followed by them. If, as I hoped, they had been sent to see what I did, rather than to stop me from doing it, I had no reason to expect trouble from them. In fact, their presence might in some ways prove a positive advantage. What mattered far more was to avoid attracting the attention of the local authorities who, as I knew all too well from past experience, would not take the same academic interest in my activities and were much more likely to upset my plans.

My first object now was to ascertain as discreetly as possible how to get to Bokhara. I believed that an occasional train still ran along what had once been the Emir's State Railway. But I was obliged to abandon this idea almost immediately, for the first person I met on emerging from the luggage office was a portly local Jewess lamenting loudly that the only train of the day had already gone and that there was no bus service. While I was condoling with her and wondering what to do next, I caught sight of a lorry laden with bales of cotton moving off down the only road in sight which, at a guess, I felt, probably led to Bokhara. It seemed a chance worth taking. A short sprint and a flying jump landed me head first in a rather loosely packed bale of cotton, from which I emerged to see one of my N.K.V.D. men running despairingly after the lorry, while his companion disappeared into the door of the Militia guard room to get help. The lorry, meanwhile, with me on board, was heading for the open country and showing a pretty turn of speed. The situation was clearly fraught with interesting possibilities.

At this point the lorry for no apparent reason stopped and a few seconds later a breathless secret policeman landed in the next cotton bale to mine. I felt reassured and hoped that his colleague would not now persist in his intention of turning out the guard and that I should be able to complete my journey to Bokhara undisturbed in this providential vehicle.

But this was not to be. The sight of two people jumping on to a lorry had put the same idea into a number of other heads. There was a rush and we were trampled over and rolled on as the lorry filled with a variegated crowd of Uzbeks, yelling, kicking and biting, as only Uzbeks can, in their efforts to get themselves on and their friends off.

All might yet have been well, had not the driver, who had now let in the clutch and was moving off again, happened to put his head round the corner and catch sight of this multitude of uninvited passengers. It was, he said, too much. One or two stowaways might pass, but not a whole crowd. We must all get off at once. There ensued a general argument which ended in the driver letting down the sides of the lorry and pushing off as many of his passengers as he could reach, while others climbed in again from the far side.

This might have gone on indefinitely, when suddenly I saw something which caused me to get off the lorry in a hurry and disappear into some trees at the side of the road, where in due course I was joined by my N.K.V.D. man. A car was coming down the road from the station. In it was my other N.K.V.D. follower and a uniformed officer of State Security.

By now the lorry, having got rid of most of its passengers, had started once again on its way. It was quickly overtaken and stopped by the police car. The driver was made to get out and cross-questioned and every bale of cotton was gone through. Meanwhile the first N.K.V.D. man, crouching beside me in the bushes, stayed, inexplicably, where he was, without giving any sign of life. As I watched the progress of the search from my hiding place, I decided that the interest which the local authorities were showing in my movements was far from reassuring. I consoled myself, however, with the thought that in due course the zeal which they were now displaying might peter out, as so many things peter out in Central Asia.

Having completed his search of the lorry and allowed the somewhat bewildered driver to proceed on his way, the Officer of State Security now climbed back into his car and drove off, leaving his plain-clothes colleague from Moscow standing in the middle of the road. From the bushes, I watched his departure with relief. I had by this time decided that my only hope of reaching Bokhara was to walk there and wondered why I had not thought of this before. I was not sure of the distance, but I had an idea that the Emir's little train was supposed to take an hour, so that it could not be very far. The road followed by the lorry was the only one in sight. Emerging boldly from the bushes I set off along it, while my escort fell discreetly in behind.

Apart from the railway station, the N.K.V.D. Headquarters, one or two cotton mills and a large and distressing structure combining all the worst points of European and Oriental architecture, Kagan can boast no buildings to justify the name of a town, and we were soon in the open country. On either side of the road, flowering fields of cotton, intersected by irrigation ditches, stretched away into the distance. From time to time, I passed groups of two or three native farmsteads amid clusters of poplars and fruit trees. Here and there, through an open gate, set in high mud walls, I could see a courtyard with a fire burning in the living-room on the far side. Uzbek houses have changed very little since the days of Tamerlane.

Every now and then the road branched and I had to decide whether to go to the left or the right. The sun was setting and the prospect of spending the night wandering about Uzbekistan looking for Bokhara in what might well be the wrong direction did not appeal to me. But I did not want to draw attention to myself by asking the way. And so I allowed myself to be guided by the endless caravans of two-humped Bactrian dromedaries in the hope that they, like myself, were bound for the former capital of the Emirs. The sweet tone of their bells sounded reassuring in the gathering darkness. Behind me my followers in their neat Moscow-made blue suits and bright yellow shoes padded along disconsolately in the ankle-deep dust.

I walked for what seemed a very long time. It was by now quite dark and there was still no sign of Bokhara. I had come to feel less well-disposed towards the dromedaries. With their vast bales of merchandise they took up the whole road, entangling me in their head ropes, breathing menacingly down my neck and occasionally lumbering up against me and pushing me into the ditch.

I was beginning to wonder if I had not after all taken the wrong road, and, if so, where it would lead me, when I noticed that the sky in the direction in which I was walking seemed slightly more luminous than elsewhere. It might, or it might not, be the reflected lights of a city. Soon the farmsteads along the road and in the fields became more numerous. On either side of me were high mud walls enclosing orchards of apricot trees. Then all at once the road took a turn, and topping a slight rise, I found myself looking down on the broad white walls and watchtowers of Bokhara spread out before me in the light of the rising moon.

Immediately in front of me stood one of the city gates, its great arch set in a fortified tower which rose high above the massive walls. Following a string of dromedaries I passed through it into the city. My knowledge of the writings of earlier travellers made it easy for me to find my way. Entering the city from the south-east, I followed the fairly straight street leading to the bazaars and centre of the town which for centuries has been followed by travellers and caravans from India, Persia and Afghanistan.

Seen thus, Bokhara seemed an enchanted city, its pinnacles and domes and crumbling ramparts white and dazzling in the pale light of the moon, and, rising high above them all, infinitely elegant and infinitely sinister, the Great Minaret, the Tower of Death. For century after century men had been cast down to their death from the delicately ornamented gallery which crowned its slender shaft. Now a great Red Flag flapped noisily from the summit.

Before me gaped one of the cavernous tunnels of the covered bazaar. Threading my way through it, I bought from a plump Uzbek merchant sitting cross-legged at the entrance of his dimly lighted shop a flat round loaf of sour-tasting black bread, some fruit and a bottle of sweet red wine, and, repairing to the garden of a nearby mosque, sat down under a bush to rest and eat. Beneath the central arch of the old mosque stood a gleaming new white marble monument to Lenin and Stalin, lavishly draped with red bunting.

As I took a reviving pull at my bottle of wine, I became aware of someone hovering uncertainly near me, and an elderly, quavering voice said, 'Please leave some for me.' Whereupon a very frail, very tattered old European Russian — a 'poor white', if ever there was one — with long drooping grey moustaches, emerged ghostlike from the shadows and stood waiting expectantly. I gave him the bottle. Tilting back his head, he raised it to his mouth. There was a sound of gurgling, and he put it down empty. Then, with a mumbled word of thanks, he shuffled off into the darkness, leaving me with the sense of having by chance supplied a much felt need. Cheered by this encounter and by my share of the wine, I took another stroll through the empty streets, and then returned to the garden, which I had decided to make my home for as long as I remained in Bokhara.

An attempt to secure a bed in one of the *chai-khanas* would have necessitated the production of documents and might well have led to trouble with the local authorities. But, so long as I did not formally announce my presence, the latter were not formally obliged to take steps to get rid of me. It was therefore my chief concern to avoid any kind of incident which would have made it necessary for me to declare my identity. And so I now installed myself as comfortably as I could under some shrubs, while my escort reluctantly followed my example a few yards away. They were not, I think, particularly pleased. They had taken a good deal more fresh air and exercise than they liked; they had been made to look at a number of ancient monuments in which they were not particularly interested; and, worst of all, their evening's work had added nothing to their knowledge of British intrigues in Soviet Central Asia.

Wrapped in my greatcoat, I passed the remainder of the night undisturbed. After midnight few of the inhabitants ventured out, and the only noises to be heard were the snarling and barking of the thousands of dogs which stray about the streets of the city, the melancholy whistling of the night-watchmen, and the flapping of the great Red Flag on the Tower of Death.

Rising at first light, I ate the rest of my loaf and then resumed my wanderings through the town. My escort had now been reinforced by an Uzbek secret policeman, an amiable native of Bokhara, with whom I soon made friends and who showed me my way about, told me in broken Russian where I could buy what I wanted and even helped me to identify some of the buildings. He was a simple, friendly soul, clearly delighted at coming into contact with a genuine foreigner, especially one so full of admiration for his birthplace.

Far more than Tashkent or Samarkand, Bokhara had remained, through all the vicissitudes of its history, a completely Eastern city Within the orbit of its high, crumbling walls there were still but few outward and visible signs of Western influence. While accepting Russian protection and surrendering to his Imperial suzerain the control of their relations with the outside world, the Emirs of Bokhara had, as we have seen, continued to enjoy absolute power within their own dominions and their capital has remained right up to the flight of the last Emir in 1920 the traditional centre of Mohammedan culture and

religion which it had been for hundreds of years. The Russian population was limited to a handful of merchants and resident officials, and
foreign travellers were not encouraged.

The process of Sovietization, which followed Bokhara's ultimate
incorporation in the Soviet Union in 1924, had proved neither rapid
nor easy. The population, it is true, were accustomed to suffer oppression
at the hands of their rulers but they were not accustomed to interference with their religion or with their age-old customs. There were
the *mullahs* to be reckoned with, whose influence with the population
was considerable, the merchants, both great and small, the landowners,
and in the hills, so it was said, a few lingering *Basmachis*. The problem
confronting the Bolsheviks in Bokhara was as thorny as any which
faced them in the whole of the Soviet Union. The solution which in
the long run they adopted was perhaps the only one possible. Bokhara
the Noble could not, it seemed, be converted into a Soviet town unless
it were razed to the ground and completely rebuilt. And so it was left as
it was and allowed to decay. While the population of most other towns
in the Soviet Union increased enormously, that of Bokhara dwindled
away until it was soon less than half of what it used to be. Scarcely a
new building made its appearance. The only changes were those
wrought by neglect, decay and demolition.

I found the city still surrounded by its massive crenellated walls with
their eleven great gates and one hundred and eighty-one watch towers.
Within these lay a labyrinth of narrow twisting lanes between high
walls. The tawny, flat-roofed houses were built of sun-baked mud
bricks. There were no windows in their outer walls, but through
occasional crannies and cracks the traveller might catch occasional
glimpses of shady courtyards and green gardens and orchards. Here
and there, square ponds surrounded by trees were filled from little
channels of water running down the sides of the streets. These in turn
were fed by Shakh Rud, the canal which flowed through Bokhara and
constituted at once the city's main water supply and main drain. To
the peculiar foulness of its water and to the parasites which flourished in
it could be attributed the prevalence in Bokhara of the notorious Sartian
Sickness, of Bokhara Boil and of innumerable other unpleasant diseases.
'There is', wrote Anthony Jenkinson, 'a little river running through the

middes of the saide Citie, but the water thereof is most unholsome, for it breedeth sometimes in men that drinke thereof ... a worme of an ell long, which lieth commonly in the legge betwixt the flesh and the skinne, and is pluckt out about the ancle with great art and cunning.' And his words were still as true as when he wrote them four hundred years ago.

In the larger streets, jostling, brightly clad crowds divided to make way for a string of dromedaries or for a high-wheeled native cart. There were not many European Russians to be seen, and the Bokharans for the most part still wore their national dress, long striped *khalats* and turbans or embroidered skull-caps. Here, as elsewhere in Central Asia, life still revolved round the *chai-khanas*, full of dignified turbaned figures, who sat cross-legged on piles of carpets, drinking green tea out of shallow china bowls, talking, bargaining and telling each other stories, while above their heads loud-speakers blared out the discordant music of the East.

In the centre of the town, near the Tower of Death, stood the two largest mosques, built in the sixteenth or seventeenth century: the Kalyan, formerly the place of worship of the Emir; and the vast Mir Arab, which once possessed the largest *medresseh*, or theological school, in Central Asia. Neither is of outstanding architectural merit, though the brilliant turquoise blue tiles of the Kalyan afford a striking contrast to the dust-coloured buildings which cluster all round it.

Like their more magnificent counterparts in Samarkand, the mosques and *medressehs* of Bokhara are built of mud bricks of different shades of pale red and brown. The design is nearly always the same: in the centre of the façade is the great central arch or *pishtak*, reaching the whole height of the building, and flanked on either side by a double row of smaller arches. In the *medressehs* the central arch forms the entrance to one or more courtyards surrounded by cloisters and rows of cells. But in Bokhara most of the buildings have lost the coloured tiles which formerly adorned them. Only the *medresseh* of Abdul Azis and that of Tamerlane's grandson Ulug Beg, which stand facing each other not far away from the Tower of Death, have retained their former splendour, their façades still bearing the intricate arabesques with which their founders adorned them.

Bokhara could once boast several hundred places of learning and worship. Of these many were still standing, but only a few were in use, and everywhere heaps of masonry and rubble testified to the processes of demolition and decay which were fast robbing the city of its remaining splendours.

Round the Tower of Death and the principal mosques lay the bazaar quarter. Not so many years ago the covered bazaars stretched for miles throughout the centre of the town. Now little is left of what was once the richest bazaar in Central Asia save the *Char-su* or clusters of domes at the points where two or more lanes intersect. In front of their stalls the remaining merchants still sit cross-legged. But individual enterprise had been all but stamped out, and even the brightly striped *khalats* were now made by seamstresses working under the auspices of some state combine or trust. Only the fruit and vegetable bazaars, with their magnificent piles of apricots, grapes and melons, retained something of their former magnificence.

Not far from the Kalyan and Mir Arab, on the north-west side of the town, rose the grim-looking Ark. Its lofty walls and crumbling fortifications cover an enormous space. The entrance gate, with its twin turrets, bore, in Russian and Uzbek, the inscription, 'Town Soviet'. In front of it, the Registan no longer presented the same animated scene as it once did.

I could have spent weeks in Bokhara, seeking out other memories of its prodigious past, mingling with the bright crowds in the streets, or simply idling away my time under the apricot trees in the clear warm sunlight of Central Asia. But my position was precarious and my time limited. Reluctantly I decided that I had better continue my journey to the Oxus and beyond it to Afghanistan.

My decision was greeted with enthusiasm by my two followers. They had never liked Bokhara, finding the alfresco existence we led there particularly trying. Now that we were leaving, they were too tired even to walk to the station, and their Uzbek colleague had to make room for all three of us in a very small bus, already crammed with local inhabitants in their padded chintz *khalats*. This took us to the point outside the walls where the Emir's little train was waiting with its antiquated engine and two or three open coaches. Up and down it, wandered a very old blind man with a straggling white beard and an elaborate and very dirty turban, chanting prayers in a high nasal wail and gathering a large crop of *kopeks* from his fellow passengers.

Eventually the train started and eventually we arrived at Kagan. The next thing was to board the first train bound for Stalinabad, the capital of Tajikstan, and passing through Termez in Eastern Turkmenistan, whence I hoped somehow to cross the Oxus into Afghanistan. This was no easy matter. To leave a through train at a point which is not a terminus is a risky move in the hazardous game of railway travel in the Soviet Union. The trains which pass through such stations are in general completely full. If there are any vacant places, they are given to travelling officials, Red Army soldiers or nursing mothers. The general public simply camp out in the station, sometimes for days on end, with their teapots and their bedding, and wait for something to turn up.

This had happened to me often enough in the past and I was determined that it should not happen to me on this occasion. I was by now on quite intimate terms with my escort, though we kept up the polite fiction that we were simply travellers whose ways somehow always happened to coincide. I accordingly explained to them where I wanted to go, adding casually that, if by any chance I should fail to obtain accommodation on the train, I should simply walk back to Bokhara, a place, I said, to which I had taken a great liking. This hint of more walking and of a prolonged stay in Bokhara, far away from their homes and from any manifestation of Soviet culture, did the trick. The station master, that most elusive of Soviet officials, was found without delay. A word was whispered in his ear, and, when the next south-bound train came in, room was somehow made for us in a hard coach. It was, we were told, the best that could be done.

The pre-war Soviet 'hard' coach, like its counterpart under the Tsars, was built to hold forty passengers and never held less, though it often holds a great many more. It was not divided into compartments. An open space ran down the middle and on either side there were three layers of planks arranged one above the other on each of which there was just room for a small man to lie at full length. A tall man, on the other hand, would find that his feet stuck far out into the central passage-way. Like everything else in the Soviet Union, hard carriages varied considerably. Some were infested with vermin. Others were perfectly clean. Sometimes bedding can be hired, but often one had to sleep on the bare boards. Sometimes they were provided with electric light. In others illumination was provided by a single tallow candle placed in the middle of the central passage. In several respects, however, all railway carriages in the Soviet Union were alike. The windows were either not made to open or, if they were, were kept tightly shut. A general conversation on a variety of subjects was constantly in progress all day and all night. And someone was always eating and drinking and usually singing.

My intention had been to get some rest on the way in order to be fresh for my impending encounter with the frontier authorities in the small hours of the following morning and I accordingly lost no time in stretching myself out on the nearest shelf and disposing myself to sleep. But this was not to be. Hard carriages are always lively places. This was the liveliest I had ever experienced. My immediate neighbours were two olive-skinned, almond-eyed characters in *khalats* and skull-caps. I had no sooner dozed off than they dug me in the ribs and introduced themselves as Tajiks. They had been in Kirghizstan, which was a much better place and they were sorry they had ever left it. Where had I come from and where was I going to? I explained that I had come from Ferengistan and was going to Afghanistan and possibly Hindustan. Though they must have spent most of their lives within a hundred miles of the North-West Frontier of India, this did not seem to convey much to them. All contact with the outer world had been long since cut off and knowledge of or interest in outside affairs had evidently waned correspondingly.

Having found out all they wanted to know about me, and having observed that 'anyone with so many belongings' (I had a kit bag and one rather disreputable bundle) must be a rich man, the two Tajiks set out to regale me with some account of themselves. They were, they said, laughing heartily, poor men, and badly treated at that. They had been sent to Kirghizia to build a road in some remote and singularly unpleasant mountains. They had been badly housed and paid only eighty roubles a month, which was not enough to live on. They were glad to have seen the last of Kirghizia. Still laughing loudly, for they were irrepressibly cheerful, they then passed round a bottle of bright pink vodka, after which they proceeded to take off the elaborate system of wrappings swathed round their feet in the place of socks. This, they explained to me, somewhat superfluously, was a thing they only very rarely did, but they thought it might interest me as a *Ferenghi*. I could not help wishing that they had postponed the operation a little longer.

After this we all went to sleep for a time, the livelier of the two Tajiks occasionally prodding his companion or myself in order to tell us of some amusing thought which had occurred to him. But not for long. Soon a Russian with a basket of vodka bottles and another basket of pink sausages appeared and announced that the shelves on which we were lying were reserved for refreshments. We replied that we had never heard of such a thing. But the consensus of opinion in the carriage was definitely on the side of the sausage-seller, and we were eventually moved, protesting loudly, to some other shelves farther up the carriage.

I now gave up all hope of sleep and spent the rest of the daylight looking out of the window. We were travelling through typical Central Asian country: pale, yellowish desert, relieved by occasional oases and ranges of low red hills, the desert across which the pilgrims used to make their Golden Journey. At intervals there were strange-looking *tumuli*. To pass the time, I discussed their origin in a desultory manner with my neighbours. These now included an elderly and benevolent Russian couple, who seemed perpetually concerned at the discomfort in which they imagined me to be, and a rather weedy young man, travelling for the first time to Central Asia to take up an appointment in Stalinabad, who kept on comparing 'all this sand' most unfavourably with the forests and villages of European Russia. We did not come to any particular conclusion about the *tumuli*.

Presently the sausages and vodka began to have their effect. A little farther up the carriage a group of travellers had formed themselves into what is known in the Soviet Union as an *ansambl*, or concert party, and were giving spirited renderings of various national songs and dances, bellowing for all they were worth and shooting out their legs in true Cossack style. Vodka flowed more and more freely and soon complete pandemonium broke loose. Even the elderly couple's benevolent smile broadened into a bleary grin. Several members of the party were entirely overcome and had to be hoisted like sacks on to the top shelves, from which at intervals they crashed ten feet to the floor, without any apparent ill effects. When we reached Termez an hour or two before dawn, the party was at its height and I felt quite sorry to leave.

For the last part of the journey the railway line had followed the course of the Oxus, passing through Eastern Turkmenistan. The far bank of the river was Afghan territory. It only remained to get across the river. I foresaw that it would take a lot of doing. I was right.

My first care, on alighting from the train at Termez, was to establish contact with the local authorities. As soon as they became aware of my presence, they would, I imagined, lose no time in getting me over the frontier and out of the way. Foreigners, I knew from previous experience, were not popular in frontier zones. And, indeed, the Militia officer at the station proved most accommodating. I was at once placed on a lorry with a mixed escort of a dozen Militiamen and N.K.V.D. troops, somehow reminiscent, in the bleak half-light that precedes the dawn, of a firing squad, and sent off to the centre of the little town with the assurance that, if I would present myself at Militia Headquarters at eight, the necessary arrangements would at once be made for me to cross the river.

At eight I was duly received by the local Chief of Militia, a corpulent Uzbek of great complacency, who explained amiably that he could do nothing until twelve because the Frontier Guards did not get up till then. I said that in the meanwhile I would do some shopping and have some food. I was provided with an official escort of one uniformed Militiaman, who was instructed, in a loud aside, that there were to be 'no personal conversations'; my unofficial escort fell in wearily behind; and, thus accompanied, I started out to explore Termez.

Like almost every other town between Tashkent and Kabul, Termez was founded by Alexander the Great, sacked by Genghiz Khan, and later visited by the Spaniard Clavijo, in whose day it was so considerable a city that the noise made by its inhabitants could be heard at Balkh, sixty miles away across the Oxus. Now nothing remains of its former splendour save for a few crumbling ruins in the country to the north of the present town. In other respects it exactly resembles any other Russian military settlement in Central Asia, having been entirely built since 1894, when the Tsar took over the fortress of Termez from the Emir of Bokhara and made it the principal Russian military post on the Afghan frontier.

Accompanied by my Militiaman, who carried my purchases for me and whose presence greatly increased my prestige with the local shop-keepers, I wandered up and down the broad dusty avenues of low whitewashed buildings and eventually succeeded in accumulating an enormous round loaf, some melons and some eggs. From this com-paratively successful expedition, I returned to Militia Headquarters and, after some further prevarication by the commanding officer, was eventually put into a car and sent down to the frontier post on the river bank, where, I was assured, all arrangements had been made for my passage across the river.

The frontier post was at Patta Hissar. For a mile or so along the river stretched in a narrow strip the barracks of the frontier troops, the officers' bungalows, and piles of merchandise awaiting trans-shipment; then, as far as the eye could reach, a jungle of reeds ten or eleven feet high, reputed to harbour tigers as well as a great deal of smaller game. The Oxus at this point looked about a mile wide, a vast muddy river full of mud flats and sandbanks, flowing between low mud banks. I have seen more exciting-looking rivers, but its name and the knowledge that very few Europeans except Soviet frontier guards had ever seen it at this or any other point on its course made up for its rather drab appearance. In the distance some blue mountains rose above the heat haze.

The captain of frontier guards, a smart-looking young Russian, received me most politely, but, on hearing that I wished to cross the river, seemed surprised and distressed. Previous experience of Soviet methods prevented me from feeling much astonishment on now realiz-ing that the town Militia had made no attempt whatever to com-municate with the frontier post. I said that it was of course unfortunate that he had not been warned of my arrival, but that I imagined that this need not delay matters. At this he looked more embarrassed than ever, and I was filled with gloomy forebodings. They were fully justified. The frontier, he said, was not working. Did he mean that it was closed, I asked. No, he said, he would not go so far as to say that; it just wasn't working. Moreover, nobody knew when it would start working again and in the circumstances he would advise me to return to Moscow and see if I could not take an aeroplane to Kabul. It would be much more comfortable. I saw that it was not going to be an easy matter to get across the river that day.

However, after an hour or two of arguing, things began to look a bit brighter. I had by now extracted from the frontier guard captain the admission that, while the frontier would in effect have been closed to anyone else, he would, in view of my official position, have been prepared in principle to let me cross it, if there had been any means of getting me across. Unfortunately there were no boats. I asked him whether he meant to tell me that there was not so much as a rowing boat on the whole of the Oxus? He replied that there were three paddle boats, but two were completely out of action and the third was undergoing a *kapitalny remont*, a complete overhaul. If I waited a day or two, it might be possible to put her into commission.

This, I felt, was a distinct advance. Sooner or later, I should get across. My immediate aim must be somehow to accelerate the *remont* of the third paddle boat. I accordingly observed in the course of conversation that on a recent visit to the Chinese border I had been told that foreigners were not allowed to linger in the frontier zones of the Soviet Union. Moreover, I had reasons of my own for wishing to be in Afghanistan that same day. From what I had heard of Soviet 'shock' methods, a group of 'stakhanovites' or 'shock-workers' should be able to put any paddle boat in order in a hour or two. Possibly, said the captain, but he must first get authority from his commanding officer.

This was a blow, for nobody knew where the commanding officer was. By about four in the afternoon, however, his authority having either been obtained or dispensed with, a 'brigade' of somewhat half-hearted-looking 'shock-workers' made their appearance and we all went down to inspect the craft which I had to choose from. Two paddle boats were obviously incapable of keeping afloat. The third, which was

called *The Seventeenth Party Congress*, though, to judge by her antiquated appearance, she must have been built long before the Communist Party had ever been thought of, was handicapped by the
absence of an engine or motor of any kind. In the end it was decided
to take the motor out of one of the other two boats and transfer it to
the third. On closer inspection it turned out to be a rather battered-
looking tractor engine from the Stalin Factory, and as it was heaved
up on to the shoulders of the shock brigade I felt glad that I was not
embarking on a more considerable voyage.

While the finishing touches were being put to *The Seventeenth Party
Congress*, I stood talking to the captain of Frontier Guards and his wife
and children, all well dressed and good-looking in a stolid Soviet kind
of way. Proudly displaying his dog, an amiable animal of uncertain
parentage, which he explained was a cross between a pointer and a
setter, the captain told me that he was a keen shot and frequently went
out, not only after Trotskists and Diversionists, with whom the frontiers of the Soviet Union were known to be swarming, but also after
pheasant and sometimes even wild pig and tigers. He was, he went on,
learning English from a work entitled *London from the top of an Omnibus*
which, he said, made him feel as if he had known Westminster Abbey
and Buckingham Palace all his life. For purposes of conversation,
however, his knowledge of the English language seemed to be limited
to the one cryptic expression: 'Very well by us!' of which he was
inordinately proud, and it was to repeated shouts of 'Very well by us!'
heartily reciprocated by myself, that some time later I embarked.

Once I was on board, the Red Flag was hoisted, the crew of seven
counted and recounted in case any should try to escape, the tractor
engine started up (an anxious moment), and we set out on our somewhat unsteady course across the Oxus. On the river bank my plain-
clothes escort stood and waved their handkerchiefs — somewhat
ironically, I thought, but then our relations had been tinged with irony
from the start. Perhaps, too, they knew what I was only to discover
later, namely, that the perfectly valid reason why the frontier was
closed was that an exceptionally virulent cholera epidemic was now
raging in Afghanistan.

The crossing took half an hour or more, the innumerable sandbanks making navigation a complicated business. From the upper floor of the two-storeyed cottage which combined the functions of bridge, engine room and sleeping quarters for the crew, I commanded an extensive view of the river and of the jungle on both shores. On the Soviet side high watch-towers projected at intervals from the jungle, and a patrol of frontier troops could be seen setting out to hunt for Diversionists. On the Afghan side there was, as far as I could see, nothing but jungle.

Such knowledge as I possessed of the point for which we were making was derived from the narrative of Colonel Grodekov, who was not at all favourably impressed by it. In his day there had been no sign of a village and all he found was three reed huts and a group of not very friendly Afghans.

Now, as we approached the Afghan bank, I saw that there were perhaps a dozen Afghans standing on it, watching us come in. Two were soldiers in uniform; the remainder wore *khalats* and turbans. In the background there were three round reed huts very like the *kibitkas* of Russian Central Asia. There were also two or three horses. Apart from these there was nothing except the jungle over which the sun was now setting. Nothing, as far as I could see, had changed since the day when Colonel Grodekov landed there just sixty years before.

At this point, it occurred to me somewhat forcibly that I had no money, very little food and could not speak a word of Persian. But I was allowed no time for second thoughts. As I looked anxiously out at Afghanistan, *The Seventeenth Party Congress* grounded with a bump; a plank was put down; I scrambled along it; my luggage was thrown after me; the engines were reversed; and that remarkable craft started off stern first for the Soviet Union as though the whole capitalist world were infected with the plague. Thus abruptly my visit to the former Kingdom of Bokhara came to an end. It had left me with a strong wish to return there.

For twenty years my wish remained unfulfilled. Then, this summer, just as this book was going to press, unexpectedly the long-awaited opportunity presented itself.

'If you wish to go to Turkestan, you will have to travel *de luxe*,' said the charming blonde young lady at the Soviet Embassy to whom I addressed myself. 'Nothing,' I replied, 'could suit me better.' And so it was as a tourist *de luxe* under the auspices of *Intourist*, the Soviet State Tourist Agency, that I set out on my return visit to Central Asia.

The giant TU-104 jet air-liner, with its sixty comfortable armchairs, its lace curtains, china figurines in glass cases, and heavy mahogany tables, covered the three thousand kilometres from Moscow to Tashkent in three and a half hours. From a height of 20,000 feet one was vaguely aware of the fields and forests of European Russia, of the sea of Aral and later, as we ate our neatly served luncheon of fresh caviar and *escalopes de veau*, of the arid expanse of the Kizil Kum. Then came the warning to fasten our seat belts, the rapid circling descent and, suddenly visible through the tilted window, the green avenues and gardens, the orchards and tree-lined water-courses of Tashkent. As the doors opened and we stepped out into the glaring sunlight of Central Asia the heat hit us like a blast from a furnace.

Perhaps it was the signs of modernization that I found everywhere, perhaps the fact that I was twenty years older, or perhaps merely the ease and speed with which the journey had been accomplished and the readily granted assent of the Soviet authorities, that made Tashkent and Samarkand seem less exciting places than they had in 1938. Even the advantage of being able to examine in detail and at my leisure the ancient splendours of Shakh Zindeh and the Gur Emir and to live in comfort while I did so, could not quite replace the thrill of being somewhere that was hard to get to.

But before I finished my trip I was to experience this also. Bokhara, I was told, was closed to tourists. No permits were issued by the police. There was no means of getting there and nothing to eat and nowhere to live when you did get there. And Bokhara was the place I wanted to revisit most of all.

For a time I toyed with the idea of simply taking a train and going there. Then another, better idea occurred to me. Making my way back to Moscow, I took advantage of a convenient diplomatic reception to get myself introduced to Mr Khrushchov. I then directed his attention to the unsympathetic attitude of his subordinates. Was it not, I asked, unreasonable and mean to place such obstacles in the way of a harmless historian? ('So now,' murmured a near-by Soviet official wearily, 'you are a historian.') But Mr Khrushchov, no doubt anxious to conclude a conversation that threatened to become tedious, hastened to agree with everything I said. In that case, I put in hurriedly, could I leave for Bokhara at once? 'Yes, yes,' he said, moving away, 'of course, of course.' I had achieved my object. Forty-eight hours later I was coming in to land at Bokhara.

Unlike Samarkand, Bokhara has not yet become an official tourist centre. But this, I suspect, is only a matter of time. Already it has been done over and tidied up almost beyond recognition. The ancient walls and gates of the city have for the most part been swept away. A number of wide, tree-lined boulevards have been driven through the maze of narrow, winding streets. Various new buildings have made their appearance and others are under construction. An hygienic water supply has replaced the insanitary Shakh Rud and an imposing water-tower now dominates the Registan. Unlikely as it seemed twenty years ago, Bokhara today is well on the way to becoming an up-to-date Soviet town.

And yet at every step I found pointers to the past: as I entered the city by the Karakul Gate, through which Dr Wolff had passed in 1844; as I climbed, in the tragic footsteps of Stoddart and Conolly, *balà*, up to the Ark, through the great gatehouse with its twin turrets, and then, by way of the steep, dark, winding passage, up to the audience chamber of the Emir. I found them, too, as I peered down into the dark depths of the *Siah Chah*, the bug pit, and the other dungeons of the Zindan, now cleaned up and tidily cemented, but still unutterably sinister; as I wandered through what remains of the Bazaar and sat in a *chai-khana*, drinking refreshing bowls of green tea in company with bearded and turbaned elders; as I came, in a museum, on a faded photograph of Finkelstein.

But it was while flying from Tashkent to Baku on my way back to Moscow that I was able to review as though in a diorama the scenes of nearly all the events I have recounted in this book. As we took off from Tashkent, this time in an ordinary low-flying aircraft that trundled along at a reasonable speed, the weather was threatening and the piled-up thunder-clouds promised a bumpy flight over the desert. Soon we had crossed the Jaxartes and were over the pale, reddish-brown expanse of the Kizil Kum; then two or three ranges of sandstone hills and, leaving Samarkand behind us on the left, we were flying along the valley of the Zerafshan. '*Bukharà!*' said the exceptionally pretty

Uzbek air hostess. And there it was, with its crumbling walls and domes and minarets, pale and dead-looking under the gun-metal glare of the sky. Then a strip of desert and then the broad muddy stream of the Oxus. And after that once more the desert, stretching away in every direction as far as the eye could reach. Suddenly, the sun came out in a blue sky with only a few fleecy white clouds. Looking down, I could see beneath me to the south unexpected patches of green — the swamps where the Murghab River runs away into the sand — and I knew that beyond them in the heat haze lay Merv. But already on the horizon was the blue barrier of the Persian mountains, rising range upon range into the distance, and a few minutes later we were landing at Askabad, a typical Russian Central Asian town: white houses in broad green avenues running at right angles to each other. The heat and the glare were terrific. At the airport the bunches of grapes hanging from the ornamental trellis were almost ripe. Turkomans in blue overalls squatted cross-legged in the rare patches of shade. At the local theatre they were giving *The Merry Widow*. It seemed a shame to miss it. But by now we were back in the aircraft; a fat Turkoman woman waved a white flag; and we flew off again westwards along the railway over Gök Tepe. There, a dozen miles or so away to the south, was the Persian frontier, and I could see the very mountain from which on January 24th, 1881, O'Donovan watched the fall of the fortress. To the north lay the wide plain across which the fugitives fled before Skobelyov's pursuing Cossacks. The desert, I noticed, was now no longer reddish-brown but of a different colour: a bleak, blackish grey, inexpressibly dreary and dismal under the blazing sun; the Kara Kum, the Black Sands. After a time the monotony was broken first by one mountain range rising abruptly from the plain and then by another: the Greater and Lesser Balkan, round which, just ninety-five years ago, Vambery and his friends had skirted on their way to Khiva. Then suddenly we caught sight of the sea. Krasnovodsk, as dreary as in Curzon's day, lay spread out beneath us with Üzün Ada and the long sandy coastline stretching away on either side. In a few more minutes we were flying far out over the blue-green waters of the Caspian, and my visit to Central Asia was over.

Strachur, July 1958

BIBLIOGRAPHY

J. Abbott: *Journey to Herat*, etc.

Madame Adam: *Le Général Skobeleff.*

G. S. Agabekov: *Cheka Za Rabotoi.*

H. Armstrong: *Grey Wolf.*

F. M. Bailey: *Mission to Tashkent.*

A. Barmine: *One Who Survived.*

D. C. Boulger: *England and Russia in Central Asia.*

F. G. Burnaby: *A Ride to Khiva.*

A. Burnes: *Cabool, Travels into Bokhara.*

O. Caroe: *Soviet Empire.*

E. H. Carr: *The Bolshevik Revolution.*

Douglas Carruthers: *Beyond the Caspian.*

J. Castagné: *Les Basmatchis.*

A. Conolly: *Journey to the North of India; Diary (India Office Library).*

G. Curzon: *Russia in Central Asia.*

J. P. Ferrier: *Caravan Journeys; History of the Afghans.*

L. Fischer: *The Soviets in World Affairs.*

K. Fraser-Tytler: *Afghanistan.*

N. L. Grodekoff: *Ride from Samarkand to Herat.*

J. Grover: *The Bokhara Victims; An Appeal to the British Nation; The Ameer of Bokhara and Lord Aberdeen.*

R. Hakluyt: *The Principal Navigations*, etc.

Jonas Hanway: *An Historical Account of the British Trade over the Caspian Sea.*

J. W. Kaye: *War in Afghanistan; Lives of Indian Officers.*

Khanikov: *Bokhara.*

G. Krist: *Allein durch das Verbotene Land.*

H. Lansdell: *Through Central Asia, Russian Central Asia.*

A. Le Mesurier: *From London to Bokhara.*

J. A. MacGahan: *Campaigning on the Oxus.*

C. Marvin: *Merv and the Man-Stealing Turcomans; The Russian Annexation of Merv; The Russians in Merv and Herat; Merv, the Queen of the World; The Russian disaster at Gök Tepe; Reconnoitring Central Asia; Conversations with Skobeleff.*

G. de Meyendorff: *Voyage d'Orenbourg à Boukhara.*

BIBLIOGRAPHY

J. & R. MITCHELL: *The Russians in Central Asia.*

LAL MOHAN: *Travels.*

NEMIROVICH-DANCHENKO: *Personal Reminiscences of General Skobeleff.*

E. O'DONOVAN: *The Merv Oasis; Merv.*

K. OKAY: *Enver Pascha: Der grosse Freund Deutschlands.*

H. PALMER: *Joseph Wolff.*

FANNY PARKS: *Wanderings of a Pilgrim in Search of the Picturesque.*

PIPES: *The Formation of the Soviet Union.*

POMIANKOWSKI: *Zusammenbruch des Ottoman-Reiches.*

F. RABENAU: *Seeckt.*

SIR H. RAWLINSON: *India and Russia in the East.*

RONALDSHAY: *Life of Lord Curzon.*

E. SCHUYLER: *Turkistan.*

M. D. SKOBELEFF: *Official Report on the Siege and Assault of Denghil Tepe.*

A. VAMBERY: *Sketches of Central Asia; His Life and Adventures; The Story of My Struggles; Travels in Central Asia; History of Bokhara.*

SIR H. DRUMMOND WOLFF: *Rambling Recollections.*

J. WOLFF: *Narrative of a Journey to Bokhara; Travels and Adventures; Journal of Missionary Labours.*

J. WOOD: *Narrative of a Journey to the Source of the Oxus.*

Blackwoods Magazine (1842).

Calcutta Review, vol. XV (1851)

The Daily News (1881-82).

Edinburgh Review (1845).

Fortnightly Review (1889).

Manchester Courier (1888-89).

New York Herald (1873-74).

Novy Vostok.

Proceedings of the Royal Geographical Society.

Royal Central Asian Journal.

Revue du Monde Mussulman (1922).

Official Correspondence in Public Record Office (F.O.60, Persia).

Official Correspondence in India Office Library.